JAMES MADISON
AND THE STRUGGLE FOR THE BILL OF RIGHTS

ALSO BY RICHARD LABUNSKI

The First Amendment Under Siege

Libel and the First Amendment

The Second Constitutional Convention

The Educated Student:
Getting the Most Out of Your College Years

PIVOTAL MOMENTS
IN AMERICAN HISTORY

Series Editors
David Hackett Fischer
James M. McPherson

James T. Patterson
Brown v. Board of Education
A Civil Rights Milestone and Its Troubled Legacy

Maury Klein
Rainbow's End: The Crash of 1929

James M. McPherson
Crossroads of Freedom: Antietam

Glenn C. Altschuler
All Shook Up: How Rock 'n' Roll Changed America

David Hackett Fischer
Washington's Crossing

John Ferling
Adams vs. Jefferson:
The Tumultuous Election of 1800

Joel H. Silbey
Storm over Texas:
The Annexation Controversy and the Road to Civil War

Raymond Arsenault
Freedom Riders:
1961 and the Struggle for Racial Justice

Colin G. Calloway
The Scratch of a Pen:
1763 and the Transformation of America

JAMES MADISON

AND THE STRUGGLE FOR THE BILL OF RIGHTS

RICHARD LABUNSKI

OXFORD

UNIVERSITY PRESS

2006

OXFORD
UNIVERSITY PRESS

Oxford University Press, Inc., publishes works that
further Oxford University's objective of excellence
in research, scholarship, and education.

Oxford   New York
Auckland   Cape Town   Dar es Salaam   Hong Kong   Karachi
Kuala Lumpur   Madrid   Melbourne   Mexico City   Nairobi
New Delhi   Shanghai   Taipei   Toronto

With offices in
Argentina   Austria   Brazil   Chile   Czech Republic   France   Greece
Guatemala   Hungary   Italy   Japan   Poland   Portugal   Singapore
South Korea   Switzerland   Thailand   Turkey   Ukraine   Vietnam

Copyright © 2006 by Richard Labunski

Published by Oxford University Press, Inc.
198 Madison Avenue, New York, NY 10016
www.oup.com

Oxford is a registered trademark of Oxford University Press

Library of Congress Cataloging-in-Publication Data
Labunski, Richard E.
James Madison and the struggle for the Bill of Rights / Richard Labunski.
p. cm. — (Pivotal moments in American history)
Includes bibliographical references and index.
ISBN-13: 978-0-19-518105-0
ISBN-10: 0-19-518105-0
1. United States. Constitution. 1st–10th Amendments—History.
2. Civil rights—United States—History.
3. Madison, James, 1751–1836.
I. Title. II. Series.
KF4749.L32 2006   342.7308'5—dc22   2006005347

1 3 5 7 9 8 6 4 2
Printed in the United States of America
on acid-free paper

For Elisa, with love and gratitude

Contents

Editor's Note

In the history of the early American Republic, we find repeated evidence that one individual, working with others, can make a major difference in the outcome of great events. It happened again and again in the new nation. A leading example was the role of James Madison in the birth of the Bill of Rights.

Richard Labunski has given us a fresh account of that familiar subject. It centers on a struggle between extraordinary men, James Madison and Patrick Henry. Their rivalry is a story with many surprising twists and turns. When James Madison became the father of the Bill of Rights, he did so with great reluctance. In 1787 he believed that a Federal bill of rights was needless, divisive, and a question that should be left to the states. The contest over the Constitution persuaded him otherwise, and the price of ratification was a promise he had to keep.

On the other side was Patrick Henry, who shared his border ancestors' deep hatred of strong government and did all in his power to defeat the Constitution. He fought James Madison every step of the way. In this story of their rivalry, we observe two very able leaders at work. Both men were driven by deep republican ideals. They were hands-on politicians, highly skilled at parliamentary tactics, electioneering campaigns, and appeals to public opinion. Even after Patrick Henry lost the battle over ratification of the Constitution in Virginia, he continued the fight, going so far as to redefine the state's congressional districts in a vain attempt to keep Madison out of the House of Representatives and to prevent him from framing a bill of rights that would reconcile many Americans to the Federal government. Patrick Henry also tried through friends in Congress to stop Madison from enacting the Bill of Rights, and fought its ratification in Virginia's House of Delegates. James Madison won most of these battles by narrow margins, but at heavy personal cost. A colleague observed that he was "haunted by the ghost of Patrick Henry."

This book reconstructs that story in rich and colorful detail. It also takes a new look at the debates over the Federal Bill of Rights and finds much of interest. In the pages of this book, we are present as one of the great American texts gradually emerges from many earlier bills of rights and from two hundred amendments proposed by the states. We are there when other very interesting amendments are put forward and defeated, as in Thomas Tudor Tucker's proposal to guarantee the right of constituents to instruct their representatives. It failed, but the debate was the first clear alignment of Federalists and Jeffersonians, well before the struggle over Hamilton's fiscal plans and the fights over foreign policy.

In the debates over the wording of the Ninth and Tenth Amendments, we also find clear evidence that most original framers of the Constitution and Bill of Rights were not themselves "originalists." By a vote of 32 to 17, they supported the idea that the interpretation of this great document should be open to growth and change in "admitted powers by implication," as James Madison himself put it. Altogether, this is a story of high drama, colorful events, great characters, and large consequences that continue to shape the world in which we live.

—David Hackett Fischer

JAMES MADISON
AND THE STRUGGLE FOR THE BILL OF RIGHTS

Introduction

AFTER THE CONSTITUTION WAS WRITTEN in the summer of 1787 and the Confederation Congress forwarded it to the states, delegates at many of the
ratifying conventions became alarmed by the planned transfer of power
to the new federal government. They worried that the states would no
longer exist as independent sovereignties and would instead become subservient to a potentially oppressive and unaccountable central government.

By June 1788, enough state conventions had approved the Constitution to launch the new government. But the bare minimum needed for
ratification was not enough. Virginia, the largest state and politically
powerful, and New York, fifth in population but of immense commercial importance, would have to join the union or it was doomed.

Imagine now what might have been:

After three weeks of passionate and intense debate, Virginia delegates
at the ratifying convention in Richmond narrowly rejected the Constitution. Led by Patrick Henry, George Mason, and other Anti-Federalists,
opponents of the Constitution demanded that a second constitutional
convention be held immediately to propose amendments to return power
to the states, where the rights of citizens would be better protected.

Couriers rushed to the New York ratifying convention with the news
that Virginia had refused to approve the plan. That gave opponents of the
Constitution the momentum they needed to prevent ratification there.

Word quickly spread around the country that with Virginia out of the new republic, its most prominent citizen, George Washington, would be ineligible for the presidency. Because so many people had agreed to the new plan only because Washington would become the first chief executive, support for the Constitution quickly eroded.

Six months later, a chaotic second constitutional convention was held. Anti-Federalists, who outnumbered supporters of the Constitution at the convention, dominated the proceedings.

The delegates could not decide what to do. Some tried to limit the convention to considering amendments to alter the structure of government and add protection for individual rights, while others wanted to start fresh with a new Constitution.

Unlike delegates to the first convention in Philadelphia, who were able to compromise, the members of the second assembly had been instructed by their state legislatures not to negotiate on important issues. The convention was hopelessly stalemated, and the delegates returned home to tell state officials that adding amendments or writing a new plan of government was impossible in the current climate.

With no viable federal government in place, states formed regional alliances and established ties to foreign nations. Northern states joined together and sided with England. Virginia, North Carolina, South Carolina, and Georgia created a southern confederacy aligned with France. Citizens in the West banded together and chose Spain as their ally so they were guaranteed access to the Mississippi River.

Instead of a unified, affluent nation, America became a land of regional confederacies, each jealously guarding its independence, endlessly bickering with neighboring states, and threatening to use the military power of its foreign partner.

WHAT STOOD BETWEEN THIS SCENARIO and the nation's eventual history was a five-foot-four, hundred-pound, shy intellectual with a quiet voice, who worried almost constantly about his health and mortality. James Madison was a most unlikely candidate for this daunting task. Yet he played a central role at the most important events that shaped the nation's founding period, including the Constitutional Convention, the Virginia ratifying convention, and the First Congress, where he worked tirelessly to see the Bill of Rights approved. Without Madison, those ten amendments, which became the foundation for individual liberty, might not have become part of the Constitution—then or perhaps ever.

This book tells the story of how Madison helped lead the republic at its infancy away from a potentially bleak future toward the democratic society that he knew could exist and that the nation has become today.

~ 1 ~

The Philadelphia Convention

AS JAMES MADISON WAITED to sign the Constitution in the historic Assembly Room where he had spent almost every day of the last four months, he knew that he and the other convention delegates—who had come from twelve of the thirteen states and were some of the most distinguished citizens of the new republic—would never again be together. Although not sentimental, the shy and soft-spoken statesman from Orange County, Virginia, must have allowed himself at least a few moments to appreciate what had been accomplished in the State House in Philadelphia during the long summer of 1787.

The magnificent room was the most hallowed place in the young nation. It was where the Second Continental Congress appointed George Washington commander in chief of the Continental Army in 1775 and the Declaration of Independence was adopted on July 4, 1776. Now, the Constitution had been debated and written and was ready to be signed within its protective walls.

The convention was emotionally and physically draining for the delegates. Despite the summer heat, the windows had to be closed because the noise of carriage wheels and horseshoes hammering against the cobblestones in the street made it difficult for the delegates to hear each other. They also had decided to meet in private so they could speak freely, float ideas, and criticize each other's proposals without

Assembly Room, Independence Hall, Philadelphia, where the Constitution was debated and signed in the summer of 1787. *(Photo by author)*

worrying about the reaction of fellow citizens in Philadelphia and back home.

The delegates sat in pairs at tables covered with solemn green cloth adorned with candles and quill pens, whose feathers curved lightly upward from the inkwells. The tables were in a semicircle, while the president's desk, draped with the same unpretentious cloth, sat on a raised platform between two large marble fireplaces at the front of the room.

George Washington quietly occupied the president's chair; so quietly, in fact, that he spoke only twice during the months the convention met. He broke his silence early in the summer to warn delegates not to let drafts of the proposed Constitution fall into the hands of others. On the last day, he endorsed a motion to increase the size of the House of

Representatives to better reflect the diverse interests of the people.[1] For the rest of the time, Washington's presence encouraged an aura of civility, even when the members of the convention energetically disagreed with each other on important issues. Occasionally, he admonished his fellow delegates by fixing his intense gaze

George Washington presided over the Constitutional Convention and helped win ratification of the Constitution and the Bill of Rights. *(National Archives)*

on those who spoke too long or offered proposals that Washington believed would not be good for the new nation.[2]

James Madison did not sit with the others during the debates. Day after day, for six to seven hours, Madison sat at the front of the room with his back mostly turned to Washington so he could face the delegates.[3] Madison wanted future generations of Americans to know why the framers had written the Constitution the way they did. Without missing a day, he took notes of almost everything said that was of importance and recorded all votes. The work, which he chose to do, was exhausting; he had to write furiously to keep up with his colleagues, who spoke at a pace that would have challenged an experienced stenographer. Later he would say that his note-taking duties during the summer almost killed him. Now the day had arrived, September 17, 1787. Madison watched as Washington stepped forward to be the first to sign his name to the Constitution. As president of the convention and the nation's most revered figure, Washington deserved that honor. Without him, there would likely have been no convention.

Washington was an imposing figure, almost larger than life. At six-foot-three, he was unusually tall for that era and almost a foot taller than Madison. To many of his grateful fellow citizens, the fifty-five-year-old general had the status of a deity. He led the colonies to victory against

The Scene at the Signing of the Constitution by Howard Chandler Christy. *(Library of Congress)*

overwhelming odds in a brutal war that lasted eight long years. Washington commanded a ragtag army that came close to defeat several times. Yet, with perseverance, luck, and help from the French, he and his troops turned the tide of the war, and the victory gave the colonies the opportunity to form a new nation.[4]

At the end of July when the convention adjourned briefly, Washington took a break from sitting for so many hours each day in the stuffy Assembly Room and traveled to the outskirts of Philadelphia with Gouverneur Morris, a Pennsylvania delegate and friend. Morris had invited him to relax by fishing for trout at a stream about eighteen miles northwest of the city.[5] It was hot and humid in downtown Philadelphia, and Washington must have looked forward to a few days in the country. But the future president had more than fishing on his mind.

Shortly after they arrived, Washington left Morris and rode the short distance to Valley Forge, a place that held painful memories for him. One of the darkest times of the war came during the winter of 1777–78, when men lacking food, clothes, shoes, and supplies struggled to stay alive against the wind and snow of the unforgiving winter.

By early winter, the ruts worn into the ground by farm vehicles during the autumn rains had turned into jagged, frozen ridges. With the roads covered with ice or packed snow, marching was difficult even for soldiers with shoes. Some men used cloth or crude moccasins made from the hides of the cattle butchered in the camp, but the flimsy footwear was no match for the harsh conditions, and the soldiers left a trail of blood on the frozen ground. As Washington rode at the rear, he saw the red tracks on the icy road. His supply officer explained they could not find enough footgear for most of the men. Washington lost 2,500 soldiers during those months.[6]

A decade later, Washington walked the grounds where his men had suffered that winter. Much of what had been his camp was now plowed fields, and the sloping hills that had been covered with snow and ice were dry and dusty. He walked through the woods where his men had sought shelter in a desperate attempt to survive. It was the only part of the original camp where the soil had not been tilled.[7]

For all the sorrow that Washington must have felt as he visited Valley Forge, he must have been pleased with how far the country had come in such a short time. Here he was, presiding over the convention that would create a new plan of government, the likes of which no nation had ever seen. If the American people would give the plan a chance, they could live in a society founded on democratic principles. Yet mixed with his hope for the future must have been a profound sense of concern and uncertainty over what lay ahead.

Six weeks after Washington's visit to Valley Forge, delegates were ready to sign the Constitution. Madison could take particular pleasure in watching Washington add his name to the document, for Madison had been largely responsible for persuading him to attend.[8] For months, the general insisted on remaining in private life at Mount Vernon. Without Washington, it looked as though the Philadelphia convention would suffer the same fate as the gathering in Annapolis on September 11 of the previous year, when delegates from five states accomplished little except to call for another convention. But Madison never gave up. He knew what to say to Washington, and when word spread that the general was going to Philadelphia, other political figures whose presence at the convention would turn out to be crucial agreed to attend.[9]

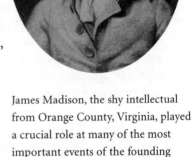

When Washington had laid down his quill, other delegates came forward, in rough geographical order from North to South, beginning with representatives from New Hampshire. Next came Massachusetts, which had nurtured the initial yearning for independence and given the nation some of its greatest leaders. But the signature of one of its most influential citizens would not grace the Constitution. Elbridge Gerry said he could not sign without betraying his commitment to do what was best for his state.[10]

James Madison, the shy intellectual from Orange County, Virginia, played a crucial role at many of the most important events of the founding period. *(National Archives)*

After delegates from Connecticut, New York, New Jersey, Pennsylvania, and Delaware added their names, James Madison signed with his fellow Virginian John Blair.[11] But this was far from a completely joyous occasion for Madison. Two delegates with great influence in his home state looked on grimly as others stepped forward to sign. Governor Edmund Randolph and George Mason had made good on their threat to not add their names to the Constitution.[12]

Madison knew from the long debates during the summer that these two Virginians had serious concerns about the proposed plan. Randolph had many objections to the Constitution. He disapproved of the Senate's role in trying impeachments, the two-thirds majority required for Congress to override a presidential veto, the size of the House of Representatives, congressional authority to create a standing army and to pass navigation laws, and the vagueness of the "necessary and proper" clause giving Congress substantial discretion to exercise powers granted in Article I, among other sections. He also wanted explicit protection for individual rights.[13] Mason objected for many reasons, including the failure to create a government that would protect the autonomy of the states and be responsive to the people, and especially because of the lack of a bill of rights.[14]

Mason was an important figure in Virginia politics. He had energetically supported independence and had developed a close friendship with his Fairfax County neighbor George Washington. One of his greatest achievements was his part in writing a declaration of rights that was approved by the Virginia constitutional convention in 1776, when the colony formally established its own government.[15] Mason's elegant language extending protection to individual liberty later influenced other states as they wrote their own bills of rights.

Mason's contributions to the nation's early years reflected his complex character. He clearly had the wrong temperament for politics. Although intelligent and articulate, Mason was also intensely private, and he considered public service an infringement on his personal freedom. He was chronically impatient, often refused to compromise on even minor details, and relished the opportunity to exploit the weaknesses in an adversary's statement of facts or reasoning in a way that often caused a backlash of resentment. He had health problems for much of his life, and they seemed to be aggravated when things did not go his way in the political arena.[16]

Mason announced during the final weeks of the Philadelphia convention that he would "sooner chop off his right hand than put it to the Constitution as it now stands."[17] Coming from Mason, such a colorful expression of disdain for

George Mason, influential political figure, energetically opposed the Constitution and tried to prevent ratification in Virginia.
(Library of Congress)

the new Constitution was guaranteed to be repeated in newspapers and to lodge in the memory of citizens and delegates to ratifying conventions.[18]

The absence of a bill of rights in the original Constitution would soon become its most conspicuous flaw, and one that supporters would be unable to successfully defend. Five days before the convention adjourned, Mason said he "wished the plan had been prefaced with a Bill of Rights . . . It would give great quiet to the people." And, Mason added, "with the aid of the State declarations [of rights], a bill might be prepared in a few hours."[19]

Roger Sherman, the sixty-six-year-old statesman from Connecticut, opposed Mason's recommendation, arguing that rights protected by state constitutions "are not repealed by this Constitution; and being in force are sufficient." Referring to the new federal Congress, he said the "Legislature may be safely trusted." Mason responded by warning that the "Laws of the U.S. are to be paramount to State Bills of Rights." Madison remained silent.[20]

With delegates voting as states, they unanimously rejected Mason's plea for a bill of rights. Fatigue was certainly a factor. The delegates had been hard at work for four months creating the Constitution. They were eager to go home to tend to personal and business matters and to report the results of their work. Some were concerned that instead of a few hours being required to prepare a list of rights, as Mason had predicted, it could take days or weeks and could lead to the unraveling of precarious compromises reached in other sections of the document.

But the primary objection to adding a bill of rights to the original Constitution was that the government to be formed under it would be one of limited powers. Unlike state governments, which had plenary authority to act on behalf of their citizens, the federal Constitution would create a government whose powers would mostly be confined to those authorized in the document. Because the plan did not repeal individual rights protected in state constitutions, and because the new general government had no authority to abuse such rights, there was no need to grant them explicit protection. Moreover, once a list was begun, it would be inevitable that some important rights would be left off. This would suggest that the federal government was authorized to abridge such rights since, it might be assumed, only the enumerated ones would be entitled to constitutional protection.

No one defended this argument more eloquently than Alexander Hamilton. He did so not at the convention but a few months later in *Federalist 84*. Hamilton wrote that a bill of rights would be "not only

unnecessary in the proposed constitution, but would even be dangerous." And he asked, "why declare things shall not be done, which there is
no power to do? Why, for instance, should it be said, that the liberty of
the press shall not be restrained, when no power is given by which restrictions may be imposed?"[21]

Mason did not have an opportunity at the convention to challenge
this position, but if the debate had continued, he would have asked a
question for which supporters of the Constitution would have no easy
answer. If Hamilton believed that the Constitution did not permit the
new government to oppress individual liberty and therefore no list of
rights was needed, why then were certain rights protected in the original
document? For example, the Constitution preserved the right to a jury
in a criminal trial and prohibited bills of attainder (laws imposing criminal penalties by a legislative body without involvement of the courts)
and ex post facto laws (punishing acts that were not criminal at the time
they were committed). Why, Mason would have asked, would the new
government be prohibited from abridging the rights not listed?

Hamilton's answer was that those sections of the Constitution "in
favour of particular privileges and rights" adopted the "common and
statute law of Great Britain, by which many other rights, not expressed,
are equally secured." And he concluded that the "constitution is itself, in
every rational sense, and to every useful purpose, a Bill of Rights."[22]

The decision not to include a list of individual rights was a misjudgment on the part of supporters of the Constitution that would have dire
consequences, some of which could be seen immediately at the Philadelphia convention. Even as the document was being finalized, several
prominent delegates demanded that a second constitutional convention
be held to correct what they considered to be serious defects in the Constitution they were writing. It had taken an extraordinary effort on the
part of many individuals to organize this first convention and to bring it
to a successful conclusion. A second convention could create political
instability, even chaos.

A few weeks before the convention adjourned, George Mason warned
that if his concerns were not addressed, "his wish would then be to bring
the whole subject before another general Convention." Gouverneur
Morris agreed, telling the delegates "he had long wished for another
Convention, that will have the firmness to provide a vigorous Government, which we are afraid to do." Governor Randolph also supported
another convention. He told his colleagues that if the final form of the
Constitution was such that he could not sign it, then "State [ratifying]

Conventions should be at liberty to propose amendments to be submitted to another General Convention which may reject or incorporate them,
as shall be judged proper."[23]

Randolph repeated this argument a week before the Constitution
was signed, interrupting the discussion of how the document should be
submitted to the states for ratification. Randolph said that "State Conventions should be at liberty to offer amendments to the plan; and that
these should be submitted to a second General Convention, with full
power to settle the Constitution finally."[24]

Randolph was determined to be heard on this subject, if not at the
convention in Philadelphia, then in the months ahead as state ratifying
conventions debated the Constitution. When his colleagues seemed to
ignore his plea and resumed their discussion of the plan for ratification,
Randolph again tried to get them to focus on a second convention. "Was
he to promote the establishment of a plan which he verily believed would
end in Tyranny?" the governor asked. He urged the delegates to support
his motion for submitting the Constitution to state legislatures, which
in turn would give it to "State Conventions having power to adopt[,]
reject or amend; the process to close with another General Convention
with full power to adopt or reject the alterations proposed by the State
Conventions, and to establish finally the Government." Benjamin Franklin
then seconded Randolph's motion without elaborating.[25] If someone of
Franklin's stature were to publicly support a second convention, the chances
that one would be called would be greatly increased. Madison's notes do
not indicate that any action was taken on the motion.

Two days before the Constitution was signed, Randolph again urged
his colleagues not to submit the document in its current form. He moved
that "amendments to the plan might be offered by the State [ratifying]
Conventions, which should be submitted to and finally decided on by
another general Convention." Randolph warned that "should this proposition be disregarded, it would . . . be impossible for him to put his name
to the instrument." Mason seconded the motion, arguing that "This
Convention had been formed without the knowledge or idea of the
people. A second Convention will know more of the sense of the people,
and be able to provide a system more consonant to it."[26]

It was left to Charles Pinckney of South Carolina to respond to the
demands for a new convention, and he did so two days before adjournment. He cautioned his colleagues that the "states will never agree in
their plans [of proposed amendments], and the Deputies to a second
Convention coming together under the discordant impressions of their

Constituents, will never agree. Conventions are serious things, and ought not to be repeated."[27]

The last to comment on the subject was Elbridge Gerry, who explained why he—along with Randolph and Mason—would withhold his signature from the Constitution. After identifying his objections to the plan, he said the "best that could be done" to fix the Constitution was to "provide for a second general Convention." The delegates, voting as states, unanimously rejected Randolph's motion.[28]

The refusal of two of Virginia's most prominent citizens to sign the Constitution was going to make ratification more difficult to secure there and in other states. Even if Randolph, the popular governor, did not actively campaign against approval of the new government, the decision to withhold his name would be interpreted as a rejection of the proposed plan and could influence citizens as they elected delegates to the ratifying conventions. Randolph's objections to the Constitution would be discussed frequently and heatedly at the Virginia ratifying convention in June.

It was troublesome enough that Gerry of Massachusetts and Randolph and Mason of Virginia had stayed until the end of the convention and then refused to add their names to the Constitution.[29] If not for the words spoken by the oldest and, except for Washington, the most respected member of the convention, even more delegates might have not signed.

Benjamin Franklin, tired, frail, and at eighty-one near the end of his long and illustrious life, had attended all but one day of the convention. He wrote a speech that his fellow Pennsylvanian James Wilson read to the delegates on the final day. Franklin said he had many concerns about the proposed government, but he was convinced that the Constitution deserved the approval of the American people and that problems with the plan could be addressed down the road.[30] He urged his fellow delegates to be open-minded and not judge the Constitution by a few phrases or sections with which they disagreed: "For having lived long, I have experienced many instances of being obliged by better information or fuller consideration, to change opinions even on important subjects, which I once thought right, but found to be otherwise. It is therefore that the older I grow, the more apt I am to doubt my own judgment, and to pay more respect to the judgment of others . . . I agree to this Constitution with all its faults, if they are such."[31]

Franklin concluded his speech with a motion written by another colleague from the host state, Gouverneur Morris. Morris wanted Franklin to offer the motion because he knew that it would be hard for the delegates to say no to him after all he had done to help win independence and launch the new government. The motion provided that the delegates sign as representatives of states and not as individuals. They would therefore not be personally committed to support ratification, and the Constitution could be said to have been approved unanimously by states at the convention. The delegates eventually accepted this suggestion when they added these words after Article VII: "Done in Convention by the Unanimous Consent of the States present ... IN WITNESS whereof WE have hereunto subscribed our Names." Franklin hoped this would allow delegates like Randolph to sign and thus "prevent the great mischief which the refusal of his name might produce." Randolph replied that it was a change of form only, and "therefore could make no difference with him."[32]

As the delegates were leaving the Assembly Room, Franklin paused and spoke quietly to those standing nearby. He said he had noticed the wood carving of a sun on the chair Washington had used while presiding at the convention. He observed that artists had a difficult time distinguishing a rising from a setting sun in their work, and he had wondered during the convention which one adorned the president's chair. With the signing of the Constitution, Franklin knew the answer: "But now at length I have the happiness to know that it is a rising and not a setting sun."[33]

The story is told that when Franklin left the Assembly Room, a woman approached him and asked, "Well, Doctor, what have we got, a republic or a monarchy?" To which Franklin replied, "A republic, madam, if you can keep it."[34] With that, the delegates left the State House for the last time as a group. Some headed to their boardinghouses to pack for the journey home, while others went to the City Tavern to dine and celebrate.[35]

James Madison would have preferred to return to Montpelier, his peaceful home with a view of the Blue Ridge Mountains in the Piedmont area of central Virginia. Except for three days in January, Madison had been away for almost a year and a half. His plantation had a growing list of financial and agricultural problems requiring his attention. Unlike many of the delegates who went home for short periods to attend to personal business during the convention, Madison was in Philadelphia every day.

But Madison could not go back to Montpelier. He was needed in New York, the capital of the new United States, where he served as a member of the Confederation Congress, the body that exercised almost all the functions of the rudimentary American government. Although the work of the Philadelphia convention was over, the most difficult challenges were still ahead. Before the proposed Constitution could be submitted to the states for ratification, it had to get through the national legislature. Madison was destined to play a key role in that effort.

The Philadelphia delegates had created a remarkable document. The issues they confronted were complex and divisive: How should power between the individual states and the new federal government be balanced? How should Congress regulate trade between the states and with other countries? How should the federal court system be structured, and what should its powers be? How should states be represented in Congress and its members elected? How should a president be chosen? And what should the new nation do about slavery?

But all the work at the convention, all the hours of debate and compromise over crucial issues, could have been futile if the delegates had not made the right decision about how the Constitution should be ratified. The framers decided that if nine states ratified the Constitution, it would go into effect for those states, and the government would begin to operate. The other states could join the union when they approved the Constitution. That plan required Congress to forward the Constitution to the states. State legislatures would then call ratifying conventions whose members would be chosen directly by the people. The Philadelphia delegates believed this was the only way to give the people the chance to decide the nation's fate.[36]

Such a strategy was risky, even though eighteen of the thirty-three members of Congress present had just finished serving as delegates at the Philadelphia convention.[37] The framers were saying, in effect, "We are sending this document to you in Congress. You cannot amend it. You cannot even debate it in a formal way. We are only giving you the opportunity to forward it to the states. When state legislatures receive the document from you, they are also prohibited from debating or amending it. Their sole function is to provide for elections to ratifying conventions where the real decisions will be made." To members of Congress and state legislatures, this mandate may have felt like a slap in the face. The nation's legislative body was being told that it would serve only as a distribution center, receiving the Constitution and forwarding copies to the states.

State legislators had previously ratified the Articles of Confederation, the nation's first Constitution. Now they were being informed, in effect, that they could not be trusted to render a fair judgment on the new plan of government. If the Confederation Congress determined that state legislatures and not state conventions should decide on ratification, some legislators would remember that the Philadelphia convention had tried to exclude them from the process, and that might make them even more hostile to the plan.

The obstacles to ratification were legal as well as political. The delegates could not formally submit the new Constitution directly to the states because the Philadelphia convention had been authorized by Congress. The idea for a convention may have begun in the states, but once eight state legislatures appointed delegates to meet in Philadelphia, and it looked like a convention might actually be held in which a majority of states were represented, Congress took charge. In February 1787, it called a convention "for the sole and express purpose of revising the Articles of Confederation."[38]

The Articles had been adopted by the Second Continental Congress in 1777 but not ratified until 1781. They proved to be woefully inadequate for the task of creating a new republic. The confederation government— what there was of it—consisted of a unicameral legislature in which each state, regardless of population, had one vote. Congress exercised limited executive and judicial functions, and it had no power to compel states to pay the money they owed to the national government so it could function properly.

More troubling was the Articles' requirement that all thirteen states give their approval before amendments became effective.[39] Because no proposed amendments ever attracted unanimous support, the nation was stuck with an unworkable and unchangeable plan of government that had to be replaced. For instance, Rhode Island and New York had each been the sole negative vote on two different amendments that would have raised desperately needed revenue.[40]

The Philadelphia delegates did not pay attention to the congressional mandate that limited their role to revising the Articles. Once the convention began work and Governor Randolph presented the "Virginia Plan" on behalf of his colleagues on May 29, it was clear that they were not going to simply rewrite the Articles. Randolph laid out a bold vision for a new government—one developed mostly by Madison—that would establish the framework for the Constitution.[41]

The writing of a new Constitution did not mean that the Articles had been repealed. No matter how widespread the agreement that the confederation government was a failure, a group of fifty-five men meeting in Philadelphia did not have the authority to revoke what was then the nation's governing document.

Some members of Congress assumed that because it had authorized the Philadelphia convention and the proposed Constitution would be submitted to that legislative body, they would be free to debate, accept, reject, or modify it. Another assumption was that Congress could determine whether the proposed plan should be forwarded to the states, and if so, how many states would be needed for ratification. This had been the subject of heated debate and disagreement at the convention. Alexander Hamilton of New York and Elbridge Gerry of Massachusetts were among those who argued that Congress would need to give its assent before the Constitution could advance to the states.[42]

No one knew better than the delegates that the proposed Constitution would drastically alter the structure of government. Much of the power of the states would be taken from them. The framers worried that state legislatures would resist giving up power to a new central government that, in the view of many citizens, was potentially oppressive and unaccountable.

Elbridge Gerry, from Massachusetts, would not sign the Constitution and urged amendments before it was ratified. He later served in the first U.S. House of Representatives. *(Library of Congress)*

Besides the practical reasons for not allowing state legislatures the chance to reject the Constitution, a more fundamental justification required giving the decision directly to the people. As Madison noted, if state legislatures ratified the Constitution, it would be like a treaty among sovereign states. If any state subsequently violated any of its provisions, the others would be able to dissolve the compact. Accordingly, Madison urged that the Constitution be submitted to "the supreme authority of the people themselves."[43] If the new Constitution emanated directly from the people, it would not be a creature of the states and would become the nation's fundamental charter of government.

The convention sent a "report" consisting of three documents to Congress: the new Constitution, the resolution setting out the recommended ratification procedure—with the request that it be submitted "to a Convention of Deputies in each State to be chosen by the People thereof"—and a cover letter of transmittal.[44]

If Congress changed one word, the Constitution would no longer be the work of the Philadelphia delegates as reflected in the thirty-nine signatures on the document. Madison recognized this when he warned that if modified in any way, it would become a "mere act of Congress, and must be . . . addressed to the Legislatures, not conventions of the States, and require ratification by thirteen instead of nine States."[45]

Some in Congress were shocked by the boldness and scope of the new plan. They had approved the convention to try to fix the Articles. Now it was clear what the Philadelphia delegates had done behind closed doors for the past four months. They had devised a greatly expanded plan of government that would dramatically change the nature of the nation's political system and drastically reduce the power and autonomy of the states.

It did not take long for opposition to arise. A few days after the Philadelphia convention adjourned, Richard Henry Lee—like Madison, a Virginian and a member of Congress—said the Constitution was a "report" from the convention that Congress was free to amend. Lee, an influential and highly respected member of the famous Virginia family, who would become one of the state's first U.S. senators, offered a lengthy set of amendments that included a proposed bill of rights and major changes that would have substantially altered the structure of the proposed government.[46]

Supporters of the Constitution knew they were the most vulnerable when it came to the absence of protections for individual rights. Madison had good reason to worry that if Lee demanded a roll call vote on his amendments, the effort could attract enough support to negatively influence public opinion. Congress could even have called a second constitutional convention to remedy what it considered to be defects in the proposed Constitution.

Madison and his colleagues were denounced for even returning to Congress. Lee criticized the willingness of the delegates from Philadelphia to vote on the very document they had just created. Lee felt so strongly about that principle that although he had been chosen to be a delegate at the Constitutional Convention, he declined to attend on the grounds that it was wrong for the members to "pass judgment at New York upon their opinions at Philadelphia."[47]

When some members of Congress attacked the delegates as having gone beyond their instructions to revise the Articles, Madison responded that Congress had asked the convention to "render the federal Constitution adequate to the exigencies of Government and the preservation of the Union." The convention decided it could not accomplish that goal by merely tinkering with the Articles.[48]

After three days of debate in New York, supporters and opponents of the Constitution arranged a compromise. Congress would not vote to approve or reject the Constitution; it would simply send the plan to state legislatures. That was an important victory for supporters of the Constitution. At the same time, Congress agreed there would be no official record of the debate and none would be distributed as would normally be the case. Everyone would then be free to interpret events as he saw fit in letters, newspapers commentaries, and other forums.

Madison was relieved when Congress decided not to take a formal vote on Lee's amendments. He told Washington that "these difficulties which at one time threatened a serious division in Congs. and popular alterations with the yeas & nays on the journals, were at length fortunately terminated" by the resolution Congress adopted unanimously on September 28.[49]

Each side got what it wanted. Madison and other supporters of the Constitution avoided having even a handful of members of Congress go on record against the plan. Such a vote would have been used by opponents to show that the nation's legislative body was divided over the proposed Constitution. Those rejecting the document, on the other hand, were able to prevent what would likely have been a formal vote of support.

Lee also benefited from the compromise. Although Congress did not take a roll call vote on his proposed amendments and they would not appear in the congressional journal, the fact that they were discussed on the floor of Congress enhanced his stature and focused attention on the amendments. In the months that followed, when Lee discussed his amendments in letters and elsewhere, he could say that they had come before Congress and deserved serious consideration.

Congress's decision to forward the Constitution was limited to the actual transmission of the document and did not address the merits of the proposed plan. The transmittal letter did not even use the word "Constitution." "Having received the report of the Convention lately assembled at Philadelphia," wrote Congress, we have "Resolved unanimously that the said report, together with the resolutions and letters accompanying the same, be transmitted to the several legislatures."

Federalists hoped the American people would assume that since Congress submitted the Constitution to the states without dissent, it did not have serious concerns about it. Washington assured Madison that few citizens would know the details of what transpired when Congress dealt with this matter and that the "appearance of unanimity in that body, on this occasn., will be of great importance."[50]

Within days of the adjournment of the Philadelphia convention, the new Constitution began appearing in newspapers around the country.

The Pennsylvania Packet, *and Daily Advertiser.*

[Price Four-Pence.]   WEDNESDAY, September 19, 1787.   [No. 2690.]

WE, the People of the United States, in order to form a more perfect Union, establish Justice, insure domestic Tranquility, provide for the common Defence, promote the General Welfare, and secure the Blessings of Liberty to Ourselves and our Posterity, do ordain and establish this Constitution for the United States of America.

ARTICLE I.

Sect. 1. ALL legislative powers herein granted shall be vested in a Congress of the United States, which shall consist of a Senate and House of Representatives.

Sect. 2. The House of Representatives shall be composed of members chosen every second year by the people of the several states, and the electors in each state shall have the qualifications requisite for electors of the most numerous branch of the state legislature.

No person shall be a representative who shall not have attained to the age of twenty-five years, and been seven years a citizen of the United States, and who shall not, when elected, be an inhabitant of that state in which he shall be chosen.

Representatives and direct taxes shall be apportioned among the several states which may be included within this Union, according to their respective numbers, which shall be determined by adding to the whole number of free persons, including those bound to service for a term of years, and excluding Indians not taxed, three-fifths of all other persons. The actual enumeration shall be made within three years after the first meeting of the Congress of the United States, and within every subsequent term of ten years, in such manner as they shall by law direct. The number of representatives shall not exceed one for every thirty thousand, but each state shall have at least one representative; and until such enumeration shall be made, the state of New-Hampshire shall be entitled to chuse three, Massachusetts eight, Rhode-Island and Providence Plantations one, Connecticut five, New-York six, New-Jersey four, Pennsylvania eight, Delaware one, Maryland six, Virginia ten, North-Carolina five, South-Carolina five, and Georgia three.

When vacancies happen in the representation from any state, the Executive authority thereof shall issue writs of election to fill such vacancies.

The House of Representatives shall chuse their Speaker and other officers; and shall have the sole power of impeachment.

Sect. 3. The Senate of the United States shall be composed of two senators from each state, chosen by the legislature thereof, for six years; and each senator shall have one vote.

Immediately after they shall be assembled in consequence of the first election, they shall be divided as equally as may be into three classes. The seats of the senators of the first class shall be vacated at the expiration of the second year, of the second class at the expiration of the fourth year, and of the third class at the expiration of the sixth year, so that one-third may be chosen every second year; and if vacancies happen by resignation, or otherwise, during the recess of the Legislature of any state, the Executive thereof may make temporary appointments until the next meeting of the Legislature, which shall then fill such vacancies.

No person shall be a senator who shall not have attained to the age of thirty years, and been nine years a citizen of the United States, and who shall not, when elected, be an inhabitant of that state for which he shall be chosen.

The Vice-President of the United States shall be President of the senate, but shall have no vote, unless they be equally divided.

The Senate shall chuse their other officers, and also a President pro tempore, in the absence of the Vice-President, or when he shall exercise the office of President of the United States.

The Senate shall have the sole power to try all impeachments. When sitting for that purpose, they shall be on oath or affirmation. When the President of the United States is tried, the Chief Justice shall preside: And no person shall be convicted without the concurrence of two-thirds of the members present.

Judgment in cases of impeachment shall not extend further than to removal from office, and disqualification to hold and enjoy any office of honor, trust or profit under the United States; but the party convicted shall nevertheless be liable and subject to indictment, trial, judgment and punishment, according to law.

Sect. 4. The times, places and manner of holding elections for senators and representatives, shall be prescribed in each state by the legislature thereof; but the Congress may at any time by law make or alter such regulations, except as to the places of chusing Senators.

The Congress shall assemble at least once in every year, and such meeting shall be on the first Monday in December, unless they shall by law appoint a different day.

Sect. 5. Each House shall be the judge of the elections, returns and qualifications of its own members, and a majority of each shall constitute a quorum to do business; but a smaller number may adjourn from day to day, and may be authorised to compel the attendance of absent members, in such manner, and under such penalties as each house may provide.

Each house may determine the rules of its proceedings, punish its members for disorderly behaviour, and, with the concurrence of two-thirds, expel a member.

Each house shall keep a journal of its proceedings, and from time to time publish the same, excepting such parts as may in their judgment require secrecy; and the yeas and nays of the members of either house on any question shall, at the desire of one-fifth of those present, be entered on the journal.

Neither house, during the session of Congress, shall, without the consent of the other, adjourn for more than three days, nor to any other place than that in which the two houses shall be sitting.

Sect. 6. The senators and representatives shall receive a compensation for their services, to be ascertained by law, and paid out of the treasury of the United States. They shall in all cases, except treason, felony and breach of the peace, be privileged from arrest during their attendance at the session of their respective houses, and in going to and returning from the same; and for any speech or debate in either house, they shall not be questioned in any other place.

No senator or representative shall, during the time for which he was elected, be appointed to any civil office under the authority of the United States, which shall have been created, or the emoluments whereof shall have been encreased during such time; and no person holding any office under the United States, shall be a member of either house during his continuance in office.

Sect. 7. All bills for raising revenue shall originate in the house of representatives; but the senate may propose or concur with amendments as on other bills.

Every bill which shall have passed the house of representatives and the senate, shall, before it become a law, be presented to the president of the United States; if he approve he shall sign it, but if not he shall return it, with his objections to that house in which it shall have originated, who shall enter the objections at large on their journal, and proceed to reconsider it. If after such reconsideration two-thirds of that house shall agree to pass the bill, it shall be sent, together with the objections, to the other house, by which it shall likewise be reconsidered, and if approved by two-thirds of that house, it shall become a law. But in all such cases the votes of both houses shall

---

The Pennsylvania Packet and Daily Advertiser, with the first printing of the Constitution, September 19, 1787. (*Library of Congress*)

Citizens who had no idea a convention had been held were now reading the Constitution and hearing about its shortcomings. Those opposed to the Constitution and working against its ratification—known as Anti-Federalists—included prominent individuals such as Samuel Adams and Elbridge Gerry of Massachusetts; Governor George Clinton, John Lansing, Robert Yates, and Melancton Smith of New York; Thomas Sumter and Thomas Tudor Tucker of South Carolina; Patrick Henry, William Grayson, Richard Henry Lee, George Mason, and James Monroe of Virginia; and Luther Martin of Maryland.[51]

As they wrote letters to friends and political acquaintances and published commentaries in newspapers, the Anti-Federalists began to have an impact on their fellow citizens, many of whom were alarmed over the potential power and lack of accountability of the new government. Federalists were learning that the absence of a bill of rights would become the most serious shortcoming in the Constitution and the hardest for supporters to explain. It would haunt Federalists during the entire ratification process.

If Madison had not been in New York, the Constitution would not likely have made it through Congress unscathed.[52] At this period in the nation's history, the presence of a few individuals like Madison or Washington at certain places and times could be crucial to the course of events. A single mishap could have changed the course of history—and at this moment, one almost did.

In those days, no one could take safe travel for granted. Roads were often primitive, and the weather frequently made travel hazardous. Stagecoaches were uncomfortable and often left passengers physically exhausted after only a few days. Coaches could travel fifty miles on a good day but were often vulnerable to disaster as they traversed roads with bone-jarring holes, mud when it rained, and other calamities such as raging streams. Carriages owned by affluent citizens were also susceptible to serious accidents.[53]

Two days after the Constitutional Convention ended, George Washington was heading home to Mount Vernon when he narrowly escaped death or serious injury. He was traveling with fellow Virginia delegate John Blair, whom Washington later appointed to the Supreme Court, when they encountered an impassible stream near the head of the Elk River in northeast Maryland. According to Washington's diary, the rain the previous evening "swelled the Water considerably," and there was "no fording it safely."[54]

Rather than wait for the water to recede, they decided to cross an "old, rotten & long-disused bridge." To lighten the load, Washington and

Blair got out of the carriage and walked across on foot. As the vehicle began to cross the bridge, the rotted-out planks collapsed under one of the horses, which fell fifteen feet to the river below. The other horse nearly suffered the same fate.

Workers at a nearby mill rushed to help. With "great exertion," as Washington noted, they were able to release the first horse from its harness and prevent the second horse from falling through the bridge. Washington realized that if both horses had crashed through the planks, the carriage and baggage would have followed, "destroy[ing] the whole effectually."[55] The vehicle was not damaged, and the future president was able to continue his journey home.

Washington's death or serious injury would have had a profound impact on ratification and the nation's future. Many who opposed the Constitution and feared the potential power of the new government were willing to give the plan a chance only because they took for granted that George Washington would be the first chief executive. Washington's reputation for personal integrity, his stature as the hero of the War of Independence, and his staunch commitment to the United States made him the ideal—and in many minds, the only—man to take the reins of government in the new nation. Americans would trust a government headed by Washington as they would not trust one led by any other politician.[56]

A week after the incident, the *Delaware Gazette* expressed the relief that many felt: "In crossing the bridge near the Head of Elk, the bridge gave way and his horse fell into the river. His Excellency had alighted in order to walk over the bridge, which fortunate circumstances probably saved a life so dear to his country."[57] The *Pennsylvania Gazette,* in an article that was widely reprinted, quoted a Virginia clergyman as saying, "God had preserved his life, to be an eminent blessing to his country," and the paper asked for the "providential preservation of the valuable life of this great and good man" so he could help establish a government that will "render safe and permanent the liberties of America."[58]

What no one knew at the time was that nine months later, delegates at the Virginia ratifying convention in Richmond would come within a few votes of doing what the Elk River had not—depriving the nation of Washington's services as the first president.

George Mason was not so lucky as he was leaving the convention. When he and fellow delegate James McHenry of Maryland were nine miles from Baltimore, their carriage tipped over on a potholed road, and both men were thrown to the ground. Daniel Carroll, a Maryland delegate to the convention, was traveling the same road and came upon

Mason and McHenry shortly after the accident. Carroll told Madison "they were both hurt—the Col. [Mason] most so—he lost blood at Baltimore."[59] Weeks later, Mason wrote to Washington that he was still in pain: "I got very much hurt in my Neck & Head, by the unlucky Accident on the road; it is now wearing off, tho' at times still uneasy to me."[60]

Meanwhile, Madison remained in New York and prepared for winter. He had plenty of things to do. John Jay, Alexander Hamilton, and he would soon undertake the huge task of writing the eighty-five essays, later known as *The Federalist,* that were meant to persuade New York voters to elect supporters of the Constitution to the ratifying convention. They were widely distributed throughout the country and are among the most important documents related to the meaning of the Constitution ever written.

Late in the fall of 1787, Madison received disturbing reports from Virginia that Anti-Federalists, led by Patrick Henry and Richard Henry Lee, were warning citizens—who would soon vote for delegates to the state ratifying convention—that the new Constitution would create a government that betrayed the principles of the Declaration of Independence and would trample personal liberties. He received similar reports from other states.[61]

Madison's friends pleaded with him to return to Virginia to respond to accusations that he had helped to write a plan for a government that his opponents argued would be dangerously powerful. His supporters desperately wanted him to be a candidate for election to the Virginia ratifying convention to be held in Richmond the following June, insisting that only when people heard from Madison directly would they reject the attacks of the Anti-Federalists. Although Madison had strongly supported the plan to have delegates to ratifying conventions elected by the people, that did not mean he wanted to be a candidate. He believed that those who wrote the Constitution should not be the ones who passed judgment on it at the conventions.[62]

As winter approached, he was determined to stay in New York. He had many tasks ahead, and he despised traveling in cold weather. He wrote to friends that he was suffering from a "bilious" condition, which often meant stomach disorder and diarrhea. That ailment, which Madison endured for much of his life, made traveling twelve hours or more a day indescribably uncomfortable. During that era, carriages and stagecoaches absorbed none of the vibrations from the road and instead sent every jolt through the bodies of the helpless passengers. When it was cold, travel was miserable even for those in good health.

Madison told his family and friends that he would stay in the capital at least for the next few months. The election for delegates in Virginia was March 24. He had no intention of being home on that day, and he would not agree to run for election to the ratifying convention.

His supporters needed him to change his mind, and time was running out. He had to be back in Orange County by the day of the election. In eighteenth-century Virginia, voters considered it an insult if a candidate did not appear at the polling place when they cast their ballots. The longer Madison stayed in New York, the less likely he would make it back in time, even if he eventually agreed to run.

As he sat in his room at the boardinghouse at 19 Maiden Lane in lower Manhattan, he opened a letter from John Dawson, a legislator and lawyer from Spotsylvania County, Virginia. Dawson, who later voted against ratification at the convention in Richmond, had surprising news for Madison. It was news that confirmed just how much trouble the new Constitution was in. Suddenly, ratification seemed less likely in Virginia, and if the largest and most important state did not join the union, the proposed plan of government was doomed.

After all the notes from friends, family, and devoted supporters, it may have been a letter from an opponent of the Constitution that convinced Madison to reconsider and return home to Virginia.

~ **2** ~

The Reluctant Candidate

AMONG JAMES MADISON'S MANY ADMIRERS, few seemed as devoted as John Dawson. Known as "Beau" for his elegant attire, the redheaded Dawson wrote a steady stream of letters to Madison between 1785 and 1812.[1] Dawson cared so much about his relationship with Madison that he often began his correspondence with an expression of regret, or even pique, if he had not received a response to his previous note. A week after the Philadelphia convention ended, he wrote, "On my arrival in this town [Fredericksburg], on the last evening, I was much disappointed in receiving no letter from you." He hoped that "our correspondence will be more regular" and said that any information Madison could provide about Congress's activities would be considered "a matter of first consequence to me."[2] He sometimes informed Madison of his travel plans so Madison would know where to send the next letter.[3]

Whether Dawson's respect and fondness for Madison was reciprocated may be lost to history. While dozens of Dawson's letters were saved by Madison and later published, Madison's letters to Dawson were apparently destroyed. That they existed is confirmed only by references in Dawson's correspondence.

Dawson was known for his "amiable deportment," and it was said that Patrick Henry was "very fond of him." He was related to James Monroe, Madison's friend and successor in the White House, through an unusual occurrence of death and remarriage. Monroe's uncle Judge Joseph Jones, who raised Monroe after his father died, was also Dawson's stepfather.[4]

From his room at Mrs. Dorothy Elsworth's boardinghouse in lower Manhattan, where he stayed with other members of the Virginia delegation to Congress, Madison corresponded with dozens of important political figures around the country. After it approved the proposed Constitution and forwarded it to the states at the end of September, Congress failed to achieve a quorum for several months. Madison was thus freed of daily legislative duties and could devote much of his time to working for ratification.

He relied on friends and political supporters in Virginia and throughout the nation to keep informed of developments in his home state and elsewhere. Dawson was an especially conscientious correspondent who told Madison about important events throughout the summer of 1787 and into the fall, as the battle over ratification began.

For months after the Philadelphia convention adjourned, Madison heard increasingly grim reports about how the Constitution was being received in Virginia and around the country. By February 1788, when Dawson's letter arrived with especially bad news, Madison knew the Constitution was in serious trouble.

The letter confirmed rumors Madison had previously heard about his formidable foe George Mason. As soon as the Constitution began appearing in newspapers, there was an immediate and visceral outpouring of disparagement and disapproval of the plan because, among other reasons, it lacked specific protection for individual liberty. The delegates at the Philadelphia convention who had not believed a bill of rights was needed were startled by the intensity of the criticism directed at their work. Citizens who might have had difficulty understanding the intricacies of the proposed plan had no problem recognizing the absence of such protection, and the weakness of the arguments offered by supporters to explain it.[5]

Although he was respected by many citizens, Mason's opposition to the Constitution and his refusal to sign the document did not go over well with his constituents in Fairfax County. Shortly after the Philadelphia convention ended, property owners in the town of Alexandria met to discuss the proposed plan. They wanted the General Assembly to move ahead quickly with ratification, and they instructed their representatives in the House of Delegates, Mason and David Stuart, to support the calling of a convention. They made it clear what they expected the convention to accomplish when they demanded that it be held "as speedily as possible, for the purpose of adopting the . . . constitution."[6]

A few days later, citizens of Fairfax County representing areas outside of Alexandria unanimously approved a resolution ordering Mason and Stuart to announce to the General Assembly that the freeholders of the county supported an immediate ratifying convention, and they ordered their representatives to vote for such a convention. The citizens of the county were understandably concerned about Mason's opposition to the Constitution, but they did not need to worry about him trying to block the calling of a convention.[7] As he told Washington in early October, the Constitution "ought to be submitted to a Convention chosen by the People . . . and shou'd any Attempt be made to prevent the calling [of] such a Convention here, such a Measure shall have every Opposition in my Power to give it."[8]

The Alexandria and Fairfax County meetings demonstrated how much opposition there was to Mason as a possible delegate to the convention. Lambert Cadwalader, a New Jersey delegate to the Confederation Congress, wrote to George Mitchell of Delaware less than a month after the Constitution was signed that "Mason will either not be chosen a Member of the State Convention or, if he is, that he will be instructed to agree to the Adoption of it [the Constitution]."[9] From Alexandria, James Hughes, a lawyer in Fairfax County, speculated that "Should Col. Mason offer himself he would hardly get twenty votes in the whole County for, he has made himself odious."[10]

Dawson had previously told Madison that the freeholders of Fairfax "have on the most pointed terms directed Colo. Mason to vote for a convention [as a member of the House of Delegates], and have as pointedly assur'd him he shall not be in it."[11] From all this correspondence, Madison may have already concluded by the end of October that Mason would not be a delegate at the convention; in any case, he believed that his constituents' opposition would restrain Mason. To a fellow Virginian, Madison wrote that "Col. Mason will exert his influence as far as he can. His County is agst. Him, and have given peremptory instructions on the subject."[12]

Madison's assessment of the political winds in Fairfax County would eventually be confirmed when two supporters of the Constitution were elected to represent the county at the Virginia ratifying convention.[13] At the end of December, Madison learned from Edmund Randolph of rumors that Mason might represent a different county at the ratifying convention: "He will be elected, it is said, for Stafford," the governor wrote in a letter in which he expressed grave concern about the prospects for ratification in Virginia.[14] When Dawson's letter of February 18 confirmed those rumors, Madison knew Mason would be heading to Richmond.[15]

With Mason at their head, the opponents of the Constitution would be in an even stronger position to persuade delegates to defeat the proposed plan. He could remind undecided or pliable delegates every day that without a bill of rights, the new government would be oppressive. Mason was in a special position to talk about that issue because of his role in writing the Virginia Declaration of Rights.

The effort by Stafford County to recruit Mason, who owned property there, had been under way for a while. As early as December, James Mercer, a former member of Congress and currently a judge of the General Court, wrote to his half brother that "it is quite my wish that the people of Stafford elect Colo. Mason for Stafford."[16] By January, Mason had decided to stand for election there, as Edward Carrington explained to Henry Knox: "Colo. Mason is decidedly discarded by a Majority of his late constituents in Fairfax County—so conscious is he that they will not elect him for the Convention that he has declared himself a Candidate for a Neighboring County, where he is invited by some characters of influence who are with him in opinion."[17]

On March 10, 1788, court day and Election Day for Stafford County, Mason told citizens there that he would oppose the Constitution, and he asked their support so that the public would hear "both sides of the story." He also criticized in unexpectedly personal terms his former colleagues at the Philadelphia convention: "My Fellow-Citizens, you have been often told of the wisdom and virtue of the federal convention, but I will now inform you of their true character—the deputies to that body from the states to the southward of us were *Coxcombs*; the deputies from Virginia you know pretty well; the majority of the deputies from the middle states were intriguing office-hunters; and those from the eastern states fools and knaves."[18]

Patrick Henry may have been especially pleased to see a group of citizens from Stafford choose Mason to represent them at the convention. Henry controlled the General Assembly when it wrote the law that governed selection of delegates to the ratifying convention. He may have had Mason in mind when he inserted in the bill a clause declaring that delegates did not have to represent their home counties, as legislators did.

Madison knew that it would not be enough for the Constitution to be approved by the minimum nine states. Virginia had to be a part of the new government for it to survive its infancy. Virginia was the most important state politically in the South, if not the nation. It was by far the largest state geographically, comprising what is today Virginia, West Virginia, and Kentucky. It had almost twice as many residents as the next largest state; its agrarian economy counterbalanced the commercial and manufacturing interests of the Northeast.[19]

Many Virginians wanted to be a part of the new nation because they worried about being on the sidelines when the new government began operations and made important decisions that would affect the country's development.[20] But there was another reason, which few people openly discussed, that made ratification all the more urgent. If Virginia failed to ratify in June 1788, and was left out of the union at its beginning, no Virginians would be eligible for office in the first national government— not even George Washington. Any new federal government without Washington as chief executive would be sorely lacking in credibility and trust.

Virginia Anti-Federalists began the campaign to defeat the Constitution as soon as the Philadelphia convention adjourned. Patrick Henry, Richard Henry Lee, William Grayson, James Monroe, and George Mason, who were among Virginia's most talented and respected political figures, were determined to stop the new plan of government.

Henry was revered for his courage in supporting independence. In 1763, the twenty-seven-year-old son of Scottish immigrants, who had practiced law for only three years, publicly criticized King George III of England and his Privy Council for declaring a law passed by the Virginia House of Burgesses to be "disallowed, void, and of none effect." The law had fixed the price of tobacco to protect Virginia's planters from creditors, public officials, and ministers of the Anglican Church, who were sometimes paid in tobacco or warehouse notes for tobacco that was ready to be shipped.[21]

Once the law was declared void, the Reverend James Maury brought a lawsuit against the collector of the parish levies to recover the balance of his 1759 salary that had been taken while the law was in effect.[22] Maury won before the presiding judge, Colonel John Henry, Patrick's father, on the issue of whether the reverend had been unfairly deprived of his salary by illegal taxation. Judge Henry had concluded, for the only time in the history of Virginia courts, that the King and his council had declared the law invalid *ab initio* (from its inception), and thus Reverend Maury was entitled to compensation. Having lost the first phase of the trial, the defendant's attorney turned the case over to his friend Patrick Henry, whose sole task was to persuade the jury, which would hear the case the next day, to award the minimum in monetary damages.

Word of Judge Henry's decision spread quickly, and a large crowd of farmers, ministers, and other citizens went to the courthouse in Hanover County, just north of Richmond, on the first day of December 1763, to hear the young Henry argue the case. If the jury awarded substantial damages, it would show that Virginia was willing to accept the authority of the Crown to veto laws passed by colonial legislatures.

In the "Parson's Cause," Henry told the jury in an hour-long speech that Virginia had the right to legislate on matters of importance, and that the British constitution did not give the Crown the authority to declare its laws void.[23] He argued that because the king had vetoed the law, "from being the father of his people [he has] degenerated into a Tyrant, and forfeits all rights to his subjects' obedience." Amid the cheers of approval were murmurs that Henry's words went too far in criticizing the king.[24] The opposing attorney strongly objected, saying that "the gentleman has spoken treason."[25] Henry's statement to the jury—coming more than a decade before the Declaration of Independence—was daring and dangerous. For such seditious utterances, he could have been arrested, tried in either America or England, and hanged.

When the jury awarded Reverend Maury only one penny in damages, the crowd erupted in celebration. Henry was carried on their shoulders across the courtyard to a nearby tavern. His father was probably as proud as he was worried about his son: "Patrick spoke in a manner that surprised me, and showed himself well informed on a subject of which I did not know he had any knowledge."[26] News quickly spread that a new voice challenging the authority of the king was being heard around Virginia and the colonies, and Henry's reputation grew.

His success in the Parson's Cause was one of the earliest chapters in the long struggle for independence in Virginia. Two years later, the twenty-nine-year-old Henry, newly elected to the Virginia House of Burgesses, introduced resolutions denouncing Parliament's taxing of the colonies through the harsh provisions of the Stamp Act.[27] Although some of Henry's recommendations were too radical for his colleagues— including one allowing Virginians to ignore laws not passed by the Virginia legislature—he became closely associated with the movement for independence. By March 1775, when Henry spoke the famous words "Give me liberty or give me death" in St. John's Church in Richmond, he had become known as a fervent supporter of freedom for the colonies, who could persuade even his opponents with his mesmerizing oratory.

Richard Henry Lee, smart, well connected, and experienced in public affairs, was highly regarded by many of his fellow Virginians. He had been among the first members of the Continental Congress to call for independence. Three decades after Lee's death, Madison, who had so vigorously opposed Lee's view of the Constitution and his efforts to stop ratification, said he was a man of "patriotic zeal," "captivating eloquence," and "polished manners."[28]

William Grayson, soon to be one of Virginia's first U.S. senators, was bright and energetic. He had many objections to the Constitution, including the lack of a bill of rights: "I think liberty a thing of too much importance to be trusted on the ground of implication: it should rest on principles expressed in the clearest & most unequivocal manner." He also believed that the Senate should have been based on population, and that the Constitution's requirement of only a majority in Congress for regulating commerce and taxing "will ruin the Southern States."[29]

James Monroe, who would become a U.S. senator, secretary of state, and president, was already gaining recognition for his intelligence and warm personality. And George Mason, who would play such a significant role in the ratification debate, was as influential as he was temperamental.

Madison did not understand at first how much of a threat these men posed to the ratification of the Constitution in Virginia and other states. If he had recognized what a difficult road lay ahead for those supporting ratification, he would not have declined initially to be a delegate to the June convention in Richmond.

He had what seemed like a principled reason for not wanting to serve in the convention. He told his brother Ambrose in early November that those who wrote the Constitution should not decide whether it would be ratified: "I am to observe that it was not my wish to have followed the Act of the General Convention into the Convention of the State; supposing that it would be as well that the final decision thereon should proceed from men who had no hand in preparing and proposing it."[30]

But Madison had discovered that other delegates who had been at Philadelphia would serve in their ratifying conventions, and he decided that it would be acceptable for him to do so. He told Ambrose in the same letter that "I shall not decline the representation of the County if I should be honoured with its appointment." He also asked his brother if he knew who the competition would be in the election.[31]

Madison's willingness to be a delegate was a crucial development in the ratification of the Constitution, but it was only the first step in a long process. He was determined to remain in New York until spring, well after March 24, when the delegates would be chosen by the voters of Orange County.

Madison had good reasons for not wanting to leave New York. Over the winter and well into the early months of 1788, traveling conditions were poor. The roads were often little more than frozen ridges of uneven ground, making a carriage or stagecoach ride even more uncomfortable than in spring or summer. With only their clothing and blankets to keep them warm, passengers were forced to ride on rough roads all day long for at least four or five days, and sometimes longer, to get from New York to Virginia.

Around every bend lay hazards that could delay the trip. A swollen river, a washed-out bridge, a ferryboat out of service, a broken wheel or axle, or exhausted horses could interrupt the journey. Inns for eating and sleeping were not always conveniently located and did not always have rooms available for the weary passengers, who were desperate for a hot meal and fireplace after they had spent hours on the road.

Madison's health made traveling especially unpleasant for him. Although he was intensely private and rarely revealed personal information in his letters—at least before the time he met and fell in love with Dolley[32]—he wrote often of his health and not infrequently said that he was not feeling well. His recurrent bouts of stomach disorder and diarrhea would have made the journey exhausting and embarrassing. If Madison required frequent stops, the other passengers would have been annoyed by the delay. It would have been humiliating for the self-conscious Madison to find a place away from the road where he could have a few moments of privacy while the others waited impatiently in the cold.[33]

It was not only the prospect of traveling in poor weather that discouraged Madison from leaving New York before the March 24 election. Madison believed that leaders did not directly solicit votes from the people. Instead, he expected that his reputation and accomplishments in public service would persuade his fellow citizens of Orange County to elect him to the ratifying convention, without his having to campaign in person or even appear in the county prior to the election.[34]

He also believed that those seeking public office should not make promises to citizens in return for their votes. If they made such commitments, they would be required to act in the interests of their supporters and not necessarily for the welfare of the community. It was his lifelong conviction that citizens should choose for government positions those of integrity and virtue who could make difficult choices that were for the long-term good of the state or country without feeling beholden to parochial or immediate demands.[35]

Madison supported limiting the right to vote to those who owned enough land to show they had a stake in the community and could exercise reasonable and independent judgment when choosing public officials. Along with many of his colleagues in the ruling class, he believed that ordinary citizens were more vulnerable to influence than the more independent members of the educated and propertied classes.[36]

Madison's attitude toward campaigning and elections reflected his complex ideas about government and how best to protect the interests of the people. He believed deeply in the principles of a republic: that government operated with the consent of the governed, and that the people were the ultimate sovereignty.[37] That view was at the heart of the Declaration of Independence and was to be the foundation of the new nation. He also wanted people to be educated so they would be knowledgeable about public affairs and could participate appropriately in their governance, no matter their social or economic status.[38] But he had serious doubts about the capacity of ordinary citizens to intelligently exercise their right to choose public officials. He worried about the majority running roughshod over the rights of those less numerous in a community, especially those of property, affluence, and education.[39]

His opinion of the ability of people to choose wisely at election time may have been clouded by his firsthand experience with voters, who sometimes behaved more like drunken partygoers than citizens performing a solemn duty. Back in 1777, when Madison ran for election to the new Virginia House of Delegates, the lower house of the legislature, he refused to go along with the usual practice of providing alcohol to voters at the polling place and around the county to win their support. He thought that the corrupting influence of liquor and other treats was "inconsistent with the purity of moral and republican principles." He was determined to introduce a "more chaste mode of conducting elections in Virginia."[40] His opponent did not have similar scruples and provided the usual beverages to prospective voters. It was the only election Madison lost by a vote of the people during his long career.

Madison was embarrassed by his election defeat, although it led to his appointment to the governor's Council of State and thus allowed him to work directly with highly influential Virginians with whom he would build a new government. Nevertheless, it bothered Madison for a long time that people rejected him because he failed to provide inducements for their vote. Although the voters of Orange County might have matured and become less unruly in the decade after Madison's defeat, there was always the possibility that he would travel all the way back to Virginia only to witness one of the brawls or drunken celebrations that periodically marred the voting in some counties.

Elections in those days were often chaotic. Sometimes crowds of inebriated voters and onlookers created such a disturbance at the polling place that it was impossible for the sheriff to conduct the election. A candidate who was present at the courthouse on Election Day could try to calm his supporters so that the voting could proceed, but it is difficult to imagine the diminutive Madison with his quiet voice successfully restraining loud and rowdy citizens who had been drinking for hours.

Because so many voters expected to be treated to liquor and food, candidates sometimes had to spend substantial sums of money to run for public office, making it difficult for those of modest means to win the election. The favorite beverage was rum punch. Cookies and ginger cake were also frequently provided. Some candidates offered picnics with barbecues, to which all of those eligible to vote were invited. After traveling long distances to get to the courthouse, voters were often tired and hungry. If they believed they were not being treated well, by either the sheriff conducting the election or the candidates, they could be surly and disruptive.[41]

In December 1755, no member was elected to the House of Burgesses—the only elected body in colonial Virginia—from Augusta County because the sheriff could not keep order during the election. "The People were so tumultuous and riotous, that I could not finish the Poll; for which Reason no Burgesses could be returned for the said County," the sheriff wrote in his report about the election.[42]

During the melee, the sheriff struck several prospective voters with a staff in an effort to control the crowd that had pushed its way into the courthouse. The sheriff later told the House of Burgesses, during its investigation of the incident, that some people had been raucous on behalf of their candidate, including one who shouted, "The Election is going against us ... [I]f we cannot carry it one Way, we will have it another: I will put a Stop to the Election." During the commotion, the sheriff was thrown onto the table holding the polling books, and it broke under him.[43]

Even George Washington had to satisfy the expectations of the voters. During a July election in Frederick County in 1758, his agent supplied 160 gallons of alcohol to 391 voters. Although this violated the law that prohibited the giving of "money, meat, drink, present, gift, reward, or entertainment . . . in order to be elected," few candidates were ever prosecuted or disqualified from taking office on such grounds.[44]

In most Virginia counties, votes were cast by voice. The sheriff called the voter's name, and the citizen stepped forward to identify the candidate he supported. After the sheriff announced the vote, the candidate, who was often sitting at the table, would rise, bow, and publicly thank the voter. Anyone nearby would know how the election was going even before the last vote was recorded. Disappointed crowds could stop the election and prevent the defeat of their candidate.[45]

No one had to register to vote in advance, and in close elections, arguments frequently erupted over the property qualifications of certain potential voters. White men at least twenty-one years old who owned twenty-five acres and a house, fifty acres unimproved, or a lot with a house in town were eligible. The sheriff could refuse to accept the vote of someone he knew to be unqualified, and each candidate had the right to challenge any voter by requiring him to swear that he met the legal requirements.[46]

The sheriff had the right to close the poll when he pleased, which could be in the early afternoon or as late as after dark. If the weather made traveling difficult, the sheriff could continue the polling the next day.[47] A losing candidate would have no choice but to try to overturn the results of the election by appealing to the General Assembly, an expensive and onerous process.

All persons who had enough land to vote were required to do so, but the law was rarely enforced. After 1785, a Virginia voter who failed to go to the polling place was supposed to forfeit an amount equal to one-fourth of his levies and taxes for the year. When the grand jury in Amherst County indicted seventy-five men for failing to vote, the county court dismissed the case.[48]

No matter what Madison's reasons were for not wanting to campaign for public office, his delayed arrival from New York alarmed his friends and supporters. Opponents of the new Constitution had tried for months to convince their fellow citizens in Orange County and around the state that the document would create a powerful and consolidated government, and that their newly won independence and not-yet-secured rights were in jeopardy. Although some opponents of the new government intentionally distorted what the Constitution said or meant, by the end of 1787 they were beginning to have an impact that could drastically affect the election of delegates to the ratifying convention and the convention itself.

The Constitution was published in Virginia newspapers beginning a few days after it was signed. By early November, the report of the Constitutional Convention had been printed twice in pamphlet editions, twice in broadsides—one- or two-page documents similar to small posters—and in at least six of Virginia's nine newspapers.[49]

It did not take long for those who objected to the Constitution to make their views known. As early as September 25, eight days after the Constitutional Convention adjourned, John Dawson wrote to Madison that "altho there are many warm friends to the plan, be assurd that the opposition will be powerful." Five days later, Governor Randolph told Madison that the opposition would be "formidable."[50]

The letters arriving at Madison's boardinghouse in New York did not just describe the objections of the now committed opponents of the Constitution. Even some correspondents Madison expected to be enthusiastic about the plan wrote of their serious misgivings about key provisions of the Constitution. Members of Madison's own family expressed concerns about how the new government would function. This was not good news for Madison. He must have thought that if his friends had such reservations about the document, his opponents would find plenty in its numerous passages with which to alarm the people.

Madison's cousin the Reverend James Madison, president of the College of William and Mary, spent much of his letter in early October praising Madison's efforts at the convention, but he objected to what he considered to be a lack of separation of powers between the executive and legislative branches, describing them as the "most unfortunate Features in the new Constn." Reverend Madison said this was a "Defect, wch. perhaps threatens Ruin to Republicanism itself." He worried that the president "may be for Life" because there were no term limits, and might prove to be "almost a Negative upon the Legislature" because of the executive's veto power. He observed that senators—who served long terms and who were appointed by state legislatures—"may also be for Life." Reverend Madison did not specifically identify characteristics of the Constitution that blended powers—including the vice president serving as the head of the Senate, and the Senate having to approve treaties and confirm high-level executive-branch officials and federal judges— but he probably had those in mind when he noted that the Senate would "occasionally [be] a Part of the Executive." Was there not, he asked his cousin, universal agreement that "it is essential to every free Govt., that ye Legislative and Executive Departments should be entirely distinct & independent?"[51]

Reverend Madison may have spared his cousin the discomfort of reading even harsher criticism of the Constitution, but he did not hold back when he wrote the same day to his brother Thomas Madison, who was married to Patrick Henry's sister Susannah. He told Thomas that by blending executive and legislative authority, the Constitution would result in a "total overthrow to every Thing like a democratic Govt.—& I think, must end if it be continued under its present Form in a certain Tyranny."[52]

Others were also troubled by the Constitution's insufficient separation of powers. Joseph Jones, a Fredericksburg lawyer who had been a member of the Continental Congress and the Council of State, complained to Madison that the "constitution of the Senate, which being both legislative and Executive and in some respects judiciary is I think radically bad." He worried that the president and Senate would be able to act on treaties and alliances, which would be the supreme law of the land, without the "concurrence of the popular branch." Jones also said that he would have preferred that a bill of rights be included because there is "so much in the execution of the Government to be provided for by the legislature and that Body possess[es] too great a portion of Aristocracy." As he gathered with fellow legislators in Richmond at the fall session, Jones warned Madison that if comments of members of the General Assembly accurately reflected the opinion of the people, then "they must be very much divided and I think the advocates for the new plan rather diminish than increase in number."[53]

While these alarming reports from Virginia made their way to Madison in New York, George Washington was observing the same trends close at hand, from his estate at Mount Vernon. He seemed optimistic in his letter to Madison of October 10 when he predicted the Constitution would be approved at the Virginia convention. But he also criticized Mason for his zealous determination to defeat the plan, and he said Mason had "rendered himself obnoxious in Philadelphia by the pains he took to disseminate his objections" among the leading members of the Pennsylvania legislature, thus causing a delay in that state's ratification process.[54] If Mason had that kind of impact in another state, it is no wonder that Washington worried about his potential effect on ratification in Virginia.

It was not long before Madison began to see how difficult the fight for the Constitution would be in his home state, and he expressed that apprehension in his letters. At the end of October, he wrote to William Short, a lawyer who had served as Jefferson's private secretary in Paris, that "Virg[ini]a I fear will be divided and extremely agitated" about the Constitution. He predicted that Randolph's and Mason's decisions not to sign would create serious problems in the state.[55]

Four days later, Madison acknowledged to Washington that the Anti-Federalists were gaining strength: "I am not without fears that their [Henry's and Mason's] combined influence and management may yet create difficulties." On the other hand, Madison remained hopeful that at least nine states would ratify, and the others would either be "left as outcasts" or be "compelled to come in."[56]

By this time, Randolph had decided to support the Constitution, having concluded that Virginia had no choice but to approve the plan and seek amendments. He also knew the situation was becoming increasingly gloomy. In a letter assessing the attitude of the General Assembly gathered in Richmond, Randolph reported that the tide is turning against the Constitution, and he added, "New objections are started daily, and the opinions of Mr. H——y [Henry] gain ground." Randolph told Madison that he had so far declined to express his support for ratification except in private. He was waiting until the General Assembly had a chance to debate the proposed plan. The governor knew that he was going to be harshly criticized for refusing to sign and noted that he and Mason, the other Virginia delegate who did not sign the Constitution, had been "spoken of illiberally at least."[57]

While members of the General Assembly discussed how and when to hold the ratifying convention, they had to decide whether to elect Randolph to another term as governor and whether to continue Madison as a member of the Confederation Congress. Although some of the criticism of the Constitution was directed at Randolph and Madison personally, the members of the General Assembly set that aside to express a vote of confidence in the two officials. On October 23, Madison was reelected to another term in Congress by "126 out of 140," and Randolph was elected to a second one-year term as governor by "137 out of 140."[58]

The General Assembly eventually voted unanimously to forward the Constitution to the ratifying convention that would meet in June, a comparatively late date that would come after most other state conventions.[59] That decision brought relief to some who predicted that supporters would need more time to shape public opinion. John Dawson wrote in November that opponents in Virginia are "many, able, and busy—Converts are daily made." He added that by "fixing the meeting of the convention to so late a day we shall be able to act on the determinations of the other states."[60]

As the fall of 1787 continued, Madison wrote letters to supporters and encouraged them to discuss with as many people as possible the arguments in favor of ratification. In mid-November, he sent Washington the first seven essays of *The Federalist* and all but admitted that he was one of the authors of the essays written under the name "Publius." He asked Washington to send the papers to his "confidential correspondents" at Richmond so they could be reprinted there.[61] Washington complied with this request, and before the end of the year, the essays began appearing in Virginia newspapers.[62]

Meanwhile, the Anti-Federalists were hard at work. Richard Henry Lee began his efforts to stop the Constitution from being ratified soon after the convention ended. He did not have to start from scratch. As Henry Knox, the Confederation secretary of war, wrote to Washington in early October, the "germ of opposition originated in the [Philadelphia] convention itself. The gentlemen [Randolph, Mason, and Gerry] who refused signing it will most probably conceive themselves obligated to state their reasons publickly. The presses will groan with melancholy forebodings, and a party of some strength will be created."[63]

When the Confederation Congress debated the proposed plan of government, Lee wanted to attach a statement to the effect that the Philadelphia convention had exceeded its authority, and to add a list of proposed amendments. He failed to persuade his colleagues to go along with either suggestion. Shortly after Congress forwarded the Constitution to the states on September 28, Lee began contacting friends and political allies, criticizing the Constitution and enclosing copies of his amendments. In a letter to Elbridge Gerry, who was in New York, Lee wrote that unless the Constitution was amended to preserve "those essential rights of Mankind, without which liberty can not exist, we shall soon find that the New plan of government will be far more inconvenient than any thing sustained under the present Government."[64]

Lee, who was one of the most important Anti-Federalists and perhaps the leading intellectual in their ranks, passionately believed that the Constitution granted so much power to the new federal government that a bill of rights was necessary to protect citizens from potentially despotic rulers.[65] Specifically, he wanted to defend the rights of conscience in matters of religion; freedom of the press; protection against unreasonable searches and seizures; the right to trial by jury in civil cases; the ban on standing armies unless two-thirds of Congress approved; the prohibition of excessive bail or fines and of cruel and unusual punishment; and the right of the people to assemble peaceably for the purpose of petitioning legislative bodies.[66]

He also believed that the Constitution should create a "council of state" or "privy council" to advise and assist the executive branch of government, whose eleven members would be appointed by the president.[67] Virginia had such a Council of State under its 1776 constitution, which had to give its approval before the governor could make significant decisions.[68]

Although Lee favored such a council at the federal level to prevent the president from becoming too powerful, some of his recommendations seemed to enlarge, not diminish, the power of the executive branch.

He argued that the Constitution should be changed to give the new council of state the authority to confirm the appointments of "all officers, civil and military" made by the president, a power granted under the Constitution to the Senate. He also supported the elimination of the vice president, whose duties would be handled by the council. The Senate, according to Lee, could choose one of its members to preside over its deliberations and did not need the vice president to perform that function. Lee also wanted to increase the size of the House of Representatives, the only branch elected by the people, so that it could protect the diverse interests of the nation.[69]

Political figures in those days often wrote letters to allies with the idea that they would eventually be published in a newspaper or other forum.[70] It was one of the few ways to influence the opinion of people who often lived in small towns and were hard to reach otherwise. When discussing his concerns about the Constitution and in proposing amendments, Lee did not want his correspondents to keep the letters private. He knew that to generate support among Anti-Federalists and have a chance to stop the ratification effort, his criticisms of the Constitution and his plan for improving it would have to be widely known.

Lee wrote to Mason at the beginning of October to explain in detail what had transpired in the Confederation Congress and to warn of the dangers of the proposed Constitution. He urged Mason to help spread the word about "a plan subversive of the present system" and recommended that Mason forward Lee's comments to Edmund Pendleton, the respected Virginia judge, whose views on the Constitution were unknown. If Pendleton could be persuaded to oppose the Constitution, his opinion would carry great weight in Virginia and influence delegates to the upcoming ratifying convention. Lee was hoping that once Pendleton had joined the Anti-Federalist cause, he would help in other states by communicating his opposition to one of his nephews, Henry Pendleton, a judge in South Carolina. He also asked Mason to contact Thomas Stone, a Maryland state senator, and "others of influence in Maryland," so that Maryland and Virginia could work together to block ratification until amendments were proposed.[71]

Lee continued his letter-writing campaign to spread the word throughout the nation that supporters of the Constitution had to be stopped. He told William Shippen Jr., a Philadelphia doctor who was married to Lee's sister Alice, that it would "put Civil Liberty and the happiness of the people at the mercy of Rulers who may possess the great unguarded powers given [in the Constitution]." He included his list of amendments and told Shippen to submit the letter to his father, William Shippen Sr., with whom Lee had served in Congress; also, Lee added, "Perhaps they may be submitted to the world at large."[72]

In a long letter to Randolph two weeks later, Lee discussed various defects and dangers in the Constitution. He told the governor that "I am perfectly satisfied that you make such use of this letter as you shall think to be for the public good."[73] Lee may have believed that Randolph would actively join the opponents of the Constitution, and he was asking Randolph to use his political connections to help disseminate Lee's letter and his proposed amendments as widely as possible.

Lee then directed his efforts toward stopping ratification in the northern states. He wrote a detailed letter to Samuel Adams of Massachusetts, with whom Lee said he had long toiled in the "Vineyard of liberty," arguing that the Constitution could be saved if states would submit amendments to Congress, which would then call a constitutional convention to add them to the proposed plan. He warned that the people had no idea that they were "being brought under despotic rule under the notion of 'Strong government,' or in the form of *elective despotism:* Chains being still Chains, whether made of gold or iron."[74] Adams, who was a hero to many in Massachusetts and New England for his efforts to win independence, would be influential if he were to actively oppose the Constitution.

It was not long before Lee's concerns about the Constitution were widely published. His amendments began appearing in newspapers in

Virginia by mid-November and around the country soon after. The *Winchester Virginia Gazette* printed them under the heading "Observations on the Plan of Government, proposed by the Convention. By R.H.L., Esquire." Three weeks later, the *Petersburg Virginia Gazette* published Lee's October 16 letter to Randolph, including his proposed amendments.[75]

Samuel Adams, the well known patriot, was generally opposed to the Constitution but eventually voted for its ratification at the Massachusetts convention. *(National Archives)*

During the fall, increasing numbers of citizens had access to Lee's scathing criticism of the Constitution. In early December, Washington informed Madison that Lee's letter to Randolph "circulated with great industry in manuscript, four weeks before it went to press, and is said to have had a bad influence. The enemies of the Constitution leave no stone unturned to encrease the opposition to it."[76] Within a short time, Lee's letter to Randolph and his list of amendments were published in eleven newspapers in six states, while the letter without the amendments was printed in a half dozen additional newspapers.[77]

Lee's comments on the Constitution were not confined to newspapers and letters. His criticisms and his proposed amendments were published in a sixty-four-page pamphlet anthology titled *Various Extracts on the Federal Government, Proposed by the Convention Held at Philadelphia.* The pamphlet, published by Augustine Davis of the *Virginia Independent Chronicle* in Richmond, included essays by supporters and opponents of the Constitution.[78]

While Lee worked energetically to spread opposition to the Constitution and to promote his amendments, Mason wrote letters and newspaper essays that reached ever-increasing numbers of citizens worried about the potential power of the new federal government. The genesis of Mason's writings in opposition to the Constitution may have been at the Philadelphia convention when, a few days before the Constitution was signed, Mason objected to the absence of a bill of rights. He was upset that the report of the five-member Committee of Style—a committee that drafted much of the final language of the Constitution and that included Madison—did not provide explicit protection for individual rights. Mason wrote his objections to the Constitution on his copy of the committee's report.[79]

Long after the convention ended, Mason was still brooding about the way he was treated in Philadelphia. As he later explained to Thomas Jefferson, Mason wanted to offer his ideas to the convention "by Way of Protest; but was discouraged from doing so, by the precipitate & intemperate, not to say indecent Manner in which the Business was conducted, during the last week of the Convention, after the Patrons of this new plan found they had a decided majority in their Favour." Mason told Jefferson that he could not understand why so many delegates to the Virginia ratifying convention were leaning toward approval: "Many are for ratifying first, and amending afterwards. This Idea appears to me so utterly absurd, that I can not think any Man of Sense candid, in Proposing it."[80]

Mason's primary objection was the lack of a bill of rights in the new Constitution. He believed sections of state constitutions protecting individual liberty would provide no security under the new government. He also argued that the House of Representatives would be "only the shadow of Representation" and that laws would generally be made by branches of government not directly elected by the people. He voiced many other objections to the plan, including the potential power of the federal judiciary to "absorb & destroy the Judiciarys of the several states." He especially regretted the absence of language protecting freedom of the press and trial by jury in civil cases, and the presence of language allowing standing armies in time of peace.[81]

Mason's energy and zeal were boundless. The October 17 edition of the *Virginia Independent Chronicle* included an article written by "Cato Uticensis," who was probably Mason, one of many political figures who wrote comments using a different name.[82] Addressing "Freemen of Virginia," Cato wrote in a long, intensely passionate, and sweeping article that the proposed plan would "annihilat[e] the Constitution of each individual state" and that the new "high prerogative government . . . is to swallow up the rest."[83]

Mason told anyone who would listen that he vigorously opposed the Constitution. By the time he returned to his seat in the House of Delegates at the end of October, news of his objections had already reached Richmond.[84] A fellow delegate, John Pierce, who represented James City County, observed that Mason was taking "the utmost pains to disseminate the reasons of his dissent, in which he has condemned every part of the Constitution, and undertaken to proving the destruction of the liberty of the people in consequence of it."[85]

Tobias Lear, Washington's private secretary, reported to John Langdon, a New Hampshire delegate to the Constitutional Convention, that Mason had given his objections "in manuscript to persons in all parts of the country where he supposed they would make an impression."[86] No one doubted Mason's passion in stirring up opposition to the Constitution, or his self-confidence. Lear noted this in an earlier letter to Langdon: "I hope the people will have too much good sense to be influenced by them [the Anti-Federalists].—Colo. Mason is certainly a man of superior abilities—he is sensible of it," and has "generally felt his own weight & influence in those publick bodies where he has acted heretofore."[87]

By the end of November, newspapers in Virginia and other states published Mason's objections. Augustine Davis's *Virginia Independent Chronicle* published Mason's views in the *Various Extracts on the Federal Government* pamphlet, along with the amendments proposed by Lee.[88]

Worried supporters of the Constitution searched for new approaches to slow the momentum of the Anti-Federalists and undo some of the damage inflicted on efforts to ratify the Constitution in Virginia and other states. From Mount Vernon, Washington began circulating to political supporters James Wilson's speech to a public meeting in Philadelphia delivered in early October, a few weeks after the convention ended, in which Wilson provided an eloquent defense of the proposed plan of government and explained why the Constitution should be approved even without a bill of rights.[89] Wilson, who later served on the U.S. Supreme Court, had been an important member of the Pennsylvania delegation at the Constitutional Convention.

Circulating Wilson's speech may have persuaded some potential delegates, but its impact was probably limited. Two weeks after Washington sent the Wilson speech to various individuals and newspapers, the *Virginia Independent Chronicle* published an anonymous commentary that called Wilson's talk a laughable performance. The writer refused to accept the assertion by supporters of the Constitution that the people would be protected without a bill of rights because the new government was one of limited powers.[90]

Even Madison's friend James Monroe, while not explicitly stating his own objections to the Constitution, told Madison in mid-October that opponents of the plan were hard at work and, combined with the decision of Mason and Randolph not to sign the Constitution, "this ensures it a powerful opposition."[91]

Under the barrage of bad publicity generated by the Anti-Federalists, supporters of the Constitution fought back with letters, broadsides, and newspaper essays and at public meetings. Citizens in the counties of Berkeley, Fairfax, Frederick, and Henrico, and in the cities of Alexandria, Williamsburg, Fredericksburg, and Petersburg, gathered to express support for the Constitution, to petition the General Assembly to call a ratifying convention, or both.[92]

As Madison read his correspondence in New York, he realized that he had to do something to stem the tide of opposition to the Constitution in Virginia. If he waited much longer, not only would too many opponents be elected to the ratifying convention, but Madison himself could be defeated at the polls and prevented from going to Richmond to argue for the document he had been so instrumental in writing. His correspondents were begging him to return to Orange County to refute what they said were lies about the proposed plan of government and his role in creating it. They hoped that hearing of such misrepresentations would help persuade the reluctant statesman to come back to Virginia. But by the end of the year, they learned that strategy was not likely to work, so they instead appealed directly to his sense of duty and honor. They also did not want to take a chance that voters would be offended by his absence from the county before Election Day.

Orange County justice of the peace Lawrence Taliaferro began this new approach by writing to Madison in mid-December with the disturbing news that some in the county were saying that Madison himself was opposed to the Constitution: "I dare say you will be gratly [greatly] suppd. [surprised] to hear that it is report'd that you Are Opos'd to the Sistum & I was told the other day that you ware [were, are] Actually writing a Pece against it." Taliaferro urged Madison to be in Orange County a few weeks before the election to prevent citizens from "being led into an Error by a few Men that seme vary ernest in doing it."[93]

Archibald Stuart was one of many friends who tried to explain to Madison how important it was for him to be in Virginia before the election. In a tone that few correspondents used in letters to Madison, Stuart appealed to his commitment to public service to help overcome his reluctance: "For gods sake do not disappoint the Anxious expectations of yr friends & let me add of yr country."[94]

Andrew Shepherd, later sheriff of Orange County, warned Madison just before Christmas that his presence was necessary to prevent "artfull persons from injecting their poison into the unwarie,"[95] while Henry Lee, a friend and member of the famous Virginia family, but one who supported the Constitution, told Madison that some in the county were "warmly opposed [to the Constitution] & may perhaps consider it their duty to prevent your election."[96]

James Gordon, who eventually served with Madison at the ratifying convention, believed that the county was "much divided" over the plan for the new government and that Madison's attendance was essential. As proof of how bad things were, Gordon informed Madison that Baptist minister John Leland was among those trying to convince citizens to oppose the new system.[97] Leland had great influence over the numerous Baptists in the area and, as he would clearly show a year later when Madison ran for election to the First Congress, could sway hundreds of voters. If Leland had doubts about the new government and could not be persuaded to support it, Madison's election to the Richmond convention was in danger. Madison had to get home to talk to Leland and others who had serious concerns about the proposed Constitution.

Even Madison's father, James Madison Sr., who did not often write to his son about politics, understood the threat that Baptist opposition posed to his election. At the end of January, the senior Madison wrote that the "Baptists are now generally opposed to it [the new Constitution] ... I think you had better come in as early in March as you can; many of your friends wish it; there are some who suspends their opinion till they see you, & wish for an explanation, others wish you not to come, & will endeavor to shut you out of the Convention, the better to carry their point."[98]

The most important of the letter writers who pleaded with Madison to get back to Virginia was Governor Randolph. He had become increasingly concerned about the future of Virginia and the nation if his home state did not ratify the Constitution and join the union.

Randolph would shortly show the kind of courage that was one of the traits Madison admired in him. At the Richmond convention, the thirty-four-year-old governor was criticized and ridiculed in unusually sharp and personal terms. Men fought duels over less caustic language than that hurled at Randolph during the three weeks of debate.[99] In an era in which inconsistency in political positions was seen as a negative attribute, it must have been hard for the governor to show up and explain why Virginia should approve a plan that only months earlier he had rejected.

Although Madison had been disappointed and distressed by Randolph's decision not to add his name to the Constitution, he still respected him and was likely influenced by his request that Madison return to Orange County. Randolph wrote to his fellow Virginian just after the first of the year: "You must come in. Some people in Orange are opposed to your politicks. Your election to the convention, is, I believe, sure; but I beg you not to hazard it by being absent at the time."[100]

William Moore, a close friend of Madison and a legislator who also served as sheriff of Orange County until 1789, learned from Madison's father that his son was not planning to return to Virginia before the election. Moore wrote to Madison at the end of January to remind him of the "disadvantage of being absent at Election to those who offer themselves to serve the Public[.] I must therefore intreat and conjure you nay commd. you, if it was in my Power, to be here in February or the first of March Next." Moore told Madison that his friends and supporters would do everything they could to help him win even if he stayed in New York, but he urged him, "[P]ray dont disappoint the wishes of your Friends and many others who are wavering on the Constitution that are anxiously waiting for an Explanation from you[.] [I]n short they want your Sentiments from your own mouth which they say will convince them of the necessity of adopting it [the Constitution]."[101]

Then the letter from John Dawson arrived. Not only did he tell Madison that Mason would likely be a delegate to the ratifying convention, he revealed that several strong candidates were running in Orange County, and thus Madison's election to the ratifying convention was "very doubtful." Encouraging Madison to return, he said, "I must therefore join your other friends and intreat your attendance at the election." He also informed Madison that James Monroe was running for delegate to the ratifying convention from Spotsylvania County.[102] Madison thus knew that the capable Monroe could be joining Henry and Mason during those difficult weeks ahead in Richmond.

After months of indecision, Madison finally agreed to return home in time for the election. Washington, who had followed these events through letters and visits from friends, must have been greatly relieved when Madison told him that he would be a candidate and would appear in person in the county: "I can say with great truth however that in this overture I sacrifice every private inclination to considerations not of a selfish nature. I foresee that the undertaking will involve me in very laborious and irksome discussions; that public opposition to several very respectable characters whose esteem and friendship I greatly prize may unintentionally endanger the subsisting connection; and that disagreeable misconstructions of which samples have already been given, may be the fruit of those exertions which fidelity will impose."[103]

On the crucial issue of whether he would personally appear in Orange County on Election Day, Madison told Washington that "if I am informed that my presence at the election in the County be indispensable, [I] shall submit to that condition also; though it is my particular wish to decline it, as well to avoid apparent solicitude on the occasion, as a journey of such length at a very unpleasant season."[104]

Overcoming his lack of enthusiasm for campaigning and the bad roads, Madison arrived in Orange County on March 23, only one day before the election. The next morning he traveled the four miles from Montpelier to the Orange County courthouse, where, for the first time in his long career, he addressed a large crowd and asked them to elect him to a position of importance.

March 24 was the third day of spring, but there was little sign of it in Virginia. The day dawned wintry and cold, and as Madison spoke to the voters, drifts of snow swirled in front of the courthouse. Madison's thin voice must have been difficult for many in the audience to hear, but he held their attention for almost two hours. He said later he had not expected the level of opposition to the new Constitution that he found in his home county. He told his friend Eliza House Trist that he was "cha-grined" to find the county "filled with the most absurd and groundless prejudices against the federal Constitution." The situation required him to "mount for the first time in my life, the rostrum before a large body of the people, and to launch into a harangue of some length in the open air and on a very windy day."[105]

Madison learned that his friends were right all along.

In the election, Madison won, and by an overwhelming margin. He received 202 votes, and his fellow delegate James Gordon, also a sup-porter of the Constitution, earned 187. The Anti-Federalist candidates trailed with 56 and 34 votes.[106] Madison must have felt extra satisfaction because one of his opponents was Charles Porter, who had defeated Madison for the House of Delegates in 1777 by providing alcohol to vot-ers. Porter received the fewest votes.[107]

Whether it had been prompted by Dawson's letter informing Madi-son about Mason, or the cumulative effect of the letters from friends and family, Madison's decision to return home for the election almost certainly meant the difference between victory and defeat. His speech to the assembled voters was eloquent enough to defeat the fears and uncer-tainties spread by the Constitution's opponents. James Duncanson told a correspondent that Madison "had converted them in a speech of an hour & three quarters, delivered at the Courthouse door before the Pol opened."[108] Another observer noted that Madison "convinced a Major-ity that he had acted as he ought & that the Constitution ought to be Adopted."[109] Cyrus Griffin, attending Congress in New York, said he was told that Madison's presence in Orange County was "absolutely neces-sary to counteract some unwarrantable proceedings."[110] Edward Carrington congratulated Madison "upon the success which attended your efforts to turn the Sinners of Orange from their wicked ways."[111]

Madison himself conceded that if he had not been at the Orange County courthouse on that day, the election might well have gone the other way: "It is very probable that a very different event would have taken place as to myself if the efforts of my friends had not been sec-onded by my presence."[112] But now Madison was on his way to Rich-mond, where he could fight for the new Constitution in person.

3

The Road to Richmond

THE DROUGHT THAT PLAGUED RICHMOND in the days leading up to the convention may have been devastating to local farmers, but it made travel easier. With so little rain, rivers and creeks could be crossed on horseback. The city had few bridges, and if heavy rainfall had preceded the convention, some delegates would not have made it to the opening sessions. From the hills overlooking the city, local residents could see clouds of dust as hundreds of horses made their way along parched roads leading to town. On horseback and in carriages, some of the most important political figures of the founding period, along with hundreds of spectators who wanted to hear the debate, made their way to the state capital.[1]

From the distance of more than two centuries, it is easy to think of the ratifying conventions as part of an orderly and predictable process that began with the signing of the Constitution in September 1787 and ended successfully with the ratification of the ninth state, New Hampshire, the following June. But in fact the process was created ad hoc and varied from state to state, and the outcome was far from certain. Unlike the delegates to the Philadelphia convention, who gathered in one place over a three-and-a-half-month period to propose a plan of government, the 1,750 men who attended the state ratifying conventions—fourteen in all because North Carolina held two—were chosen in hundreds of elections that varied from town meetings in New England to countywide elections in most other states in a process that lasted almost three years.[2] All of this took place in an era in which transportation was slow and arduous and communications systems were primitive by today's standards.

Many steps were involved: The Confederation Congress, upon receiving the proposed Constitution from the Philadelphia delegates, forwarded the document to the states for their consideration. Each state legislature had to call an election for delegates to the convention, decide on their eligibility, and determine the qualifications of citizens voting in the election. Anti-Federalist legislators, concerned about the diminished power of the states under the new system, could create mischief at every step.

Once laws establishing the process for selecting delegates to the conventions had been enacted, candidates came forward to communicate their views on the Constitution to their fellow citizens, and elections had to be conducted. Explaining a long and complex document that was difficult for many people to understand was challenging enough. When opponents and supporters finessed troublesome sections of the proposed plan or intentionally distorted what it said, the debate became more convoluted. Finally, ratifying conventions were held, where delegates decided whether to approve the Constitution.

The long journey toward ratification in Virginia had begun the previous October with the General Assembly's decision to hold the convention. Soon, however, disputes arose. In November, what should have been a routine administrative matter that had been "overlooked" during the debate over the timing of the convention suddenly turned into a heated and divisive argument over amendments to the proposed Constitution.[3]

The decision to hold the convention seven months later in June 1788, a relatively late date in the ratification period, generated vigorous debate. Both sides realized that every decision, including when to have the convention, could affect the outcome in Virginia and other states. Even at this early stage, Madison believed that citizens throughout the country were watching to see how Virginia approached the ratification issue. He told Edmund Pendleton at the end of October that "the example of Virginia will have great weight," and added, "It would be truly mortifying if any thing should occur to prevent or retard the concurrence of a State [Virginia] which has generally taken the lead on great occasions."[4]

When Francis Corbin introduced a resolution in the House of Delegates on October 25 calling for the ratifying convention, the Anti-Federalists were ready.[5] Patrick Henry immediately objected because Corbin's resolution implied that the convention would be limited to an up or down vote on the Constitution. Henry did not question the need for a convention, but he wanted it made clear that its delegates would have the discretion to propose amendments either before or after ratification. There were "errors and defects" in the Constitution, Henry argued, that had to be corrected for the plan to be acceptable to Virginia and the nation.[6]

Corbin would not budge as he energetically defended his resolution. His colleague George Nicholas, who represented Jefferson's home county of Albemarle, supported Corbin by objecting to Henry's motion on the grounds that it gave the false impression the legislature had debated the Constitution and had reached the conclusion that amendments were necessary. In fact, Nicholas said, "there was a decided majority in its favour" in Virginia.[7]

George Mason, who had just taken his seat in the House, rose to second Henry's motion to amend the Corbin resolution. He promised to explain more at "a proper season" but said that after he had "deeply and maturely weighed every article of the constitution . . . he could not approve it."[8] He demanded that the ratifying convention have the authority to propose amendments.

The argument continued until John Marshall, with "his usual perspicuity"—in the words of the *Virginia Gazette*—recommended that the Constitution be submitted to the convention delegates "for their free and ample discussion."[9] The delegates must have concluded that this proposal neither suggested that the General Assembly had reviewed the Constitution and had objections to it, nor precluded consideration of amendments at the convention, for they unanimously approved Marshall's resolution. The Senate endorsed the measure six days later.[10] Not only would Henry get the opportunity in June to discuss amendments, he also would have the chance to convince his fellow delegates that Virginia should require changes to the Constitution before ratifying it.

The decision to allow amendments gave those opposed to the Constitution a potent weapon, but supporters had little choice. Governor Randolph believed that if the delegates had been prevented from considering amendments, the General Assembly would have refused to schedule the meeting. He told Madison after the resolution passed the House that if the convention had not been able to "freely . . . discuss and deliberate on the constitution," it "would have been rejected and the spirit of union extinguished."[11]

Nevertheless, Madison was worried that the Virginia resolution would send precisely the wrong message to other states: that the Constitution could be amended by state conventions. "Virginia has set the example of opening a door for amendments, if the Convention there should chuse to propose them," he wrote to Jefferson in early December.[12] Madison had good reason to be concerned that other state conventions would consider proposing amendments now that Virginia had authorized its convention to do so. Once state conventions agreed to debate amendments, there was no guarantee that a clean ratification would come first and that amendments would be discretionary. With amendments on the table, opponents of the Constitution at state conventions could argue that ratification with suggested amendments would be a hollow gesture because the new Congress would be free to ignore such recommendations. Only when ratification was contingent upon the approval of amendments would Congress have to seriously consider them.

Supporters maintained that the entire ratification process could be jeopardized if state conventions attached amendments as a condition of their approval. A conditional ratification by any state would probably not have counted toward the nine required to officially sanction the Constitution and launch the new government. Until the Constitution had been ratified, the new Congress would be unable to meet to consider amendments.

Madison and other supporters feared that once state conventions began writing amendments, the number of suggested changes would quickly multiply. Most states would propose amendments that advanced their own interests. Some of the most important sections of the proposed Constitution—which had resulted

Thomas Jefferson, although in Paris as minister to France, urged the adoption of the Bill of Rights and helped persuade James Madison to support what became the first ten amendments. *(National Archives)*

from long debate and delicate compromises at the Philadelphia convention—would be drastically changed if such amendments were adopted. When Congress eventually met, it would have to sort out hundreds of amendments, knowing that the failure to give them sufficient attention would permit a state to withdraw its conditional ratification. Madison wrote to George Nicholas two months before the Virginia ratifying convention that "Conditional amendments or a second general

Convention, will be fatal." Just the delay to consider such amendments was, to Madison, "too serious to be hazarded."[13]

Madison was also greatly concerned about Governor Randolph's support for a second constitutional convention. He knew firsthand what it had taken to organize and conduct the first convention, and he was understandably worried about what a second would do. A few months before the Virginia ratifying convention met, he tried to persuade Randolph to reconsider his position. Madison told the governor that a "conditional ratification [by Virginia] or a second convention appears to me utterly irreconcileable in the present state of things with the dictates of prudence and safety . . . [A] second experiment [convention] would be either wholly abortive, or would end in something much more remote from your [Randolph's] ideas and those of others who wish a salutary Government, than the plan [Constitution] now before the public." Madison told Randolph that those determined to defeat the Constitution would use the new convention to "carry on their schemes, under the mask of contending for alterations." Madison especially worried about efforts by prominent Virginia Anti-Federalists—such as Patrick Henry, Richard Henry Lee, and George Mason—to coordinate plans for a new convention with opponents of the Constitution in New York: "Every danger of this sort might be justly dreaded from such men as this state [Virginia] and N. York only could furnish, playing for such a purpose, into each others hands."[14]

Madison had the same message for Jefferson, informing the U.S. envoy in Paris that the "Constitution and the Union will be both endangered" if a second convention were to be held. Madison did not expect the "same spirit of compromise will prevail" in a second convention to produce the "amicable result" of the first. As he had told Randolph, those who had "latent views of disunion" could use a demand for new amendments as a way of attaining their goals.[15] Madison later wrote to Jefferson that the "great danger in the present crisis is that if another Convention should be soon assembled, it would terminate in discord, or in alterations of the federal system which would throw back *essential* powers into the State Legislatures . . . At present the public mind is neither sufficiently cool nor sufficiently informed for so delicate an operation."[16] Madison used even stronger language in his next letter, describing to Jefferson the potential dangers of another convention. He told his fellow Virginian that it would be "composed of men who will essentially mutilate the system, particularly in the article of taxation . . . An early Convention is in every view to be dreaded in the present temper of America."[17]

Madison hoped that George Washington would use his prestige to help stop the Virginia General Assembly from formally calling for a second convention. He told him before the fall session of 1788 that "If an Early General Convention cannot be parried, it is seriously to be feared that the system which has resisted so many direct attacks may be at last successfully undermined by its enemies."[18] A few weeks later, Washington informed Benjamin Lincoln, the lieutenant governor of Massachusetts, that the letter approved by the New York legislature seeking support from other states for a convention was "intended to bring on a general Convention at too early a period . . . to set every thing afloat again." Washington added, "I wish I may be mistaken in imagining, that there are persons, who, upon finding they could not carry their point by an open attack against the Constitution, have some sinister designs to be silently effected."[19]

Washington was not as alarmed as Madison, but he was still concerned about a possible convention. A week later Washington told Jefferson that he was not worried about most of the amendments that were being discussed "except that which goes to the prevention of direct taxation." Washington said the new federal government must have the means to "do justice to the public creditors and retrieve the National character."[20]

Governor Randolph resisted Madison's gentle efforts to get him to reconsider his position on a second convention. Randolph relayed the news that even Madison's cousin the Reverend James Madison "espouses with warmth an early convention." The governor hoped that the "valuable parts of the constitution may suffer no ill from the temper, with which such a body [a second convention] will probably assemble."[21] Still, he insisted that the risk was worth it to secure additional amendments.

Newspapers carried some of the letters arguing for and against another convention. "Cassius III" wrote to Richard Henry Lee in the *Virginia Independent Chronicle* that the first convention met "unrestrained by any local matters, and felt itself at liberty to concede any thing to each other, that they found necessary to the general good." But in a second convention, "every state will propose its amendments, and certainly not forget . . . its own particular interest." Later in the essay, however, Cassius seemed more supportive of a convention: "Because two-thirds of the legislatures of the different states have a right to demand another convention for the purpose of amending it [the Constitution] and if the [federal] government should be oppressive, it will be known and felt by each legislature, consequently we may safely rely on their exercising this right."[22]

The Cassius essay was devoted primarily to answering Richard Henry Lee's objections to the Constitution, but the writer, in recognizing the availability of a second convention, may not have thought through the implications of such a gathering. To organize a new convention under Article V, nine of thirteen states would have to petition Congress. Because ten of thirteen states would have to ratify amendments proposed by the convention, the bare minimum of nine requesting the convention might not have been enough to see the process through.

Article V is silent on the form and scope of the petitions. The petitions would likely vary, with some states explicitly listing the amendments they were demanding, while others would limit the petition to calling for a convention to consider amendments.[23] A key issue that would have to be resolved was whether the convention could consider only those amendments included in the petitions.

States would then have to choose delegates to attend the convention. State legislatures would most likely reserve for themselves the right to select them. Many of the delegates to the second convention would arrive with specific instructions on what amendments to support or oppose. Some states would deny their delegates any discretion to compromise on issues directly affecting them.

Article V does not say how such a convention would be conducted. Some convention delegates would not want to be confined to the list submitted in the petitions. There would be squabbles over whether amendments need to be approved by a majority or supermajority at the convention and over other procedural issues. Committees would have to sort through the hundreds of suggestions submitted by the states and to write the language of specific amendments.

Once the convention decided on amendments, Congress would—if it followed the language of Article V—forward them to the states. The Constitution gives Congress the option of choosing whether the amendments will be ratified by state legislatures or state conventions. If Congress chose conventions, states would decide whether delegates to the conventions would be appointed by the legislature or elected by the people. There would be intense demand from citizens for the right to elect delegates to the convention. The campaigns for election to the conventions would last at least several months. Then the conventions would need to be held, and after what would likely be lengthy debates, votes would be taken on whether to ratify the proposed amendments. A frantic effort would be undertaken by delegates at one convention to find out what was transpiring at others.

Madison and other supporters of the Constitution tried another approach to stopping a convention by pointing out that it would take much longer for a convention to propose amendments than the First Congress. During the time the convention process dragged on, state governments and foreign nations would not know the eventual form the Constitution would take. Because a second convention would likely consider both personal rights and structural amendments, it was possible that changes would be proposed that would drastically alter the relative power of the states and the new federal government. Foreign nations would be hesitant to lend money during a period of such instability, and the danger that some states would form regional confederacies would be increased.[24] Only days before the Virginia General Assembly formally requested a convention, Madison told George Lee Turberville that a second convention would propose too many amendments and would consider itself "as having greater latitude than the Congress appointed to administer and support as well as to amend the system." Madison doubted that "the deliberations of the body [a second convention] could be conducted in harmony, or terminate in the general good." As Madison also explained to Henry Lee, amendments were "much more attainable from Congress than from attempts to bring about another Convention."[25]

After the Virginia General Assembly voted to request a convention, Madison reported to Jefferson that two-thirds of the legislators were "enemies to the Government." He wanted Jefferson to know that some friends of the Constitution also supported amendments, but "they wish the revisal to be carried no farther than to supply additional guards for liberty, without abridging the sum of power transferred from the States to the general Government." The opponents, on the other hand, were "zealous for a second Convention, and for a revisal which may either not be restrained at all, or extend at least as far as alterations have been proposed by any State."[26]

The House had selected the fourth Monday in May for the ratifying convention to begin, but the Senate changed that to the first Monday in June. The decision to have the convention after all but a few other states had held theirs was significant. Both sides saw an advantage in the late start. Federalists needed time to generate support for the Constitution, and many of them believed that as more states ratified, it would be increasingly difficult for Virginia to stay out of the union.[27] Opponents expected that as the debate ensued in other states, the defects of the document would become clearer, and the convention delegates would be more inclined to oppose ratification or at least require amendments.

John Dawson, who as a member of the House of Delegates tried to keep Madison informed about the legislative debate in Richmond, wrote that if the General Assembly had insisted on an early convention and not allowed amendments, the Constitution would have been defeated. Dawson told Madison that the late start of the convention would allow Virginia to "act on the determinations of the other states, and to determine ourselves as circumstances may point out."[28]

Watching all this from Mount Vernon, Washington was not sure which side would be helped by the long wait for the convention. He told John Langdon of New Hampshire that "whether putting it off to so late a period will be favourable or otherwise, must be determined by circumstances, for if those States whose conventions are to meet sooner should adopt the plan I think there is no doubt but they will be followed by this, and if some of them should reject it, it is very probable that the opposers of it here will exert themselves to add this State to the number."[29]

In addition to scheduling the convention, the General Assembly had to decide who would be eligible to serve as delegates and which voters would be qualified to elect them. Each of the eighty-four counties could send two delegates, while the borough of Norfolk and the city of Williamsburg would have one each. While legislators had to be residents and property owners in the county that they represented, the delegates to the convention were not subject to that restriction.[30] (That decision would allow George Mason to represent Stafford County at the ratifying convention when his fellow citizens in Fairfax County, who strongly favored the Constitution, would not elect him.) In deciding who would be eligible to vote for delegates, the General Assembly extended the right to those who were currently eligible to cast a ballot in legislative elections.[31]

It was soon discovered that something was missing from the law approved by the General Assembly at the end of October. The resolution calling for a convention did not provide for the expenses of convention delegates. On the last day in November, the House of Delegates debated how to compensate those who would travel to Richmond and spend most of the month of June debating the Constitution.[32]

Anti-Federalists, who controlled the General Assembly by a substantial margin, saw an opening. They agreed that the delegates to the June convention had to be paid, but they also adopted, over strenuous objections from pro-Constitution members, the policy of reimbursing delegates who incurred expenses by traveling to confer with convention delegates in other states. Anti-Federalists clearly believed that defeating the Constitution required a multipronged attack and that communication with other

opponents around the country was essential. They wanted both to influence those in other states and to learn what objections to the Constitution
were raised at other ratifying conventions. Their hope was that as concerns mounted in other states, Virginia's delegates would become increasingly apprehensive about approving the new plan of government.

But the Anti-Federalists did not stop there. One of them, Samuel
Hopkins Jr., who represented Mecklenburg County in the House of Delegates, introduced a resolution not only to provide for "the expences or
allowance" of delegates to the June convention but also to reimburse
"deputies to a federal convention, in case such a convention should be
judged necessary."[33]

Supporters of the Constitution had reason to be concerned. It was
troublesome enough that the delegates in June would be able to propose
amendments, thus suggesting that the largest state believed that immediate changes to the Constitution were needed. Now Virginia was going
on record as implicitly planning for a second constitutional convention
to add amendments to the work of the Philadelphia delegates even before the Constitution was ratified. Madison criticized these efforts by
the General Assembly: "The only surprize I feel at the last steps taken
with regard to the new Constitution, is that it does not strike the well
meaning adversaries themselves with the necessity of some anchor for
the fluctuations which threaten shipwreck to our liberty."[34] And he knew
that everything his state did on this subject would be important: "The
vote of [Virginia] . . . will either dismember the Union, or reduce her
[Virginia] to a dilemma . . . mortifying to her pride . . . [There is] difficulty and danger in every Stage of [this] . . . experiment."[35]

The debate raged over the next few weeks. The House of Delegates,
meeting as a committee of the whole, initially approved the resolution
allowing delegates to the ratifying convention to propose amendments,
confer with other states, and, if necessary, appoint deputies to a second
constitutional convention. After the debate, the final bill that would enact Hopkins's proposal deleted explicit references to a second convention or to delegates conferring with other conventions. Still, the amended
bill was vague enough for the Anti-Federalists to claim that the General
Assembly had reserved the right to send delegates to a second convention.
It provided for "Such reasonable expenses as may be incurred in case the
[ratifying] Convention . . . should deem it necessary to hold any Communications with any of the sister states . . . or should in any other manner
incur any expence in collecting the sentiments of the union respecting the
proposed Federal Constitution."[36] The bill was passed unanimously on

December 11, and the Senate, which also had a majority opposed to the Constitution, accepted the measure the next day.

Patrick Henry thought this language left too much to chance because it did not specifically authorize the paying of expenses of those attending a second federal convention. He knew that if Virginia formally recognized the potential need for a second convention, it would greatly enhance the demand for such a gathering, which had already been made by leading figures around the country, including Governor Randolph. Henry declared his intention to propose a bill specifically about a second convention. The *House Journal* does not provide details about the proceedings of the committee of the whole, but apparently enough members objected to including an explicit funding provision for a second constitutional convention that it was removed from the language of the final legislation. Henry would have to be content with the imprecise language of the original bill.[37]

Archibald Stuart, a member of the House, recognized the advantage of not explicitly stating whether expenses should be paid for delegates to attend a federal convention. He told Madison that it was better that the law providing for payment to the delegates "be made in General terms which should not discover the sense of the house on ye Subject." Stuart was also relieved that most other states would have already decided whether to approve the Constitution by the time of the June convention, "for I now have my doubts whether She [Virginia] would afford them as usual a good Example."[38]

The General Assembly requested the governor to transmit copies of the new law to the executives and legislatures of other states so Virginia's preparation for its ratifying convention would be known around the country.[39] The Anti-Federalists also arranged for couriers to rush by horseback between Richmond and other state conventions to make sure opponents of the Constitution had information about developments in other states as quickly as possible.[40] They expected that if another state either rejected the Constitution or ratified it contingent upon the approval of amendments, it would bolster their side at Virginia's ratifying convention.

By the time Virginia voted on the Constitution, three other states—Massachusetts, South Carolina, and New Hampshire—had ratified with recommended amendments. Supporters of the Constitution frequently cited the "Massachusetts compromise"—the decision to ratify the Constitution while formally requesting specific amendments, but not as a condition of ratification, and named for the first state to take such action—as a reasonable way to win approval of the new plan while at the same time allowing a state to urge the new government to seriously consider proposed amendments.[41]

Federalists were not sure how the Massachusetts plan would affect the ratification debate in the remaining states. A little over a week after Massachusetts ratified the Constitution, Madison sent Washington a newspaper article with a description of the compromise. He told Washington that "the amendments are a blemish, but are in the least Offensive form." Washington thought that the example offered by Massachusetts might be helpful, telling Madison that "the decision . . . is a severe stroke to the opponents of the proposed Constitution in this State [Virginia]." Madison was still concerned about the message that the Massachusetts convention had sent. He wrote to Washington the next day that by approving recommended amendments, Massachusetts "has not rejected the Constitution; but it has failed to adopt it."[42]

From Paris, Thomas Jefferson had initially recommended that after nine states ratified the Constitution, the four remaining states should withhold their approval until a bill of rights was added, but he later changed his mind.[43] In May, he told Edward Carrington that the "plan of Massachusetts is far preferable [to the remaining states withholding their ratification], and will I hope be followed by those who are yet to decide."[44] A few days later, he told another correspondent that "I am now convinced that the plan of Massachusetts is the best that is, to accept, and to amend afterwards." And Jefferson predicted that if the states after Massachusetts followed the same procedure, the "essential amendments" would be obtained.[45]

Newspaper coverage was generally supportive of the idea that ratification should include recommended amendments. Fifteen to twenty-six newspapers printed various versions of an article that contained this statement: "The true friends to union, that is, to liberty, happiness and national glory, are those who wish to go hand in hand with Massachusetts—adopt the constitution as they have done—*and then* propose such amendments as may be thought necessary."[46]

The five states that approved the Constitution before Massachusetts might have adopted with recommended amendments as a way to appease the opposition if there had been sufficient votes to compel the creation and approval of a list of amendments. In Pennsylvania, for example, where resentment over the way they were treated at the convention enraged opponents and motivated them to widely disseminate their criticisms and campaign around the nation against the Constitution,

approval of their amendments as recommendations could well have diminished their feelings of bitterness. The minority report of the Pennsylvania convention was publicized in newspapers around the country,
adding to the anxiety over the new federal Constitution—particularly
its lack of a bill of rights.[47]

As delegates gathered at various conventions, information about what
other states were doing became increasingly valuable. If one convention
rejected the Constitution, postponed the final decision, offered amendments, or approved the new government contingent on such amendments, it could have a substantial impact on meetings in other states.
Supporters and opponents exchanged information through letters, newspapers, and in person, but generally, accurate and timely information
about the ratification process in other states was hard to come by.[48]

Although the ratification process could hardly be described as
smooth, by May 23, 1788, when South Carolina ratified, eight of the nine
states required for the Constitution to become effective had already given
their approval, less than nine months after the convention in Philadelphia
adjourned. Because eight states already had accepted the Constitution—
and a ninth, New Hampshire, ratified while the Virginia convention
was taking place—the proposed plan was about to become official.
But if Virginia and New York—states with almost a third of the nation's
population and vital in both political and economic terms—were to
reject its defining document, the new nation would have little chance
of success.[49]

It was Virginia's turn first. If it did not approve the Constitution, the
nation might have degenerated into regional confederacies—with or
without New York's eventual approval—with those confederations likely
forming foreign alliances.[50] "That there are some . . . who wish to see
[the] States divided into several confederacies," observed George Washington, "is pretty evident."[51] In the South, Virginia, Kentucky, and North
Carolina may have banded together, to be joined later by South Carolina
and Georgia.[52]

As they prepared for the convention in Richmond, the delegates realized the importance of their upcoming work. Many of them had fought
in the war, and they understood the sacrifice that had brought them to
Richmond to debate a republican form of government unknown to the
rest of the world.

But whatever support the Constitution enjoyed as the convention
began did not eliminate the apprehension many people felt when they
saw how few personal rights were specifically protected in the docu-

ment. Where was freedom of speech or press or religion? Protection against the government illegally seizing evidence and using it against a criminal defendant? The right not to be forced to provide incriminating statements? The right to a jury trial in civil cases? With the carnage of the war fresh in their minds, many had visions of a despotic central government emasculating the states and amassing so much power that people would live not as free citizens of a new, enlightened country but once again as subjects of a constitutional monarchy and without the ability to reform or overthrow the government. Patrick Henry warned the delegates at the Virginia convention that under the proposed plan, "Congress will have an unlimited, unbounded command over the soul of this Commonwealth [Virginia]. After satisfying their uncontrouled demands, what can be left for the States?" More forcefully, Henry told the convention a few days later that the new government would "destroy the State governments, and swallow the liberties of the people, without giving them previous notice."[53]

The extensive writings of the Anti-Federalists on the shortcomings of the Constitution and their passionate belief that the proposed plan betrayed the principles of the Declaration of Independence were widely read during the ratification period, and their ideas contributed significantly to the nation's constitutional evolution.

As would be vigorously discussed at the Virginia convention, Anti-Federalists believed that the Constitutional Convention had proposed a government that would consolidate power to the detriment of the states and the rights of the people. After years of agonizing experience with the Crown and royal governors, many citizens did not trust centralized authority. They rejected Madison's argument that the new government was not a threat because it would be both federal and national—federal, in that it would preserve the independence of the states and leave them substantial power to govern on matters of local concern, and national, in that it derived its powers directly from the people and was therefore the caretaker of the nation's ultimate sovereignty.[54] They dismissed such declarations as an effort to win ratification and not as a sincere explanation of the new system.[55] They believed that without strong, independent state governments, individual liberty would be in constant danger from federal officials. They treated as folly the assertion that the new government would exercise authority only in areas explicitly granted by the Constitution, and that states retained all powers not surrendered.

At the Virginia convention, Governor Randolph would try to answer the opponents' argument that the new government would be too powerful. When Henry made that charge, Randolph replied: "He says that every power is given to the General Government, that is not reserved to the states. Pardon me if I say the converse of the proposition is true. I defy any one to prove the contrary. Every power not given it by this system is left with the States."[56]

Opponents of the Constitution also ridiculed the claim that a bill of rights was unnecessary and actually counterproductive because the new government had no authority to deprive individuals of personal liberty, and thus a list of rights would be incomplete and would imply the federal government had authority in those areas not specified.[57]

Federalists, including Madison, had what they considered to be good reasons for opposing a bill of rights.[58] Although he had been silent in the final days of the Philadelphia convention when George Mason tried to have amendments protecting individual liberty added to the Constitution, Madison's correspondence made it clear that he believed immediate changes to the document were not needed and could be harmful. Federalists argued that the states were the primary source of protection of liberty and would remain so. Thus it was unnecessary to identify the rights that the new government could not abridge, because it did not have such authority in the first place.

Madison had written disparagingly about a bill of rights for several years. In *Federalist 38*, he unconvincingly dismissed the need for a list of rights on the grounds that Anti-Federalists could not agree on what protections they wanted and that the "confederation has no bill of rights," presumably proving that the nation could manage without one.[59] In *Federalist 44*, Madison observed that the Constitution prohibited the states from interfering with certain rights, but that additional rights should be protected against state infringement; he conspicuously neglected to add that citizens needed such protection from the federal government as well. In *Federalist 46*, he implied that a bill of rights was unnecessary because the states could protect citizens from an oppressive federal government. He also argued, in *Federalist 48*, that a bill of rights would not do much good because states had already proved they were able to infringe personal liberty despite explicit protection in state constitutions or a declaration of rights.

Over time, with the gentle but firm persuasion of Thomas Jefferson and others, Madison softened his opposition to a bill of rights.[60] During his campaign for election to the Virginia ratifying convention and to the First Congress, Madison freely admitted that he had never understood why so many opposed the Constitution because it lacked an explicit enumeration of rights. He eventually adopted a mostly neutral attitude, arriving at the position that as long as amendments did not touch the structure of government and alter the delicate compromises reached at the Philadelphia convention, amendments could be beneficial and could be safely added now that the Constitution had been ratified. Madison eventually recognized that they would offer some additional protection to personal liberty, would comfort those still vigorously opposed to the Constitution, and would provide the necessary incentive for North Carolina and Rhode Island to join the union.[61]

As Anti-Federalists argued against approval of the Constitution, their words became part of a national debate that engaged a wide range of political leaders and ordinary citizens, many of whom understandably wanted guidance on whether the new plan should be adopted.

Elbridge Gerry of Massachusetts, who had refused to sign the Constitution in Philadelphia, wrote the most widely distributed—and presumably read—tract against the Constitution. Under the title "Hon. Mr. Gerry's Objections," his essay first appeared in the *Massachusetts Centinel* on November 3, 1787, and was subsequently printed forty-six times, more than any other Anti-Federalist essay. Gerry's criticisms of the Constitution—including the lack of representation of the people in the government, indefinite and dangerous powers of the national legislature, the blurring of executive and legislative power, and especially the lack of a bill of rights—would be debated at length at the Virginia convention. Gerry argued that the proposed plan did not provide for viable state governments but instead created a consolidated national government.[62]

Other Anti-Federalists, such as Richard Henry Lee and George Mason, and the dissenters at the Pennsylvania ratifying convention, saw their views of the Constitution widely distributed, while others had less success. Some essays were published only once, and thus likely had limited impact. Fewer than 150 essays were reprinted at least twice.[63] The well-known essays of "A Federal Farmer"—who was suspected to be Richard Henry Lee for many years, but evidence now suggests was someone else—were reprinted only five times.[64] Despite the limited circulation of some materials, the Anti-Federalists were able to share their views with a geographically diverse audience.

Because they were arguing against a completed document and did not have one of their own, Anti-Federalists had an almost impossible task. Scattered around the country at a time of primitive transportation and communication, they had to persuade citizens and delegates to ratifying conventions that the proposed plan was so risky that either it should be rejected completely or the ratification process should be suspended until amendments were proposed by a second convention.

Opponents of the Constitution in Virginia were the most active in demanding amendments. Shortly after the Philadelphia convention ended and Congress forwarded the Constitution to the states, Richard Henry Lee sent Samuel Adams a detailed explanation of the defects of the Constitution—particularly the lack of protection for individual rights—and told the Massachusetts patriot that a new convention could make necessary changes: "Why may not such indispensable amendments be proposed by the [state ratifying] Conventions and returned With a new plan to Congress that a new general Convention may so weave them into the proffer'd system as that a Web may be produced fit for freemen to wear?" Lee wondered why there was such a hurry to approve the current version of the Constitution, "as if the subject of Government were a business of passion, instead of cool, sober, and intense consideration."[65]

A week later, Lee notified Randolph that he was joining the call for a second convention, asking the governor, "If with infinite ease, a convention was obtained to prepare a system, why may not another with equal ease be procured to make proper and necessary amendments?" Lee reminded Randolph that "Good government is not the work of a short time, or of sudden thought." He asked the governor to join him in proposing amendments and to "suggest the calling of a new convention for the purpose of considering them."[66]

A few months later, however, Lee was having second thoughts about whether a convention was the best way to obtain amendments. He recommended that the Richmond convention pass a motion giving Virginia, if it ratified the Constitution, the discretion to rescind that ratification if amendments were not forthcoming. He told George Mason shortly before the convention that amendments "may be obtained from the new Congress without endangering a total loss of the proposed constitution." Lee suggested that if amendments were not proposed within "two years after the meeting of the new Congress, that Virginia shall, in that case, be considered as disengaged from this ratification." It would be safer, Lee said, for Congress to propose amendments because it could be done "without risking the convulsion of conventions."[67]

As the drive for a second convention gained momentum, supporters of the Constitution began to worry that enough states would ask that a convention be held prior to ratification or that a sufficient number would formally petition Congress under Article V if the Constitution had been ratified. Federalists knew that a second convention could be disastrous. Edward Carrington was one of the first to sound the alarm, telling Thomas Jefferson that unlike the delegates at the first convention, those at the second would arrive with specific and inflexible orders from their state legislatures, thus making compromise difficult. A new convention would be "clogged with instructions and biassed by the presentiments of their constituents," Carrington warned.[68]

Considering the obstacles, the Anti-Federalists were remarkably successful in forming a coherent ideology and identifying what they considered to be serious flaws in the Constitution.[69] Their best opportunity to successfully challenge adoption of the proposed plan would come in Virginia. Some of their most celebrated leaders—Henry, Mason, Monroe, and Grayson, among others—would carry the torch during the twenty-three days of debate. Richard Henry Lee, among the most important and widely known opponents of the Constitution, would have been another influential voice at the convention, but he worried that his health would suffer during the warm weather in Richmond. Mason and others tried to convince Lee to attend by offering election to a "safe seat" in Fauquier County, where Lee would only have to do limited campaigning, and by encouraging him to stay overnight outside of Richmond, where his health would be less imperiled. Lee rejected the offers and worked in opposition to the Constitution from a distance.[70]

George Mason was disappointed that Lee would not be at the convention. His brother Arthur Lee told him that "Col. Mason laments very much, that you do not stand for the Convention. He says there will be no one in whom he can confide." Arthur Lee also worried that many people would interpret his brother's decision not to go to Richmond as abandoning the cause because he was afraid it could not be won.[71]

All of the major criticisms of the Constitution—the lack of a bill of rights and separation of powers, the consolidating nature of the new government and the diminished role of the states, concerns about taxation, the worry about a standing army in peacetime, the lack of representation of citizens—would be debated at length at the Virginia convention. It was as if Richmond were hosting a national forum to consider the ideas that had developed around the country in the months since the Constitution was signed.

And this convention would provide center stage for some of the most important political figures of the era. Despite advancing age and health problems, Patrick Henry would stand on his feet for hours at a time while exhorting, scolding, and occasionally berating his fellow delegates. He had no faith in the supporters' promise that if Virginia approved the

Constitution unconditionally, they would see to it that the First Congress offered amendments. In Henry's view, the Philadelphia delegates had made it almost impossible to change the Constitution. "To encourage us to adopt it [the Constitution], they tell us that there is a plain easy way of getting amendments: When I come to contemplate this part, I suppose that I am mad, or, that my countrymen are so: The way to amendment, is, in my conception, shut," declared Henry.[72] He considered the idea of approving the Constitution first, then asking for amendments, "absurd": "I am at a loss what to say. You agree to bind yourselves hand and foot—For the sake of what?—Of being unbound. You go into a dungeon—For what? To get out. Is there no danger when you go in, that the bolts of federal authority shall shut you in?"[73]

Henry did not know at the time that New Hampshire would become the ninth state to ratify, on June 21, 1788, four days before Virginia's ratification vote. With New Hampshire's approval, the Constitution went into effect, replacing the Articles of Confederation. Any convention held outside the provisions of Article V—even if organized by such prominent Anti-Federalists as Henry and Lee, and endorsed by supporters of the Constitution such as Governor Randolph—would have no legal standing. Furthermore, if Virginia rejected the Constitution and remained out of the union, it could not petition Congress under Article V to call a convention for the purpose of proposing amendments, and it could not vote to ratify or reject amendments proposed by Congress.

Henry hoped that if Virginia rejected the Constitution, or ratified contingent upon the proposing of amendments by either a convention or the First Congress, one of two developments would take place: The states that had not yet voted on the Constitution would freeze the ratification process by also demanding amendments before giving their approval; or some states that had already ratified would be so moved by Virginia's principled stand in defense of civil liberties that they would rescind their endorsement until amendments were offered.[74]

Henry was not alone in pushing for a second convention. Virginia eventually joined New York, North Carolina, and Rhode Island in demanding that one be called to recommend a bill of rights. In other states, Anti-Federalists favoring a new convention may not have had a majority of votes, but they constituted considerable pluralities in their legislatures and ratifying conventions where petitions to Congress were considered.

On Monday, June 2, 1788, the Virginia ratifying convention officially began its work. Over the next twenty-five days, the delegates and spectators would witness a thorough, passionate, and often heated debate about the Constitution.

~ 4 ~

The Virginia Ratifying Convention

On Shockoe Hill in downtown Richmond, Alexander Maria Quesnay de Beaurepaire built what he hoped would be a grand academy of arts and sciences. Quesnay, a French soldier who arrived in 1777 at the age of twenty-two to help the American colonies win independence and served as a captain in Virginia, had deep affection for the United States.[1] After the war, he envisioned centers of learning and culture—similar to the academies of Europe—throughout the new nation. His Richmond academy would attract scholars from around the world who would teach music, art, fencing, foreign languages, geography, arithmetic, and the physical sciences. More practical crafts would be taught as well, including embroidery, needlework, and writing.[2] To help support the academy's educational programs and enrich the cultural life of Richmond, Quesnay arranged for the building to also serve as a theater.[3] He wanted the great plays of the day to be performed by local and touring companies for the five thousand inhabitants of the growing city, who had few opportunities for such enlightened entertainment.

Quesnay had tried unsuccessfully to establish an academy in other cities, but his efforts were welcomed in Richmond. On June 24, 1786, the cornerstone for the new building was laid "under a salute of cannon" in a ceremony that attracted a "numerous assemblage of ladies and gentlemen," including the mayor and other leading political and social figures of the city.[4] The first stone was consecrated with corn, wine, and oil, and a second stone was laid to the east as part of a structure that would occupy "Academy Square," on the north side of Broad between Twelfth and Thirteenth streets. Quesnay was pleased that his efforts finally resulted in the building of his academy: "After years of perseverance, I had the satisfaction to witness the imposing ceremonies with which the laying of the corner-stone of the Academy was honored."[5]

Quesnay would never see his dream become a reality. Shortly after the "New Academy" opened on October 10, he returned to France to shore up financial support for his Richmond endeavor and for the institutions he also planned for Baltimore, Philadelphia, and New York. But with growing tensions that led to the French Revolution, he was unable to raise additional funds. He later served as the commander of the Parisian militia and did not return to the United States. His Richmond academy never became a place of study and teaching. It was converted permanently to a theater and later destroyed by fire.[6]

Just before Quesnay's departure, the New Academy saw the performance of the first of many plays that would be produced in the building, which could accommodate a larger audience than any other in Richmond. It was thus fitting that the Virginia ratifying convention would be held there, for the "drama" that would take place during those crucial weeks in June 1788 would surpass in importance any fictionalized work that was performed within its walls. The new nation's survival likely depended on the outcome.[7]

The convention began on June 2, 1788, in the capitol building that was still under construction, but it was immediately apparent that the 170 delegates and several hundred spectators would not fit into those tight quarters. On the second day, everyone moved across the street to the Quesnay Academy—this "Spacious and Airy Building sufficiently large to accommodate all the Members," in the words of one delegate, where the convention met until it adjourned on June 27.[8] A wooden structure with a brick foundation, the academy was the largest nonchurch building in Richmond.[9]

Citizens came from throughout the state to see many of the leading figures of the revolutionary and founding era debate the Constitution. The galleries were packed with those willing to put up with the often sweltering conditions created by the typically warm and humid June.[10] As Alexander White, a Federalist delegate from Frederick, observed, "We have every day a gay circle of Ladies—to hear the debates—and have the pleasure of believing them all Federalists."[11] Hundreds of additional spectators stood in the passages and in the doorways.[12] Some had closed their businesses in Richmond in order to attend.[13] In Fredericksburg, there was so much interest in the convention that "all the Town are at this moment, looking out for Intelligence by the Stage[coach] this Evening."[14]

They came to see James Madison and Patrick Henry; Governor Edmund Randolph, who would soon reveal whether he now supported the Constitution after having refused to sign it at the Philadelphia convention; Edmund Pendleton, the aging and revered president of the state's highest court, presiding as chair of the convention, whose prestige and inspiring comments helped the convention complete its work when it looked like it might break apart; George Mason, the controversial yet widely respected author of the Virginia Declaration of Rights; John Marshall, who almost on his own would establish the Supreme Court as an equal branch of government through his thirty-five years of service as chief justice; James Monroe, a future U.S. senator, secretary of state, and president, who would reluctantly vote against ratification; George Wythe, the "Socrates of Virginia" and the first professor of law in America, who taught some of the leaders of the revolutionary era and would have important responsibilities as the chair of the committee of the whole;[15] William Grayson, who would serve as one of Virginia's first U.S. senators, and whose "powers of humor, wit, sarcasm, [and] ridicule . . . were unrivaled;"[16] and George Nicholas, rotund and disheveled, and little known today, yet a powerful voice in support of the Constitution at the convention.

The audience would also hear from Virginia attorney general James Innes. His career and legacy were cut short by an early death, which was likely related to his huge size. Innes was so large that he could not ride an ordinary horse or sit in a normal chair. He made one of the convention's most impassioned and impressive speeches in support of the Constitution.[17] With his voice of "unbounded power and of great compass," Innes's words so stirred Patrick Henry that he offered his only genuine praise of an opposition speech during the convention, and one of the few in his career.[18]

The delegates would spend many hours together. From June 2 to 27, 1788, they met every day except Sunday, starting at either 9:00 or 10:00 A.M., and usually adjourning at 4:00 P.M. As the first order of business, the delegates unanimously selected the highly respected jurist Edmund Pendleton as the chairman of the convention. Unassuming and unpretentious, Pendleton was an ideal choice. He was the president of the Virginia court of appeals, equivalent to the chief justice of a state supreme court. He also had impressive legislative experience, having served in

Edmund Pendleton, respected Virginia judge
and political figure, presided over the
Virginia ratifying convention.
(Library of Congress)

the House of Burgesses, in the House of Delegates (including as Speaker), and as a member of Congress. As far back as the previous October, George Washington had recognized the importance of having Pendleton attend the convention, for he "espouses the Constitution so warmly as to declare he will give it his aid in the Convention, if his health will permit."[19]

Presiding over the convention would prove to be tiring for the sixty-six-year-old Pendleton. Eleven years earlier he had fallen off his horse and dislocated his hip, leaving him disabled. Two months after the accident, he told a friend that he "hope[d] to be soon on foot." More than three months later, he was still optimistic: "I continue to walk only on crutches, but have some feelings flattering to my hopes of my being one day able to walk alone."[20] But his positive attitude could not overcome the damage that had been done to his body. For the rest of his life, he could walk only with crutches, and he often needed assistance.

The accident may have created other health problems. In 1786, Pendleton developed a wheezing condition and shortness of breath that was diagnosed as asthma.[21] During the middle of the Richmond convention, he had to be excused for a day because a storm created conditions that were too damp for him to endure. When not presiding over the committee of the whole, Pendleton took his seat as a member of the convention, with his fellow delegates allowing him to speak without standing, in deference to his infirmities.[22]

The delegates had not come to Richmond just to make speeches. Each side wanted desperately to win by convincing enough of their colleagues to approve or reject ratification of the Constitution. Not surprisingly, because so much was at stake at the convention—the outcome would profoundly affect Virginia and the rest of the nation—there were sometimes heated disputes over what should have been routine matters.

On the first day of the convention, an intense disagreement arose over the official recording of the speeches. David Robertson, a prominent lawyer from Petersburg, had been chosen, apparently by Federalists, to keep a record of the debate. Federalist delegate George Nicholas offered a motion to allow Robertson and an assistant to "take down the minutes of the house." Patrick Henry and George Mason strongly objected, arguing that because the reporters were not members of the convention, they could not be trusted to publish an accurate transcription of the speeches. They further noted that "such reporting had traditionally been ruled a breach of privilege by the British House of Commons." Mason later criticized Robertson for having the "Audacity to desire the Sanction of Convention Authority for his work, even before he began it, and got a Member [Nicholas] to make a Motion for that Purpose." But once Mason and Henry exposed—in Mason's words—"the Impropriety and Absurdity of it," Nicholas became "ashamed of it [the motion], & withdrew it."[23]

The Anti-Federalists hoped that objections to the Constitution voiced at the Richmond convention would be widely reported and would inspire opponents around the nation to continue working against approval of the proposed government. That is why it concerned Mason and Henry that Robertson and his assistant "were strangers—that it was an important trust [position] for any one—for not only the people at large might be misinformed, but a fatal stab might be given to a gentleman of the house from a perversion of his language."[24] Mason later told his son, before the records of the convention were published, that he did not expect the record of the debates to be "authentic," and that the "Short-Hand Man [Robertson], who took them down, being a *federal* Partizan, they will probably be garbled, in some such Partial [partisan] Manner."[25]

Robertson had wanted to sit at a table directly in front of the presiding officer so he could easily hear the debate, but instead was required to take a seat in the gallery. The delegates allowed him to take shorthand notes, which he was permitted to publish without the official sanction of the convention.[26]

It was perhaps to be expected that there would be such an argument. This was the first time in the history of Virginia that debates in an assembly had been recorded. The suspicion that Robertson "was in the interest of the Federalists" may explain why opponents of the Constitution declined to ask him to correct the record even when they believed his report did not accurately reflect their speeches. According to William Wirt Henry, Patrick's grandson, the Anti-Federalists did "themselves the greatest injustice" by not correcting the record. The supporters of the Constitution, on the other hand, periodically revised Robertson's report.[27]

Whatever inaccuracies may have found their way into the report of the convention—and most of what we know about the debates comes from Robertson's notes—may not have been the result of a partisan effort to favor the Federalists. It would have been difficult for anyone to write down the thousands of words spoken each hour during the convention. With energetic orators like Patrick Henry, it was especially difficult to make an accurate record of their speeches.

William Henry, who wrote a history of the convention that is understandably complimentary of his famous grandfather, said that Robertson "confess[ed] his inability to follow him [Patrick Henry] in his overpowering bursts of eloquence, and the incompleteness of the report . . . falls far short of doing him justice." St. George Tucker, who observed Henry speaking at the convention and would have looked to see how much effort Robertson and his assistant were making to keep up with the debate, said that Henry's speeches were "taken in shorthand, [but] I do not think them accurately taken."[28]

Henry's speeches may have been difficult to write down, but that did not prevent Robertson or anyone else from hearing him. Henry was fifty-two, but, in the words of his grandson, "ill health had given him the appearance of an old man, and this added greatly to the impressiveness of his appeals to the body [convention]." When Henry spoke, a "death-like silence prevailed, and the eager listeners did not fail to catch every syllable he uttered." According to his grandson, Henry's "mental powers were as great as ever, and the deep interest he took in the subject under debate caused him to exert them to the utmost."[29]

Edmund Winston, a delegate from Campbell County who voted against ratification, said that while Henry was speaking "there was a perfect stillness throughout the House, and in the galleries. There was no inattention or appearance of weariness." But when other members spoke, according to Winston, the delegates and audience would in "half an hour be going out or moving from their seats."[30]

It was time for the convention to begin. On the morning of June 2, Pendleton gave his first address as the presiding officer, appealing to the delegates to "calmly reason With each other, as Friends, having the same end in view, the real happiness of our Constituents, avoiding all heats, Intemperance & Personal Altercations . . . Let us probe the Plan to the Bottom, but let us do it with Candor, temper & mutual forbearance."[31] These words from a respected member of the founding generation may have had their intended impact because, although the debate was often heated and at times personal, the convention completed its work in little more than three weeks.

Upon returning the next morning, the delegates debated one of the most important procedural issues. At the urging of Richard Henry Lee—who was concerned that Federalists would insist on an early vote, as they had successfully done in Pennsylvania and Maryland—George Mason recommended that the Constitution be discussed clause by clause, paragraph by paragraph, before a decision was made on the ratification question.[32] Both sides agreed to this motion because they saw it as an advantage. Anti-Federalists may later have regretted this strategy because if they had demanded an early decision on ratification, they might have had enough votes to require amendments as a condition of approving the Constitution. After he learned of these developments from Madison and others, Washington, who was at home at Mount Vernon, said the decision not to vote on the Constitution until a line-by-line examination had been completed was "as unexpected as acceptable to the Federalists; and their ready acquiescence seems to have somewhat startled the opposition for fear they had committed themselves."[33]

But Washington had other concerns. He worried that the detailed treatment would take so much time that the convention would run beyond June 23, when the General Assembly was scheduled to meet. Because more than sixty delegates were members of both bodies, Washington thought the opponents would use this as a "mere colorable pretext for an adjournment."[34] If the ratifying convention disbanded before approving the Constitution, it would be interpreted as a rejection of the proposed government.[35]

Madison, meanwhile, was uneasy about the potential impact of the legislative session on the ratifying convention for another reason. He knew that when legislators arrived in Richmond, they would be able to tell delegates at the convention that the people were strongly opposed to the Constitution, and because the delegates would have been mostly confined to the capital city, they might be influenced by such a claim. As Madison explained to Alexander Hamilton, who was in New York at its convention, the General Assembly "consists of a considerable majority of antifederal members . . . As individuals they may have some influence, and as coming immediately from the people at large they can give any colour they please to the popular sentiments at this moment, and may in that mode throw a bias on the representatives of the people in Convention."[36]

On the third day of the convention, Patrick Henry rose to discuss the proposed Constitution for the first time. Henry would dominate the floor over the next three weeks, speaking on all but five of the convention's twenty-two days, as many as eight times in one day, and almost a quarter

Patrick Henry, a leading opponent of the Constitution, did everything he could to prevent ratification and James Madison from being elected to the U.S. House. *(Library of Congress)*

of the total speaking time of all the delegates.[37] His performance was apparently a marvel to watch, for Henry had great instincts for political theater and natural gifts that would be the envy of any stage actor, including a powerful voice and gestures that seemed to command the attention of the delegates and audience. Henry's memorable phrases attacking the Constitution and the sinister plans of those who wrote it filled the New Academy. His dark, piercing eyes and long, straight nose seemed to launch his intense gaze toward anyone he addressed. He could mesmerize even his opponents. As Federalists watched Henry, they could only imagine the impact that he might be having on the delegates who would decide the fate of the Constitution.[38] Everyone knew that the elections in March had created a closely divided convention and that no more than a few votes would make the difference. Madison wrote frequently that the margin would be only three or four votes.[39]

Henry's attacks on the Constitution were often broad, sweeping, and grandiose, and were sprinkled with exaggerated warnings of the dire consequences that lay ahead if the Constitution was approved. One moment his arguments could be general, unfocused, and overlapping; at other times he was precise in identifying and disparaging sections of the proposed plan he believed to be especially dangerous. Henry was not a deep political thinker. He preferred not to focus on the details of the Constitution or engage in philosophical discussions of how best to create a republic. He left it to other Anti-Federalists, particularly George Mason, to discuss the specific sections of the Constitution that most troubled its opponents. Instead, Henry relied on emotional appeals, enhanced by his penchant for theatrics, to convince wavering delegates that the document presented a threat to the liberties for which Virginians had so courageously died. He repeatedly called for a new convention that would offer a plan to preserve the autonomy of the states and to protect individual rights.

When he addressed the delegates on that Wednesday morning, he did not get off to a good start. The great orator may have captivated the audience and many of the delegates, but he was about to discover that his magic did not work very well on Pendleton. Henry began with an unexpected request: He wanted the law that Congress had passed the previous year authorizing the Constitutional Convention and the appointment of deputies to be read aloud. Pendleton quickly realized what he was up to. Henry believed that the Philadelphia convention had acted beyond its mandate by writing a new Constitution and not simply revising the Articles. He wanted the chance to prove that the work of the delegates in Philadelphia had no legal basis and thus did not deserve the approval of the Richmond convention.

A lesser figure might have been intimated by Henry, but not Pendleton. He respected Henry's long commitment to independence, but as chairman of the convention, Pendleton sternly admonished him for trying to undermine the ratification debate: "We are not to consider whether the Federal Convention exceeded their powers . . . Although those Gentlemen were only directed to consider the defects of the old system, and not devise a new one; if they found it so thoroughly defective as not to admit a revision, and submitted a new system to our consideration, which the people have deputed us to investigate, I cannot find any degree of propriety in reading those papers."[40] Pendleton would not allow the convention to be sidetracked by the issue of whether the delegates in Philadelphia had exceeded their authority. Henry realized his misjudgment and quickly withdrew his motion.

The delegates, meeting as a committee of the whole, then began a detailed discussion of the Constitution. Although they had agreed to consider the document beginning with the first clause, it was not long before some delegates—usually the opponents—refused to stick to the issue at hand and instead greatly enlarged the debate to include whatever part of the Constitution they wanted to discuss. This would last throughout much of the convention. The day would begin with reference to whatever section of the Constitution was considered during the previous session, but then one or more delegates would digress by launching a more general attack or statement of support. Not surprisingly, in the twenty-two days of debate, the convention did not cover every section of the Constitution. It did, however, conduct the most thorough discussion of the proposed plan of any of the ratifying conventions.

George Nicholas, who represented Albemarle County in the House of Delegates and the ratifying convention, gave the opening address for the supporters of the Constitution. His brilliant mind was not complemented by physical characteristics. His appearance was described as "far from prepossessing. His stature was low, ungainly, and deformed with fat. His head was bald, his nose curved . . . and his voice, though strong and clear, was without modulation."[41] In a speech that lasted several hours, Nicholas laid out the provisions of Article I by describing the features of the legislative branch. He explained that the people would elect the members of the House of Representatives and that the Constitution imposed only age and residence requirements on its members, and therefore it did not limit membership to those of wealth or property. A branch of government that was accountable to the people, he argued, could not be oppressive and would respond to the wishes of the citizens. Because they would have to face voters every two years, members of the House would consult "scrupulously the interests of their constituents."[42] And with senators appointed by state legislatures and presumably reflecting their interests, Congress would be sensitive to the needs of both the people and the states.

The power of the "people's house" would be a recurring theme throughout the convention. Opponents strenuously argued that although members of the House would be directly accountable to the people, the House itself had limited powers. For example, the president and Senate decided on the appointment and confirmation of high-level executive department officials and federal judges and on the negotiation and approval of treaties. Many opponents feared that senators, appointed by legislatures to six-year terms, would be the aristocratic branch protecting the interests of the affluent.[43] Because every state, no matter its size, would have equal representation in the Senate, the influence of small states would be greatly disproportionate to their population. Many delegates at the Richmond convention also worried about the blending of executive and legislative functions—including having the vice president preside over the Senate—because, they believed, history had taught that separation of powers was essential to making government accountable.

As soon as Nicholas sat down, Henry rose to give his first detailed speech of the convention. He immediately departed from the agreement to discuss the Constitution clause by clause. His first words signaled the themes that he would return to throughout the convention: "The public mind, as well as my own, is extremely uneasy at the proposed change of Government." Henry said that before the Philadelphia convention, "a general peace, and [a] universal tranquility prevailed in this country." Now, he "conceive[d] the republic to be in extreme danger." To Henry, the danger was a "proposal that goes to the utter annihilation of the most solemn engagements of the States." He warned that the plan would create a "consolidated" government, the danger of which was "very striking." In Henry's view, the plan would emasculate the states and create a dangerously powerful national government. While being careful not to personally disparage the reputation of the individuals who wrote the Constitution—at least on this day—he could not resist criticizing the Philadelphia delegates for going beyond their mandate: "The Federal Convention ought to have amended the old system—for this purpose they were solely delegated: The object of their mission extended to no other consideration."[44]

When Henry talked about consolidated government, he and other Anti-Federalists meant that once Virginia joined the new union, it would cease to be an autonomous political entity; furthermore, once it entered into such arrangement, it would be legally obligated to remain no matter how oppressive the new government had become. The Articles of Confederation had been a compact that states could voluntarily join and leave if they felt the union was not in their best interest. The Constitution, on the other hand, with its preamble proclaiming "We the People" to be sovereign, would create a legal entity whose laws would be supreme throughout the land and in which the independence of the states would be drastically curtailed.[45]

For Henry, this was a relatively short speech. When he sat down, the governor of Virginia, Edmund Randolph, took the floor. Delegates and spectators must have focused on his every word. Governor Randolph's decision in Philadelphia not to sign the Constitution had been a serious blow to its supporters. Now, speculation abounded over whether he would be for or against the proposed plan in the debate at Richmond. If he continued his opposition to the Constitution, it would likely influence some of the delegates, perhaps enough to defeat the proposed plan. If he supported the Constitution, it would bolster the Federalist cause—but to do so he would have to explain why he now endorsed a document that he had refused to add his name to only ten months before. It would be one of the most important speeches Randolph would ever give, and of immense

Edmund Randolph, governor of Virginia, refused to sign the Constitution but later supported ratification at the Virginia convention. *(Library of Congress)*

importance to the deliberations of the ratifying convention.

The thirty-five-year-old Randolph had been governor for almost two years when the convention met. He had dark hair, dark eyes, and a generally even disposition and was respected by many who disagreed with him on important issues. He later would become the first attorney general of the United States and for a short time secretary of state. He and Madison enjoyed a lifelong friendship.

Randolph vigorously defended his decision at the Philadelphia convention not to sign the Constitution. He recognized that his actions at the Constitutional Convention had created problems for supporters of the plan; nevertheless, he said, "if the same were to return, again I would refuse."[46]

But since then, Randolph admitted, he had come to see the potential of the plan to create a stable republic. He was now convinced that if the Constitution was rejected by the Richmond convention, it would mean dissolution of the union, and to Randolph, that was unacceptable: "When I withheld my subscription, I had not even a glimpse of the genius of America, relative to the principles of the new Constitution." He also recognized that someone in his situation might try to obscure the reasons for having first opposed the Constitution and now endorsing it, saying, "I freely indulge those who may think this declaration too candid, in believing, that I hereby depart from the concealment belonging to the character of a Statesman." But now was not the time for such concerns, Randolph argued, because the "spirit of America depends on a combination of circumstances, which no individual can controul, and arises not from the prospect of advantages which may be gained by the arts of negociation, but from deeper and more honest causes." He expressed admiration for the willingness of many Virginians to take a chance on a new government, asking, "Who, arguing from the preceding history of Virginia, could have divined that she was prepared for the important change?"[47]

Randolph said he would elaborate on his reasons for having opposed the Constitution in Philadelphia when the Richmond convention discussed the appropriate sections, and he expressed relief that the ratifying convention had the authority to propose amendments. "Amendments were consequently my wish," he said. But he also believed that because the Virginia convention was scheduled so late in the ratification process, it was no longer practical for the delegates to require that amendments be approved before Virginia agreed to join the union: "The postponement of this Convention, to so late a day, has extinguished the probability of [previous amendments] without inevitable ruin to the Union, and the Union is the anchor of our political salvation."[48] Randolph's conclusion that amendments were needed, but that they had to be obtained after Virginia ratified the Constitution, was in direct opposition to Henry's argument that it made no sense to ratify first and then hope the new government would allow changes.

Randolph covered much ground as the delegates and spectators now realized he had decided to support the Constitution. He disagreed with Henry about the effectiveness of the previous government under the Articles of Confederation and said it could not function without sufficient authority: "Was it not a political farce, to pretend to vest powers, without accompanying them with the means of putting them in execution?" He denounced the requirement of the Articles that all thirteen states approve any amendments and noted the problems with allowing a single state, no matter how small, to thwart of the wishes of all the others.[49]

He then directly addressed Henry's assertion that the preamble to the Constitution should not say "We the People," but instead should say "We the States," to show that the states would be preserved in the new system. To Randolph, this went to the heart of the matter: "I ask why not [We the People]? The Government is for the people . . . What harm is there in consulting the people, on the construction of a Government by which they are to be bound?" He called Henry's objection to the preamble one of the "most trivial objections that will be made to the Constitution." Finally, anticipating the criticism that he knew would come over his decision not to sign but to now endorse the plan, Randolph said that he did what he thought was right: "In this whole of this business, I have acted in the strictest obedience to the dictates of my conscience, in discharging what I conceive to be my duty to my country. I refused my signature, and if the same reasons operated on my mind, I would still refuse; but as I think that those eight States which have adopted the Constitution will not recede, I am a friend to the Union."[50]

The governor was sensitive about what he considered personal attacks on his character. On June 9, for example, when Henry criticized Randolph for being inconsistent in his views on the Constitution, Randolph responded harshly: "I find myself attacked, in the most illiberal manner, by the Honorable Gentleman [Henry]. I disdain his aspersions, and his insinuations. His asperity is warranted by no principle of Parliamentary decency, nor compatible with the least shadow of friendship; and if our friendship must fall—*Let it fall like Lucifer, never to rise again* . . . He has accused me of inconsistency in this very respectable assembly. Sir, if I do not stand on the bottom of integrity, and pure love for Virginia, as much as those who can be most clamorous, I wish to resign my existence."[51]

Randolph would become increasingly weary of such criticism for having modified his position on the Constitution. One observer noted that "nothing can exceed the teeming violence with which Mr. Henry and Col[.] Grayson combat the constitution—except the ability with which Mr[.] Maddison and Governor Randolph advocate it. Mr. Henry used such harsh language [when criticizing Randolph] . . . that the house compel'd him to ask that gentleman's pardon."[52]

Randolph must have known that he would be involved in a vigorous debate. He not only had changed his mind about the Constitution, he had decided to be one of the leaders at the Richmond convention who would engage in long and often difficult discussions about the proposed plan of government. Randolph was determined to be on the convention floor every day, refuting arguments made by Henry and other opponents, and advancing the position that the Constitution must be ratified without the requirement of previous amendments.

This commitment would come at the expense of his duties as governor. Randolph was understandably tired by late afternoon after a full day of attending—and often speaking at—the convention. Letters piled up unanswered on his desk at the governor's office, and he did little to prepare for the upcoming legislative session. As governor, he was expected to entertain delegates and other visitors at his home in the evening—mostly to talk about public business—which he continued to do, but that left little time to spend with the family.[53]

While Randolph defended his position on the Constitution and urged ratification, he also continued the demand he had made in Philadelphia, that a second convention be held to propose amendments. Anti-

Of VIRGINIA CONVENTION.

*Extract of a letter from a gentleman of the first in-
formation, dated Petersburg, June 9, 1788, received per a vessel in 5 days from Norfolk.*

" I have been attending the debates of our
Convention thefe feven days. Much eloquence
has hitherto been difplayed on both fides on the
important queftion—But I may venture to affure
you, there will be a MAJORTIY—a fmall one—
in favour of the Conftitution."

By this veffel we further learn—That the Convention, on the 9th inft. were debating the Conftitution by paragraphs—That Mr. Maddifon,
Col. Lee, and Gov. Randolph, in favour of the
Conftitution, fpoke the three firft days, and that
on the fourth Mr. Mafon began on the oppofition,
and fpoke a fhort time, after which Mr. Patrick
Henry rofe, and fpoke all that day (Thurfday) all
Friday, Saturday, Monday, Tuefday, and Wed-
nefday, and was ftill fpeaking on Thurfday, the
date of our information—That there are many
fhining charaflers in the Convention— Rutledge,
Blair, Jones, Lee, Henry, Wythe, and
    " *Maddifon* among the reft,
    Pouring from his narrow cheft,
    More than Greek or Roman fenfe,
    Boundlefs tides of eloquence." &c. &c.
and that the Convention would fet about three
weeks.

Massachusetts Centinel, report on Virginia ratifying convention, June 25, 1788.
(Author's newspaper collection)

Federalists at the Richmond convention and Governor Randolph may not
have agreed on much, but they did share the view that Virginia should
work with other states to organize a second convention. Early in the Richmond proceedings, Patrick Henry told the delegates that under Article V
it would be nearly impossible to secure amendments, and that a second
convention was needed prior to ratification. First, he doubted whether
Congress would propose them: "The most unworthy characters may get

into power and prevent the introduction of amendments." Then, Henry argued, even if two-thirds of state legislatures submitted petitions, there was no guarantee that a convention would be called. And he doubted that even if a convention proposed amendments they would be ratified: "There must necessarily be some designing bad men: To suppose that so large a number as three-fourths of the States will concur, is to suppose that they will possess genius, intelligence and integrity, approaching to miraculous." Henry reminded the convention that "four of the smallest States, that do not collectively contain one-tenth part of the population of the United States, may obstruct the most salutary and necessary amendments."[54]

George Nicholas, who supported the Constitution, tried to reassure Henry and other Anti-Federalists at the convention, telling them that if Congress refused to approve amendments, a second convention could be called. He added, "It is natural to conclude that those States who will apply for calling the Convention, will concur in the ratification of the proposed amendments." Nicholas seemed overly optimistic when he said that the delegates to the new convention "will have their deliberations confined to a few points;—no local interests to divert their attention;— nothing but the necessary alterations."[55]

Francis Corbin, another supporter of the Constitution, told opponents at the Virginia convention that if they insisted on ratification contingent upon the approval of amendments, a second constitutional convention would have to be immediately called to propose them. "Admitting this state [Virginia] proposes amendments previous to her adoption [of the Constitution], must there not be another Federal Convention? Must there not be also a Convention in each state? Suppose some of our proposed conditions to be rejected, will not our exclusion out of the Union be the consequence?"[56]

George Mason followed Randolph with a lengthy speech about the dangers of a national government. Along with Henry, Mason would carry the greatest burden of promoting the Anti-Federalist side. He was one of the most important figures in Virginia politics. Patrick Henry's youngest son, John, told the story of how Henry and Mason made their way each morning from the Swan boardinghouse a few blocks away. Despite the warm weather, Mason "was dressed in a full suit of black, and was remarkable for the urbanity and dignity with which he received and returned the courtesies of those who passed him."[57]

As he would explain repeatedly to the delegates, Mason was especially incensed about the power of proposed government to tax citizens directly. For months the Anti-Federalists had been raising the prospect of aggressive federal tax collectors swooping down on vulnerable citizens to take from them whatever money the state tax authorities had left behind. He argued that the ability to lay direct taxes against the people would "entirely change the confederation of the States into one consolidated government . . . [which] is totally subversive of every principle which has hitherto governed us. This power is calculated to annihilate totally the State governments." Mason supported an amendment whereby "Congress shall not exercise the power of raising direct taxes till the States shall have refused to comply with the requisitions of Congress."[58] Anti-Federalists would return many times during the convention to the authority of the federal government to directly tax citizens.

Mason also echoed the belief of many Anti-Federalists that a country as large geographically as the United States could not be governed as a republic: "There never was a Government, over a very extensive country, without destroying the liberties of the people . . . [M]onarchy may suit a large territory, and despotic Governments ever so extensive a country . . . but popular Governments can only exist in small territories."[59] He challenged his fellow delegates to cite one example in history to the contrary.

Mason also criticized the relatively small size of the House of Representatives, the only branch of government elected by the people: "Sixty-five members cannot possibly know the situation and circumstances of all the inhabitants of this immense continent." He added, "It would be impossible to have a full and adequate representation in the General Government; it would be too expensive and too unwieldy." Mason was convinced that once the House began meeting, it would resist efforts to add more members, which he believed necessary for the body to represent the diverse interests of the people. He gave Virginia as an example, where ten members of the House would be elected. He wondered why those individuals would agree to increase the size of the House and thus decrease the relative power that each would exercise. He said they would never "lessen their own power and influence . . . for the greater the number of men among whom any given quantum of power is divided, the less the power of each individual."[60]

Unlike his colleague Patrick Henry, Mason was candid about the ineffectiveness of the government under the Articles of Confederation. He wanted a stronger central government. But removing the power to directly tax citizens would, in Mason's view, preserve the autonomy of the states while at the same time encouraging them to act in good faith by providing the money that the federal government needed to carry out its functions.[61]

It was late in the afternoon on Wednesday. Delegates and spectators had listened to several long speeches in what must have been a sweltering theater. At that point, James Madison rose to discuss the Constitution for the first time at the convention.[62] He had missed the first day, having arrived Monday evening.[63] The delegate from Orange County declined at this point to answer Mason's charges that the federal government's power to directly tax citizens would make it dangerously powerful, that a republic could not be maintained in a large country, and that the House would be unresponsive to the will of the people. He said, simply, that the House of Representatives was to be elected by the people, whose members "depend on their good behaviour for re-election." He reminded the delegates that the convention had decided to review the Constitution in order, and he said he would discuss these matters in detail at the appropriate time.[64]

Madison's brief statement, coming at the end of a long day, belied the central role he would play at the convention. He would be supported by eloquent and respected Federalists such as Randolph and Nicholas, but the greatest burden of answering Henry's broad charges and the detailed criticisms of George Mason and others would fall on his shoulders. Although many of the delegates were well educated, experienced, and accomplished, no one could equal Madison's deep understanding of government and politics. He was the one who would consistently refute Henry's arguments against the proposed plan. When Henry made broad statements denouncing the Constitution, Madison answered with logical and detailed responses. Madison did not try to—indeed, could not hope to—match Patrick Henry's commanding voice and animated gestures, but instead he offered considered responses that refuted Henry's facts and decisively undermined his arguments, without being confrontational. Madison sometimes accepted one of Henry's premises, but he then convincingly demonstrated that the outcome would be the opposite of what Henry predicted.

Underlying the debate during the three weeks of the convention was a strong yet unspoken code of honor. In an era when "reputation" was as precious as property, a fine line existed between a vigorous debate in which a delegate could energetically criticize an opponent's argument and a personal attack for which apologies had to be issued or wounded feelings of honor had to be avenged. Duels might be fought over such perceived insults. As the debate raged on and fatigue and the uncomfortable conditions took their toll on the delegates, each side made statements that offended the other. With passions running high and so much at stake, the personal attacks would escalate and threaten to disrupt the convention.

On Thursday, Henry Lee of Westmoreland County directly criticized Patrick Henry, the first time someone had done so at the convention. "Light-Horse Harry" Lee, so named for his daring exploits during
the Revolutionary War, had been a college classmate of James Madison
and was a close friend. The future governor of Virginia and the father of
Robert E. Lee first expressed admiration for Henry, for "the honors with
which he has been dignified, and the brilliant talents which he has so
often displayed, [which] have attracted my respect and attention." But
Lee was disappointed by the combative tone that Henry had already used
in denouncing the proposed plan: "Instead of proceeding to investigate
the merits of the new plan of Government, the worthy character informed us of horrors which he felt, of apprehensions in his mind, which
make him tremblingly fearful of the fate of the Commonwealth." And
Lee asked, "Was it proper to appeal to the fear of this House? I trust he is
come to judge and not to alarm."[65]

Henry then talked for almost the entire afternoon, beginning with a
somewhat sarcastic retort to Lee, saying that Henry wished he were "possessed of talents, or possessed of any thing, that might enable me to
elucidate on this great subject." During his long address, Henry refused
to limit his remarks to the section of the Constitution that was supposed to be before the body. He insisted that Virginia reject the Constitution until it was substantially amended to limit the powers of the central
government and preserve the autonomy of the states. Just because eight
other states had ratified did not mean that Virginia should make the
same mistake, he argued.[66]

As any great orator would be, Henry must have been intensely focused on what he was trying to say to the convention. But as he was
speaking, he noticed that his son, whom he had left at home to protect
the family during his absence, had entered the convention hall. The delegates and spectators must have wondered why Henry interrupted his
remarks to the convention and whispered something to fellow delegate
John Dawson, who was sitting nearby. He said, "Dawson, I see my son in
the hall; take him out." Dawson soon returned with the news that Henry's
wife had safely delivered a son, Alexander Spotswood, and that mother
and children were doing well.[67] Unfortunately, the record does not indicate whether the proud father announced the news to the convention.

After Henry finally sat down, an exasperated Governor Randolph
observed that "if we go on in this irregular manner, contrary to our resolution, instead of three or six weeks, it will take us six months to decide
this question."[68]

The next day, Friday, June 6, belonged to the Federalists. As he had two days before, Governor Randolph said that any position he had taken on the Constitution was motivated solely by his devotion to liberty and his lack of interest in preserving his reputation: "If I have not succeeded in securing the esteem of my countrymen, I shall reap abundant consolation from the rectitude of my intentions." Sprinkled throughout his long address were references to his pure motivations in wanting to see the nation begin on a solid foundation. To Randolph, the failure to approve the Constitution would now mean disunion and would "throw away all those blessings we have so earnestly fought for."[69] He added defensively, "Pardon me if I discharge the obligation I owe to my country by voting for its adoption."

Having laid the foundation that he hoped would allow his arguments in favor of ratification to be judged on their merits—unburdened by his previous objections to the plan—Randolph strenuously argued that the approval of eight states meant Virginia no longer had any choice but to ratify the document. Randolph believed that given the cumulative support for the new plan, as shown by the approval of all but one state needed for ratification, Virginia would hurt itself and cripple the new nation if it refused to give its approval: "I am convinced that the Union will be lost by our rejection."[70]

Considering Randolph's passion on this subject, it is not surprising that he was incensed by Henry's assertion a day earlier that Virginia should not be influenced by the ratification of other states. Clearly annoyed at Henry's statement and his failure to adhere to the agreement to discuss the Constitution section by section, Randolph said that "many ... things have been alledged out of order—instead of discussing the system regularly, a variety of points are promiscuously debated in order to make temporary impressions on the members." He then indirectly questioned Henry's ability to look at the issues fairly: "Let us argue with unprejudiced minds."[71] This was one of several times when Randolph and Henry made statements that were personal and confrontational.[72]

In his speech that Friday morning, Randolph returned to familiar themes of the Federalists in arguing that given its abundant resources, the nation's potential for economic success was being wasted by the inability of the confederation government to secure adequate funding and to manage a national economy. He objected to the repeated assertions of Henry and other opponents that the nation was at peace and that prosperity would soon follow. If there were no union, the states would become "competitors and rivals," the governor claimed. He also warned that without a sufficiently powerful national government, the nation was susceptible to attack from foreign and domestic enemies.[73] States like Virginia, on their own, could not protect themselves against foreign nations. Only with the support of other states could Virginia have an army and navy to defend itself.

Randolph also discussed the federal judiciary, described in Article III, although the convention had not yet finished Articles I and II. The governor believed that an independent federal judiciary would be a source of protection for individual liberty and not oppressive. He pleaded with the delegates to recognize the need for a national government that would have "stability and give us security."[74]

Randolph urged the delegates to recognize that the confederation government was no longer viable. "It is gone, whether this House says so, or not. It is gone, Sir, by its own weakness," he told the convention at the end of his address. He argued, as would Madison at the convention and most convincingly in *Federalist 10,* that a geographically large nation could be governed as a republic and not a monarchy, and that the liberty of the people would be preserved in a government if freely chosen by them. "Extent of country, in my conception, ought to be no bar to the adoption of a good Government," Randolph said.[75]

Although he had been standing for three hours and talking loudly enough for the delegates and the gallery to hear him, Randolph concluded with some of the most passionate words spoken at the convention: "I believe, that as sure as there is a God in Heaven, our safety, our political happiness and existence, depend on the Union of the States; and that without the Union, the people of this and the other States, will undergo the unspeakable calamities, which discord, faction, turbulence, war, and bloodshed, have produced in other countries." He encouraged his fellow delegates to think about how this important debate and opportunity would be viewed in the future: "Catch the present moment— seize it with avidity and eagerness—for it may be lost—never to be regained. If the Union be now lost, I fear it will remain so forever."[76]

An anonymous writer from Richmond helped spread the word that Randolph had made this important speech, noting, "The governor has declared he will support the Constitution—he spoke for three hours today before he sat down."[77]

Bushrod Washington, the future president's nephew, who represented Westmoreland County at the convention, wrote to his uncle that Randolph, after pointing out the Constitution's defects, had "painted in a masterly and affecting manner the necessity of a more solid union of the States."[78] George Washington was able to pass this news to John Jay, whom he told that Randolph "is reported to have spoken with great pathos ... [and] declared, that, since so many of the States had adopted the proposed Constitution, he considered the sense of America to be already taken & that he should give his vote in favor of it without insisting previously upon amendments." Washington was confident that Randolph would have "considerable effect with those who had hitherto been wavering."[79]

Madison then rose and began what was a very long and must have been for him a physically exhausting speech. It was the first time he addressed the convention at length. If he was to influence the handful of undecided and wavering delegates, he had to make a good impression, both with the logic of his arguments and in his personal appeal to those whom he was asking to set aside their reservations about the proposed plan and vote to approve the Constitution.

It was probably early afternoon when Madison began his talk. His voice, thin and quiet compared to Henry's, immediately demonstrated how inadequate his speaking skills were for disseminating the work of his powerful mind. The stenographer noted, as he would several times during the debates, that Madison "spoke so low that his exordium [introductory comments] could not be heard distinctly."

Madison must have been nervous. This was far from the ideal environment for the man from Orange County. He had impressed the members of Governor Patrick Henry's executive council in 1777–78 because he could work and interact with them as part of a small group. He excelled as a member of small legislative bodies, especially in committee work, when he could display his understanding of history, government, and politics without having to give "public" speeches. Edward Coles, who served as President Madison's private secretary and later as the second governor of Illinois, wrote that Thomas Jefferson had often observed that if Madison had been a member of the House of Representatives after it had become a large body, "he never would have been distinguished." Madison, Jefferson noted, needed to sit behind closed doors in small groups, where the proceedings were conducted "in a conversational manner." That "enabled him ... to get the better of his modesty [and] take an active and distinguished part." Often Madison would shun the opportunity to speak on the floor of the state or federal legislature, preferring instead to work behind the scenes.[80]

Those with a good view of Madison as he spoke to the delegates in the Quesnay Academy would likely have seen, in the words of Edward Coles written many years later, a man who was "in his dress not at all excentric or given to dandyism, but always appeared neat and genteel." Coles had heard that early in Madison's life he sometimes wore light-colored clothes, but "from the time I [Coles] first knew him . . . when I was a child . . . I never knew him to wear any other colour but black." At the Richmond convention, he likely wore "his breeches short with buckles at the knees, black silk stockings and shoes with strings," as Coles had frequently seen him dress. Madison often wore powder in his hair, "which was dressed full over the ears, tied behind, and brought to a point above the forehead, to cover some degree of his baldness."[81]

Coles says that Madison stood five feet six inches, several inches taller than most contemporaries and biographers have estimated to be his height. He had a "small and delicate form" and "rather a tawny complexion, bespeaking a sedentary and studious man." He often wore a three-pointed black hat in which he would sometimes store his notes for speeches.[82] Madison's hair was "originally of a dark brown colour; his eyes were bluish, but not a bright blue; [and although] his form, features and manner were not commanding . . . few men possessed so rich a flow of language."[83]

Madison began this important speech by trying to focus the debate in a way that would play to his strengths. He decided not to confront Henry by challenging his general criticisms of the Constitution, which Henry had attempted to support with vague references to specific sections and misrepresentations of what the Constitution said or the Philadelphia delegates meant. Instead, in a direct rebuff to the Anti-Federalists, Madison demanded that the opponents provide evidence and examples when they claimed that the Constitution would destroy the nation's newly won liberty. He encouraged "calm and rational investigation" and added, "I hope that Gentlemen, in displaying their abilities, on this occasion, instead of giving opinions, and making assertions, will condescend to prove and demonstrate, by a fair and regular discussion—It gives me pain to hear Gentlemen continually distorting the natural construction of language."[84]

Madison cautioned the delegates not to be misled by unsupported criticisms of the proposed plan, saying, in effect, that they should reject broad challenges to the Constitution unless supported by proof grounded in a reasonable interpretation of its words. Madison observed that Henry "told us, that this Constitution ought to be rejected, because it endangered the public liberty . . . Give me leave to make one answer to that observation—Let the dangers which this system is supposed to be replete with, be clearly pointed out. If any dangerous and unnecessary powers be given to the general Legislature, let them be plainly demonstrated, and let us not rest satisfied with general assertions of dangers, without examination."[85]

Madison challenged Henry's argument that the nation was at peace and capable of prosperity: "I wish sincerely, Sir, this were true. If this be their happy situation, why has every State acknowledged the contrary? Why were deputies from all the States sent to the General Convention? Why have complaints of national and international distresses been echoed and re-echoed throughout the Continent? Why has our General Government been so shamefully disgraced, and our Constitution [the Articles of Confederation] violated?"[86]

If Madison could show that Henry's attacks on the Constitution were inconsistent and conflicting, some delegates would lose confidence in his argument that the proposed plan was unnecessary and dangerous. Demonstrating such contradictions would suggest that Henry's criticisms were not well thought out and should be viewed suspiciously.

On that Friday afternoon, Madison began his effort to undermine Henry's argument with these seemingly deferential words: "I must confess, I have not been able to find his [Henry's] usual consistency, in the Gentleman's arguments on this occasion."[87] One of Henry's primary arguments against the Constitution was that it made the approval of amendments too difficult, if not impossible. Henry argued that requiring such a high level of consensus on the part of Congress and the states to propose and ratify amendments was unrealistic, and that after the document was in effect, the people would be unable to convince their representatives to make changes to address threats to their liberty.

Madison found what he called a "glaring" inconsistency in Henry's attack on Article V (the amending provision) of the Constitution. Madison attacked this view first by noting that only nine states were required to put the new Constitution into effect to "abolish the present inadequate, unsafe, and pernicious Confederation!" He then reminded Henry that the Articles of Confederation could only be amended with the unanimous consent of the states, and that "the smallest State in the Union [Rhode Island] has obstructed every attempt to reform the government—That little member has repeatedly disobeyed and counteracted the general authority." And he asked Henry, "Would the Honorable Gentleman agree to continue the most radical defects in the old system, because the petty State of Rhode-Island would not agree to remove them?" He found contradictory his opponents' argument that the Articles provided a better system of government, when the new Constitution offered an orderly and politically feasible method for amending the new charter of government.[88]

Madison said that the confederation system had left the nation vulnerable to attacks from abroad and within: "Without a general controuling power to call forth the strength of the Union, to repel invasions, the country might be over-run and conquered by foreign enemies—Without such a power, to suppress insurrections, our liberties might be destroyed by domestic faction, and domestic tyranny be established." According to Madison, under the proposed Constitution "powers are not given to any particular set of men—They are in the hands of the people—delegated to their Representatives chosen for short terms. To Representatives responsible to the people, and whose situation is perfectly similar to their own:— As long as this is the case we have no danger to apprehend."[89]

Madison observed that in other countries, freedom had often been lost because a central government was too weak to exercise power in the best interests of the whole nation, telling the convention that "the loss of liberty very often resulted from factions and divisions;—from local considerations, which eternally lead to quarrels . . . [I]nternal dissentions . . . have more frequently demolished civil liberty, than a tenacious disposition in rulers, to retain any stipulated powers." At the same time, the proposed Constitution, Madison argued, also preserved the autonomy of the states. Disagreeing directly with Henry, Madison said this "Government is not completely consolidated, —nor is it entirely federal [preserving the power of the states]. Who are the parties to it? The people—but not the people as composing one great body—but the people as composing thirteen sovereignties."[90]

Madison said that the legitimacy of the proposed system would come directly from the people, while the new government would also maintain much of the structure of the current system: "The existing system has been derived from the dependent derivative authority of the Legislatures of the States; whereas this is derived from the superior power of the people." He cited as an example the election of senators by state legislatures, arguing that if the proposed government were to be "completely consolidated, the Senate would have been chosen by the people in their individual capacity, in the same manner as the members of the other House." The members of the House, because they would be elected by the people, would direct their "deliberations . . . to the interests of the people of America," while senators, appointed by state legislatures, would "not soon forget the source from which they derive their political existence." He concluded by recognizing that the proposed system was "of a complicated nature, and this complication, I trust, will be found to exclude the evils of absolute consolidation, as well as of a mere confederacy . . . [T]he general [government] will never destroy the individual [state] Governments."[91]

Madison's speech impressed many of his colleagues, including fellow delegate Bushrod Washington, who reported that Madison had spoken "with such a force of reasoning, and a display of irresistible truths, that opposition seemed to have quitted the field." But Washington was not sure Madison had changed very many minds: "I am not so sanguine as to trust appearances, or even to flatter myself that he made many converts. A few I have been confidently informed he did influence, who were decidedly in the opposition."[92]

When Madison sat down, George Nicholas carried on the Federalists' efforts to persuade undecided and wavering delegates. He first expressed surprise that the debate had been so far-ranging, because he had expected a clause-by-clause discussion of the plan. He characterized Henry's arguments about the dangers of the new government as "inconclusive and inaccurate" and said Henry's arguments came down to this: "The powers given any Government ought to be small." Nicholas believed that the powers given to a government should be "proportionate" to its purpose, and that it was "necessary to give powers to a certain extent, to any Government." Henry had argued that the people had the right to determine their government. Nicholas responded with Henry's own words: "He tells us, that the Constitution annihilates the Confederation. Did he [Henry] not prove, that every people had a right to change their Government, when it should be deemed inadequate to their happiness?" Nicholas answered Henry's assertion that governments never willingly give up power by arguing that the states were doing just that by agreeing to the creation of a new central government. He told the delegates and the gallery that the plan would not create an oppressive tax system, and that the House of Representatives would be accountable to the people through direct and frequent elections.[93]

Nicholas then reminded Henry that the new Constitution not only provided for Congress to propose amendments but also gave such power to the states. Under Article V, if two-thirds of state legislatures petitioned Congress to hold a convention for the purpose of proposing amendments, it would be required to do so. Such amendments would then have to be approved by three-fourths of state legislatures or state conventions, the same level of consensus required of amendments proposed by Congress.

Nicholas suggested that this provided a safeguard against unforeseen problems in the new Constitution and demonstrated the flexibility of the plan: "The Convention shall be called, will have their deliberations confined to a few points;—no local interests to divert their attention;—nothing but the necessary alterations.—They will have many advantages over the last Convention. No experiments to devise; the general and fundamental regulations being already laid down."[94] Delegates who had serious misgivings about the proposed Constitution were being reminded that the plan provided its own method of amendment.

When Nicholas concluded, the convention adjourned for the day. It had been a remarkable week in the Quesnay Academy. Probably no one in the gallery had been disappointed by the discussion or failed to appreciate its importance. James Breckinridge, a surveyor from Botetourt County, told his brother that the debates "exceed, if possible my expectations; they have been elaborate, elegant, eloquent, & consequently entertaining and instructive." He said Patrick Henry's "eloquence and oratory far exceeded my conception," and in "such an Assembly he . . . [was] better adapted to carry his point & lead the ignorant people astray than any other person upon earth; Madisons plain, ingenious, & elegant reasoning is entirely thrown away and lost among such men."[95]

Most of the week had been dominated by Federalists, led by Randolph, Madison, and Nicholas. In the early days of the convention, Patrick Henry had been less aggressive than might have been expected. An anonymous letter that appeared in several newspapers noted that Henry "seems anxious to reserve his strong hold till he can decoy *Maddison* and *Randolph* to declare all they have to say."[96]

Perhaps Henry had underestimated the energy and passion of his adversaries or was trying to sense the strength and direction of their arguments before he counterattacked. In any case, the next day he returned to the offensive with a vengeance. Saturday opened with more speeches from supporters of the Constitution. Then Henry rose. His speech, addressing the charges that he had exaggerated the dangers of the proposed system and that his arguments were inconsistent, was a withering assault on the Constitution. It signaled Henry's determination to dominate the rest of the convention.

Henry and his fellow delegates would vigorously debate many of the most important issues arising from the proposed plan: the powers of the new government and the impact on the states; the lack of a bill of rights; the threat posed by federal judges with lifetime tenure; the future of slavery; access to the Mississippi River and other trade issues; the power of the president and the Senate to negotiate and approve treaties; the authority of the federal government to impose taxes; the size of the House of Representatives; and the power of the president. They also debated one of the most important and divisive issues: Should Virginia require that amendments protecting individual rights be added to the proposed Constitution as a condition of the state's ratification?

Henry focused numerous times during the convention on access to the Mississippi River, an issue of immense importance to the West and to those concerned that John Jay had been willing to negotiate away the right to navigate the river in return for benefits from Spain.[97] To some delegates, the possible closing of the Mississippi was more important than amendments to the Constitution. Henry's remarks on that subject were of particular interest to the fourteen delegates from the Kentucky territory, who had been subjected to a barrage of Anti-Federalist sentiment before the convention. Madison believed those delegates could decide the outcome of the ratification vote.[98]

Henry hoped the proposed plan would be defeated if he could persuade even a handful of delegates. A week after the start of the convention, Henry told a correspondent that "four-fifths of our inhabitants are opposed to the new scheme of government . . . Indeed, in the part of this country [Virginia] lying south of the James River, I am confident nine-tenths are opposed to it." Yet, Henry explained, "Strange as it may seem, the numbers in the convention appear equal on both sides, so that the majority, which way soever it goes, will be small." Henry suggested that supporters of the Constitution had won election to the Richmond convention by misleading their constituents: "The friends and seekers of power, have, with their usual subtilty wriggled themselves into the choice of the people, by assuming shapes as various as the faces of the men they address on such occasions."[99]

William Grayson also thought the outcome would be decided by only a few votes. As he explained in a letter a week after the convention began, "Our affairs in the convention are suspended by a hair; I really cannot tell you on which side the scale will turn; the difference . . . will be exceedingly small indeed."[100]

If Henry was correct that the delegates sent to Richmond did not represent the strong sentiment against the Constitution, it may be explained in part by the nature of the election districts. All counties, regardless of size, sent two delegates to the convention. William Wirt Henry, Patrick Henry's grandson, believed that the smaller eastern counties, which were largely Federalist, had been overrepresented at the convention when compared to the interior counties, which were mostly Anti-Federalist. Presumably, if counties had elected delegates based on population, more opponents than supporters would have been sent to Richmond.[101]

On that Saturday afternoon, Henry's determination to prevent ratification was evident as he gave one of his longest speeches. He argued that Virginia should stay out of the union until needed amendments were proposed by a second convention or by Congress, and that because of Virginia's size and importance, the other states would respond by also demanding changes to the Constitution.

Madison and other Federalists were equally committed to preventing the rejection of the Constitution. In what could be considered a veiled criticism of Henry, Madison said that the weakness of the present system had "manifested itself . . . to such a degree as admits of no doubt to a rational, intelligent, and unbiased mind."[102]

The long week was finally over, and delegates would have looked forward to Sunday, their one day off. It had become clear that Madison would carry much of the burden of convincing wavering delegates that they should vote to ratify without requiring amendments as a condition. He needed to be there every day to explain what was discussed at the Philadelphia convention, to answer the arguments of the opponents, and to make the case for the Constitution.

Then, as the delegates and spectators arrived in the Quesnay Academy on Monday for the start of the second week of the convention, something was different. Straining to see the face of every arriving delegate, supporters of the Constitution would have become increasingly apprehensive as the time for resuming the debate approached. With the pounding of the gavel and the call to order, Patrick Henry was about to give one of his longest and most vitriolic speeches.

Someone would have to answer Henry's attacks on the Constitution, but it would not be James Madison. As this important day began, his seat was empty.

5

The Ratification Vote

OVER THE WEEKEND, James Madison had become ill. He wrote to Alexander Hamilton that the "Heat of the weather . . . has laid me up with a bilious attack: I am not able therefore to say more than a few words."[1] Madison was probably suffering again from severe stomach discomfort. He would have had a difficult time leaving his boardinghouse room and was likely weak from diarrhea and dehydration. The already shy Madison would have been humiliated if he returned to the convention in this condition and his fellow delegates and the audience saw him frequently get up from his seat and exit the floor. This was not good news for supporters of the Constitution. If the frail Madison were to be seriously ill during the Richmond convention, it could affect the ratification vote.

Federalists must have been relieved to see Madison return on Tuesday, but he was still not feeling well. He wrote to Rufus King that "I have been for two days & still am laid up with a bilious attack. Writing is scarcely practicable & very injurious to me." To Tench Coxe, he explained he could not respond to his letter right away because "for several days preceding yesterday [I] was confined to my room. I am now able to resume my seat in the Convention; though am extremely feeble." By the end of the week, Madison was feeling better. He told Washington, "I am tolerably well recovered" from the "bilious indisposition which confined me for several days."[2]

But then, only a few days later, Madison was again not well. He wrote to Hamilton that "I have been partially recovered since my last [letter to you] but to day have a . . . relapse. My health is not good, and the business [of the convention] is wearisome beyond expression." Madison later missed three more days because of the same illness. A week before the ratification vote, he apologized to Rufus King for not responding more quickly to his letters, telling him, "I have been much indisposed & continue so in a degree which barely allows me to co-operate in the business." He also told Washington, "I find myself not yet restored & extremely feeble."[3]

His friends began to worry about his health. Cyrus Griffin, president of the Confederation Congress and a fellow Virginian, told Madison, "We are all extremely uneasy at your Indisposition—how much to be regretted indeed! And particularly when such important matters are under deliberation—but I hope that kind Heaven has restored you before this day [June 18], to be a farther blessing and honor to your Country!" Although Hamilton was busy at the New York ratifying convention, he told Madison that "I fear something from your indisposition."[4]

No matter how Madison was feeling, the debate in the Quesnay Academy continued furiously, a rhetorical brawl that overpowered occasional attempts to keep it confined to an orderly discussion of the articles. The president of the convention, Edmund Pendleton, did not try to limit the discussion to a section-by-section examination of the Constitution, which was the original plan. He may have believed that if the convention considered the proposed document so methodically, it would take several months, and much time would be wasted talking about uncontroversial sections. Without strict direction from Pendleton, delegates often discussed whatever part of the Constitution they wanted, repeated points they or other delegates had made, and covered numerous topics within the same speech.

On Monday, June 9, when Madison was absent, Patrick Henry shocked the convention by announcing that one of Virginia's most respected political figures opposed the Constitution. He did not mention Thomas Jefferson by name at this point but described him as "an illustrious citizen of Virginia, who is now in Paris." Then Henry proclaimed that "This illustrious citizen advises you to reject this Government, till it be amended. His sentiments coincide entirely with ours." As if the delegates and audience had forgotten the contributions Jefferson had made to Virginia and the nation, Henry added, "His character and abilities are in the highest estimation—He is well acquainted in every respect, with this country."[5]

Henry suggested that Jefferson was so disappointed in the Constitution's failure to provide for explicit protection of personal rights that the author of the Declaration of Independence was recommending that the Richmond convention reject the proposed plan until such amendments were added. As Henry explained: "At a great distance from us, he remembers and studies our happiness. Living in splendor and dissipation, he thinks yet of Bills of Rights . . . Let us follow the sage advice of this common friend of our happiness."[6]

Federalists must have wondered how Henry knew that Jefferson, who was still in Paris, opposed the Constitution in its current form. Henry had access to a letter Jefferson had written on February 7 to Alexander Donald, a Richmond tobacco merchant and close friend of Jefferson. In the letter, Jefferson said, "I wish with all my soul that the nine first Conventions may accept the new Constitution, because this will secure to us the good it contains, which I think great & important." But Jefferson added, "I equally wish that the four latest conventions, whichever they may be, may refuse to accede to it till a declaration of rights be annexed." If four states took this action, Jefferson wrote, "this would probably command the offer of such a declaration, & thus give to the whole fabric, perhaps as much perfection as any one of that kind ever had." Jefferson then listed the rights he wanted to see included, such as "freedom of religion, freedom of the press . . . trial by juries in all cases, no suspensions of the habeas corpus, no standing armies . . . [T]hese are fetters against doing evil which no honest government should decline."[7]

Because of how long it took for letters to get from Paris to Virginia, no one in the Quesnay Academy on June 9 knew that Jefferson had changed his mind. On May 27, he wrote to Edward Carrington that he now favored the path that Massachusetts had taken, namely, ratifying the Constitution with recommended amendments. As Jefferson explained, "The plan of Massachusetts is far preferable, and will I hope be followed by those who are yet to decide." A few days later, he wrote to William Carmichael that "I am now convinced that the plan of Massachusetts is the best that is, to accept, and to amend afterwards."[8]

Surprisingly, no Federalist immediately challenged Henry's interpretation of the Jefferson letter. Randolph followed Henry that day and delivered a passionate speech to the convention, but he did not confront him over this strategy for persuading undecided delegates.

The next morning Randolph, who had not seen Jefferson's letter to Donald, expressed outrage on the convention floor that Jefferson would be used this way. Perhaps the governor paid a visit to the ailing Madison at his boardinghouse the night before and told him what Henry had said. Madison may have been infuriated by Henry's methods and encouraged Randolph to speak out. Everyone knew Randolph was directing his remarks at Henry when he said, "I trust that his [Jefferson's] name was not mentioned to influence any member of this House. Notwithstanding the celebrity of his character, his name cannot be used as authority against the Constitution." Randolph added, "I have had no letter from him [Jefferson]. As far as my information goes, it is only a report circulated through the town, that he wished nine States to adopt, and the others to reject it, in order to get amendments."[9]

Edmund Pendleton also criticized Henry for invoking Jefferson this way. He told the convention that he had seen the Donald letter, and that Jefferson advocated adoption of the Constitution by nine states "because he thinks it will secure to us the good it contains, which he thinks *great* and *important* . . . but he would not wish that a schism should take place in the Union on any consideration. If then we are to be influenced by his opinion at all, we will ratify it, and secure thereby the good it contains." According to Pendleton, the amendment process could then be used to remove "those inconveniences which experience shall point out."[10]

Henry would not let it go. This time using Jefferson's name— "The Honorable Gentleman [Pendleton] has endeavored to explain the opinion of Mr. Jefferson our common friend, into an advice to adopt this new government"—Henry again argued that Jefferson was recommending that Virginia reject the Constitution to force the addition of a bill of rights. Madison had heard enough. He was no doubt greatly irritated that his friend had been used this way. He told the convention, "I believe that were that Gentleman [Jefferson] now on this floor, he would be *for* the adoption of this Constitution. I wish his name had never been mentioned.—I wish every thing spoken here relative to his opinion may be suppressed if our debates should be published. I know that the delicacy of his feelings will be wounded when he will see in print what has, and may be said, concerning him on this occasion."[11]

After listening to Henry, Randolph, Pendleton, and Madison talk about Thomas Jefferson, some delegates may have been confused about Jefferson's position on ratification by the Virginia convention. But as the debate continued, some of the nation's future leaders made it clear how they stood.

Early in the second week, James Monroe spoke for the first time. He began his extended comments by telling the convention, "I cannot avoid expressing the great anxiety which I feel upon the present occasion—an anxiety that proceeds not only from an high sense of the importance of the subject, but from a profound respect for this august and venerable assembly." After discussing how easily governments can decay and become oppressive and after tracing the evolution from British colonies to free states, Monroe observed that the government was now in the hands of "one order of people only—freemen; not of nobles and freemen." It was his "most earnest wish and fervent prayer" that government remain in the hands of the people. He then discussed at great length the history of democracy in Greece and in other nations. When Monroe read long quotes from works on ancient civilizations, the stenographer summarized, but did not transcribe, the statements. As Monroe continued discussing various nations over the course of human history, the delegates on the floor and the spectators in the sweltering galleries must have been eager for him to make his points in favor or opposition to the Constitution. His speech that day lasted more than three hours.[12]

Monroe finally turned to the powers of the proposed government. He recognized the need for a new federal government with authority over national affairs, including "one great power . . . [the] absolute controul over commerce." The only power Monroe would remove from the federal government was that of direct taxation, arguing that its other powers were sufficient without it. He characterized such authority as "unnecessary [and] impracticable under a Democracy; and if exercised, as tending to anarchy, or the subversion of liberty, and probably the latter." In Monroe's view, the federal government would have plenty of money from other sources such as duties on imports and exports, sale of land and other natural resources, and, if necessary, loans. He anticipated that the federal government would grow to dominate the states, and he worried about the nation's most capable leaders assuming positions in the federal government and leaving the states with those less qualified. He concluded by again affirming his opposition to taxation: "I am strongly impressed with the necessity of having a firm national Government, but I am decidedly against giving it the

James Monroe, Revolutionary War hero, voted against ratification of the Constitution and opposed his friend James Madison for election to the U.S. House. (*National Archives*)

power of direct taxation; because I think it endangers our liberties. My attachment to the Union and an energetic government, is such, that I would consent to give the General Government every power contained in that plan, except that of taxation." He also expressed strong support for attaching a bill of rights to the Constitution.[13]

John Marshall, delegate to the Virginia ratifying convention and a member of Congress, would have his greatest influence as chief justice of the United States for thirty-four years.
(Library of Congress)

After Monroe sat down, the future chief justice of the United States, John Marshall, addressed the convention for the first time. The thirty-two-year-old Marshall had practiced law from the close of the war to the Richmond convention, pausing to serve in the House of Delegates. He was over six feet tall and had "piercing black eyes and dark, unkempt hair." His clothes always seemed rumpled. He was well liked—historian Grigsby said "his habits were convivial almost to excess"—and as an accomplished lawyer, he likely commanded substantial attention whenever he spoke at the convention.[14]

Marshall urged the delegates to vote for the Constitution and confronted one of Henry's primary arguments. He said that if Henry was correct that amendments would be difficult to obtain after Virginia ratified, they would be equally difficult to obtain if Virginia refused to approve the Constitution. Marshall discussed at length the weaknesses of the confederation government, and he refuted Monroe's argument about taxation. To Marshall, a system by which the federal government requested money from the states was untenable: "Requisitions cannot be effectual. They will be productive of delay, and will ultimately be inefficient. By direct taxation, the necessities of the Government will be supplied in a peaceable manner without irritating the minds of the people. But requisitions cannot be rendered without a civil war—without great expence of money, and the blood of our citizens."[15]

The next day, June 11, Madison had to disagree with his friend James Monroe without hurting his feelings. Madison knew that his fellow

Virginian was sensitive to criticism and would be especially so in a public forum like the ratifying convention. Nevertheless, Madison, after referring to Monroe as "the Honorable Gentleman" and my "honorable friend," rejected the argument that the new government would have sufficient funds without imposing direct taxes. He considered it crucial that the federal government have enough revenue to carry out its functions and grow in relation to the states.[16]

On the same day, William Grayson gave his first speech at the convention. Representing Prince William County, Grayson would soon be one of Virginia's first U.S. senators. Grayson had been educated at Oxford and had read widely the works of the major political thinkers, including Adam Smith, whose *Wealth of Nations* greatly influenced him when he was young. Washington recognized his "spirit and intelligence" and invited him to join his military staff. His distinguished service included fighting in several of the most important battles of the war.[17] After the war, he served in the Confederation Congress.

Grayson was described by contemporaries as an accomplished debater and the "handsomest man in the Convention." At six feet tall and weighing 250 pounds, he had a commanding physical presence. His eyes were "black and deep-seated; his nose large and curved; his lips well formed, disclosing teeth white and regular . . . [and] a fine complexion gave animation to the whole."[18] He spoke in a strong, pleasing voice, and his wit and sense of humor held the attention of delegates and spectators alike. After Henry and Mason, Grayson was the most important Anti-Federalist delegate at the convention.

Grayson addressed the delegates more than two dozen times, discussing what he considered to be dangerous defects in the Constitution. He warned of "adopting measures which we apprehend to be ruinous and destructive." He ridiculed the assertion of Randolph and others that doom was around the corner unless the Constitution was adopted: "We are now told that we shall

William Grayson, an energetic opponent of the Constitution, became one of Virginia's first U.S. senators. *(Library of Congress)*

have wars . . . that every calamity is to attend us . . . the Indians are to invade us . . . to convert our cleared lands into hunting grounds—And the Carolinians from the South, mounted on alligators, I presume, are to come and destroy our corn fields and eat up our little children!"[19]

Grayson argued that the Confederation government had brought peace, but he also had ideas on how it could be improved. He advocated a "President for life, choosing his successor at the same time—A Senate for life, with the powers of the House of Lords—And a triennial House of Representatives, with the powers of the House of Commons in England." He decried the proposed power of the federal government to directly tax citizens and said that should tax collectors, supported by the army, come to take their bounty, "by this Constitution, the sword is employed against individuals[;] by the other [Confederation government] it is employed against the States, which is more honorable."[20]

As the convention moved into its closing days, the Constitution's lack of a bill of rights became the focus of some of the most heated and important debates. No issue created more problems for the Federalists. In an important letter from Paris, Thomas Jefferson had told Madison at the end of December that he generally favored the Constitution. He mentioned the organization of the government into three branches, the election of members of the House by the people, the authority to levy taxes, and the veto power of the president as among its best features. He said he was "captivated" by the compromises between large and small states that had allowed the writing of the Constitution to be completed.[21]

But Jefferson expressed disappointment and concern because it lacked a bill of rights. He listed the omission of specific protection for freedom of religion, for freedom of the press, and against standing armies as serious deficiencies. He rejected James Wilson's argument, representing the "official" position of Federalists, that protection for individual rights in state constitutions was sufficient: "To say, as [M]r. Wilson does, that a bill of rights was not necessary because all is reserved in the case of the general [federal] government which is not given, while in the particular ones [state governments] all is given which is not reserved, might do for the Audience to whom it was addressed, but is surely a gratis dictum opposed by strong inferences from the body of the instrument [the proposed Constitution], as well as the omission of the clause of our present confederation which had declared that in express terms."[22] Jefferson was referring to Article II of the Articles of Confederation: "Each state retains its sovereignty, freedom and independence, and every power, jurisdiction and right, which is not by this confederation expressly delegated to the United States in Congress assembled."

Jefferson noted that state constitutions varied significantly in the rights they protected, and thus citizens could not rely on those documents to limit the power of the federal government. In a line that was to be repeated widely, Jefferson argued that a list of protections should have been included: "A bill of rights is what the people are entitled to against every government on earth, general or particular, & what no just government should refuse or rest on inference."[23] Madison did not directly answer Jefferson by saying that a bill of rights was unnecessary and could create potential problems, although that was his view at the time.

Although a bill of rights was mentioned by various speakers during the first two weeks of the convention, it received substantial attention in the final days. On June 16, nine days before the delegates voted on whether to approve or reject the Constitution, George Mason rose to talk about this vital issue. He had special authority to speak about the bill of rights. Mason had been the principal author of the Virginia Declaration of Rights in 1776, and he had argued energetically at the Philadelphia convention that the original Constitution must include a set of amendments protecting individual liberty.

Mason said that nothing in the proposed plan specifically held that the states were to retain powers not granted to the federal government. Furthermore, the Constitution granted Congress sweeping powers to make all laws "necessary and proper" to carry out its duties. Thus, according to Mason, the Constitution did not prevent Congress from interfering with freedom of the press and other rights. He wondered what would happen if Congress became too powerful: "Now suppose oppressions should arise under the Government, and any writer should dare to stand forth and expose to the community at large, the abuses of those powers. Could not Congress, under the idea of providing for the general welfare, and under their own construction, say, that this was destroying the general peace, encouraging sedition, and poisoning the minds of the people? And could they not, in order to provide against this, lay a dangerous restriction on the press?"[24]

George Nicholas immediately responded with the usual argument of the Federalists. He said the Constitution did not require the states to give up the protections provided in their constitutions: "It is a simple and plain proposition. It is agreed upon by all, that the people have all power. If they part with any of it, is it necessary to declare that they retain the rest? . . . If I have one thousand acres of land, and I grant five hundred acres of it, must I declare that I retain the other five hundred? . . . After granting some powers, the rest must rest with the people."[25]

Mason had a swift rebuttal. Although the government of Virginia "was drawn from the people," a list of rights explicitly protecting individual freedoms was included in the state bill of rights. "Why should it not be so in this Constitution?" he asked. "Artful sophistry and evasions" would not satisfy him, and he added that he could see "no clear distinction between rights relinquished by a positive grant, and lost by implication. Unless there was a Bill of Rights, implication might swallow up all our rights."[26]

Henry knew that the Constitution's supporters were especially vulnerable on this issue, and he tried to convince wavering delegates that the absence of a bill of rights was so important that it required rejection of the Constitution. Rising to his feet as soon as Mason finished, Henry said, "The necessity of a Bill of Rights appears to me to be greater in this Government, than ever it was in any Government before."[27]

Citing the example of Great Britain and the power long wielded by kings, Henry argued that unless a right is reserved to the people by some express provision, it is "relinquished to rulers." Virginia, Henry noted, even with a developed system of elections and representation, still chose to explicitly protect certain rights in its constitution: "She most cautiously and guardedly reserved and secured those invaluable, inestimable rights and privileges, which no people, inspired with the least glow of patriotic love of liberty, ever did, or ever can, abandon." To Henry, the states under the new system would be greatly weakened. Thus it made no sense to provide protection against those governments but not against the new government: "You have a Bill of Rights to defend you against the State Government, which is bereaved of all power; and yet you have none against Congress, though in full and exclusive possession of all power! You arm yourselves against the weak and defenceless, and expose yourselves naked to the armed and powerful. Is not this a conduct of unexampled absurdity?"[28]

Henry wondered aloud why the Philadelphia convention had not proposed a bill of rights along with the Constitution and argued that one must be added now. He noted sarcastically that a "Bill of Rights may be summed up in a few words. What do they [Federalists] tell us?—That our rights are reserved.—Why not say so? Is it because it will consume too much paper?" And he warned that without a bill of rights federal officials could "go into your cellars and rooms, and search, ransack and measure, every thing you eat, drink and wear."[29]

Finally, after a week's additional discussion of various issues, the delegates prepared for the key vote on whether amendments to the

Constitution should be required before Virginia gave its approval. Governor Randolph framed the issue by stating that approval of the Constitution was "necessary to avoid the storm which is hanging over America," and that the decision to propose "previous or subsequent amendments, is now the only dispute . . . But I ask[,] Gentlemen, whether as eight states have adopted it, it be not safer to adopt it and rely on the probability of obtaining amendments, than by a rejection to hazard a breach of the Union?"[30]

By the end of the convention, fatigue and frustration eroded the usual decorum and carefully chosen words. On June 23, Henry Lee had finally heard enough of George Mason's attacks on the proposed plan. He boiled over in exasperation. Lee did not just disagree with Mason's criticisms of the Constitution. He denounced Mason's comments as likely to incite those who were determined to wreck the proposed system: "My feelings are so oppressed with the declarations of my honorable friend, that I can no longer suppress my utterance. I respect the Honorable Gentleman, and never believed I should live, to have heard fall from his lips, opinions so injurious to our country, and so opposite to the dignity of this Assembly. If the dreadful picture which he has drawn, be so abhorrent to his mind as he has declared, let me ask the Honorable Gentlemen, if he has not pursued the very means to bring into action, the horrors which he deprecates? Such speeches within these walls, from a character so venerable and estimable, easily progress into overt acts, among the less thinking and vicious." And Lee warned that if Mason and other opponents defeated the Constitution, they might be responsible for bringing about some of the very evils they were predicting would plague the nation if the document was approved: "I pray you to remember, and the Gentlemen in opposition not to forget, that should these impious scenes commence, which my honorable friend [Mason] might abhor, and which I execrate, whence and how they began. God of Heaven avert from my country the dreadful curse."[31]

The day before the vote, Patrick Henry again appealed to the delegates to reject the Constitution until amendments could be written and offered to a subsequent convention. Randolph responded that such an outcome would result in the dissolution of the union: "Previous amendments are but another name for rejection. They will throw Virginia out of the Union, and cause heart aches to many of those Gentlemen who may vote for them." He added, "If, in this situation, we reject the Constitution, the Union will be dissolved, the dogs of war will break loose, and anarchy and discord will complete the ruin of this country."[32]

After George Mason again criticized the power granted to Congress under the proposed Constitution to regulate commerce and navigation, John Dawson gave his only speech of the convention. It was an important moment because Dawson may have reflected the view of some of the wavering delegates, who were sufficient in number to determine the outcome.

Dawson had been a longtime admirer of Madison and, as we have seen, considered him a friend. He had declared to the voters of Spotsylvania County before he was elected to the convention that he was opposed to the Constitution, but it was reasonable for Madison to hope that Dawson had reconsidered. For three weeks at the convention, Dawson had listened to Madison and other Federalists explain what the delegates at the Philadelphia convention had done, what the phrases of the proposed plan meant, and what the consequences would be of rejecting the Constitution or approving it contingent upon amendments. When Dawson stood to deliver his speech, Madison must have listened with anticipation. If Dawson announced he would vote in favor in ratification, it would likely mean that the supporters had successfully made their case. If he was opposed, it likely reflected a lingering distrust of the plan on the part of many of the swing delegates. In short, if Dawson spoke against the Constitution, it would bode ill for the next day's vote.

Dawson's speech, thoughtful and articulate, lasted more than an hour, and it was obvious that he had carefully prepared his remarks. He did not enjoy the stature of many of the delegates to the convention. He was a conscientious member of the General Assembly, with a friendly personality that spawned friendships among leading figures on both sides of the debate, but there was nothing about his background that required great deference to his views. Although he apologized for taking the time of the delegates, he nevertheless gave an impassioned and forceful address. To the dismay of the Federalists, he announced he would vote against ratification.

Dawson supported many provisions of the proposed plan, but his primary objection was that it would create a consolidated government that would leave the states too weak. He said early in his speech that he wanted to be able to support the Constitution. He recognized, as had many others during the convention, the serious shortcomings in the Articles of Confederation. Even so, after careful consideration, Dawson said, "I was persuaded that, although the proposed plan contains many things excellent, yet by the adoption of it, as it now stands, the liberties of America, in general; the property of Virginia in particular; would be endangered." He believed that not only would the new government have sufficient powers to become oppressive, it could govern over so vast a land only by infringing on the rights of the people. He asked whether the new system would "convert the Thirteen Confederate States into one consolidated government—and whether any country, as extensive as North-America, and where climates, dispositions, and interests are so essentially different, can be governed under one consolidated plan, except by the introduction of despotic principles."[33]

Dawson echoed the views of many opposed to the Constitution when he criticized the lack of a bill of rights: "That sacred palladium of liberty, the freedom of the press . . . has not been expressed."[34] He criticized the lack of protection against standing armies in peacetime and the failure to include trial by juries in civil cases. He urged his fellow delegates to require amendments prior to approving the Constitution.

With Dawson's speech concluded, James Madison rose to give the last Federalist speech of the day. He must have been thinking about the potential influence of Dawson's views on undecided delegates. Madison implored his colleagues not to consider a second federal convention to propose amendments. He noted that the "mutual deference and concession" that had marked the Philadelphia convention would be absent from a second convention: "It is a most awful thing that depends on our decision—no less than whether the thirteen States shall unite freely, peaceably, and unanimously, for the security of their common happiness and liberty, or whether every thing is to be put in confusion and disorder!"[35]

Madison recognized that a list of forty amendments had been circulating among Anti-Federalists at the convention. Twenty related mostly to a bill of rights, while another twenty provided largely for structural changes in the proposed government. "Will not every State," Madison asked, "think herself equally entitled to propose as many amendments?" If a second convention had to sort out hundreds of amendments, it would be unlikely to match the accomplishments of the Philadelphia convention. Madison warned those opposed to the Constitution that if they insisted on another convention, they might end up with something worse than the plan they opposed: "I would declare it [liberty and happiness of the people] more safe in its present form [the proposed Constitution], than it would be after introducing into it that long train of alterations which they call amendments."[36]

Then an extraordinary event took place. After Madison sat down, Henry argued, as he had many times during the convention, that amendments could be obtained prior to ratification. But this time, instead of a delegate responding to Henry, a force beyond the convention answered him. As Henry spoke, a powerful thunderstorm burst over the Quesnay Academy. Rain lashed the windows, and violent claps of thunder drowned out Henry's speech, forcing him to end it abruptly.[37]

Observers who wrote about the thunderstorm—and many remembered it even years later—believed that its occurrence had something to do with Henry's fiery oratory. Spencer Roane, Patrick Henry's son-in-law, wrote around 1817 that Henry, in describing the dangers of the proposed Constitution, "presented such an awful picture, and in such feeling colors, as to interest the feelings of the audience to the highest pitch—when lo! a storm at that moment arose, which shook the building in which the Convention was sitting, and broke it up in confusion. So remarkable a coincidence was never before witnessed, and it seemed as if he had indeed the faculty of calling up spirits from the vasty deep."[38] Perhaps sensing that some higher force had heard enough debate, after the storm subsided, the delegates agreed to vote on the Constitution the next day.

The convention had completed its clause-by-clause consideration of the Constitution, although many of the less controversial provisions of the plan had been either ignored or given limited consideration. George Wythe proposed that the committee of the whole write a ratification resolution and that a list of amendments be prepared that could be presented to the new Congress.[39]

The next day, the twenty-fifth, delegates heard some of the most eloquent speeches of the convention. Several members who had listened silently to the debate for three weeks spoke for or against ratification. In between their statements, Madison assured the delegates that if the convention ratified the Constitution without requiring previous amendments, he and his fellow supporters would remain at the convention and vote on amendments to be recommended. (Some Anti-Federalists had worried that the moment they lost the initial vote, Federalists would leave Richmond, and thus no quorum would exist for approving amendments.) Madison reminded the delegates that Article V of the Constitution provided an orderly method for approving amendments. The alternative of not approving the Constitution and insisting on prior amendments was "pregnant with such infinite dangers, that I cannot contemplate it without horror."[40]

Madison was followed by James Monroe, who argued again in favor of ratifying contingent upon the approval of amendments. He strongly believed that once Virginia joined the union and the Constitution went into effect, the new government would find a way to prevent the adoption of the additional amendments. He noted that changes protecting individual rights would not harm the proposed plan: "Do they change a feature of the Constitution? They secure our rights without altering a single feature."[41]

Then James Innes, the state attorney general and the sole delegate from Williamsburg, gave his only speech of the convention. For Innes, who was huge in size and needed special accommodations to sit at the convention or travel, standing to give a long speech must have been physically draining, yet he spoke for an hour or more. He argued that the people of Virginia sent the delegates to Richmond after they had the opportunity to review the Constitution. They would not have seen the proposed amendments, yet would have no choice but to abide by them: "If you propose previous amendments as the condition of your adoption, they may radically change the paper [the Constitution] on the table, and the people will be bound by what they know not. Subsequent amendments would not have that effect. They would not operate till the people had an opportunity of considering and altering them, if they thought proper." No one during the convention had framed the issue quite this way, and Innes urged his fellow delegates to approve the Constitution without requiring amendments.[42]

Not surprisingly, Patrick Henry had the last word.[43] He appealed one last time to delegates not to ratify the Constitution without requiring the approval of amendments. He urged the delegates to support amendments in a "manly, firm and resolute manner." But in comments that were unexpectedly conciliatory, Henry also said that if he turned out to be on the losing side, he would not oppose the new system: "If I shall be in the minority, I shall have those painful sensations, which arise from a conviction of being overpowered in a good cause. Yet I will be a peaceable citizen!—My head, my hand, and my heart shall be at liberty to retrieve the loss of liberty, and remove the defects of that system—in a constitutional way.—I wish not to go to violence, but will wait with hopes that the spirit which predominated in the revolution, is not yet gone, nor the cause of those who are attached to the revolution yet lost—I shall therefore patiently wait in expectation of seeing that Government changed so as to be compatible with the safety, liberty and happiness of the people."[44]

Henry apparently believed that the vote would be close and he might not prevail. His remarks sounded like the words of a seasoned politician preparing to fight another day. But Madison and his allies could not count on victory. Henry's emphasis on continuing his battle in a "constitutional way" meant to Madison that opponents would use "every peaceable effort to disgrace & destroy" the Constitution and would immediately ask state legislatures to petition Congress under Article V to call a second constitutional convention. As Madison told Hamilton just after the convention ended, "My conjecture is that exertions will be made to engage 2/3ds of the Legislature in the task of regularly undermining the government." He wrote to Washington the same day to warn that Henry's plan would be to organize a second convention through the petition process or to "get a Congress appointed in the first instance that will commit suicide on their own Authority."[45]

The crucial vote was at hand. The delegates and spectators who had witnessed this remarkable debate over the past few weeks knew how much was at stake. They were about to see history being made, not just of the commonwealth of Virginia, but of the nation. It would be a moment that few of them would likely forget.

The delegates would vote first on the question of whether ratification would be conditional. Approval of this motion would delay Virginia's admission into the new nation for at least several years. Henry and the Anti-Federalists were not proposing simply that Virginia accept the Constitution after the amendments approved at the ratifying convention were submitted to the other states. They demanded that Virginia remain out of the union until Congress—now operating under Article V of the Constitution—either proposed amendments to the states or organized a constitutional convention upon receiving petitions from two-thirds of the states that had already approved the Constitution. Even then, under the Henry proposal, Virginia would not join the union until either state legislatures or state conventions—under Article V, Congress was to choose the ratification method—approved the amendments and they became part of the Constitution.

It was early afternoon on Wednesday, June 25, 1788. The delegates had spent three weeks debating and arguing over the proposed plan of government. It had come to this moment of decision. If the first motion passed, no second vote would be taken. It had long been apparent that Virginia would not outright reject the Constitution. But if it approved the motion, Virginia would be on record as having ratified contingent upon the adoption of amendments. Supporters had argued throughout the convention that such a vote was the same as rejection of the Constitution.

As the roll call began, it became clear that the vote was going to be very close. During the convention, the delegates from the territory of Kentucky were thought by some to have the decisive votes for or against ratification. William Grayson had predicted a week before that Anti-Federalists "have got ten out of 13" of the Kentucky members.[46] Many hours had been spent discussing control of the Mississippi River and western expansion in an effort to appeal to those delegates and to assure them that the new system would be favorable to the territory when it became a state.[47] Anti-Federalists had worked for months—some even traveling to Kentucky—to convince those delegates that if the Constitution was approved, northern states would surrender to Spain control of the Mississippi, on which the western territories depended for navigation.[48] Some delegates believed that the river would be closed to American shipping for many years.[49] John Marshall, Madison, and others had argued on several occasions that approving the Constitution would greatly strengthen the new United States in its negotiations with Spain over access to the river.[50]

Finally, the first resolution was before the convention: "Resolved, That previous to the ratification of the new Constitution of Government recommended by the late Federal Convention, a declaration of rights asserting and securing from encroachment the great principles of civil and religious liberty, and the unalienable rights of the people, together with amendments to the most exceptionable parts of the said Constitution of Government, ought to be referred by this Convention to the other States in the American confederacy for their consideration."[51]

The clerk began the roll call alphabetically with the name of each of the eighty-four counties and the cities of Norfolk and Williamsburg. First up, Accomack County, on the Eastern Shore, whose two delegates split their votes. Then Albemarle, Jefferson's home county, which, as expected, gave two votes opposing the motion requiring amendments before ratification. Delegates from Amelia and solidly Anti-Federalist Amherst County next cast four votes for the resolution. Bourbon County, the first one of the Kentucky counties to be called, had one delegate missing, but the one present voted in favor, indicating trouble for supporters of the Constitution if the rest of the Kentucky delegation voted the same way. Then six more votes for Patrick Henry and the Anti-Federalists were cast by delegates from Brunswick, Buckingham, and Campbell counties.

Madison's sensitive stomach must have been churning as he heard the delegates announce their votes. Out of the first twenty-three cast, fourteen votes were in favor of the resolution. At this point, it looked as if the Anti-Federalists might have enough support to require amendments before ratification.

Delegates and spectators waited anxiously for the Kentucky counties to be called. Early in the roll call, supporters of the Constitution would have been comforted when the delegates from Fayette County split their votes and the two delegates from Jefferson County, named in 1780 for then-governor Thomas Jefferson, voted against the motion. But those were the last of the votes from Kentucky's seven counties for Madison's side.

After the lengthy roll call, the final vote was tallied. By a margin of 88 to 80, the delegates rejected the motion to ratify contingent upon amendments being approved by Congress or a new convention and being ratified by the states. At last, the Federalists had momentum in their favor. They knew that victory was theirs if no more than three delegates changed position during the actual vote on the Constitution.[52]

The resolution confirming ratification was before the body. It read in part: "Whereas any imperfections which may exist in the said Constitution ought rather to be examined in the mode prescribed therein for obtaining amendments, than by a delay with a hope of obtaining previous amendments, to bring the Union into danger; Resolved, That . . . the said Constitution be ratified."[53]

Around 2:30 P.M., the delegates began the roll call vote on the Constitution itself.[54] Everyone would have kept track of the tally as the delegates announced their votes. It may well have taken close to an hour for the votes to be gathered.[55] By a margin of 89 to 79, the delegates approved the ratification motion with amendments recommended but not required as a condition of the convention's assent. The Federalists had won. Madison must have felt great excitement, not to mention enormous relief. He no longer had to think about the dire consequences of an outright rejection or an approval contingent upon amendments.

The celebrating would have to wait, for there was still more to do. After the ratification vote, Federalists kept their word that they would remain at the convention so amendments could be considered. George Wythe, the respected law professor, was named as head of a committee that would prepare a list of amendments that would accompany the ratification resolution. Patrick Henry, James Madison, George Mason, and John Marshall were added to the twenty-person group.

Two days later, on June 27, the final day of the convention, the Wythe committee presented its report. Many of the amendments were based on those proposed by an informal committee chaired by George Mason that had met early in the convention to discuss changes they wanted to see in the Constitution. Mason had forwarded his group's list to Anti-Federalists in New York on June 9, hoping that opponents in Virginia and New York could work together. In addition to reporting the forty amendments, the committee—comprised of eleven Federalists and nine Anti-Federalists—proposed a detailed resolution to explain that the Virginia convention had ratified the Constitution after "having fully and freely investigated and discussed the proceedings of the Federal Convention, and being prepared as well as the most mature deliberation hath enabled us, to decide thereon." The resolution then included a statement that would later form the core of the First Amendment: "No right of [religious] denomination, can be cancelled, abridged, restrained or modified, by the Congress . . . acting in any capacity, [or] by the President . . . except in those instances in which power is given by the Constitution for those purposes: and that among the other essential rights, the liberty of conscience and of the press cannot be cancelled, abridged, restrained or modified by any authority of the United States."[56]

Twenty of the amendments focused mostly on personal rights, while another twenty dealt generally with the establishment and powers of the new government. Among the amendments relating to a "Declaration or Bill of Rights," as it was called in the resolution from the Wythe committee, were statements that there exist certain natural rights, among them the "enjoyment of life, and liberty, with the means of acquiring, possessing and protecting property; and pursuing and obtaining happiness and safety"; that all power derives from the people; that the legislature must give its assent before laws are suspended; that the right to a fair trial and to confront witnesses shall not be infringed; and that no one will lose liberty or property except by the law of the land. Other amendments protected against unreasonable searches and seizures, prohibited a tax or other kind of fee on voting, asserted the right of the people to keep and bear arms, and protected freedom of speech and the press.

The second set of amendments reserved to the states powers not granted to the new government; provided for a larger House of Representatives; prohibited Congress from interfering with the conduct of elections; prevented Congress from imposing direct taxes on the people unless the federal government failed to raise sufficient funds from duties on imports and only after requisitioning such funds from the states; provided that commercial treaties be ratified by two-thirds of the entire Senate and not just those present; prohibited a standing army during a time of peace except with the approval of two-thirds of both houses; and limited the jurisdiction of the federal courts.[57]

The Wythe committee also included a statement, which was approved by the convention, urging the members of the new House and Senate from Virginia to seek ratification of the forty amendments through the process established in Article V. The convention asked that until the amendments were adopted, Virginia's congressional delegation "conform to the spirit of these amendments as far as the said Constitution will admit."[58]

After meeting briefly on Thursday to allocate reimbursements to the officers of the convention, the delegates gathered on Friday, June 27, the final day, to approve the list of amendments offered by the Wythe committee. The delegates approved the report without their individual votes being recorded.[59]

Delegates demonstrated their continuing concern about the power of the new government to lay taxes by taking a separate vote on one of the amendments. The third structural amendment said that Congress would have to inform the governor of each state as to how much tax money that state's citizens owed based on the census. This notice would give the states an opportunity to pass an "effectual" law to raise the required funds, thereby eliminating the need for federal tax collectors to acquire the money directly. The motion to strike the amendment was defeated by a margin of 85 to 65; thus the proposed amendment remained in the list. Madison voted yes to eliminate the amendment, while Pendleton voted against the motion. The substantial number of votes against removing this amendment showed that even some of the Constitution's supporters were uneasy about the taxing power of the new government.[60]

Madison described many of the proposed amendments as "highly objectionable," with the direct taxation amendment "one of the most so." As he told Hamilton right after the convention ended, "It was impossible to prevent this error."[61] Of course, Madison also understood that since the amendments were only recommendations to Congress, their actual content was not crucial at this stage.

That evening, after the convention had adjourned, a group of Anti-Federalists met in the chamber of the Virginia Senate. George Mason, who organized the gathering, wanted opponents of the Constitution to prepare a statement—perhaps similar to the minority report that had been issued by Pennsylvania Anti-Federalists—to alert citizens to the dangers ahead now that the new plan had been approved. Some attending the meeting were reluctant to embark on such a course. Years later, an observer recounted that some of the Anti-Federalists there believed that the document would "irritate, rather than quiet the public mind."[62]

A decision was made to go find Patrick Henry and invite him to the gathering. When Henry arrived, he urged the group to abandon its effort to create trouble for the new government. He said "he had done his duty strenuously, in opposing the Constitution, in the *proper place*,—and with all the powers he possessed. The question had been fully discussed and settled, and, that as true and faithful republicans, they had all better go home! They should cherish it, and give it fair play—support it too, in order for the federal administration might be left to the untrammeled and free exercise of its functions."[63] After he spoke, the group dispersed without taking any formal action.

Henry was up to something. After the extraordinary effort he had undertaken before and during the convention to prevent ratification, it seemed out of character for him to urge his disappointed colleagues to accept the outcome and help establish the new government. Only a few weeks earlier Henry had told General John Lamb of New York that he would support the creation of a society dedicated to continuing opposition to the Constitution even after the Richmond convention. The idea of such a society had been discussed at a meeting in May in New York organized by Governor Clinton, an ardent Anti-Federalist. Henry urged the formation of such a group if opponents were unsuccessful in Richmond: "If they [supporters] shall carry their point, and preclude previous amendments, which we have ready to offer, it will become highly necessary to form the society you mention. Indeed, it appears the only chance to secure a remnant of those invaluable rights which are yielded [displaced] by the new plan." And Henry knew who should head such an effort in Virginia. As he told Lamb, "Colonel George Mason has agreed to act as chairman of our republican society. His character I need not describe. He is every way fit."[64]

With his sharp political instincts, Henry must have sensed that the public would be critical of him and other opponents if, after losing the fight against ratification in Richmond, they were to openly campaign to undermine the establishment of the new system. Virginia had just agreed to join the new nation. It would have been unseemly for some of its leading political figures to add to the already difficult challenges that the state faced as it prepared to participate in the new government. Rather than continue the fight that had been lost in the convention, Henry wanted to focus his attention on helping elect to state and federal office Anti-Federalists who could promote his goals.

Henry's sense of the political winds turned out to be correct. In the days that followed the convention, newspapers carried letters criticizing Mason for attending the evening meeting and for planning to disrupt the process of acceptance of the Constitution under the guise of wanting to communicate with his constituents about what had taken place at the convention. As one anonymous commentator observed, "What principles actuate *some* of the flaming opposers of the Federal System, may be discovered in the late conduct of the Hon. Mr. Mason . . . he introduced a fiery, irritating manifesto—which he would have sent out to divide the State, had it not been for the patriotism of a majority of the persons assembled—who seeing the serpent in the grass, exposed it, and prevented any thing of the sort taking place."[65]

For Madison, the Richmond convention had been a moment of triumph, but he was no doubt exhausted. George Washington, writing from Mount Vernon, must have sensed this, because he invited Madison to rest at his plantation. He said that relaxation was important to Madison's health, and he advised him to "take a little respite from business and to express a wish that part of the [Madison's] time might be spent under this Roof . . . Moderate exercise, and books occasionally, with the mind unbent, will be your best restoratives. With much truth I can assure you that no one will be happier in your company."[66] Madison accepted Washington's invitation. He made his way to Mount Vernon on July 4 and spent three days there before continuing to New York, the nation's temporary capital, to resume his work as a member of the Confederation Congress.

Madison recognized the important role that Washington had played at the ratifying convention, although he never appeared in Richmond. Washington's correspondence praising the Constitution and expressing strong opposition to conditional ratification would have been shown to various delegates. It also helped significantly, in the view of Patrick Henry's grandson, that everyone expected Washington to be the first president. That had "great influence in carrying the Constitution," said the younger Henry. William Grayson noted that "were it not for one great character [Washington] in America, so many men would not be for this government." Grayson expressed the concern about what would happen after Washington was gone: "We do not fear while he lives, but we can only expect his fame to be immortal. We wish to know who, besides him, can concentrate the confidence and affections of all America." James Monroe later wrote that "General Washington's influence carried this government."[67]

One of the most remarkable characteristics of the Virginia ratifying convention was the failure to discuss something that was probably on everyone's mind but that no one mentioned. If Virginia had declined to ratify or ratified contingent upon amendments being approved, it would not have joined the union, and George Washington could not have been the first president. None of the thousands of words spoken on the floor of the Quesnay Academy over the three weeks of the convention referred to Washington being ineligible for the presidency. Perhaps it would have been improper for a supporter of the Constitution to invoke Washington's name by proclaiming that if the proposed plan was defeated, the nation would be deprived of the services of Virginia's most famous citizen. It was more likely that supporters wanted to use Washington's letters to Madison and others to try to influence wavering delegates, and making the comment on the floor of the convention about Washington's ineligibility for the presidency would have given the appearance that Washington was trying to benefit from his efforts to influence delegates. Throughout his life, the proud and often stubborn general was adamant about never taking action that looked like it was meant for personal gain.

Interpreting the debate that had taken place inside the Quesnay Academy continued years after the convention had ended. William Wirt Henry wanted his grandfather's legacy to accurately reflect his many attributes. He fervently believed that the emphasis on Patrick Henry's eloquence at the convention sometimes obscured the sharp mind behind those hours of speeches delivered over the three weeks of the convention. "It is true," William Henry wrote, that "Mr. Madison argued with great logical powers, and that he was a prince among logicians. But it is not true that Mr. Henry was simply eloquent. He also displayed great logical powers." To William, the question of whether to secure amendments prior to or after ratification, on which Madison prevailed, was largely a matter of "policy, and was not carried by logic." With the approval of forty amendments by the convention, it could be said that "the arguments of Mr. Henry on this question were, in fact, the more logical, as was demonstrated by the event." John Marshall later said that while Henry was "a great orator, he was that and much more, a learned lawyer, a most accurate thinker, and a profound reasoner." And in an especially strong compliment, considering the source, Marshall said that of the "men I have known [who] had the greatest power to convince, I should perhaps say Mr. Madison, while Mr. Henry had without doubt the greatest power to persuade."[68]

Henry's remarkable work at the convention had inspired some who had witnessed the great orator, including Spencer Roane, his son-in-law, who wrote that the "Decision [ratifying the Constitution] has been distressing & awful to great Numbers of very respectable Members." He added, "Mr. Henry has given exemplary proofs of his Greatness, & in the opinion of many, of his Virtue. I have myself heard some Touches of Eloquence from him wch. wd. almost disgrace Cicero or Demosthenes."[69]

Newspapers around the country and in Virginia praised the delegates for their work. The *Winchester Virginia Gazette* observed that "so much eloquence, it is thought, has never been displayed in any one assembly in America, and will do great honor to the federal cause, whatever may be the event." The *Virginia Independent Chronicle* said, "The calm, cool, and deliberate manner in which this important subject has been investigated, will be a lasting monument of national gratitude to those venerable statesmen, who have so eminently distinguished themselves in forming this new plan of government."[70]

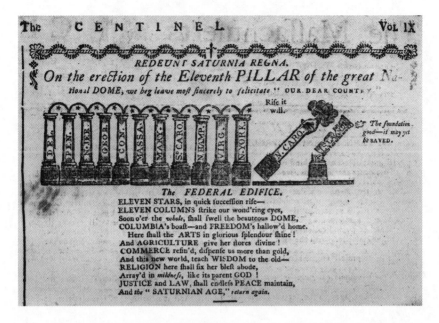

The C E N T I N E L. Vol. IX

REDEUNT SATURNIA REGNA.

On the erection of the Eleventh PILLAR of the great National DOME, we beg leave most sincerely to felicitate " OUR. DEAR COUNTRY."

Rise it will.

The foundation good—it may yet be SAVED.

The FEDERAL EDIFICE.

ELEVEN STARS, in quick succession rise—
ELEVEN COLUMNS strike our wond'ring eyes,
Soon o'er the whole, shall swell the beauteous DOME,
COLUMBIA's boast—and FREEDOM's hallow'd home.
Here shall the ARTS in glorious splendour shine !
And AGRICULTURE give her stores divine !
COMMERCE refin'd, dispense us more than gold,
And this new world, teach WISDOM to the old—
RELIGION here shall fix her blest abode,
Array'd in mildness, like its parent GOD !
JUSTICE and LAW, shall endless PEACE maintain,
And the " SATURNIAN AGE," return again.

Massachusetts Centinel, "The Federal Edifice," August 2, 1788. (*Library of Congress*)

With New Hampshire's approval of the Constitution on June 21, the new Constitution went into effect. Virginia's ratification on June 25, and New York's on July 26, by a vote of 30 to 27, meant that two of the most important states would be part of the union. It had been a struggle, but the new republic, at least for the moment, was on a sound footing.

With key figures in Virginia still opposed to the Constitution and likely embittered by their experience in Richmond, there was the potential for problems in launching the new government. The next crucial phase would be the Virginia General Assembly's fall session, when it would meet to enact laws for the election of members of the new U.S. House of Representatives and to choose two U.S. senators. Patrick Henry's conciliatory comments at the convention in the final days and his address to the Anti-Federalists at the meeting organized by George Mason should not have misled anyone about Henry's plans. He wanted the new Constitution to be implemented on his terms. By preventing his adversary, James Madison, from taking a seat in the new Congress, Henry could not only avenge his defeat at the ratifying convention, he would keep Madison from introducing amendments that would fall far short of the radical changes that Henry so passionately wanted. From the opening gavel of the Virginia legislature, it was clear that Henry was firmly in control.

~ 6 ~

The Anti-Federalists Fight Back

IN THE FINAL DAYS of the ratifying convention, Patrick Henry told his fellow delegates and the hundreds of spectators packed into the galleries that he would accept defeat gracefully. He pledged to be a "quiet citizen" who, having fought the good fight against what he was convinced would be a dangerous federal government, was now ready to accept the new system.[1] He expressed the same sentiment to Anti-Federalists attending the meeting organized by George Mason on June 27 at the state capitol building and in letters to friends and supporters.[2]

Despite his conciliatory tone, Henry never intended to support the new government. From the moment the ratifying convention approved the Constitution without requiring amendments, Henry was ready to carry out a scheme to undermine the new system.[3] His motivation was political and personal. He still believed that sweeping amendments must be added to protect the liberty of the people and return power to the states. And he was determined to reclaim his honor by punishing his longtime nemesis, James Madison.

While Henry was unsuccessful at the convention, he was far from helpless. He controlled the Virginia General Assembly, and he knew that when it convened in the fall of 1788, he could use the prestige and political influence of Virginia to help organize a second constitutional convention, as Article V of the Constitution, now in effect, provided. Henry could also work to keep Madison out of the First Congress.

Patrick Henry genuinely believed that Madison either opposed the immediate addition of a bill of rights or at least was sufficiently luke-warm that he would not energetically support such an effort. In Henry's view, if Madison offered a bill of rights to mollify the people, the pro-posed amendments would be more than useless. Such recommenda-tions, Henry argued, not only would fail to provide the safeguards that citizens needed and deserved, they also would take the place of more radical amendments that would alter the relative power of the federal government and the states. According to Henry, amendments guaran-teeing a larger role for the states and a list of personal freedoms, as of-fered by the Wythe committee and approved by the Virginia ratifying convention on its last day, were needed to ensure the sovereignty of the states and to protect the rights of the people.[4]

After the ratifying convention adjourned on June 27, word spread quickly around the nation that Virginia had approved the Constitution. The news had been anticipated anxiously by both supporters and oppo-nents of the Constitution. Its potential impact on the New York ratifying convention, which was meeting in Poughkeepsie, was considered to be so important that Alexander Hamilton had arranged for an express rider to rush the news from Richmond to New York.[5] At the New York convention, Anti-Federalists had a substantial majority, but the news of Virginia's rati-fication tipped the balance in favor of the Constitution by a slim margin.[6]

Virginia's approval also signaled the end of the effort by opponents to prevent the adoption of the Constitution. Their best hope now was to secure the election of federal officeholders who would advance the ideas that Anti-Federalists had advocated during the ratification debate and, if possible, obtain amendments to the Constitution. Newspapers and letters spread not only the news of Virginia's approval but also the list of forty amendments the convention had endorsed. Within three weeks, Americans throughout the nation knew the results of the convention, and they had a chance to consider Virginia's proposed amendments along with those of other states.[7] Much of the newspaper commentary decried the absence of a bill of rights in the Constitution, while several newspa-pers praised Madison's efforts at the convention.[8] The *Pennsylvania Mer-cury*, for example, wrote that Henry's "declamatory powers" were "vastly overpowered by the deep reasoning of our glorious little Madison."[9]

On October 20, 1788, the General Assembly convened in Richmond. It would be a session of immense importance. During the next few months, the Virginia House of Delegates—in which Anti-Federalists had at least a fifteen-seat majority—and the Senate would formally petition Congress for a second constitutional convention, elect the state's first U.S. senators, establish a process for choosing electors for the upcoming presidential election, and create ten congressional districts from which members of the new U.S. House would be chosen. All of these actions were under the direct control of Patrick Henry, a member of the House of Delegates. His influence over the legislature was so evident that George Washington observed that "He has only to say let this be Law—and it is Law."[10]

Supporters of the Constitution were hopelessly outmatched, not only in terms of numbers but also because of a lack of political experience. Fifty delegates who had been at the ratifying convention were members of the General Assembly; a majority of them were Anti-Federalists. While Henry, William Grayson, and James Monroe—who had all participated energetically in the debate at the Quesnay Academy—were members of the General Assembly, James Madison, George Nicholas, John Marshall, and Edmund Pendleton were not. Among Federalists, only the youthful Francis Corbin, who had spoken several times in support of the Constitution at the ratifying convention, was now a member of the General Assembly.

Corbin showed his lack of political skills by trying to make a humorous point at Henry's expense during the debate in the House of Delegates. Instead, he insulted Henry, causing resentment among Henry's supporters and embarrassment among the Federalists. The twenty-nine-year-old Corbin was born to wealthy parents who had remained loyal to England. He spent the war years studying at Cambridge University and other British academies and returned to Virginia only after the war had ended. At one point on the floor of the House, Henry, in arguing that Virginians did not trust the new Constitution, said he was ready to "bow, with the utmost deference, to the majesty of the people." In response, Corbin forcefully denied that the people were dissatisfied with the Constitution and desired immediate amendments. For a relatively young and inexperienced political figure to directly challenge Henry this way was controversial enough; Corbin made it worse.

Mocking Henry's words that he would bow to the majesty of the people, Corbin then executed—in the words of Henry's grandson—a "most graceful bow" in Henry's direction. Not knowing when to stop, Corbin continued to argue that Henry had "set himself in opposition to the people throughout the whole course of this transaction," and that the ratification at the convention showed the people "wished the adoption of the constitution as the only means of saving the credit and honour of the country." After Corbin said that Henry had placed himself at the head of those opposed to the Constitution, he returned to Henry's phrase of "bowing to the people," then undertook "another profound and graceful bow." Oblivious to the negative impression he was making on members of the House, Corbin continued challenging Henry, derisively repeating his words, then bowing again.

Henry's friends and supporters were shocked and considered "such an attack on a man of his years and high character as very little short of sacrilege." All eyes were probably on Henry as he rose slowly and pointed out that he (Henry) had been raised among "planters and other plain men of similar education" and had not been given the advantage of a privileged education such as young Corbin had enjoyed. Henry suggested that while Corbin was learning to bow in exclusive British schools, he himself was "engaged in the arduous toils of the revolution." Henry continued for some time, with a mocking deference to Corbin, and then finally ended not with the graceful bow of which he was capable but with a bow that was "ludicrously awkward and clownish, as took the house by surprise and put them in a roar of laughter." Henry had spoken for fifteen or twenty minutes, while Corbin "hung his head" and "sank at least a foot in his seat."[11] Corbin's misjudgment certainly did not encourage Anti-Federalists to be conciliatory toward their outnumbered opponents.

Corbin had crossed swords with a man of immense ability and complex character traits. Henry believed genuinely that the Constitution would create a government with the potential to be oppressive, but he was so committed to the causes he championed throughout his life that he belittled the views of those with whom he disagreed, often refusing to compromise—for fear of showing any sign of weakness—or to recognize that his proposals might not be in the best interests of the nation.

It is difficult to know what made Henry so thoroughly committed to defeating the Constitution. He did not keep a journal, saved few letters, and did not hold on to drafts of his numerous speeches, whose content had to be reconstructed, often years later, from the memory of those who had heard him. Henry seemed unconcerned about how history would treat him. He would have been better known had he accepted some of the positions that he was offered during his career, including delegate to the Constitutional Convention in Philadelphia, U.S. senator, secretary of state in the Washington administration, and chief justice of the United States, all of which he declined.[12]

Some insight into his character is provided by his great-grandson Edward Fontaine. Born fifteen years after Henry's death, Fontaine kept a journal for four decades—beginning when he was seventeen—in which he collected anecdotes about Henry from three of Henry's daughters, his oldest grandson (Edward's father), and his friends and acquaintances. Fontaine wanted to correct many of the inaccuracies found in the first biography of Henry, published by William Wirt in 1817. Fontaine would be disappointed that his journal was not used in future editions of Wirt's book; a later biographer of Patrick Henry did use some of Fontaine's recollections in his work.[13]

Fontaine's short work, completed in 1872, reveals that Henry wrote poetry, spent an hour each day in prayer and meditation, and, although he had been a tobacco planter, so disliked tobacco smoke that servants and visitors were careful not to indulge in that habit before going to see him for fear he would notice the scent left over from a tobacco pipe. Fontaine wrote that Henry's nervous system, which deteriorated over the years, made the smell of smoke "very disagreeable to him." He could tell instantly if someone was smoking somewhere in the house.[14]

Henry was six feet in height, weighed about 160 pounds, and had dark and curling hair. His features were "classical, more Grecian than Roman, & his countenance commanding, but capable of every variety of expression." To Henry's family and friends, his most remarkable feature was his eyes, which were "deeply set, & well shaded—the color hazel & blue, but bright or dark, benign or piercing at will, & reflecting instantly every emotion . . . of [his] . . . soul."[15]

Henry rarely consumed alcohol and was so alarmed over how much drinking he saw in the years after the war that he encouraged the consumption of "small beer," an inexpensive drink with low alcohol content. During his final terms as governor—he served five one-year terms as chief executive—he made sure that samples of the beer were available in his office.[16]

Henry believed strongly in religious freedom. Born to parents of modest means who were members of the Protestant Episcopal Church of which his uncle was a minister, Henry once defended for no fee two Baptist ministers who were imprisoned for preaching. This commitment inspired Fontaine to describe Henry as a "protector of the oppressed, & an invincible champion of Freedom, that made him the most honored & dearly loved man that ever lived."[17]

In the mornings, Henry would exercise his voice and strengthen his lungs by calling to servants who were a half mile away. Fontaine was told that the tones of his voice were "melodious as the notes of an Alpine horn."[18]

According to his great-grandson, Henry's health was damaged by his work regimen. "Confinement to his books, intense thought, & the want of active physical exercise while he was impregnating his mind for the delivery of his wonderful speeches, shattered his nervous system," wrote Fontaine. Yet despite his infirmities, when Henry was giving a public address, the "venerable man seemed to forget his age."[19]

Henry had little formal education. His schooling was over at the age of fifteen, but even before then, he did not seem very interested in his studies. When he was in his early teens, his father took a greater role in Patrick's education. A few years later, though, Patrick was done with the domestic schooling provided by his father and was working at a country store. His lack of promising prospects at that point did not discourage him, for at the age of eighteen he married his first wife, Sarah Shelton. Sarah's father gave Patrick three hundred acres and the chance to farm tobacco, which he did not do very well.[20] After her death in 1775, Henry married Dorothea Dandridge, twenty-one years his junior.[21]

He was apparently a loving father—he had seventeen children over a period of forty-three years, six in his first marriage and eleven in his second, and seventy grandchildren—but like most aspects of his personal life, his affection for his children was kept from public view. Fontaine said that Henry "wrote poetry beautifully" and often composed sonnets adapted to Scotch songs for his daughters to sing and play. But as soon as his children finished singing, Henry would destroy the paper on which he had created the poems out of fear that "such compositions if published would injure his reputation as a Statesman, & lessen his influence with the people of Virginia."[22]

Henry had limited military duties during the war. He served briefly as a colonel of a Virginia military regiment and commander-in-chief of the Virginia militia. Even then, he was more interested in politics, having won election to the Virginia convention that would write the state's first constitution in 1776. Soon afterward, the convention elected Henry as Virginia's first governor.[23]

This complex and driven man was a formidable opponent for Federalists in the General Assembly. They could do little to stop the legislature from taking actions that they considered detrimental to the interests of the people, including formally petitioning Congress to hold a second convention. The Anti-Federalists were joined in this effort by Governor Randolph, who had long advocated such a convention, and who was delighted when New York's Circular Letter arrived in July requesting Congress to organize a convention "at a Period not far remote," which the governor turned over to the House of Delegates on October 20.[24]

Randolph's support for a second convention was genuine, but he never thought through the potential problems such a gathering could create and the consequences of adding what might be dozens of amendments to the Constitution.

As the fall session was getting started, Henry announced that he would "oppose every measure" for implementing the new Constitution until the legislature called for a federal convention. He argued that "the most precious rights of the people if not cancelled are rendered insecure" by the Constitution. Charles Lee, brother of Henry Lee, wrote to Washington to criticize Henry's efforts to prevent a smooth transition to the new government until amendments were requested: "The language of this [Henry's] resolution contains a direct and indecent censure on all those who have befriended the new constitution holding them forth as the betrayers of the dearest rights of the people." Washington recognized the dangers ahead when he wrote to Benjamin Lincoln that there was "no room for the advocates of the Constitution to relax in their exertions; for if they should be lulled into security, appointments of Antifederal men may probably take place."[25]

With Henry and the other Anti-Federalists dominating the legislature, there was little doubt that it would endorse New York's efforts. At the same time, it was surprising that some supporters of the Constitution did not see the potential harm of such a convention. George Lee Turberville, who represented Richmond County in the House of Delegates from 1785 to 1789, told Madison that a convention was "talked of even by the staunchest friends to the new Constitution, to close With N York & propose another convention to amend." Four days later, Turberville wrote again to tell Madison that there was "Much talk of closing with New York in her proposal for a new convention. Prima facie—I see no impropriety in it."[26]

If Turberville had been at the Constitutional Convention in Philadelphia and witnessed the debate that led to Article V, he would not have been so nonchalant about the possibility of a second convention. Instead, like Madison, who had witnessed and participated in the debate, Turberville would have warned of the dangers of such a gathering and instead recommended that Congress propose amendments.

The amending provision of the Constitution—which was critical in securing ratification because no bill of rights could have been proposed by Congress without it—received relatively little attention from the delegates. Some at the Constitutional Convention even suggested that no amendment mechanism was needed. After all, of the original thirteen states, the constitutions of five of them contained no such provision.[27] Perhaps because these state constitutions were written during a time of revolutionary fervor, their framers may have believed that replacing a constitution rather than amending it provided the best way to institute a new government when—to paraphrase the Declaration of Independence—it became destructive of the people's rights.[28]

The first time the issue of amending the Constitution was raised was four days after the Philadelphia convention began, when Governor Randolph presented the Virginia Plan. Resolution XIII of the plan suggested that "provision ought to be made for the amendment of the Articles of Union whensoever it shall seem necessary, and that the assent of the National Legislature ought not to be required thereto."[29] The convention did not discuss the amending process again until early June, when Elbridge Gerry said he favored a process for amending the Constitution, arguing that the "novelty & difficulty of the experiment requires periodical revision."[30]

A week later, Article V began to take shape. According to Madison's notes, "several members did not see the necessity of the Resolution [XIII of the Virginia Plan] at all, nor the propriety of making the consent of the Natl Legisl. unnecessary." George Mason strenuously objected to any suggestion that an amending provision should be left out of the Constitution, insisting that the "plan now to be formed will certainly be defective, as the Confederation has been found on trial to be. Amendments therefore will be necessary, and it will be better to provide for them, in an easy, regular and Constitutional way than to trust to chance and violence." Mason worried about giving Congress the sole power to propose amendments: "It would be improper to require the consent of the Natl. Legislature, because they may abuse their power, and refuse their consent [to amendments] on that very account."[31] The delegates agreed that the Constitution would include an article on amendments, but they postponed a decision on what the role of Congress would be.

What became the amending section of Article V was written mostly by the Committee of Detail, which was given the responsibility of drafting the actual language of the Constitution to reflect the votes and debates of the convention. Because so many of the resolutions agreed to by the delegates in the first months of the convention were general in nature, the committee had substantial discretion when transforming those resolutions into specific language. The committee included for the first time a provision requiring Congress to call a convention to "revise or alter" the Constitution upon the submission of petitions from two-thirds of the states. Perhaps in reaction to Mason's statement about an oppressive Congress obstructing constitutional reform, the committee did not give Congress the authority to propose amendments or call a convention on its own. When the convention—voting by state—unanimously adopted the committee's language, Gouverneur Morris objected to excluding Congress. He did not want Congress to have to wait for the states to request such a gathering, arguing that the "Legislature should be left at liberty to call a Convention, whenever they please."[32]

Only a week before the Constitution was signed, the delegates again debated Article V. The convention accepted Gerry's recommendation that the amending provision be reconsidered because of the possibility that a majority of states could "bind the Union to innovations that may subvert the State Constitutions altogether."[33] Alexander Hamilton, who had been away for much of the summer and who, at times, seemed disinterested in the proceedings when he was there, made an important and likely influential argument that Congress should be more involved in the amending process.[34] He persuaded his colleagues that it would be dangerous to leave it solely in the hands of state legislatures and argued that Congress should be able not only to propose amendments but to call a convention as well. He told them that "the State Legislatures will not apply for alterations but with a view to increase their own powers. The National Legislature will be the first to perceive and will be the most sensible to the necessity of amendments, and ought also to be empowered, whenever two-thirds of each branch should concur to call a Convention."[35]

The delegates agreed to reconsider the previously approved version of Article V, and they debated the role of Congress and state legislatures in proposing and ratifying amendments. One of the crucial decisions they made was to narrowly reject the requirement that two-thirds of states ratify proposed amendments, choosing instead the stricter requirement of three-fourths.[36]

Madison, who was busy taking notes and had said little during this discussion, felt compelled to ask several important questions that the delegates either were too tired to answer or assumed future generations would work out. He wanted to know: "How was a Convention to be formed? by what rule decide? what the force of its acts?"[37] Madison was troubled by the lack of guidance provided by the Constitution on how a second convention would be organized and conduct its business.

After the delegates added several additional sections—guaranteeing states their representation in the Senate and protecting the importation of slaves until 1808—Article V was approved. The amending section of the Constitution was finally in place, but not everyone was pleased with it. George Mason objected to the exclusion of the people from any role in directly proposing or ratifying amendments. Two days before the convention adjourned, Mason said that "no amendments of the proper kind would ever be obtained by the people, if the Government should become oppressive."[38]

At that time, Madison could not have anticipated that in the next year his home state and New York would formally petition Congress to hold a convention. When Article V was being debated in Philadelphia, Madison was less attuned to the potential problems of such an assembly. After Morris and Gerry moved to add a provision to Article V to require a convention on the application of two-thirds of the states, Madison suggested that such a provision was not necessary: He "did not see why Congress would not be as much bound to propose amendments applied for by two thirds of the States as to call a Convention on the like application." But then he agreed that an alternative to Congress proposing amendments would be acceptable, telling his colleagues that "he saw no objection however against providing for a Convention for the purpose of amendments, except only that difficulties might arise as to the form, the quorum &c. which in Constitutional regulations ought to be as much as possible avoided."[39]

Now, Madison was greatly disturbed by reports from Richmond that the General Assembly at its fall 1788 session had formally petitioned Congress for a convention and called upon other states to join its efforts. He must have been especially dismayed that friends of the Constitution did not have a better idea of the potential consequences of a convention.

In a detailed letter responding to Turberville's inquiry, Madison set out his concerns. He acknowledged that the Constitution was "not a faultless work," and he told Turberville he wished amendments had been included before the Constitution was completed in Philadelphia. Some changes, Madison noted, could be added with little controversy, but those that had "both advocates and opponents" should "receive the light of actual experiment, before it would be prudent to admit them into the Constitution."[40]

Madison gave four reasons why a convention should not be called: First, delegates at such a convention would disagree about the merits of the proposals and the proper method for obtaining them; thus there would be "unquestionably a number of States who will be so averse and apprehensive as to the mode, that they will reject the merits rather than agree to the mode." Second, although Article V required Congress to call a convention upon receiving petitions from two-thirds of the states, all states would probably have to participate in such a convention for it to be successful. In Congress, on the other hand, the process for enacting amendments was much simpler and less cumbersome: A single legislator could introduce amendments, and members of Congress, unlike delegates to a convention, could act without instructions from their state legislatures. Third, a convention would not be as restrained as Congress because the legislature is chosen to "administer and support as well as to amend the system." Therefore, "If a General Convention were to take place for the avowed and sole purpose of revising the Constitution, it would naturally consider itself as having a greater latitude than the Congress . . . [I]t would consequently give greater agitation to the public mind; an election into it would be courted by the most violent partisans on both sides . . . [and] would no doubt contain individuals of insidious views who under the mask of seeking alterations popular in some parts . . . might have a dangerous opportunity of sapping the very foundations of the fabric." Madison knew from experience how difficult it was to reach consensus at a constitutional convention: "Having witnessed the difficulties and dangers experienced by the first Convention which assembled under every propitious circumstance, I should tremble for the result of a Second, meeting in the present temper in America."[41]

Finally, Madison worried that Europe would consider a second convention to be a "dark and threatening Cloud hanging over the Constitution just established, and perhaps over the Union itself." He believed that foreign nations would be reluctant to develop relations with the United States during this period of uncertainty. He cited a loan from Holland that was granted only because that country expected the Constitution to be "speedily, quietly, and finally established."[42]

Madison also knew that the calling of a convention would require substantially more time than that required for Congress to approve amendments. Two-thirds of states would have to submit petitions to Congress. Congress would then have to schedule a convention. Delegates to such a convention would have to be selected by either state legislatures or voters. They would have to convene, agree on potentially dozens of amendments, and then, as required by Article V, submit those amendments to state legislatures or state conventions for ratification. In some states, where legislatures met infrequently, governors would have to call a special session to prevent a long delay in considering proposed amendments. If Congress chose state conventions, ratification would be delayed while elections were held to choose the delegates to such a convention. Months would pass while the elections were conducted and the conventions organized. This entire process could take several years, during which time there would be great uncertainty about the future of the Constitution and the nation.

Despite the complexity of such a multistage process, Anti-Federalists in the Virginia General Assembly argued that it would take longer for Congress to propose amendments, or that Congress would propose amendments that were not radical enough, something they considered worse than mere delay. Included in the resolution approved by the legislature was this statement: "The anxiety with which our Countrymen press for the accomplishment of this important end [securing amendments], will ill admit of delay. The slow forms of Congressional discussion and recommendation, if indeed they should ever agree to any change, would we fear be less certain of success. Happily for their wishes, the Constitution hath presented an alternative, by admitting the submission to a Convention of the States. To this therefore we resort, as the source from whence they are to derive relief from their present apprehensions."[43] Anti-Federalists clearly believed that a convention, to which state legislatures would likely send carefully instructed delegates, would propose amendments to limit the power of the new federal government that Congress would not offer.

As the House met as a committee of the whole, Henry introduced a resolution to appoint a committee to draft a request to Congress for a convention, to answer the New York Circular Letter, and to ask other states to join the effort to organize a convention. Federalists on October 30 offered a substitute motion: No convention would be called, but Congress would be encouraged to propose amendments to "conform to the true spirit" of the Virginia Declaration of Rights and other amendments approved by the Virginia ratifying convention.[44] The Federalists' motion was defeated 85 to 39. Supporters of the Constitution also did not want the Virginia legislature to send a letter to other states asking them to petition Congress for a convention, so they offered a substitute letter that would call on states to pressure Congress to propose amendments. This motion was defeated 72 to 50, demonstrating the solid control of the House of Delegates by the Anti-Federalists. The Henry resolution was then approved by a voice vote.[45] As George Lee Turberville described their efforts, "the Cloven hoof begins to appear . . . [I]ntrigue antifederalism and artifice go hand in hand."[46]

Supporters of the Constitution tried again when the report of the committee of the whole was presented to the full house. They argued that the ratifying convention preferred amendments offered by Congress, and that the "Assembly ought not to divert the course of their pursuit."[47] The House rejected the pleas of the Federalists and adopted the committee's resolution and letters to the other states.[48] After the Senate made minor changes to which the House agreed, the resolution was completed and sent to the governor so he could forward it "to the new Congress, as soon as they shall assemble," and the letters to the other states sent "without delay."[49]

Henry had very little opposition to his efforts in the House. Richard Bland Lee, a supporter of the Constitution, told Madison at the end of October that Federalists in the legislature "being all young & inexperienced—form but a feeble band against him." Lee had hoped to modify Henry's motion, "so as to divest it of its inflammatory dress—or to postpone its operation to such a distant period as to give the people of America a fair experiment of the government." But the supporters failed, as George Lee Turberville told Madison: "The triumph of Antifederalism is compleat."[50]

On the last day of the Virginia ratifying convention, the delegates had approved a motion asking "their representatives in Congress to exert all influence and use all reasonable and legal methods" to obtain ratification of the forty amendments "in the manner provided by the fifth article of the said Constitution."[51] The General Assembly, on November 20, 1788, approved a resolution to be "presented to Congress . . . requesting that Honorable Body, to call a Convention of deputies from the several States" to consider the amendments they recommended and to "report such amendments, as they shall find best calculated to answer the purpose."[52] This was approved after the Constitution's ratification in June 1788 by the ninth state. Once the Constitution went into effect, Congress could not call a convention on its own but would have to wait until states submitted petitions.

Madison was appalled that the legislature of his state had formally requested a second constitutional convention. He probably did not expect that enough other states would follow Virginia's and New York's lead to force a new convention right away, but he thought it highly irresponsible for legislators to take any chance that the Constitution would be altered by potentially dozens of amendments offered through such a gathering. As he explained to Henry Lee: "The measures pursued at Richmond are as impolitic as they are otherwise exceptionable—if alterations of a reasonable sort are really in view, they are much more attainable from Congress than from attempts to bring about another Convention. It is already decided that the latter mode is a hopeless pursuit."[53]

Having formally requested a second convention, the General Assembly turned to other business. Under Henry's direction, it approved a "Disabling Act," a laudable measure undertaken for questionable reasons. The law prohibited federal officeholders—persons "who shall hold any legislative, executive, or judicial office, or other lucrative office whatsoever, under the authority of the United States"—from holding any state office. Federalists believed that their opponents pushed through this legislation in order to increase the number of officeholders and thus add to the cost of government, believing this would enrage taxpayers who were already worried about the cost of the new system.[54] Perhaps not surprisingly, some Federalists voted for it when it was approved 71 to 52. Edward Carrington, who opposed the bill, probably echoed the views of many Federalists when he said that the "design [of the Disabling Act] is doubtless to create discontents against the Federal Govt. from the numbers of additional Officers which must be employed amongst the People, indeed to embarrass the U.S." Carrington recognized that in the short run, the law might generate some opposition. But over time, he thought, if the states had to develop competent public officials and not rely on those who also serve the federal government, "It will ultimately ... greatly abridge [enhance] the importance of the State, for the U.S., being disbarred from conferring their powers upon State Officers, will induce the most able of these [officials] into their service."[55]

The next step in creating a functioning republic was the election of competent and conscientious individuals to public office. The makeup of the First Congress would be especially important. Its members would create the new republic's executive departments, enact criminal laws, and establish a federal judicial system. Just as significant, almost everything the First Congress did would set a precedent. The *Virginia Centinel*, published in Winchester, discussed this shortly after the ratifying convention adjourned: "The election of a President, and Delegates from each state to form the first Congress, are matters of the utmost importance to every free citizen. On the choice of these persons depends our future well-being and prosperity.—Men of approved talents and strict integrity should be sought for to fill those important stations—men who would sacrifice every thing at the shrine of liberty."[56]

Many of the Constitution's supporters felt it would be vital to have Madison as a member of the First Congress, and some wanted him to be in the more prestigious Senate. There would be only twenty-two members initially—Rhode Island and North Carolina had not yet ratified the Constitution—and with six-year terms, Madison would be freed from the obligation of frequent campaigning, something he disliked, and could concentrate on the long-term interests of the nation. In the smaller chamber, Madison was likely to have more influence.

Madison himself had serious reservations about serving in the Senate. He expected that senators, as members of the more "aristocratic" branch, would have to maintain a lifestyle that was beyond his means.[57] Montpelier, his plantation in Orange County from which he had been frequently absent for several years, had not made him a rich man. Senators, he expected, would expend substantial sums entertaining important guests such as fellow members of Congress, officials in the executive branch, and foreign visitors.

His hesitation to serve in the Senate was more than financial. Madison found appealing the idea of serving in the House, where he would be elected by and directly represent the people. He did not see as contradictory his wanting to serve in the House while still hating to campaign and ask for votes. He likely found more appealing the prospect of being accountable to his fellow citizens from a seat in the House than being beholden to the state legislature, which selected senators. As early as August, his friend and fellow delegate to the ratifying convention from Orange County, James Gordon, asked Madison in which body he would like to serve. His supporters needed to know Madison's preference as soon as possible so they could plan their effort to persuade the General Assembly to follow their recommendation.[58] By the middle of October, Madison was telling friends, including Governor Randolph, that he favored election to the House because "if I can render any service there, it can only be to the public, and not even in imputation, to myself."[59]

But Madison also speculated that if he sought election to the House, he would be spared the distasteful process of having to actively campaign, perhaps believing his friends would arrange for him to run in a district heavily populated by Federalists: "[My preference for the House] is somewhat founded on the supposition that the arrangements for the popular elections may secure me agst. any competition which wd. require on my part any step that wd. speak a solicitude which I do not feel, or have the appearance of a spirit of electioneering which I despise."[60] Within a few months, Madison would learn just how wrong he was.

George Washington was alarmed at the prospect of two Anti-Federalists representing Virginia as the first U.S. senators, and he wanted Madison to seek that office. Washington told Madison's friend and fellow member of the Confederation Congress Edward Carrington that only Madison had the stature to have a chance of being chosen by the General Assembly for the Senate, and that considering the importance of that body under the Constitution, Madison's services would be of "more importance than in the other House."[61]

Edward Carrington was a member of the Virginia House of Delegates who strongly supported the Constitution and corresponded frequently with Madison. *(Library of Congress)*

Carrington told Madison a few days later that Anti-Federalists were planning to elect two of their own to the Senate, and that Patrick Henry would be one of them if he agreed to serve, although Carrington knew that Henry was hesitant to accept such a position. Only Madison, in Carrington's view, had a chance of being elected: "I am convinced that it will be in vain to try any Federalist but yourself, & am decidedly of opinion that you ought to be put in nomination."[62]

As the General Assembly continued its work, Governor Randolph heard reports that Henry and his Anti-Federalist colleagues were planning something that could create a lot of problems for the fledgling government. The governor reported to Madison that Henry would decline the offer to serve in the Senate because, in Randolph's words, he was "unwilling to submit to the oath." But Randolph had also been told "that he appears to be involved in gloomy mystery." The governor was not sure what Henry was up to, but he worried that "Something is surely meditated against the new constitution, more animated, forcible and violent, than a simple application for calling a convention."[63]

Randolph could have been referring to any number of actions planned by the Anti-Federalists, including the creation of districts to elect members of the new U.S. House. Madison was even more pointed in his criticism of Henry when he responded to Randolph's letter. He said the opponents were "permanently hostile, and likely to produce every effort that might endanger or embarrass it [the new government]." He believed the "secret wish of his [Henry's] heart was destruction of the whole System."[64]

Although Madison had told his supporters that he preferred election to the House, efforts continued in Richmond to put his name in nomination for the Senate. As late as October 29, a week before the General Assembly elected senators, Richard Bland Lee was still hopeful that the legislature would set aside partisanship and choose the best people to serve Virginia in the new Senate. He said that both supporters and opponents of the Constitution were "sufficiently sensible of the propriety of preferring gentlemen of the first merit and integrity to offices of such importance, without regard to their theoretic opinions on Government." But Madison knew better. By November 2, with the vote for senators a few days away, he told Governor Randolph that "whatever my inclinations or those of my friends may be, they are likely to be of little avail . . . I take it for certain that a clear majority of the Assembly are enemies to the Govt. and I have no reason to suppose that I can be less obnoxious than others on the opposite side."[65]

Despite the bleak prospects, Randolph informed Madison that "your friends have resolved to nominate you; being well assured, that their labours will not be in vain." With members of the House of Delegates and the Senate each casting two votes, there would be a maximum of 388 votes.[66] Randolph expected that the fifty Federalists in the General Assembly would vote for Madison and waste their second vote by choosing someone who was not nominated, while at least some of the uncommitted delegates would vote for Madison. Thus there was a chance he would be elected.[67]

The General Assembly selected Saturday, November 8, as the day to choose Virginia's first senators. They would be elected by a joint ballot of the House and Senate. Two days before the vote, the House of Delegates nominated three candidates for the two seats: Richard Henry Lee, William Grayson—both of whom had spoken out strongly against the Constitution—and Madison.[68]

Upon Madison's nomination, Henry immediately urged his fellow delegates to reject the man from Orange County, commenting that Madison's opinions were "so adverse to the opinions of many members."[69] Henry had already told the assembly that "no person who wishes the constitution to be amended should vote for Mr[.] Madison to be in the senate."[70] Then Henry seized upon a remark by one of Madison's supporters in the House of Delegates, who said that Madison would resist Virginia's efforts to repeal the section of the new Constitution giving the federal government the power to directly tax the people. "There[,] gentlemen," said Henry, "the secret is out: it is doubted whether Mr. Madison will obey instructions." Henry said on the House floor that citizens were so opposed to Madison that his election to the Senate would have produced "rivulets of blood throughout the land."[71]

When a committee of House members met with a committee of senators on Saturday, the votes were counted. Randolph was greatly disappointed: "To the mortification, and grievous discontent of the advocates for order and truth, the numbers were for R.H. Lee 98, for W.G. 86, for J.M. 77."[72] Randolph was surprised 164 members voted, not having expected that many to participate, and that some Madison supporters were absent.[73] Edward Carrington told Madison that 62 votes were given singly to him. He was convinced that "two thirds of the Assembly are Anti's who meditate mischief against the Govt."[74]

Carrington told Madison he should not feel dishonored by the vote, and considering the overwhelming majority in the General Assembly opposed to the Constitution, it was impressive that he received "so great a ballot." Randolph also assured Madison there was no shame in having been defeated: "Were I to decide what would be agreeable to my own feelings, the anxiety, and affection which were discovered by your friends in doors [in the legislature], and your favourers without [outside the legislature], I would prefer the situation of the unsuccessful candidate." Francis Corbin told Madison that if he could see the legislators in action, he "would agree with me . . . that it is honorable not to be Esteem'd by them . . . They are all become abominable and gone astray."[75]

One of Madison's closest friends and supporters, Henry Lee, a Federalist from Westmoreland County, was glad that Madison had been defeated for the Senate, and he hoped that he would also lose the election to the House. He wanted Madison to accept a prominent position in the Washington administration, perhaps as secretary of state, a position that eventually went to Thomas Jefferson. If Jefferson had declined the appointment, which he thought seriously about doing, Madison would likely have been chosen. Lee said he discussed this with Washington, and the general agreed that Madison should be a part of the administration. Even if Lee's assessment was accurate, Washington had already expressed disappointment at Madison's not being chosen for the Senate and was not confident of his prospects for being elected to the House.[76]

Madison, although probably disappointed at being snubbed for a Senate seat—even if he preferred the House—was nevertheless glad to see how much support he received from legislators who disagreed with him about the Constitution. He told Randolph that he was surprised that his "name should have been honored with so great a vote as it received." He also speculated that the House race would be very difficult: "I shall not be surprised if the attempt should be equally successful to shut the door of the other House agst. me, which was the real object of my preference."[77]

Patrick Henry scoffed at the idea that the Federalists were entitled to at least one of the Senate seats. In a letter congratulating Richard Henry

Lee, Henry said that Virginia would not see the successful adoption of the amendments proposed at the ratifying convention "if one of her senators had been found adverse to that scheme. The universal cry is for amendments, & the Federals are obliged to join in it."[78]

Having approved the petition for the second convention, passed the Disabling Act, and chosen U.S. senators, the General Assembly had two more important matters to deal with. It had to provide for the selection of presidential electors and create congressional districts from which the first members of the U.S. House would be chosen. Because Washington enjoyed such strong support and was going to be the unanimous choice as the first president, the creation of districts for the choosing of presidential electors was relatively uncontroversial.

On September 13, five weeks before the Virginia General Assembly convened, the Confederation Congress approved an ordinance to provide for the choosing of electors for president. It picked the first Wednesday in January for appointing electors, the first Wednesday in February for those electors to gather in state capitals to cast a ballot for president, and the first Wednesday in March for Congress to begin proceedings under the new Constitution. The Virginia General Assembly responded to the congressional directive by dividing Virginia's eighty-five counties into twelve districts, with each district choosing one presidential elector. Citizens who could vote for members of the General Assembly were qualified to choose a presidential elector.[79] After the appointment of a committee to draft such a bill and several minor revisions by the House and Senate, the General Assembly approved the measure on November 17.

Other states had decided to select their presidential electors either at large or with a combined district/at-large system. Virginia chose instead to have all twelve presidential electors elected by district. The detailed law listed the counties that would comprise each presidential elector district, assigned the responsibility for conducting the election to the sheriffs in each county, provided a penalty for those who failed to vote, and prohibited the distribution of food or drink to influence the election.[80]

In the presidential election, Madison's home county of Orange was placed in a district with the counties of Albemarle (Thomas Jefferson's home county), Amherst (controlled by the Anti-Federalist Cabell family, with William Cabell Sr. running for presidential elector against Federalist Edward Stevens), Buckingham, Culpeper, Fluvanna, and Spotsylvania (James Monroe's home county). Stevens won 686 to 604.[81] The *Philadelphia Independent Gazetteer,* publishing a dispatch from Petersburg, Virginia, criticized the lack of participation by voters in choosing a president:

THE ANTI-FEDERALISTS FIGHT BACK

"In many counties, we are told, not more than one half, and in some, not one fifth of the people, attended to vote on that important occasion [the choosing of presidential electors on January 7] . . . [It is] beneath the character of freeman to neglect so glorious a privilege." The paper urged citizens to pay greater attention to such matters on February 2, Election Day for choosing members of the U.S. House.[82]

The size of the first House of Representatives and the apportionment among the states had been determined by the delegates at the Constitutional Convention in Philadelphia. Article I of the Constitution provided that the number of representatives "shall not exceed one for every thirty Thousand," with every state having at least one member. Until a national census could be conducted, the Constitution gave New Hampshire three representatives, Massachusetts eight, Rhode Island one, Connecticut five, New York six, New Jersey four, Pennsylvania eight, Delaware one, Maryland six, North Carolina five, South Carolina five, and Georgia three. Virginia would have the largest House delegation, with ten members.[83]

The bill to provide for election districts for House members was introduced in the General Assembly on November 5. This was Patrick Henry's opportunity to avenge his defeat by Madison at the Virginia ratifying convention. By artfully drawing the boundaries of the state's congressional districts, he and his allies hoped to prevent Madison's election to the House of Representatives. A week later, after discussing the bill in the committee of the whole, the House of Delegates added several amendments. The next day the House approved the final bill. After the Senate and House worked out some details, the bill became law on November 20, thus creating ten congressional districts.

In laying out the district in which Madison would have to run, Henry and his Anti-Federalist colleagues strung together several counties they knew to be hostile to Madison. His home county of Orange was included with Albemarle, Amherst, Culpeper, Fluvanna, Goochland, Louisa, and Spotsylvania.[84] Madison's supporters had tried to get the more Constitution-friendly Fauquier County included, but they were outvoted.[85]

The General Assembly fixed the date for the congressional election as February 2.[86] Depending on the weather, simply visiting all of the district could be a stiff challenge for any candidate. The district would extend from Amherst in the southwestern part of the state (at the foot of the Blue Ridge Mountains) to Spotsylvania in the northeast.

Henry knew which counties to include based in part on how their delegates had voted at the Richmond convention. Out of the sixteen delegates from the eight counties, only five voted to ratify the Constitution.

Two of those were from Orange County, two from Albemarle, and one from Louisa County. Henry could be fairly certain based on those votes that Madison would have a very difficult time getting elected in the district. George Lee Turberville told Madison that Henry and the Anti-Federalists were determined to keep him out of Congress: "The object of the majority [of the House of Delegates] has been to prevent yr. Election in the house of Representatives . . . by forming a district (as they supposed) of Counties most tainted with antifederalism in which Orange is included—& then by confining the choice of the people to the residents in the particular district." Edward Carrington told Madison that the "Anti's have leveled every effort at you."[87]

George Washington, watching all this from Mount Vernon, knew that the congressional district would mean trouble for Madison. After Madison's defeat for the Senate seat, Washington said, "It is now much dreaded by [supporters of the Constitution] . . . that the State (which is to be divided into districts for the appointment of Representatives to Congress) will be so arranged as to place a large proportion of those who are called Antifederalists in That Station [district]." Burgess Ball, who lived near Fredericksburg, told Madison that the counties are "arranged so, as to render your Election, I fear, extremely doubtful, the greater no. [number] being Antifederal."[88]

Several of the counties in Madison's district were under the political control of prominent Anti-Federalists. Amherst, for example, was dominated by the Cabell family. Henry knew that not only were the Cabells strongly opposed to the Constitution, on Election Day they would motivate citizens opposed to Madison to get to Amherst, the county seat, to vote against him. French Strother, who represented Culpeper County in the legislature and who was highly influential in that populous county, had voted against ratification at the Richmond convention.

Creating a district overflowing with Anti-Federalists would not advance Henry's goals if Madison could seek election from another part of Virginia, as George Mason had done when he was elected to the ratifying convention from Stafford County, next door to his home county of Fairfax.

Henry was determined to prevent Madison from running in the Tidewater region of Virginia, or some other area more supportive of the Constitution. To that end, the Anti-Federalists in the General Assembly inserted a provision that required any candidate for the House to be a resident of the district from which he was running for twelve months before the election. Federalists introduced a motion to strike that language, but Henry and his colleagues would have none of it. The motion was defeated 80 to 32.[89] The final language meant that voters could only choose someone who had been a "bona fide resident for twelve months within such District."[90]

Virginia's residency requirement appeared to violate the first article of the Constitution the state had just so laboriously ratified. Article I requires that members of the U.S. House be residents of their states, but not of a particular district.[91] Although the Constitution gives states the power to regulate the conduct of elections, it does not permit them to alter the eligibility of those who seek election to Congress. Maryland enacted a similar residency law in 1790. In 1807, a committee of the U.S. House—the House determines the qualifications of its members under the Constitution—decided the matter by concluding that Maryland's residency law was unconstitutional.[92] Almost two hundred years later, in a case involving term limits, the Supreme Court confirmed that states cannot alter the eligibility of House members.[93] But such reaffirmations of Article I were in the future, and for now Madison's enemies had won a key tactical victory.

Henry had good reason to include the residency requirement. The Reverend James Madison, his namesake's second cousin and the president of the College of William and Mary in Williamsburg, invited the future president to seek election from that area of Virginia in order to ensure his success. Reverend Madison made this offer even before he knew which counties would be included with Orange in the congressional district. After expressing disappointment in the decision not to send Madison to the Senate, he told his cousin, "I thought it might not be improper to inform you, that your Election appears certain in the lower Part of the Country [Virginia], provided you permit yourself to be nominated." He told Madison that if the General Assembly required ownership of property for someone to run in a district, there were "Lots in this Town [which] may be had at a very low Rate."[94]

Governor Randolph also offered to help Madison get around the residency law. Edward Carrington had discussed the matter with Randolph, and Carrington reported to Madison that the governor wanted him to "take every chance for securing your election in the State, [and] he intends to Offer you for the district [the district south of Henrico County between the James and York rivers]." Carrington had talked about this with several others who were of the opinion that the residency requirement was "not within the power of the Legislature, and that it will avail nothing in Congress, where the qualifications of Members are to be judged."[95]

The residency requirement and the offers from his supporters put Madison in a difficult position. If he was elected from a district that did not include Orange County, Anti-Federalists could challenge his eligibility in the First Congress. It would lead to hearings before a congressional committee and speeches by his supporters and opponents on the House floor that could go on for an extended period. Even if Madison succeeded in retaining his seat, there would be a lingering question over whether he was elected legitimately. Although he did not refer to the possibility of such a prolonged battle in Congress, anyone as concerned about his reputation as Madison would certainly have dreaded the prospect that his debut in Congress might be consumed by a debate over his right to be there.

Carrington also offered advice that Madison wisely ignored. Recognizing Madison's intense dislike for campaigning, Carrington urged him to stay in New York and not worry about returning to Virginia in the months leading up to the election. He told Madison his supporters had been prepared for the possibility of his "non appearance" in the district, and he said, "Your coming would answer no purpose in forwarding your Election—each County will have several active Characters in your behalf. I now give it as my opinion that you ought not to come." Carrington told Madison that Randolph agreed with this recommendation, presumably because the governor wanted Madison to run in the district south of Henrico County.[96] Carrington also believed the residency requirement was directed toward Madison: "I am inclined to think that the Anti's inserted this with a view to you."[97]

To further thwart his adversary, Henry also persuaded the General Assembly to reappoint Madison to the lame-duck Confederation Congress.[98] Henry did not arrange Madison's reelection to Congress because of his admiration for his legislative skills. He knew that out of a sense of duty, Madison would stay for some time in New York, far from the district where he should have been campaigning. George Lee Turberville told Madison this in mid-November: "I do verily believe that Mr. Henry Voted for you to Congress this time with no other View but to keep you from Country [Virginia] until some more favor'd man, some minion of *his* or of *his* party shall have had an opportunity to supplant yr. Interest."[99]

Madison did not seem to mind being reappointed to Congress. He told Randolph he preferred to stay in New York for the winter. He was working on a project, which he did not disclose, that required access to the papers of Congress. But he also knew that his friends wanted him to return soon to Virginia for "counteracting the machinations agst. my election into the H. of Reps."[100]

A few days after Madison was defeated for the Senate, he began to get some idea what strategy the Anti-Federalists would use against him in the election for the House. Henry told his fellow legislators in the House of Delegates that Madison was "not to be trusted with *amendments* since [he] had declared, that not a letter of the Constitution cou'd be spared."[101] The claim that Madison thought the Constitution was perfect, or at least that he would actively oppose amendments in the First Congress, was an easy charge for the Anti-Federalists to spread. During the next several months, Madison heard from people who said they had been told he opposed amendments and they were troubled by that position. Religious groups in the congressional district—such as the Baptists—were especially concerned about the lack of protection in the Constitution for religious freedom, and they were greatly disturbed by the news that Madison did not believe such an amendment was necessary.

The harried Federalist minority in the House of Delegates had suffered one defeat after another. Even Madison's appointment to the lame-duck Congress, which Madison's allies almost all voted for because they did not want him to suffer another public rejection, was, they knew, probably a blow to his chances of winning a seat in the new House of Representatives.

Some Federalists were outraged at the way they were treated in the General Assembly. Turberville complained about Henry in particular: "The Man who leads a *mob* majority . . . is the most cruelly oppressive of all possible Tyrants." Supporters argued strenuously that the Anti-Federalists in the legislature did not represent the views of most Virginians, and they—the Federalists—had taken the high ground and had made the best case they could. Richard Bland Lee was confident that Virginians would see how supporters of the Constitution countered the proposals offered by Henry in the General Assembly, and eventually Federalists would be rewarded for their efforts: "The minority is so respectable . . . [it] will not only turn the tide of sentiment in our favor in this state, but will destroy the effect of . . . [Anti-Federalist proposals] in other states." Carrington shared the same view, as he told Madison: "I think the Feds [supporters of the Constitution] have exhibited themselves in a light before the Eyes of the people . . . [I]ndeed the palpable untruths contained in the drafts [the measures requesting a second convention] ought to fix the condemnation of the people upon them [Anti-Federalists.]"[102]

Henry and the other Anti-Federalists had one more important task if they wanted to increase the likelihood that Madison would be defeated. They needed a well-known and respected opponent to run against him. As early as mid-November, Madison's friends speculated as to who the likely opponent would be. Governor Randolph thought that either French Strother from Culpeper County, who had served in the House of Delegates for fifteen years and the state senate for another eight, or Madison's longtime admirer John Dawson would run. Carrington heard the names of Strother and William Cabell Sr., the powerful leader of Amherst County, as possible candidates.[103]

The Anti-Federalists' decision to ask James Monroe—the war hero and widely respected political figure—to run against Madison was likely made between November 15 and 18. On the fifteenth, Carrington wrote a detailed letter to Madison about the House election. He included information as to which counties would be in the district and thought Strother or Cabell might run, but he did not mention Monroe. Three days later, he again wrote to Madison, and this time he said that in the last few days, "there has arisen some reason to suspect that Colo. Monroe will be the Man." And he added a warning to Madison about his friend and future opponent: "Let me apprise you that you are upon no occasion of a public Nature to expect favors from this Gentleman." A week later, Carrington wrote to confirm that Monroe would be the opponent: "I have already apprised you of the *political* hostility of Monroe, and it will be well for you to pay some regard to it."[104]

William Cabell took credit for persuading Monroe to oppose Madison in the election. In trying to generate support for Monroe's candidacy, he sent out a general appeal to voters and said he was a "man who possesses great abilities integrity and a most amiable Character ... whom I Prevaled on to offer in our District."[105]

Madison had a difficult decision to make. He could stay in New York and continue working on whatever project he was engaged in, or return quickly to Virginia to campaign and refute the charges that he was opposed to amendments. One of the factors he considered was his health. He was suffering from hemorrhoids, as he described to George Washington: "I have for some time past been much indisposed with the piles. They have not yet entirely gone off; and may possibly detain me for some days longer."[106] Traveling was difficult enough when one was healthy; sitting for days in a carriage with such a condition would have been extremely uncomfortable.

Beyond his health concerns, Madison did not want to return to Virginia to campaign. He must have believed that at this point in his career, with all his accomplishments, he should not have to go all the way to Virginia, and then travel around the district in the dead of winter to solicit votes. He expected that the people of the district would vote for him based on his experience and reputation. He told Washington that he had been asked by several of his supporters to return to the district, and he was "apprehensive that an omission of that expedient [returning home to campaign], may eventually expose me to blame." Nevertheless, he reminded Washington how much he disliked asking for votes: "At the same time I have an extreme distaste to steps having an electioneering appearance, altho' they should lead to an appointment in which I am disposed to serve the public." Madison even worried that returning to the district would not help his efforts, saying he was "very dubious . . . whether any step which might seem to denote a solicitude on my part would not be as likely to operate against as in favor of my pretensions." He had expressed the same sentiment to Henry Lee, when he said, "[E]ven the electioneering appearance of a trip to Vira. [Virginia] . . . is not a little grating to me."[107]

Still, the letters from supporters urging him to return to Virginia kept coming. Alexander White said whatever business Madison had with the Confederation Congress could not be important enough to prevent him from returning home to campaign. He also told Madison that if he ran in another district, his opponents would create problems over the way he was elected. He said if Madison chose that course of action, it would "enable the opposers of the Government to inflame the minds of the People beyond anything which has yet happened." Orange County sheriff Andrew Shepherd told Madison the "Sooner your personal appearance could be in those Countys [in Madison's home district], the better."[108]

By December 8, when Madison wrote a long letter to Thomas Jefferson, he had agreed to return to Virginia and actively campaign for Congress. He told Jefferson, who was serving in Paris as minister to France, that he had been nominated for the Senate, but that Henry was "omnipotent in the present legislature" and had blocked his election. Besides attacking "my federal principles," Henry had taken "equal pains in forming the Counties into districts for the elections of Reps. to associate with Orange such as are most devoted to his politics, and most likely to be swayed by the prejudices excited agst. me." He told Jefferson that he did not expect much to come from his decision to campaign: "I conclude that my going to Virga. will answer no other purpose than to satisfy the Opinions and intreaties of my friends. The trip is in itself very disagreeable both on account of its electioneering appearance, and the sacrifice of the winter for which I had assigned a task which the intermission of Congressional business would have made convenient at New York."[109]

Madison knew that he had a difficult road ahead. Not only would he be campaigning in a district created to include substantial numbers of Anti-Federalists, Monroe was already hard at work, writing "Myriads of Letters to the different Counties."[110] Madison's friends warned him that Monroe's supporters would undertake the "most active unceasing endeavors . . . to secure his election."[111] To some of Madison's supporters, who respected Monroe, it was a sad occasion. Joseph Jones told Madison, "I am sorry to find two persons for whom I have real friendship in opposition as candidates for the district."[112]

As Patrick Henry headed home to tend to family matters, he must have felt great satisfaction over what had been accomplished in the General Assembly.[113] He had prevented Madison from being elected to the Senate; created a congressional district overflowing with Anti-Federalists; pushed through a residency requirement that kept Madison from running in another district; arranged for him to be reelected to Congress so he would be away from Virginia for several crucial months; sponsored a disabling act to increase the number of officials on the public payroll in an effort to turn citizens against the new government; and helped recruit a stellar candidate, James Monroe, to run against Madison.

On February 2, voters would not only choose a congressman, they would decide whether the new republic would have a bill of rights proposed in an orderly manner by the First Congress or amendments offered by a second constitutional convention. By the time Madison arrived in Orange County just after Christmas, only five weeks remained before the election. They would be among the most important weeks in his life and the life of the nation.

~ 7 ~

The Election

DURING THE LONG CARRIAGE RIDE between New York and Virginia, James Madison had time to think about all that had been accomplished since the end of the War for Independence. He had been a witness and participant at the most important events leading to the birth of a new government. Now he needed to look ahead to the country's future and his own. A year earlier, he had reluctantly agreed to return to Virginia to stand for election to the ratifying convention, arriving in Orange County only one day before the March 24 election, which he won easily but admitted later he could have lost had he not appeared. This time, with so much at stake, he planned to arrive home just after Christmas, five weeks before voters would choose between him and James Monroe for representative in the new Congress.

Madison arrived in Alexandria, Virginia, on Thursday, December 18, a week before Christmas. From there, he wrote to his father to ask for help in arranging transportation home. He needed a carriage to be brought to Fredericksburg on Friday of the following week, after he had finished his planned visit to Mount Vernon over the holiday. Madison also told his father that he continued to suffer from an ailment that made traveling "very troublesome" and thus he could not journey by horseback.[1] The next day he made it to Washington's estate, where he spent a relaxing seven days.[2] Neither man left a written record of what they discussed during the holiday visit, but surely the upcoming election would have been a prime subject.

Madison would have a very difficult five weeks ahead of him. Patrick Henry had done an extraordinary job of creating a congressional district in the Piedmont area of central Virginia that would be hostile to Madison and his supporters.[3] When the General Assembly approved the districts in November, the fifth one listed comprised eight counties, including Madison's home county of Orange and Monroe's Spotsylvania. The others were Albemarle, located southwest of Orange, where Jefferson's Monticello and the University of Virginia are located; Amherst, to the southwest of Albemarle and at the edge of the Blue Ridge Mountains; Culpeper, just to the north of Orange; Fluvanna and Goochland, located between Albemarle County and the city of Richmond; and Louisa, to the south and east of Madison's home county.

Virginia's counties were frequently divided to create smaller counties as citizens complained about the great distances between their homes and the county seat where they conducted business and saw friends and family. The eight counties in the congressional district of 1789 are twelve counties on today's map and would include the present-day counties of Madison, Nelson, Greene, and Rappahannock.[4] Culpeper County, for example, which played such an important role in the election between Madison and Monroe, would have included the 389 square miles of the present-day county, plus the 327 square miles of Madison County that was formed from Culpeper in 1793, and the 267 square miles of Rappahannock County that was separated from Culpeper in 1833. Thus in 1789 Culpeper County would have been 983 square miles, requiring some voters to journey as far as thirty miles to get to Fairfax, the county seat.[5]

To choose the counties that would make up the congressional district, Patrick Henry looked to the results of the voting in March when citizens elected delegates to the Virginia ratifying convention. Almost all the candidates had announced in advance whether they favored or opposed the Constitution. Henry assumed that voters would express their view of the proposed plan by voting for the candidate who most closely represented their position.

The term "gerrymandering" was not added to the nation's political vocabulary until 1812, when Massachusetts governor Elbridge Gerry was accused of contriving an election district to favor his party. In that respect, Patrick Henry was ahead of his time. He assembled—in the nation's first congressional election—a district for the primary purpose of keeping one candidate, James Madison, out of office.[6] Henry's Anti-Federalist

MADISON AND MONROE CAMPAIGN FOR CONGRESS, JANUARY–FEBRUARY 1789

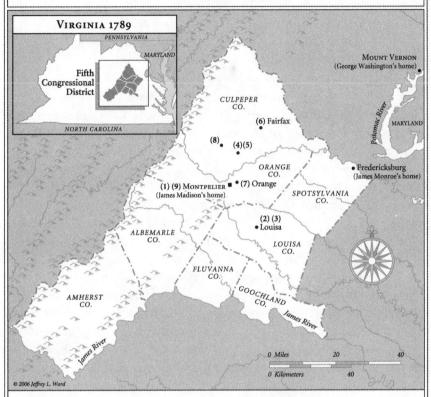

VIRGINIA 1789

PENNSYLVANIA

MARYLAND

Fifth Congressional District

NORTH CAROLINA

MOUNT VERNON
(George Washington's home)

CULPEPER CO.

(6) Fairfax

(8) (4)(5)

Potomac River

MARYLAND

ORANGE CO.

Fredericksburg
(James Monroe's home)

(1) (9) MONTPELIER • (7) Orange
(James Madison's home)

SPOTSYLVANIA CO.

(2) (3)
• Louisa

ALBEMARLE CO.

LOUISA CO.

FLUVANNA CO.

GOOCHLAND CO.

AMHERST CO.

James River

James River

0 Miles   20   40

0 Kilometers   40

© 2006 Jeffrey L. Ward

TIMELINE

1) Circa December 27, 1788
James Madison arrived at Montpelier after spending a week with George Washington at Mt. Vernon.

2) January 11, 1789
James Monroe traveled to Louisa County to address a group of Baptist ministers who came from throughout the congressional district. He also addressed citizens on court day in Louisa, the county seat.

3) January 13, 1789
Madison was in Louisa County where he wrote letters to supporters.

4) January 17, 1789
Reverend George Eve defended Madison at a meeting in Culpeper attended by Anti-Federalists.

5) Mid-January
Madison and Monroe traveled together to Culpeper to address a Lutheran congregation.

6) January 22, 1789
Monroe visited Fairfax, the county seat of Culpeper County.

7) January 26, 1789
Madison and Monroe spoke together to citizens in Orange, the county seat of Orange County.

8) End of January
Madison and Monroe spoke to a "nest of Dutchmen" at what is today the Hebron Church in present-day Madison County.

9) On the way home to Montpelier from the church, Madison suffered frostbite on his nose from the extreme cold.

colleagues applauded his creative efforts. When George Mason learned which counties were in the district, he predicted Madison's defeat.[7]

Albemarle was the only county besides Orange where both of the delegates to the Richmond convention voted to ratify the Constitution. George Nicholas and his brother Wilson Cary Nicholas were probably elected by substantial margins in Albemarle County, although there is no record of the actual vote.[8]

But in Amherst County, which had long been controlled by the Cabell family, the outcome in the voting for the ratifying convention was so lopsided that Madison could expect few, if any, votes from residents of that county in his race for Congress. William Cabell, a planter and the patriarch of the group—who served in the Virginia legislature almost continuously from 1756 to 1789—and his son Samuel were overwhelmingly elected to the ratifying convention. William Cabell received 327 votes, while Samuel J. Cabell received 313. The next closest candidate had 23 votes. The *Virginia Independent Chronicle* said that the Cabells had "declared themselves opposed to the Federal Constitution in the present form" in advance of the election.[9]

In Culpeper, the most populous of the eight counties and one of the most important in the congressional race, Federalists were outvoted, probably by substantial margins, when citizens chose French Strother and Joel Early to represent them at the ratifying convention. Strother was a planter who represented Culpeper in the House of Delegates for fifteen years and in the State Senate for another eight. He was an influential opponent of the Constitution. Early was a planter who served in the House of Delegates. He may have been more neutral about the plan initially but was persuaded to oppose the Constitution in order to win election to the convention and gain political power.[10]

Louisa was the only county in the congressional district to split its votes at the ratifying convention. William Overton Callis voted in favor of the Constitution, while William White was opposed. A petition had been filed in early June disputing the election that had sent White to the Richmond convention. It argued that some who voted for him did not own property in the county or were otherwise ineligible. After the poll closed, White had 199 votes, while Federalist Richard Morris had 195. After several hearings in Louisa and a committee investigation at the ratifying convention, fourteen of White's voters were disqualified, thus apparently giving the victory to Morris. Eventually, under the press of other business, the convention decided not to pursue the matter and allowed White's tainted victory to stand. Fortunately for supporters of the Constitution, they did not need the vote Morris would have cast had he been seated at the convention.[11] Henry probably believed that Louisa was at least closely divided on the Constitution, and that because of its contiguous position in relation to the rest of the counties in the district, it should be included.

In Orange County, James Gordon Jr. and James Madison were elected by wide margins: Madison, 202; Gordon, 187; Thomas Barbour, 56; and Charles Porter, 34.[12] Although Orange County was generally supportive of the Constitution, Henry had to add it to the district to force Madison to run there.

In Spotsylvania County, James Monroe and John Dawson, both friends of Madison, were elected over Federalist candidates. Right after they were chosen, citizens presented them with a letter saying they had "confided to your care and management the greatest trust in our Power to delegate."[13] Although the document expressed concerns about the Constitution and asked for changes, it authorized Monroe and Dawson to support ratification if nine states had already given their approval by the time the Richmond convention decided the issue. New Hampshire became the ninth state to ratify on June 21, but the delegates did not learn of that state's action until after they had voted on June 25. It seems unlikely, based on their statements at the Richmond convention, that either Monroe or Dawson would have voted to ratify if they had been informed of New Hampshire's decision.

Information about elections in the other counties in the district is limited. On April 2, 1788, the *Virginia Centinel* listed counties as being for or against the Constitution, and it identified Fluvanna as against and Goochland as "doubtful."[14] All four delegates from those counties voted against ratification at the Richmond convention.[15]

Madison's supporters in the General Assembly had tried to add Fauquier County—northeast of Culpeper—to the district, but Henry knew that it was generally supportive of the new Constitution, and he would not allow its inclusion. In the Fauquier election, the two Federalist candidates won 225 and 210 votes, while the Anti-Federalists earned 145 and 98.[16]

The counties varied significantly by the number of residents. According to the 1790 U.S. Census, the eight counties in the district had a total nonslave population (men, women, and children) of 50,857, or an average of 6,357 per county.[17] Culpeper was by far the largest, with 13,879 residents. Fluvanna had the smallest population, with 2,455. Orange County, which would give almost all its votes to Madison, had 5,500 residents, while Amherst, which was solidly Anti-Federalist, had 8,407. James Monroe's home county of Spotsylvania had 5,319.

To be eligible to participate in the congressional election, voters were required to be male, to be twenty-one years old or older, and to own either fifty acres of property or twenty-five acres with a house. Land tax records for the year 1789 reveal which citizens owned sufficient property.[18] In the district as a whole, 5,189 men appeared to be eligible to vote.

Those citizens had two exceptional candidates seeking their support. If those hostile to the Constitution had not had a strong alternative to James Madison, they might have voted for him anyway because of his long experience in public affairs and the belief that someone of stature should represent the state in the new U.S. House. But in James Monroe they had another impressive candidate whom they could support to demonstrate their concern about the new Constitution. Monroe—a war hero, an experienced legislator, and a delegate to the ratifying convention—had attributes that Madison lacked, and he was an energetic candidate.

Seven years younger than Madison, Monroe had a distinguished record in the Revolutionary War. He crossed the Delaware with Washington to take part in the Battle of Trenton, where he was seriously wounded. Governor Thomas Jefferson later appointed him military commissioner of Virginia with the rank of lieutenant colonel. By contrast, Madison's military experience was brief. He was commissioned a colonel in the Orange County militia but because of his health did not see combat.

Madison and Monroe provided quite a contrast when they stood next to each other at campaign appearances. At slightly over six feet, with broad shoulders and a large frame, Monroe looked the part of a Virginia statesman.[19] He was known for his warm personality. One of Thomas Jefferson's early biographers wrote that "Few persons ever knew Monroe intimately, who did not love him. There was a downrightness— a manliness—a crystal-like integrity in his character, which constantly grew upon associates." Jefferson was quoted as saying that Monroe was so perfectly honest that "if his soul were turned inside out, not a spot would be found on it." By contrast, Madison was shy and reserved. Some thought he was cold and distant.[20]

Monroe was initially hesitant to run. His uncle and stepfather, Joseph Jones, told Madison after the election that he had tried to stop Monroe from seeking the congressional seat. Jones wanted to make sure Madison knew he had remained neutral during the campaign: "The truth is I avoided all interference as I esteemed You both in the light of friends and dissuaded Monroe from offering; but the party as it is called had too much

influence with him, for though he resisted for a time they at length prevailed on him to come forward . . . I thought then Monroe was wrong."[21]

Monroe wanted his fellow citizens to know he agreed to run not
because of personal ambition but to satisfy those who thought he could
contribute to the new government and help propose amendments. He
told Jefferson shortly after the election that "those to whom my conduct
in publick life has been acceptable, press'd me to come forward in this
Govt. on its commencement; and that I might not lose an opportunity
of contributing my feeble efforts, in forwarding an amendment of its
defects, nor shrink from the station those who confided in me [would]
wish to place me, I yielded."[22]

James Monroe had strong feelings about public service and honor,
but he was also thin-skinned when it came to criticism and was quick to
interpret disagreements with his political decisions as personal attacks
on his character. He would remember for a long time those occasions
when he thought his talents and potential were not appreciated. He was
especially incensed over having been excluded from the Constitutional
Convention of 1787, when he had actively sought a position in the Virginia delegation. He blamed Governor Randolph for his exclusion, and
he also thought that Madison had something to do with it. On July 27,
1787, he complained to Jefferson about the way he was treated: "The
Governor [Randolph], I have reason to believe is unfriendly to me &
hath shewn (If I am well inform'd) a disposition to thwart me; Madison,
upon whose friendship I have calculated, whose views I have favord, and
with whom I have held the most confidential correspondence since you
left the continent, is in strict league with him & hath I have reason to
believe concurrd in arrangements unfavorable to me; a suspicion supported by some strong circumstances that this is the case, have given me
great uneasiness."[23] Monroe may have thought that service in the First
Congress would be a way of erasing the blemish on his record for having
not been chosen for the Constitutional Convention. He may also have
seen the congressional race against his friend as a way of avenging whatever slights he believed he had suffered as a result of Madison's actions,
although there is no evidence that Madison tried to keep Monroe off the
delegation to the Philadelphia convention.[24]

If Monroe had lingering feelings of bitterness toward Madison, he
gave no indication of them when he wrote to him for the first time after
having shared those thoughts with Jefferson. Instead, Monroe briefly
mentioned several shortcomings in the new Constitution and discussed
some financial matters.[25]

Monroe actually had serious reservations about the proposed Constitution. He primarily objected to the authority of the federal government to directly tax citizens, as he had explained at the ratifying
convention. He also criticized the absence of a bill of rights, the lack of
direct accountability of the Senate and the president, the extensive jurisdiction of the federal judiciary, the equal representation of the states in
the Senate, and the president's ability to seek reelection indefinitely,
among other issues. He vowed to support a bill of rights if elected.[26]

Monroe's decision to run for Congress was complicated by his long
friendship with Madison, which extended to purchasing land together.
Jefferson, who had helped teach Monroe the law, considered both of
them to be close friends. He told Madison about Monroe in a 1784 letter
when Monroe was serving in the Confederation Congress: "The scrupu-
lousness of his honor will make you safe in the most confidential communications. A better man [there] cannot be."[27]

That same year, Madison made what would be his longest trip, to
upstate New York. Along the way, he saw vast tracts of land in the Mohawk
Valley that could be purchased inexpensively but would, he thought, be
worth much more within a few years. The soil was rich, a branch of the
Hudson River was nearby for easy navigation, and it was likely that the
land would soon be inhabited by a great number of settlers. Madison
had been looking for a way to achieve greater financial independence,
and he expected that investing in the Mohawk Valley would help him
reach that goal.[28]

Madison wanted to purchase the land with his friend Monroe. He
also asked Jefferson to help secure financing in France, where he was
serving as minister, and to invest with them in the property. In 1785, after
asking Washington's advice about the potential value of the land, he and
Monroe agreed to buy a thousand acres for $1.50 per acre between what
is now Utica and Rome.[29] Madison and Monroe wanted to purchase
more, but Jefferson was unwilling to ask for help from French finan-
ciers. Within a few years, Monroe—who was in financial trouble most
of his life—needed to raise money, and Madison agreed to buy out his
share at a reasonable profit. Madison held on to the land for six more
years, obtaining a profit of 200 percent. It was not, however, enough
money to make him financially secure.[30]

Monroe's friendship was important to Madison, and they were able
to stay friends despite the difficult campaign because they did not treat
their political differences as personal. As Madison told Jefferson after
the election, "It was my misfortune to be thrown into a contest with our

friend, Col. Monroe. The occasion produced considerable efforts among our respective friends. Between ourselves, I have no reason to doubt that the distinction was duly kept in mind between political and personal views, and that it has saved our friendship from the smallest diminution."[31] Many years after the election, Madison told a friend that "Perhaps there never was another instance of two men brought so often, and *so directly at points* [of disagreement], who retained their cordiality towards each other unimpaired through the whole. We used to meet in days of considerable excitement, and address the people on our respective sides; but there never was an *atom of ill will* between us." Madison said of Monroe that "few men have ever made more of what may be called *sacrifices* in the service of the public. When he considered the interests or the dignity of the country involved, his own interest was never regarded."[32]

Madison and Monroe would campaign under very challenging conditions. During the five weeks leading up to the voting, when they traveled around the district, the weather was unusually cold and snowy. The often miserable conditions made it difficult for the candidates to see very many citizens in person.

Francis Taylor, Madison's second cousin, who lived in Orange County, often included a brief description of the weather in his diary entries. He noted that on December 18, when Monroe was in the district campaigning but Madison had just arrived at Mount Vernon for his Christmas visit with Washington, it was a "cold morning—snowed in the evening, hid the earth." The next day it was "windy and cold," followed by "very cold weather and [a] hard frost" the next few days. When Madison returned to Orange just after Christmas, he was greeted by "rain about 1 o'clock [that] froze as it fell" that "continued the rest of the day." The next day the "trees and ground [were] covered with ice."[33]

According to Taylor, on January 2, "hail and rain in the night [created a] great deal of ice and Sleet in the morning—cloudy, dark rainy weather Sleet the whole day." The sleet continued for two more days. Those venturing out would have had a difficult time keeping their carriages from sliding off the narrow roads or their horses from slipping on the ice. As awful as the sleet and cold were for those traveling, they were probably not as much of a hazard as the three inches of hail that fell on January 13. Even the next day, the hail was still on the ground and was "hard enough to bear a man." During the final days of the campaign, the poor weather continued. It snowed again on January 22, accompanied by hail, rain, and sleet. It snowed on the twenty-eighth, and all day on

3 About noon went to Court house. Madison got 16 votes to day — Hear he had 256 to 103 in Culpeper 174 to 105 in Albemarle. Capt Conway & C Taylor came home with us the former staid. The weather was very cold yesterday, more mild to day. quite clear. 4 hogs killed — 2 left for M Perry.

6 My father rode to Court house & heard that Col Madison got a majority of 104 votes in Louisa and a majority the first day in Goochland — Had a Cow killed which weighed ab^t 60 # Quarter I Issued a Marriage Licince to Kennoth Sutherland & Ruth Webster — Daniel Webster security — they had been to J Taylor's who had set off to day with Col Pendleton to Charlottesville, where the Shff are to meet to morrow to compare the votes for the member of Congress from this district

Francis Taylor, James Madison's cousin who lived in Orange County, recorded political events in his diary. These pages are from February 3 and 6, 1789. (*Library of Virginia*)

the thirtieth. The last weekend in January, the awful weather conditions turned worse, snowing two days before the election for a total accumulation of ten inches, with dangerously low temperatures.[34]

Although there were no modern-day polls measuring the mood of the voters, politically active citizens made predictions about the relative strength of the candidates in the counties. A supporter of Madison who lived in Monroe's Spotsylvania County, Burgess Ball, wrote on December 8 that some counties were against Madison, while others would be supportive: "Culpeper, you know, is much at ye. [the] disposal of one man [French Strother], and it is pretty certain that he means to exert himself in favor of your opponent . . . This county [Spotsylvania], I'm in hopes, will be at least as much for you as against you . . . In Louisa I'm told you will be pretty successful, at least one half being in your favour—

As to Albemarle, you can there lose but few, but in Amherst, you will get few or none—Your own county [Orange] we hope will stand with you."[35]

Several of Madison's friends stressed the importance of visiting Culpeper as soon as possible. Richard Bland Lee wrote to Madison on December 12 that Culpeper was so important that Madison should go to the county courthouse on Election Day out of respect for voters there and to show his interest in the county: "If you were to visit the Counties previous to the election and attend the Culpeper election yourself—I think there would be little doubt of your success."[36] Culpeper was going to be important in the election, but if Madison agreed to appear there on February 2, he risked offending his Orange County neighbors, whose support he needed and who expected the hometown candidate to be there on Election Day. Monroe also knew how important Culpeper would be, and apparently he had planned to be there for the election.[37]

David Jameson Jr., who represented Culpeper in the House of Delegates, thought it so important that Madison visit the county that he wrote to Madison's younger brother William to ask his help in persuading the candidate to travel there. Jameson included a note for Madison that he wanted William to forward to him as soon as possible. He told William that his brother's appearance was needed to "prevent Malicious and groundless insinuation and every undue influence . . . [W]e all know how inveterate his Enemies are and he must join us to prevent false prejudices . . . I think this County requires particular attention." Jameson's letter informed James Madison that Monroe was planning to visit Culpeper on the next court day to "explain the *Constitution* to the *People* and erase any false impressions from their minds," and he invited Madison to appear on the same day.[38] Monroe visited Culpeper about ten days before the election, one of several trips to the county.[39]

Jameson knew how limited Madison's time was but said he was "convinced every advantage will be taken by your Adversaries . . . Your being here will prevent false representations of your Sentiment and extravagant deviations on the minds of the People." Jameson understood that Madison was hesitant to directly challenge his critics, but he urged him to aggressively refute their charges: "When we find there are evil minds using every measure which Envy or Malice can Suggest to our prejudice it frees us from that restraint we otherwise should feel."[40]

A few weeks later, George Nicholas, a ratification supporter who had represented Albemarle at the Richmond convention, provided more intelligence on the campaign. Nicholas encouraged Madison to think carefully about how to use the limited time he had before the election.

He said Madison had to make his sentiments known to the citizens of the district: "Justice to yourself and your country both require that this should be done in an effectual manner. Every art has been used to prejudice the minds of the people against you." Nicholas accused Patrick Henry and French Strother of spreading lies about Madison's involvement in proposing the new government. According to Nicholas, residents of the district were told that "you tricked this country [Virginia] . . . by the manner in which you first proposed a general convention [in Philadelphia] to our legislature; that you had a chief hand in sending forth the constitution from the Convention without the amendments generally wished; and that you are now opposed to all amendments."[41]

Nicholas thought Madison had only two options if he hoped to be elected to the First Congress: "Either . . . you . . . visit the different counties on their court days, or . . . publish an address to the people. The first will be the most disagreeable and the least likely to have good effect as from the season of the year it cannot be expected that many will attend . . . [T]he latter mode if the address is printed and in sufficient numbers will convey your sentiments to every freeholder's fire side." Nicholas thought it was especially important that Madison's views be published in newspapers. He believed that having been denied a Senate seat, if Madison was also shut out of the House of Representatives, it would send a signal to the nation that both the legislature and the people of Virginia objected to the Constitution.[42]

Nicholas provided Madison with the names of prominent individuals—several were members of the House of Delegates—to whom he should write to explain his position on the Constitution and proposed amendments. Nicholas expected that they would disseminate the contents of the letters. He also assessed the mood of the voters in some of the counties in the district: "Amherst 3/4ths at least against you; Albemarle a majority in your favor but not as great as I could wish; Fluvanna at most divided; Goochland a majority against you . . . Louisa a small majority in your favor."[43]

Unsurprisingly, in view of the debates at the ratifying convention, the most important issue in the campaign for Congress was the Constitution's lack of a bill of rights. Patrick Henry and the Anti-Federalists repeatedly asserted that Madison thought the Constitution was perfect, and that he was adamantly opposed to amendments to protect personal liberty. David Jameson told Madison that word had spread in Culpeper that if he was elected, he would not sponsor such amendments: "I am informed by good Authority that . . . [Anti-Federalist Joel] Early reported that you

were against any Amendments whatever, conceiving the Constn. a perfect one."[44] Jameson's comment was one of many that reached Madison
during the campaign.

Initially, Madison's support for adding a bill of rights to the Constitution could be described as lukewarm. Along with most Federalists,
Madison believed that it was unnecessary to define which rights the new
federal government—one of limited powers—could not abridge, because
it had no authority under the Constitution to interfere with any. More
important, Madison firmly believed that the new government should
have a chance to operate for a while before changes were made.

At the same time, Madison was a pragmatic politician. He knew
that Anti-Federalists were committed to organizing a second constitutional convention, which he regarded as far more dangerous than amending the existing document. He hoped that if amendments were proposed
that would safeguard individual liberty—even if they did not also reduce the power of the federal government—the movement for a second
convention would lose momentum. He doubted whether amendments—
which he described as "parchment barriers"—would really restrain the
government if it was determined to abridge the liberties of citizens, but
he saw little harm in offering a declaration of rights. Moreover, it was
critical, in Madison's view, that amendments be proposed by Congress
and not by a convention.

Madison's primary challenge in the campaign was to let people know
he did not oppose amendments. As he told Washington a few weeks
before the election, "It has been very industriously inculcated that I am
dogmatically attached to the Constitution in every clause, syllable & letter, and therefore not a single amendment will be promoted by my vote,
either from conviction or a spirit of accommodation. This is the report
most likely to affect the election, and [the] most difficult to be com-
bated with success, within the limited period."[45]

He offered what amounted to a campaign pledge that if he was
elected, he would sponsor a bill of rights in the First Congress and work
diligently toward its passage. Several groups in the district needed to be
assured that Madison was genuinely committed to working for a bill of
rights. Baptists, who would play a crucial role in the election, wanted
Madison's pledge that he believed an amendment protecting religious freedom was necessary and he would work toward its approval in Congress.

Madison's willingness to support a bill of rights has often been seen
as nothing more than political expediency. In this interpretation, he knew
that in order to win election in a district heavily populated with those

opposed to the Constitution and demanding amendments protecting individual rights, Madison had to say he was in favor of a bill of rights, regardless of his personal views.

Madison's most important statement about his position on a bill of rights before the congressional campaign was included in a letter to Jefferson on October 17, 1788, shortly before the Virginia General Assembly met to create districts for election of members of the new House. Jefferson had criticized the Constitution's lack of such amendments the previous December, when he wrote "that a bill of rights is what the people are entitled to against every government on earth, generally or particular, & what no government should refuse or rest on inference."[46]

Madison recognized that even among advocates of the Constitution, there were some who "wish for further guards to public liberty & individual rights . . . though there are many who think such addition unnecessary." He then explained to Jefferson that he supported a bill of rights, but at best halfheartedly: "My own opinion has always been in favor of a bill of rights; provided that it be so framed as not to imply powers not meant to be included in the enumeration. At the same time I have never thought the omission a material defect, nor been anxious to supply it by *subsequent* amendment, for any other reason than that it is anxiously desired by others. I have favored it because I supposed it might be of use, and if properly executed could not be of disservice."[47]

He then offered four reasons why he had "not viewed it in an important light": Rights not given up were reserved to the people; an amendment on religious freedom and other subjects could be either too broad or too narrow and not offer sufficient protection to those rights; state governments would be "jealous" of the powers granted to the new federal government and would thus provide a check on its power "which has not existed" before; and a bill of rights might not be effective.[48]

The last point occupied much of the rest of his long letter to Jefferson. In Madison's view, majorities—both in the citizenry and in the legislature—might not be deterred by a list of protections when they were determined to violate individual rights: "Repeated violations of these parchment barriers [a list of rights] have been committed by overbearing majorities in every State. In Virginia I have seen the bill of rights violated in every instance where it has been opposed to a popular current."[49]

He cited the protection for religious liberty as an example. Madison believed that even with the strong statement of religious freedom in the Virginia Declaration of Rights and the Jefferson-written Statute for Religious Freedom, the legislature would still have approved a law that

would, in effect, have made the Church of England the "official" religion
of the commonwealth if a majority of the people had been in favor of
the measure.[50] If most Virginians were of one religious sect, Madison
would not expect a few sentences in the Declaration of Rights to prevent
the majority from imposing its will on a religious minority. He believed
the government might not necessarily be the source of oppression; it
might well come from the majority in a community. Thus a bill of rights
written on paper would not deter that majority. Nevertheless, Madison
recognized that government could be a source of oppression, and an
explicit statement of rights could be helpful.[51]

Jefferson had a strong response. He said that a bill of rights always had
the potential to control government oppression: "Tho it is not absolutely
efficacious under all circumstances, it is of great potency always, and rarely
inefficacious."[52] And he added the crucial element in the enforcement of
such rights that Madison had neglected to discuss: "In the arguments in
favor of a declaration of rights, you omit one which has great weight with
me, the legal check which it puts in the hands of the judiciary. This is a
body, which if rendered independent, & kept strictly to their own department merits great confidence for their learning and integrity."[53]

Madison's "conversion" over the bill of rights—going from initial
opposition, to the lukewarm acceptance expressed in the letter to
Jefferson, to enthusiastic endorsement as a way of increasing support
for the new Constitution—did not happen overnight. He remained silent at the Philadelphia convention when George Mason, five days before the Constitution was signed, said he "wished the plan had been
prefaced with a Bill of Rights ... [I]t would give great quiet to the people;
and with the aid of the State declarations, a bill might be prepared in a
few hours."[54] Madison was still not in favor of a bill of rights at the Virginia ratifying convention.[55] But by the time the General Assembly created the congressional districts in the fall of 1788, he recognized that
even supporters of the Constitution were in favor of adding amendments to protect personal liberty. He told Jefferson that the "friends of
the Constitution, some from an approbation of particular amendments,
others from a spirit of conciliation, are generally agreed that the System
should be revised. But they wish the revisal to be carried no farther than
to supply additional guards for liberty, without abridging the sum of
power transferred from the States to the general Government." Later in
the letter, Madison appeared to have set aside his opposition to a bill of
rights. He said such amendments could do much good, and he predicted
that if Congress responded to well-meaning advocates of a bill of rights

by proposing such protections, it would "give to the Government its due popularity and stability."[56]

Four of the letters Madison sent to various individuals that were meant for wider distribution during the congressional campaign—including publication in one or more of the newspapers serving the district—have survived. Three discuss his views of a bill of rights at length. He probably wrote more letters in the hope of reaching people scattered throughout the large district.

The most important of the letters was the one he wrote on January 2 to the Reverend George Eve, a Baptist minister and the pastor of the Blue Run Church of Orange County, located a few miles from Montpelier. As they had been during the election to the ratifying convention the previous March, Baptists would be a crucial constituency for the election to Congress. During the final months of 1788 and the beginning of 1789, Baptists and other groups had been repeatedly told by Anti-Federalists that Madison did not want the Constitution changed, and that he opposed an amendment explicitly protecting religious freedom. Baptists in the Fredericksburg area and religious groups in Culpeper County had also been told that Madison would oppose all amendments, including one to protect liberty of conscience.[57]

Madison's relationship with Baptists in Orange and surrounding counties had been generally positive. Shortly after he returned home in 1772 from three years at the College of New Jersey, he criticized the harassment and imprisonment in Culpeper and Orange counties of Baptist clergymen who had preached without a license.[58] For many years, Virginia law had regulated the holding of religious services. Not only had Baptists violated the law, they made disparaging remarks about the Anglican Church, the "official" church of the commonwealth. A Baptist elder had been jailed for praying in a private home, while his host was also imprisoned. Another clergyman was arrested in the pulpit. The Reverend Elijah Craig was imprisoned in Culpeper County for preaching dissenting doctrine and was later jailed in Orange County for the same offense.[59] The extent of Madison's efforts on their behalf is not well known, but for someone so young and new to public affairs, it was courageous to criticize their persecution.[60]

As early as December 1773, when Madison was twenty-two, he asked in a letter to his college friend William Bradford whether Virginia needed an established religion: "Is an Ecclesiastical Establishment absolutely necessary to support civil society?"[61] He also wanted to know from Bradford how much religious freedom was granted in Pennsylvania. This was the first known statement by Madison challenging the prevailing view that a state church was necessary to maintain control by the British Crown.[62] Madison had already come to the conclusion that religious liberty was essential to a free society. In the same letter to Bradford, Madison criticized the way Baptists were treated: "That diabolical Hell conceived principle of persecution rages among some . . . This vexes me the most of any thing whatever."[63] Not long afterward, he told Bradford that he hoped the Virginia legislature would enact laws to protect all religions, although he was not optimistic that harassment of Baptists would end. He noted that "the rights of Conscience . . . is one of the Characteristics of a free people."[64]

Three years later, Madison was elected a delegate from Orange County to the Virginia Revolutionary Convention, which met beginning May 6, 1776. When he was appointed to the thirty-six-member committee that would draft a declaration of rights, Madison had the chance to make his views on religious liberty part of the commonwealth's fundamental law. George Mason, whose reputation for a sharp mind and advanced writing skills were well known, was given primary responsibility for drafting the document. Madison's wording promoting religious freedom was eventually included in the last article of the Virginia Declaration of Rights, which was approved by the convention on June 12, 1776.[65] This effectively ended the Anglican establishment in Virginia, and as of January 1, 1777, there was no more funding for the church.[66]

It is likely that Madison thought carefully about how he wanted to refute the allegations against him in the letter to Pastor Eve. He knew that religious freedom was of grave concern to Baptists throughout the state. They had been heavily involved in successful efforts to repeal the law incorporating the Anglican Church in Virginia, and they had a significant presence in Orange and other counties in the district.[67] By 1790, the 204 Baptist churches in Virginia had more than twenty thousand members.[68]

In his letter, Madison did not show the irritation he may have felt about having to explain why he was entitled to the support of Baptists and other religious groups, considering his long and public commitment to religious freedom. He began by acknowledging the "prevailing reports . . . not only that I am opposed to any amendments whatever to the new federal Constitution, but that I have ceased to be a friend to the rights of Conscience." He explained to Reverend Eve that at first he did not think explicit protection of religious and personal freedom was necessary: "I freely own that I have never seen in the Constitution as it now stands those serious dangers which have alarmed many respectable Citizens. Accordingly, whilst it remained unratified, and it was necessary to unite the

States in some one plan, I opposed all previous alterations as calculated to throw the States into dangerous contentions, and to furnish the Secret enemies of the Union with an opportunity of promoting its dissolution."[69]

But with the Constitution ratified and the new government soon meeting, Madison contended, it was appropriate to consider amendments: "Circumstances are now changed: The Constitution is established . . . and amendments, if pursued with a proper moderation and in a proper mode, will be not only safe, but may serve the double purpose of satisfying the minds of well meaning opponents, and of providing additional guards in favour of liberty." He then turned to the subject that would have most interested Reverend Eve: "It is my sincere opinion that the Constitution ought to be revised, and that the first Congress . . . ought to prepare and recommend to the States for ratification the most satisfactory provisions for all essential rights, particularly the rights of Conscience in the fullest latitude, the freedom of the press, trials by jury, security against general warrants &c."[70]

What he did not tell Reverend Eve was that as a member of the House of Delegates in 1785, Madison had anonymously written the elegant and passionate "Memorial and Remonstrance," a document arguing in favor of religious liberty and against state-subsidized religion that was printed and read throughout the nation.[71]

The General Assembly in 1785 came close to passing a general assessments bill that would have provided funding for teachers of Christianity, but its primary purpose was to provide financial support to the Anglican Church in Virginia. When opponents were able to temporarily postpone final approval of the bill through a last-minute parliamentary maneuver, Madison embarked on a campaign with others to mobilize the public against the measure. About eighty petitions with more than ten thousand signatures of citizens from throughout the state were delivered to members of the General Assembly. Unlike today, when such petitions would be just one of many factors in a legislator's decision to support or oppose a bill, in eighteenth-century Virginia, petitions were taken seriously by elected officials as a representation of the sentiments of their constituents. Opponents argued that not only was the proposed law contrary to Article XVI of the Virginia Declaration of Rights of 1776 and republican principles, it was contrary to the view that government should not choose among religions.[72]

Madison had good reason for hiding his authorship of the Memorial, which he did not explicitly acknowledge until 1826, when he was seventy-five.[73] Like most authors when seeking anonymity, he wanted the arguments in the document, and not the political affiliations of the writer, to be the focus of attention. Madison also did not want to alienate important people—whose support he would need on other matters— who energetically promoted the assessments bill as a way of helping the Anglican Church. Patrick Henry, who was governor, strongly supported the proposed law, although his absence from the House of Delegates deprived his side of one of its most eloquent spokesmen. Richard Henry Lee and Edmund Pendleton also supported the bill, although they were not members of the General Assembly. Pendleton told Lee that "I am not able to discover . . . any thing which can justly alarm any other society [non-Christians] for a general assessment to support religious teachers . . . yet . . . some very sagacious gentlemen, can spy designs [in the law] to revive the former establishment [of the Church of England]."[74] By the time the General Assembly considered the bill again in the fall of 1785, Madison and other opponents had mounted an overwhelming effort, and the proposed law was set aside without a vote.[75]

Not surprisingly, Madison told Eve that he preferred that Congress and not a constitutional convention propose the amendments. Amendments would be considered more quickly if Congress offered them, he explained. Also, some states would oppose the calling of a convention but would support amendments if proposed by Congress. Finally, Madison argued that Congress "will probably be careful not to destroy or endanger" the new government. But a convention, "meeting in the present ferment of parties, and containing perhaps insidious characters from different parts of America, would at least spread a general alarm, and, be but too likely to turn every thing into confusion and uncertainty."[76]

The effect of the letter on Baptists, especially in populous Culpeper County, where they had suffered persecution, was probably significant. Reverend Eve would have received the letter slightly less than a month before the election, and that would have given him enough time to share Madison's sentiments about a proposed amendment on religious freedom with congregations throughout much of the district and in person at scheduled services. Madison also sought the support of the Reverend John Leland, the leader of the Virginia Baptists and a resident of Orange County, who had also lived in Culpeper. Reverend Leland had been helpful in securing Madison's election to the ratifying convention.[77] He also had "great influence" in Louisa and Goochland counties, in the words of one of Madison's supporters, yet there was concern over whether he would exert much effort to help Madison get elected.[78]

Monroe also knew that religious groups were an important constituency. On January 11, he traveled to Louisa County, where he hoped to talk with Baptist ministers from throughout the district who were having a "political" meeting to discuss the election and the candidates' commitment to religious freedom. While in the county, Monroe also planned to speak to citizens on court day. Madison learned of Monroe's plans from Benjamin Johnson, who later represented Orange County in the House of Delegates. Johnson wanted Madison to attend the meeting of the ministers in Louisa and offered to pay for a special messenger to bring Madison the date and place of the meeting as soon as it could be learned.[79]

Both candidates understood the importance of religious groups on the outcome of the election. They traveled together to Culpeper, about twenty miles north of Montpelier, to address a Lutheran congregation there. Given the winter weather, Madison and Monroe doubtless would have liked to speak to their audience in the meetinghouse, but instead they gave their speeches from the portico outside. Perhaps the crowd drawn by the two men—already renowned as leaders of the new nation—was too large, or perhaps the Lutherans held that politicking should not be conducted in a place of worship. In any case, after the religious service had ended, Madison and Monroe stood outside in the face of a strong wind and addressed the group on the future of the new nation.[80]

This was one of several joint appearances over a two-week period. On January 26, Madison and Monroe spoke to Madison's friends and neighbors in Orange County.[81] They then traveled another day to a church where they spoke to the congregation. Many years after Madison had retired from public life, he told the story of visiting this church to his friend Nicholas Trist. It was apparently the Hebron Lutheran Church in present-day Madison County, which until 1792 was part of Culpeper County. Madison said he and Monroe went to see members of the congregation "who generally went [voted] together, and whose vote might very probably turn the scale."[82] Madison then continued the story: "We [he and Monroe] met there at a church. Service was performed, and then they had music with two fiddles. They are remarkably fond of music. When it was all over, we addressed these people, and kept them standing in the snow listening to the discussion of constitutional subjects. They stood it out very patiently—seemed to consider it a sort of fight, of which they were required to be spectators."[83] On the way home, Madison suffered from the extreme cold, recalling years later that "I then had to ride in the night, twelve miles to quarters; and got my nose frost-bitten, of which I bear the mark now."[84]

During the final weeks of the campaign, Madison received news from Benjamin Johnson that the letter to Reverend Eve was having the desired effect. Johnson attended a meeting in Culpeper where Joel Early, the fervent Anti-Federalist from that county, accused Madison of having said at the Philadelphia convention that the Constitution "had no defects, and that it was the nearest to Perfection of any thing that Could be obtained."[85] Early claimed that he could prove this allegation if records of the convention were released.

Reverend Eve, who had gone to the meeting to defend Madison if it became necessary, did so energetically. According to Johnson, "Mr. Eve took a very Spirited and decided Part in your favor, he Spoke Long on the Subject, and reminded them of the many important Services which you had rendered ... in particular the Act for establishing Religious Liberty [in the Virginia Declaration of Rights] ... [and] he thought they were under Obligations to you, and had much more reason to place their Confidence in you, than Mr. Monroe."[86]

Because of how difficult it was for the candidates to get around the district, written communication in the form of letters and newspaper commentaries, and the support of friends in disseminating information about their positions on key issues, became increasingly important. Madison's ability to write clearly and eloquently helped him explain his complex views about the Constitution and whether a bill of rights should be added. As George Nicholas had suggested, Madison wrote letters to influential citizens around the district, hoping they would help disseminate his views.

On January 13, Madison was in Louisa County when he wrote an important letter to Thomas Mann Randolph, who lived in Goochland County.[87] It was intended to be widely distributed throughout the district. Madison particularly wanted Randolph to correct the record when it came to his view of amendments and the perfection of the Constitution. He asked Randolph to distribute the information in the letter "as opportunities may fall your way, to set the misinformed part of your county right."[88] Randolph did more than communicate Madison's views to fellow citizens of Goochland County. He arranged for the *Virginia Independent Chronicle*, based in Richmond, to publish the letter, which it did on January 28, five days before the election.[89]

Madison told Randolph that he was in favor of amendments to the Constitution and always believed "it could be improved in several points, although I never could see the dangers which alarmed many." Madison also said that when he was at the convention in Philadelphia, he had been "an unsuccessful advocate in the General Convention, which framed the instrument, for several of the very amendments, since recommended by this [Virginia] and other States."[90] This statement seems disingenuous.

[*In our last, we mentioned that the Hon. Mr. MAD-ISON (of Virginia) had expreſſed himſelf in favour of amendments to the New Conſtitution—we now give the letter on which we grounded our in-formation.*]

"LOUISA, *Jan.* 13, 1789.

"DEAR SIR,

"BEING informed, that report has aſcribed to me many opinions relating to the publick truſt, for which I am a candidate in this diſtrict, and being unable to rectify the miſtakes by per-ſonal explanations, I have thought it proper to give written communications of my real opinions, to ſeveral of my acquaintances, in your and the other counties. It has been with reluctance in every inſtance, that I have taken ſuch a liberty ; and in none have I felt more, than in troubling you with the grounds, on which my ſervices are offered. Whatever hopes I may indulge, that my opinions are not materially inconſonant to yours, and that my pretenſions, may not in other reſpects be diſapproved by you, I have no parti-cular warrant for either, that renders an apology unneceſſary. The beſt, perhaps, I can make, is the one which departs leaſt from the truth ; that as far as my opinions, and pretenſions, may not receive your approbation, I rely on your candour, for a proper interpretation of the motives, with which they are communicated ; and that, as far as I may be favoured in both reſpects, with your approbation, you will not only excuſe the liberty I take, but feel ſufficient inducements, as oppor-tunities may fall in your way, to ſet the miſin-formed part of your county right.

who will object to the mode of a Convention, without being averſe to amendments in them-ſelves) as moſt ſafe, and as moſt economical. It will not have eſcaped you, however, that the queſtion concerning a General Convention, does not depend on the diſcretion of Congreſs. If two-thirds of the ſtates make application, Con-greſs cannot refuſe to call one ; if not, Congreſs have a right to take the ſtep.

With the greateſt eſteem and reſpect, I am, dear Sir, your obedient, and humble ſervant,

J. MADISON, jun.

Massachusetts Centinel, March 4, 1789. James Madison, when seeking election to the U.S. House, wrote this letter to voters on January 13, 1789, pledging support for a bill of rights. *(Author's newspaper collection)*

If Madison had tried to persuade his colleagues in Philadelphia to include a list of amendments protecting individual rights, there is no evidence of this in the debates, which he recorded, or in his letters. In fact, when George Mason pleaded with the delegates at the Convention to add a bill of rights, Madison remained silent, and Mason's motion was defeated.[91]

Madison repeated to Randolph his view that until the Constitution was ratified, it was premature to consider amendments, and thus place the country on a "dangerous road to public confusion." Now that it had been ratified, Madison was in favor of amendments that "will either make it better in itself; or without making it worse, will make it appear better to those, who now dislike it." Madison pledged that if elected to Congress he would work for safeguards for "all those essential rights, which have been thought in danger." As he had done with other correspondents, Madison listed several rights that should be explicitly protected and eventually were included in the proposed bill of rights. He repeated the assertion that Congress, not a convention, should propose amendments.

A few days after writing to Randolph, Madison received what may have been the first encouraging news on how the campaign was going. Henry Lee wrote to tell him that although reports concerning the election had been "unfavorable" in some parts of the district, "accounts have gradually been more pleasing." Lee reported that in Culpeper, Madison's friends were "successfully active in your support, & and that [French] Strother the champion for your competitor fades in his influence daily." Lee was even encouraging about Madison picking up at least some votes in Amherst, where his friends were "struggling to break the weight of the Cabals [Cabells], & altho they will not be able to give you a majority there, they will add considerably to your poll."[92]

Madison was also encouraged by the results of the polling for presidential electors on January 7. Edward Stevens, who supported the Constitution and Madison for Congress, won more votes in Albemarle, Spotsylvania, Orange, and Culpeper counties than his Anti-Federalist rival, William Cabell. In several of those important counties, the victory for Stevens was by a wide margin. Madison thought that the results of the presidential election demonstrated there was more support for the Constitution among the people than among their legislators. That could mean good news for his election, but he admitted to Washington that he could not predict how the February congressional elections would turn out.[93] He expected that the election for the U.S. House would be a "better key to the sense of the Community."[94]

Madison's efforts were probably helped by two newspaper commentaries. On January 15, the *Virginia Herald,* based in Fredericksburg, published a commentary addressed to citizens of the congressional district that was highly complimentary of Madison. The anonymous writer heralded Madison's work in the House of Delegates four years earlier when he successfully fought against the bill that would have forced residents to contribute to the support of the established religion. The author reminded voters of Madison's commitment to such freedom, recalling how Patrick Henry had endorsed such a tax to help the Anglican Church: "You would at this moment have been groaning under the intolerable miseries produced by this law" if not for Madison. "Let me awaken both your recollection and your gratitude to the merits of Mr. Madison, for his able memorial on your behalf, to the Assembly, against this law, and his unwearied exertions in the house."[95]

The writer urged voters in the district to recognize how important this election was to the nation: "Believe me, you were never called on to give your votes on a matter of such infinite concern. It is not every age, nor every country [state], which can furnish a man of equal endowments and virtues with the one you have it in your power to chuse. Virginia cannot boast his equal." And the writer added that it was impossible to believe that the voters would not elect him: "I will not harbour such a sentiment—human nature is not capable of such ingratitude."[96]

The *Virginia Independent Chronicle,* a Richmond paper, published an equally laudatory letter a week before the election. "Republican Federalist" decried the distortions of Madison's record and sentiments that had taken place during the last month. The writer wanted to refute the allegations of those who were "endeavoring by the grossest misrepresentations of facts, to debase a fellow-citizen [Madison] in the public estimation, for no other reason, than because he has with the firmness, and independence of a free man, maintained sentiments, which he conceived conducive to the true interests of the American States."[97]

Madison himself penned a note to residents of Spotsylvania County and presumably other counties in the district that appeared in the *Virginia Herald* in Fredericksburg on January 29, only a few days before the election. It was a summary of familiar themes he had discussed in letters and in other forums. He said he "always conceived that the constitution might be improved," and explained that prior to ratification he was opposed to amendments. Now that the Constitution would go into effect, he supported "amendments as will, in the most satisfactory manner, guard essential rights, and will render certain vexatious abuses of power impossible."⁹⁸ The same day a long letter, signed by Madison and addressed to George Thompson of Fluvanna County, appeared in the *Herald*. It explained Madison's position on many of the most important provisions of the Constitution and his support for amendments.⁹⁹ Madison discussed the need for the federal government to have the power to tax citizens directly, especially if money was required to wage war; the importance of such a tax to keep duties on imports from being too large and hurting the economy of the southern states if Congress had to rely on voluntary requisitions from the states; and how Virginia depended for its financial and physical security on a strong national government.¹⁰⁰

Also influential was a series of essays from the writer "Decius," who was prolific and controversial. Decius wrote twenty-three articles in the *Virginia Independent Chronicle*, published between January 7 and July 15. In turn, the Decius articles spawned numerous, and often heated, responses. Several of the Decius essays concerned the congressional election between Madison and Monroe. The writer argued that Madison's opponents were "not content with venting their own spleen on a particular citizen [Madison], whose public merits were the secret envy of the head of the prevailing party [Henry], they endeavored to pour the bitter gall of personal hatred into the hearts of the people at large. And even dissatisfied with the impressions which their own public rejection of that man was likely to make on the peoples minds, their inventions were put to the rack to form a district so as to prevent them from choosing him themselves."¹⁰¹

The articles, the letters, the personal appearances, and the efforts of friends to spread the word about Madison's commitment to a bill of rights were paying off. George Nicholas, who had been so helpful in promoting Madison's candidacy and keeping him informed of developments, wrote in the final week of the campaign that things were looking up, but that Madison's supporters must continue to work hard in the final days. He reminded Madison that his opponents would do anything to defeat him, and he encouraged him to be more aggressive: "Delicacy is out of the question with such men and you do not do yourself justice in not exposing them . . . Do not now omit any thing to ensure success."¹⁰²

Culpeper County could swing the election, in Nicholas's view. He told Madison, "Your friends increase daily here and your majority will be much greater than when I wrote to you before." Edward Stevens reported that Monroe was planning to be in Culpeper on Election Day, and he urged Madison to appear there as well. Nicholas agreed that Madison's presence in Culpeper was vital, and he even encouraged Madison to invite Monroe to be there with him if he felt that was the proper thing to do. Madison apparently took Nicholas's advice and visited Culpeper with Monroe sometime at the end of January.[103]

It had been a grueling five weeks for Madison. He wrote probably dozens of letters, traveled to his county seat in Orange several times, and went at least once to Louisa and Culpeper counties and perhaps to other counties where there is no record of his appearance. He hated traveling in winter and loathed asking for votes, but he did both in an effort to win election to the U.S. House.

The weather conditions on Election Day, February 2, 1789, were brutal, making travel to the county seat uncomfortable and potentially dangerous. According to a weather log kept at Montpelier, the temperature at sunrise that day was two degrees with clear skies.[104] The weather was unusually cold all over Virginia. According to a meteorological journal kept by Madison, three years earlier on February 2, the temperature at sunrise was thirty-eight degrees with "somewhat cloudy" skies.[105] In Fredericksburg, the temperature on Election Day was ten degrees below zero; at Mount Vernon, George Washington recorded that the mercury did not rise above the bubble of the thermometer.[106]

The cold weather was bad enough, but on Friday, three days before the election, it began snowing around noon and "continued all day," according to Francis Taylor. It snowed until the next day. By then, Taylor noted, it was ten inches deep. As soon as the snow stopped, the temperature plunged.[107]

For those riding for hours in unheated carriages and on horseback to get to their county seat to vote, the trip posed considerable risk. The slightest wind would have cut through their flimsy clothes of homespun linen and wool, and at those temperatures any exposed skin would have been vulnerable to frostbite or hypothermia within a few hours. Their hands and feet would have been the first extremities susceptible to the bitter cold, then their faces and ears. People may not have been the only ones to suffer. Horses without proper shoes risked serious injury as they made their way across paths of jagged ice and frozen branches hidden beneath the snow.

Even under the best conditions, those coming from the most distant parts of a county would have traveled almost all day to get to the courthouse. With the weather so awful, some probably decided not to make the trip or turned back. It was unusual for Virginia to conduct elections in weather this bad.[108] The normal temperature for central Virginia in January and February is in the mid- to upper forties.

A weather log kept at Montpelier, James Madison's home. On Election Day, February 2, 1789, the temperature at sunrise was two degrees. (*American Philosophical Society*)

Considering the weather and the long distance that some had to travel to the county seat, turnout was fairly high. Districtwide, 2,280 votes were counted, or 44 percent of the total eligible. If another 315 people had voted, turnout would have been 50 percent.

Turnout rates varied significantly by county. The highest was in Amherst, a county solidly opposed to Madison, with 74 percent participation (391 of 526 eligible voters casting a ballot). Spotsylvania, which would also be expected to vote overwhelmingly for him, was second with a 61 percent turnout. The lowest was Fluvanna with 23 percent. Madison would have been disappointed by Orange County's participation rate of only 38 percent.

The voting was supposed to take place only on February 2. Virginia law did not authorize sheriffs—who were in charge of conducting elections and reporting the results—to permit voting on more than one day. The General Assembly had stated as much in its election law.[109] But perhaps because of the weather and the difficulty voters had in traveling to their county seats, sheriffs in several counties allowed the voting to extend more than one day. In his diary entry on February 2, Francis Taylor noted that he "went . . . to election for Delegate to Congress from this district. In Orange Col Madison got 200 votes—Monroe 9." The next day, Taylor wrote that "about noon went to Court house. Madison got 16 votes to day." On February 6, Taylor wrote that Madison "got a majority of 104 votes in Louisa and a majority the first day in Goochland."[110] This was not the first time this had happened. Several sheriffs had allowed voting for presidential electors the previous month to extend over two or three days.[111]

The unbearably cold temperatures and ten inches of snow on the ground would have tested the commitment of the most dedicated citizen. Those who made it to their county courthouses probably understood the importance of sending a person like Madison to the First Congress, but they could not have known how much was at stake.

When the votes were counted, Madison was victorious. He received 1,308 votes to Monroe's 972, a margin of 336 votes, or 57 to 43 percent. Culpeper, with a turnout rate of 39 percent, contributed significantly to his margin of victory. That county gave more than twice as many votes to Madison as to Monroe, 256 to 103. As expected, Anti-Federalists delivered their votes for Monroe in Amherst, but Madison still managed to earn 145 votes out of 391 there.[112] Madison won his home county 216 to 9, and although he lost Monroe's county of Spotsylvania, he received a respectable number of votes, 115 to Monroe's 189. In the end, he won Albemarle, Culpeper, Louisa, and Orange, and lost Goochland by one vote.[113]

Even Monroe seemed pleased that Madison had won. In a letter to Jefferson a few days after the election, he described the congressional district and noted that Madison "prevail'd by a large majority of about 300. It wod. [would] have given me concern to have excluded him." He wanted Jefferson to know that he was not embarrassed by the loss: "As I had no private object to gratify so a failure has given me no private concern."[114]

Thirty-five years after the election, the son of a prominent Monroe supporter in Culpeper County wrote to the then-President Monroe to tell him that his father believed the cold and snow had prevented some of his supporters from mountainous areas of the district from getting to their county seats to vote and that without the snow, Monroe would "in all probability . . . [have been] the successful candidate."[115]

Madison understood how important his campaigning had been to his success. He told Edmund Randolph: "I am persuaded . . . that my appearance in the district was more necessary to my election than you . . . calculated . . . My absence would have left a room for the calumnies of Antifederal partizans which would have defeated much better pretensions than mine. In Culpeper which was the critical County, a continued attention was necessary to repel the multiplied falsehoods which circulated."[116]

Madison's supporters were excited and relieved that he would be in the First Congress. Edward Carrington wrote to him shortly after the election to say how important it was that he had campaigned in person: "Ac-

	Eligible to Vote (at least 50 acres)	Madison	Monroe	Total Votes	Turnout	Total Non-Slave County Population (1790 U.S. Census)
JAMES MADISON/JAMES MONROE ELECTION TO THE U.S. HOUSE OF REPRESENTATIVES IN THE FIRST CONGRESS FEBRUARY 2, 1789						
County						
ALBEMARLE	840	174	105	279	33%	7,006
AMHERST	526	145	246	391	74%	8,407
CULPEPER	932	256	103	359	39%	13,879
FLUVANNA	464	42	63	105	23%	2,455
GOOCHLAND	520	132	133	265	51%	4,397
LOUISA	807	228	124	352	44%	3,894
ORANGE	599	216	9	225	38%	5,500
SPOTSYLVANIA	501	115	189	304	61%	5,319
TOTAL	5,189	1,308	972	2,280	44%	50,857

cept my most Cordial congratulations my good Friend upon your success in your Election—it is an event which I am convinced would not have taken place a fortnight sooner, had it been then tried, and I am equally well convinced, that had you staid away, it would not have happened at all." Remembering how much Madison disliked campaigning, Carrington said he was "exceedingly glad you [Madison] acted in opposition to your own & my sentiments in Coming to Virga." Carrington also recognized how important Madison's letters had been: "I did not suppose it possible for your personal attendance in the district to produce an extensive change, limited as your movements must be in so short a time—your letters however have done much good." Carrington reported that Madison's letters had helped gain some of the 145 votes he received in Amherst—even though it was dominated by Anti-Federalists—and that a former member of the House of Delegates had been very helpful in Goochland.[117]

Carrington made many of the same comments to Henry Knox but added that "Mr. Madison had every species of misrepresentation respecting both himself & the Constitution to combat in his district—do not understand me as charging [blaming] Monroe—his [Monroe's] party however were exceedingly industrious."[118]

James Duncanson of Fredericksburg, who supported the Constitution, was surprised that Madison had campaigned so energetically: "Mr. Madison returned from Congress some Weeks before the Election came on, & exerted himself a good deal, at least more than I expected."[119]

Miles King, who represented Elizabeth City County in the House of Delegates and voted for ratification at the Richmond convention, wrote to congratulate Madison on his election and to say he was "truly sorry you were not one of our Senators . . . I well know your Object is the good of your Country . . . I hope Congress will take up the Amendments proposd. by the States and do What is Necessary without there being a New Convention."[120]

George Lee Turberville, a longtime Madison supporter, was equally effusive: "I congratulate you on the triumph of Federalism in our Native State." He said that the election of a majority of seven or eight Federalists of the ten members of the House from Virginia "must strike dumb" the statements made by Anti-Federalists at the last General Assembly session, when Patrick Henry and others argued that "four fifths of the state" was opposed to the Constitution.[121]

And George Nicholas, who had been a strong advocate of the Constitution at the Richmond convention and helpful during the congressional campaign, told Madison it was "with great pleasure that I received the accounts of your election." Nicholas said that the strong showing of Federalists in Virginia proved that the people supported the Constitution.[122]

George Washington must have also been greatly relieved that Madison had won. Writing to the soon-to-be mayor of Philadelphia, Washington did not comment specifically about Madison's victory but was delighted that "all the political maneuvers which were calculated to impede, if not prevent the operation of the new government, are now brought to a close until the meeting of the new Congress." Washington was also pleased that almost all of the newly elected members of the House from Virginia were "decided friends to the New Constitution." Washington later wrote to Madison that he had heard of his election "by a respectable majority of the suffrages of the District for which you stood," and he invited him to visit Mount Vernon when Washington returned from a trip.[123]

Patrick Henry said nothing in writing about Madison's victory, although it would be safe to conclude that he was bitterly disappointed that the district he had so carefully created elected his adversary to the House. In March, he told William Grayson that the Federalist majority in Congress would not propose the amendments necessary to limit the power of the new government: "Federal and anti seem now scarcely to exist . . . Our highest toned Feds say we must have the amendments, but the Enumeration stops at Direct Taxation . . . Treatys . . . Trade &c."[124]

Madison himself did not express in writing any great feelings of triumph after overcoming so many obstacles to win the House seat. In his first letter after the election, he told Tench Coxe that "I am glad to find your calculations [of strong support for Federalists] for the House of Representatives so favorable." Then, in Madison's low-key manner, he said that in Virginia the election "has exceeded the hopes of most of the federalists, and totally disappointed the adverse party."[125] He was even more restrained when he wrote to Jefferson about his victory. He included his name as "J. Madison" on a list of "successful candidates" for the House, although he also told Jefferson that he and Monroe had remained friends despite the difficult campaign.[126]

The victory must have given Madison great satisfaction—even if he did not clearly indicate this in his letters—but as with so many of his accomplishments, he had little time to celebrate. In about a month, the First Congress would convene. Madison had made a promise to the citizens of his district and state that he would work diligently to support amendments to protect individual liberty. As he made his way to New York, he might have been forgiven for thinking that his most arduous trials were behind him. The Constitution was written and ratified, a president and Congress had been elected, and the new government was to begin operation. Supporters of the Constitution would have substantial majorities in the new House and Senate

Although he must have anticipated some opposition to his call for a bill of rights, he may have assumed that since Anti-Federalists had long argued that the Constitution needed such amendments, and his own Federalist colleagues generally supported the idea, his efforts would enjoy widespread support.

He would soon learn that he had another difficult challenge before him.

~ 8 ~

Madison Introduces the Bill of Rights

NEW YORK CITY desperately wanted to be the permanent capital of the new nation. The city had been the home of the Confederation Congress since 1784, and New Yorkers understood that the prestige, access to government officials, and financial benefits that came to the capital would be of great value to the whole state. The city's recovery from seven years of British occupation during the Revolutionary War, when it suffered several major fires and lost half of its population and commerce, was helped significantly by the presence of the federal government. New York was determined to make members of Congress feel welcome when they arrived in April and May of 1789 to form the new government.[1]

Even the state's Anti-Federalists, many of whom had wanted to prevent ratification at the New York convention in July 1788, agreed to approve the Constitution only because Federalists had strongly hinted that the city would likely become the permanent seat of government.[2] Anti-Federalists knew that if New York did not join the union, its largest city would have no chance of hosting the new government.

New York officials worried, with good reason, that Philadelphia would persuade lawmakers to return to that city, which was the home of the First Continental Congress in 1774 and where the Confederation Congress had met for nine years. Representative John Page of Virginia said that New York "is not half so large as Philadelphia; nor in any man-

ner to be compared to it for Beauty & Elegance." Benjamin Rush, a prominent Philadelphia physician, wrote a long letter to John Adams in early
spring to remind him of his home city's many amenities and virtues,
including that "Philadelphia is the centre State of the Union: she is wholly
& *highly* federal."[3] Another Pennsylvanian, Timothy Pickering, said that
"In Philadelphia, the Congress will find convenient lodgings & public
buildings—provisions good, elegant, plenty & cheap—& the most extensive libraries adapted to the use of public bodies, that are to be found
on the Continent."[4] Those libraries appealed to John Adams, who as vice
president would be expected to be involved in the selection of a permanent capital. He told Benjamin Rush that "I love Philadelphia quite as
well as New York, and the noble Libraries there [in Philadelphia] would
be a Strong temptation to me."[5]

Some southern officials were unenthusiastic about Philadelphia as
the permanent capital, but they were even less willing to send their representatives as far north as New York. Traveling to New York often required long journeys over land and water. When the weather was dry, a
trip from Boston took up to four days, with twelve passengers crammed
into a stagecoach—with three sitting on each bench—and on the road
from 4:00 A.M. to 10:00 P.M. each day. Those who could not endure the
hardship of a stagecoach trip ventured to New York by boat. For members of Congress from Connecticut and other New England states, sea-
sickness was a common malady. After long days at sea, at the end of the
journey, those travelers had to endure "Hell's Gate," the turbulent whirl-
pool where Long Island Sound met the East River.

Members traveling from New Jersey and other mid-Atlantic states
had to change coaches several times and endure as many as five ferry
crossings. During the first few years of Congress, legislators from Georgia and South Carolina were delayed going to New York and back home
when their ships foundered off the Delaware coast.[6] The dispute over
the location of the nation's capital was finally resolved in 1790 by a compromise that created the District of Columbia, but as the First Congress
met, those negotiations were still in the future.[7]

As members of the new House and Senate arrived in New York, they
were greeted by cheering crowds, banquets and tributes hosted by city
officials, and invitations to social gatherings. Streets had been repaved,
new docks were constructed on the Hudson and East rivers, and homes
that had been burned during the war were rebuilt. Newspapers urged
the city to install better street lighting and employ a larger police force
for what was called the "seat of the American empire."[8] Senator Oliver

Ellsworth of Connecticut told his wife that "No pains have been spared by the inhabitants of this place to provide for the reception of Congress & to render their stay here agreeable."[9]

The massive renovation—which had begun the previous September as soon as Congress chose New York as the temporary capital—was possible in such a short time because the city was still very small, only a tiny fraction of its size today, occupying the southernmost tip of Manhattan. It extended from the Battery northward barely one-third of the way to Greenwich Village and east along the East River only as far as the present site of the Manhattan Bridge, although city streets were platted up to the site of the Williamsburg Bridge. Even Greenwich Village, where Senator Richard Henry Lee of Virginia lived during the congressional sessions, was considered out of town.[10]

The revitalized city did not impress everyone. Representative Elias Boudinot of New Jersey told his wife that "we arrived safe in this dirty City [New York]—The difference of the wholesome Country Air, from the Stench of the filthy Streets was so apparent, as to effect our smelling Faculties greatly."[11] Representative George Clymer of Philadelphia said that for the first month he was in New York, he was "not in good health, from the extreme badness and unwholesomeness of the air."[12] Representative Michael Jenifer Stone of Maryland also complained about the unhealthy conditions, telling Tench Coxe that "I have been sick Ever since I came to New Yorke—The air—The Water—and the Scents of the Town have made War upon my weakly Frame."[13] Senator William Maclay of Pennsylvania was convinced that New York's weather had damaged his health: "I never had a series of worse health than since I came here . . . One of my knees is now swelled a third above the common Size with the Rheumatism, a disorder for which, I am told, this place is famous."[14]

The heat and humidity also bothered legislators as the summer wore on. Representative Clymer said in early July, "I am yet to be convinced that a New York summer is cooler than our own [in Philadelphia] having scarce ever felt hotter weather any where than we have had for a week past— perhaps it is the effect of greater moisture in the air upon my constitution to render me less able to bear heat than at home." He later noted that the "thermometer has daily stood from 88 to 91 the effect of which together with the fumes of a non-elastic air has been fatal to many people."[15] Clymer was not the only person to say that people had died because of the warm temperatures and humid air. A merchant from Maine, who was doing business in New York during the hottest summer months, said in mid-August, "Such has been the intenseness of the heat in this city . . . [for the last week]that several people (I believe 6 or 8) have dropped dead in the street, either by its direct influence, or by the consequence of drinking too freely of cold water . . . [At 91 degrees it is] several degrees hotter than was ever known here by the oldest person living."[16]

Even the streets, which New York officials had tried to improve before Congress began its work, received low marks from some legislators. John Page said that "the Streets here are badly paved, very dirty & narrow as well as crooked."[17] Senator Maclay complained about having to navigate New York's streets while fulfilling social obligations almost every night: "I really found considerable difficulty in discharging [social] obligations of this Kind, by hunting up thro all the Winding Alleys (a Pennsylvanian cannot call them Streets) of this crooked Town."[18]

Not every member of Congress was unhappy about New York. Many appreciated the overall quality of the boardinghouses and food, as well as the theaters and other entertainment venues. New York's John Street Theater was a favorite place of amusement for many legislators and local citizens. In 1789, the theater offered seventy-four comedies, farces, comic operas, tragedies, and other entertainment, which many members of Congress could not see at home.[19]

At the same time that the city offered entertainment, it was also described by some as a respectful and solemn place. Senator Ellsworth observed that "there are here not only many churches, for every denomination of christians, but, so far as I have visited them, which is pretty extensively, they are well filled." The senator also noted that "what has added much to my pleasure has been the great decency & appearance of devotion with which divine service is attended."[20]

Ellsworth was impressed with how religiously devout many women were in New York. He thought his wife would enjoy hearing more about the women in the city: "You will naturally enough conclude from the favourable opinion I entertain of the New York Ladies that my acquaintance with them is not a universal one. There are many I confess of whom I shall never be able to give you any account." A New Hampshire senator noticed the clothes New York women wore, explaining to one of his daughters that "I do not know of any new fashions in this place. The ladies dress much as they did last year, excepting the crowns of their hats are raised a story or two higher."[21]

About half of the legislators had left their wives and children at home.[22] In their correspondence, some members of Congress expressed sadness at being away from their families. Representative Boudinot of New Jersey wrote to his wife, Hannah, at midnight after a long day of work, and said he wished she were in New York so he could share the day's events with her: "Had I my charming Wife to repay me, by her tenderness when the business of the day was done, it would add an invaluable pleasure to all my Engagements." A week later, he wrote an affectionate note to Hannah on their anniversary: "This Evening I am alone, and the important Day could not pass without Serious Reflections of Gratitude & Praise—I congratulate my beloved Wife, on the anniversary of one of the most happy Transactions of my Life—Twenty five Years have not induced repentance—Twenty five revolving Suns have not changed the Joy nor lessened the Prize."[23]

What impressed most of the arriving legislators was the transformation of what had been City Hall into a grand federal building. The enlargement of the eighty-five-year-old structure at the corner of Wall and Nassau streets was supervised by the architect Pierre L'Enfant. It was the largest construction project in New York City at the time. Two hundred artisans, carpenters, and unskilled laborers worked for almost eight months on the project.[24] Senator William Paterson of New Jersey told his wife that the building was "elegant" and that it "far exceeds any Thing of the Kind I have seen; and all join in declaring, that there is Nothing equal to it in this Country." The French minister to the United States, Comte de Moustier, described it as "a monument that can serve as

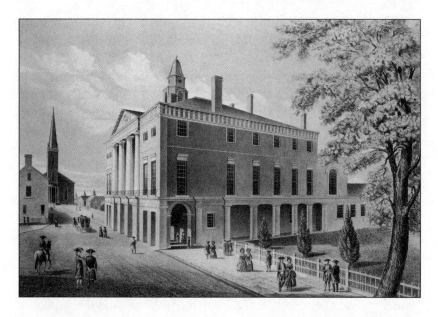

Federal Hall, at the corner of Wall and Nassau streets in lower Manhattan. It was here that the First Congress met and the Bill of Rights was proposed. *(Library of Congress)*

an allegory for the new Constitution . . . Both have been entirely changed by their framers."[25] The three-story building—which measured 95 feet in width and 145 feet at its longest point—had a great history, having hosted the trial of newspaper editor John Peter Zenger in 1735, the Stamp Act Congress in 1765, and later, the Continental and Confederation congresses. George Washington took the presidential oath on its balcony.

Visitors using the main entrance walked onto the marble floor—with the marble "very lofty and well finished"—into the three-story vestibule and could see above an "ornamented" skylight under a cupola.[26] Off the vestibule was the chamber of the House of Representatives, a two-story, richly decorated octagonal room. The Senate chamber, also two stories, was forty by thirty feet. Two staircases in the front lobby, one of them reserved for members of Congress, provided access to the upper floors. L'Enfant had apparently done an excellent job of renovating the building while preserving its older features.[27]

The House and Senate were supposed to convene in the first week of March, but it took a month before enough members arrived to form a quorum. Those who were on time became increasingly apprehensive as each day passed with only a few congressmen and senators trickling into the city. They wondered why it was taking so long for members of the new government to arrive. All but three states—New York, North Carolina, and Rhode Island—had conducted elections during the time period set by the Confederation Congress in its election law. North Carolina and

Chamber of U.S. House of Representatives, Federal Hall, 1789. *(Library of Congress)*

Rhode Island had not joined the union, and New York's delay was caused by a stalemate in its General Assembly, whose two houses were controlled by opposing factions.[28] On March 4, the day Congress was to convene, only eight senators (out of twenty-two) and thirteen representatives (out of fifty-nine) took their seats.[29] A week later, no additional senators had arrived. Members worried that the nation would think the newly elected federal representatives did not take their positions or the new government seriously. Representative Fisher Ames of Massachusetts—who played a prominent role in the first session—complained that "we lose £1,000 a day revenue. We lose credit, spirit, every thing. The public will forget the government before it is born."[30] Members of Congress already in New York wrote letters to governors and their absent colleagues urging them to get to the capital as quickly as they could. In the meantime, Congress—which had so much to do—could not conduct official business.

Finally, on April 1, the House had enough members for a quorum. Ames was impressed with the quality of many of them: "Though I am rather less awed and terrified at the sight of the members than I expected to be, I assure you I like them very well. There are a few shining geniuses; there are many who have experience, the virtues of heart, and the habits of business."[31]

The House members immediately began work by choosing a Speaker, selecting a staff, and beginning the process of establishing the rules under which they would operate. Five days later, with the arrival of the twelfth senator, the Senate had a quorum. Among the Senate's first duties was to count the electoral votes that would make George Washington the first president.

James Madison knew from past experience that achieving a quorum would take weeks, so he spent time in Virginia before leaving for New York on March 2. After delays caused by bad weather and stops in Baltimore and Philadelphia, he arrived on March 14. Pleasant weather greeted him, with a temperature of forty-one degrees and clear skies. Madison was returning to the place where he had stayed while serving in the Confederation Congress, Vandine and Dorothy Elsworth's boardinghouse at 19 Maiden Lane, near the water at the southern end of the island. Three colleagues from Virginia—John Page, Alexander White, and John Brown—as well as two members from Pennsylvania, also lived there during the new government's first session. White had heard that the Elsworth place was the "best House for Company and Entertainment in the City."[32]

The House and Senate would operate under different rules, and it did not take long for the Senate to act like the "aristocratic" branch many had assumed it would be. The Constitution was silent on whether the new Congress must open its doors to the public. The only requirement was for each house to publish a journal of its proceedings. The House voted to open its galleries, including to journalists who would provide important information about the deliberations of the House, while the Senate chose to meet in secret. The Confederation Congress had met behind closed doors for all the years of its existence, as had the Constitutional Convention in Philadelphia. The House's decision to open its galleries so citizens could witness the debates was almost unprecedented among legislative bodies around the world. As late as 1775, the British Parliament still tried to prosecute printers who had dared to publish excerpts of the debate, although visitors were permitted in the gallery. By the time the Constitution was written in 1787, American legislatures allowed access to and publication of their proceedings. The Senate would not open its sessions to the public for five years.[33]

The members of the First Congress had a tremendous amount of work ahead of them. Their first challenge was to approve the rules by which they would conduct themselves. A legislative body cannot function without rules, yet reaching consensus on such matters can be difficult. Although rules largely deal with procedural matters, they also affect what laws will be adopted and the content of those laws. The House and Senate also had to determine how to keep records of their deliberations and votes, to choose officers, to settle disputed elections of some of their members, and to create the committees that would handle much of the business of each chamber.

The new Congress did not have the luxury of time for a long discussion about procedures. The nation's business was pressing. Congress knew that it had to approve a revenue system so the federal government would have enough money to carry out its functions. It needed to pass "impost" laws that taxed imported goods—the primary source of money for the new government—and it had to do so quickly enough to collect taxes on the goods carried on ships arriving during spring and summer, the busiest seasons for such commerce. Although the new nation was in dire need of a stable taxation system, the First Congress took months to enact one, bogged down in such minutiae as whether rum should be taxed higher than molasses. As a result, goods arriving during the busy spring and summer shipping season of 1789 went untaxed, costing the government thousands of dollars.[34]

Congress had to establish executive departments so President Washington would have a cabinet to help him carry out the functions of the executive branch. It also had to create a system of public credit and payment, and to decide whether the federal government or the states would pay Revolutionary War debts.

The federal court system—of which the Constitution created only the Supreme Court—was still to be formed. Once the court system was in place and judges were confirmed by the Senate, Congress would have to enact federal criminal laws because until it did so, the federal government was unable to punish those committing federal crimes. Laws related to congressional pay, naturalization, patents and copyrights, Indians, pirates, and the location of the permanent seat of government were all to be written.[35] The power of the president to remove executive officials appointed by him and confirmed by the Senate was also going to be debated at length.[36]

The early weeks of the First Congress must have been tiring for many members. The hours seemed reasonable—members of both houses generally met from eleven in the morning until three or four in the afternoon, except when committee meetings were held at 9:00 A.M. or when they had a rare 6:00 P.M. meeting—but the demands on their time and the conditions under which they worked were often exhausting, and they had to work with almost no staff.[37]

Representative Boudinot of New Jersey told his wife of his routine: "I am up at 7 oClock or a little after; spend an hour in my Room—dress & breakfast by half past 8—in Committee at 9—from thence immediately to the House—adjourn at 3 oClock—In Committee ag. [again] at 6—return at 8—and write till 12 at Night—This has been my Course for some Time, except when I dine out, which to me is harder Service."[38]

Members were invited, and usually obligated, to attend numerous dinners and social gatherings throughout the week. Some were hosted by prominent political figures including other members of Congress, officials of the executive branch, and influential citizens. President Washington hosted a weekly levee and other engagements. Declining such an invitation could be considered an insult to the host and could negatively affect one's career. These dinners—featuring rich meals and desserts and often substantial amounts of alcohol—could last late into the evening. Someone in a single night could be served hot and cold punch before dinner, turkey, roast beef, other kinds of beef or mutton, oysters and clams, fish, a variety of vegetables, Madeira or Spanish wines, and spruce beer or cider, not to mention buttered toast, cheese, and nuts that may also have been available. Desserts included ice cream, trifle, whipped syllabub, and an array of tarts.[39]

Congressmen or senators fulfilling social obligations might stagger back to the boardinghouse late in the evening, satiated by the huge meal, and slightly or completely inebriated, only to arise the next morning, often at 7:00 A.M., to get dressed, eat breakfast, and then walk or ride to Federal Hall for a 9:00 A.M. committee meeting.

Once at the legislative building, they would encounter constituents from home, fellow members of Congress who wanted to discuss pending legislation, and "lobbyists" interested in the outcome of bills. The members would answer letters, read the newspaper, and then settle in for a day-long debate on, say, the impost bill in what was, during warm weather, a sweltering legislative chamber.[40]

The debates in the House—the only body allowing visitors—quickly became a source of great interest to the public. Some of the most distinguished figures of the founding period were members of the House, and for citizens who had never before had the opportunity to witness a federal legislative body in session, viewing the debates became a pastime and a ritual. The House galleries were packed with people. Though only men could serve in government, many women took a keen interest in the debates. Both women and men crowded the galleries, often talking with their friends for hours at a time or loudly cracking nuts—apparently a favorite snack of Congress-watchers.[41]

Members of the House must have been thinking about all that they had to accomplish when James Madison rose from his seat on May 4, just a month after a quorum was attained, to announce that he would introduce a discussion of amendments to the Constitution on May 25. Madison did not speak for long that day. He wanted to give notice that he would present a list of amendments and participate in the ensuing debate. He recognized that other business before the House might postpone that discussion, but he was hoping that the most urgent matters could be dealt with over the next few weeks so that the body could then concentrate on proposing changes to the Constitution.

In the weeks leading up to Madison's announcement on May 4, he had been busy preparing amendments and helping Washington to establish the executive branch. Washington, who lacked a cabinet when he was inaugurated on April 30, relied heavily on his fellow Virginian, whom he deeply respected and whose intellect he admired.[42] He asked Madison for advice on many important subjects, including matters of presidential style and etiquette, the president's relations with the Senate, and appointments to public office.[43] Madison was so influential that some have described him as "prime minister" during the first six months of the administration.[44]

Washington showed Madison a draft of a speech—it had been written by Washington's secretary, David Humphreys—that he wanted to deliver to Congress as his first inaugural address. The draft was seventy-three pages long and crammed with suggestions for Congress. Delicately, Madison told Washington that the draft was much too long and that it was inappropriate to list specific legislative recommendations. Instead, Madison advised the president to deliver a short address that emphasized his general aspirations for the new republic. Madison did, however, insert into Washington's speech a section that he hoped would launch a successful debate on amendments, helped along by the new president's enormous prestige. Years later, Madison observed that only because of Washington's respect for Humphreys did the president even consider giving the speech: "Nothing but an extreme delicacy towards the author of the Draft, who, no doubt, was Col. Humphreys, can account for the respect shewn to so strange a production."[45]

Washington delivered the address in the Senate chamber to a joint session of Congress on April 30, 1789. His remarks on the subject of amendments were obliquely phrased: "Besides the ordinary objects submitted to your care, it will remain with your judgment to decide how far an exercise of the occasional power delegated by the fifth article [the amending article] of the Constitution, is rendered expedient at the present juncture by the nature of the objections which have been urged against the system, or by the degree of inquietude which has given birth to them."[46]

Washington declined to propose specific changes, telling Congress that "I shall again give way to my entire confidence in your discernment and pursuit of the public good." Like Madison, though, he gave his support to amendments that would enhance personal liberty but leave untouched the basic structure of government. Washington urged legislators to be careful what alterations they proposed: "For I assure myself that whilst you carefully avoid every alteration which might endanger the benefits of an United and effective Government, or which ought to await the future lessons of experience; a reverence for the characteristic rights of freemen, and a regard for public harmony, will sufficiently influence your deliberations on the question."[47]

The low-key approach to amendments in the inaugural address reflected Washington's view that he should not tell Congress what to do. In any case, the president was one of those who did not see the need to amend the Constitution as urgent, though he recognized that some changes might be desirable. He said as much to Madison a few weeks after assuming office, after Madison had shown him the amendments.

"I see nothing exceptionable in the proposed amendments," responded Washington. "Some of them, in my opinion, are importantly necessary, others, though of themselves (in my conception) not very essential, are necessary to quiet the fears of some respectable characters and well-meaning men. Upon the whole, therefore, not foreseeing any evil consequences that can result from their adoption, they have my wishes for a favorable reception in both houses."[48] Although Madison might have wished that Washington's reference to amendments in his inaugural address had been more specific and less tentative and deferential, for his purposes the most important point was that the president had clearly endorsed the concept of revising the Constitution. Having Washington associated with his cause was invaluable to Madison. Later, he would often use the president's letter to help persuade his colleagues that they should follow Washington by supporting amendments.

Members of the House, after hearing Washington's inaugural address, decided they should reply to the president. Probably without knowing that Madison had been involved in writing Washington's speech, the House appointed him to the committee to draft the response, giving Madison the chance to generate additional support for his proposed amendments.

The House's response began with congratulations on Washington's election and compliments for his long service to the nation, and then responded to his call for consideration of amendments: "The question arising out of the fifth article of the Constitution will receive all the attention demanded by its importance; and will, we trust be decided, under the influence of all the considerations to which you allude."[49]

The Senate also wrote a response to Washington's address. The president in turn replied to each chamber. Madison had a hand in Washington's answers, continuing the unusual role of composing both sides of the correspondence. With Madison's help, the new president went on record as supporting amendments.[50]

Madison expected that Washington's endorsement would start the drive to win approval for constitutional amendments. To propose them would require a supermajority, two-thirds in favor in each house, but with both chambers overwhelmingly in Federalist hands—only ten of fifty-nine House members and two of twenty-two senators were confirmed Anti-Federalists—he probably anticipated substantial support.[51]

Early in the session, before amendments were discussed, Madison had to deal with a challenge that would arise repeatedly during the long summer and that threatened to derail his effort to propose amendments: the competing drive to call a second constitutional convention. On May

5, a fellow congressman from Virginia, Theodorick Bland—an ally of Patrick Henry—presented to the House Virginia's petition calling for a second convention to consider "the defects of this Constitution that have been suggested by the state Conventions, and report such amendments thereto, as they shall find best suited to promote our common interests, and secure to ourselves and our latest posterity, the great and unalienable rights of mankind."[52]

Bland was an energetic Anti-Federalist. A doctor from Prince George County who had served in the Confederation Congress and the Virginia House of Delegates, he had voted against ratification at the Virginia convention. He had often opposed Madison and was apparently so popular in his district that Federalists put up only token opposition in his race for Congress.[53]

The next day John Laurance, a representative from New York City, placed before the House New York's resolution asking for a new convention to propose amendments securing personal rights. He did not explain why a Federalist, who would presumably be opposed to a second convention, introduced the document. Laurance may have been simply carrying out an obligation he believed he owed the state legislature to deliver the resolution.[54]

The introduction of the two petitions drew Madison into a debate he certainly would have preferred to avoid. His primary purpose in offering amendments was to prevent the calling of another constitutional convention. Now he was faced with having to discuss two petitions for just such a convention, one from his home state, and one from the state that was hosting the national government. Madison had to be careful not to dismiss them too quickly by suggesting that the petitions should simply be filed, without Congress taking any action on them. On the other hand, if Congress took the petitions too seriously, it could encourage other states to submit their own, with the possibility that enough would do so to reach the two-thirds required by Article V for the calling of a convention.

Bland wanted the Virginia petition and list of amendments proposed by the ratifying convention to be submitted to the committee of the whole House so they could be considered along with Madison's amendments. Representative Elias Boudinot, the influential Federalist from New Jersey who had once been the president of the Confederation Congress, argued that the petitions and amendments should be available for members to consult, but that Congress should not take formal action until a sufficient number of states had presented them.[55]

Bland was not satisfied. He argued that whether or not other states "would come forward," if the House had Virginia's petition before it when amendments were considered, "it might have some proper influence in their decision, tho' it were not accompanied by other applications."[56]

Madison said that the House should respect the decision of the Virginia General Assembly to request a second convention, but that any formal action should be consistent with the requirements of the Constitution. He noted that "Congress had no deliberative power with respect to a convention." When two-thirds of states requested such a gathering, Congress was "bound to call one." Until enough states did so, the House and Senate have "no power whatever to enter into the subject—The best mode was to let it [the Virginia petition] lie upon the table till a sufficient number of applications appeared."[57] Considering that Madison had played a significant role in the debate at the Philadelphia Convention that led to the final language of Article V, his reasoning no doubt carried weight with many of the members of the House.

This could have been the end of the discussion, but Bland and Boudinot continued to disagree about what should be done with the petitions. Boudinot did not see how it would be "paying any respect to Virginia to commit their application to a body which had no power to deliberate or decide upon it," while Bland said again that if the House accepted the petitions and considered them along with the proposed amendments, there would be no violation of the Constitution. As the argument continued, Representative Elbridge Gerry of Massachusetts suggested that the debate over the treatment of the petitions should wait until the amendments themselves were discussed.[58] Finally, with Madison and Bland agreeing, the House decided to enter the petitions into the journal and keep the originals on file in the clerk's office, thus taking no immediate action on them.

On May 4, shortly after the legislative session had begun, Madison gave his colleagues notice that on the fourth Monday of the month, he would introduce the proposed amendments.[59] His announcement was greeted with frustration by some citizens in the gallery and probably some legislators as well—because they had a hard time hearing him. Jefferson had said Madison had a difficult time in large forums because of his shyness. Tristram Lowther, a merchant from North Carolina in New York on business, wrote to James Iredell—who would soon be appointed to the Supreme Court—that he had "formed the highest expectation" for Madison, but "I have had very little oppy. [opportunity] of forming an opinion for whenever he has spoke while I have been attending it has been in so low a tone of voice that I could not well distinguish what he said his voice appears to be too defective to appear to advantage [in] so large a room."[60] That may have been one reason Madison was unhappy about the way his speeches were recorded and reported in newspapers. He complained to Edmund Randolph that "the reasonings on both sides are mutilated, often misapprehended, and not unfrequently reversed."[61]

When May 25 arrived, the scheduled discussion of the amendments was again postponed because of other important business. Even though Madison must have been irritated by the delay, he did not seem too concerned when he wrote to Thomas Jefferson that "The subject of amendments was to have been introduced on monday last; but is postponed in order that more urgent business may not be delayed." He told Jefferson the House would soon consider a "Bill of rights, incorporated perhaps into the Constitution ... with a few other alterations most called for by the opponents of the Government and least objectionable to its friends."[62]

This time, Madison was willing to wait only a few weeks. On June 8, he addressed the House at length on the subject of amendments.[63] He had been preparing for this speech for a long time. It reflected his evolution from opposition to a bill of rights, to lukewarm support, to a firm determination to "advocate them [amendments] until they shall be finally adopted or rejected by a constitutional majority in the House."[64]

Madison recognized that the House had much other pressing business, but he cautioned that if "we continue to postpone [the discussion of amendments] from time to time, and refuse to let the subject come into view, it may occasion suspicions, which, though not well founded, may tend to inflame or prejudice the public mind, against our decisions." He worried that the public would think that "we are not sincere in our desire to incorporate such amendments in the constitution as will secure those rights, which they consider as not sufficiently guarded."[65]

The evidence as to how strongly Madison believed in the amendments he was proposing to Congress is not completely clear, and historians have long debated this issue. For instance, in the outline he prepared for his June 8 address, he wrote, "Bill of Rights—useful—not essential—."[66] But this language does not appear in the text of his address. On the contrary, the primary theme of his presentation was that amendments were of vital importance. That phrase in the outline may have been a reference to the view held by others that a bill of rights was not needed, a position that Madison acknowledged several times in his speech: "I am aware, that a great number of the most respectable friends to the government and champions for republican liberty, have thought such a provision, not only unnecessary, but even improper ... [or] dangerous."[67]

James Madison's notes for his speech on the Bill of Rights in the U.S. House, June 8, 1789. (*Library of Congress*)

Whatever the speculation about how sincerely he wanted to see a list of rights added to the Constitution, it is clear that Madison's words and actions during those difficult months strongly suggest that by this time he genuinely supported amendments. It is hard to believe that political expediency, keeping his word to local constituents, or a wish to assuage the concerns of those who remained opposed to the new government would be enough to motivate an individual to endure what Madison would go through during the summer of 1789. Only a genuine conviction that such rights were necessary and important could have generated the passion and commitment that Madison poured into his campaign for amendments—an effort that would demand enormous patience, tenacity, and all of his legislative skills.

As he introduced the amendments, Madison said, "[I]t will be proper in itself, and highly politic, for the tranquility of the public mind, and the stability of the government, that we should offer something, in the form I have proposed, to be incorporated into the system of government, as a declaration of the rights of the people."[68] His speech reflected his deeply held belief that in a republic, the people are sovereign, and whatever misgivings Madison may have had about the propriety of adding a bill of rights had to yield to the desire that citizens had expressed during the ratification process for such protection. Madison did not explicitly state in the June 8 address that the amendments themselves were so essential to the nation's well-being that they must be added to the Constitution regardless of how much support they had among citizens. On the contrary, he stressed that the demand for amendments by the nation's citizens required Congress to respond, and that the failure to do so—on such a fundamental issue as this—would make it clear that the new government was not going to operate with the consent of the governed and reflect the will of the people. Madison's decision to enfold the amendments in the principle that they were passionately sought by the people did not indicate a failure on his part to envision the potential of the amendments to greatly enhance individual rights.[69]

Madison moved that the House constitute itself as a committee of the whole so it would have the flexibility to discuss his proposals unencumbered by rules of parliamentary debate. He also wanted to be able to make his own detailed case to every member of the House. If the proposal was sent to a committee, its report—which Madison could not control—would form the basis of discussion when the amendments returned to the House floor.

Madison had barely finished offering his motion—and had not yet even introduced the amendments themselves—before Representative

James Jackson of Georgia, a Federalist, and Representative Aedanus Burke of South Carolina, an Anti-Federalist, vigorously objected on the grounds that it was "improper to enter on such a subject till the government was perfectly organized and in operation."[70] They argued that discussion of the amendments would take too much time and delay other important business such as the establishment of the judiciary, the executive departments, and the revenue system. They were joined by Representative William Loughton Smith of South Carolina, a Federalist, who stressed that enacting a revenue law required "constant and uninterrupted attention till compleated" and suggested that a select committee be appointed to consider amendments. He said that Madison "had done his duty: He had supported his motion with ability and candor, and if he did not succeed he was not to blame."[71]

These objections meant trouble for Madison. Jackson, a lawyer from Savannah, was elected as a Federalist and thus might be expected to join Madison's efforts. Instead, Jackson echoed the views of many of his colleagues by arguing that it made no sense to amend the Constitution until "we have some experience of its good or bad qualities." He added that "The Constitution may be compared to a ship that has never yet put to sea—she is now laying in the dock—we have had no tryal as yet; we do not know how she may steer . . . Upon experiment she may prove faultless, or her defects may be very obvious—but the present is not the time for alterations." Without a stable system of raising revenue, Jackson argued, the Constitution would be "of very little importance in itself."[72] Ironically, Madison would have made a similar argument himself prior to his conversion to the view that amendments were now needed.

To Madison's insistence that the American people expected the First Congress to deal immediately with amendments protecting personal liberty, Jackson replied that citizens would be irritated by the delay caused by such a discussion: "Should amendments now be taken up, it will be months perhaps before we can get through with them—mean time the important interests of our constituents are sacrificed."[73]

Other members of the House also objected to considering amendments for many of the same reasons. Representative Roger Sherman of Connecticut, who had played a prominent role at the Philadelphia convention and had actively supported ratification, argued that "taking up the subject of amendments at this time would alarm more persons than would have their apprehensions quieted thereby."[74]

Sherman served in the Continental Congress and on the committees that drafted the Declaration of Independence and the Articles of

Confederation. Although he had no formal education, he published on such subjects as astronomy, philosophy, and poetry and studied law. He was later a member of the Connecticut legislature and a judge. Following his one term in the U.S. House, he was a senator until his death in 1793.[75]

Representative John Vining, an influential Federalist from Delaware who had served in the Confederation Congress, wanted the House to finish discussing the revenue and judiciary systems before considering amendments. He believed that the American people were eager for the government to begin functioning and would be extremely disappointed if laws carrying out basic responsibilities were not approved first. He went so far as to argue that Article V required that two-thirds of House members favor the consider-

Roger Sherman, an influential member of the Constitutional Convention, later served in the First Congress and urged his colleagues not to add amendments to the Constitution. *(Library of Congress)*

ation of amendments before they were debated. Representative Benjamin Goodhue, a Federalist from Salem, Massachusetts, was another House member who held it unnecessary to take up amendments so soon.[76]

Madison must have been alarmed by the comments of his Federalist colleagues, from whom he had expected more support. He noted with asperity that Jackson was "certainly right in his opposition to my motion for going into the committee of the whole, because he is unfriendly to the object I have in contemplation."[77] He urged his colleagues to begin the debate, reminding the House that states had submitted amendments approved at their ratifying conventions that they wanted considered, and many citizens had supported ratification only because they were told the First Congress would immediately take up amendments. Citizens who remained actively opposed to the new government, Madison cautioned his colleagues, could create many problems during the nation's formative years if they believed their concerns about a bill of rights were not taken seriously.[78]

Jackson offered a motion to postpone consideration of amendments until March of the following year. That motion was withdrawn when Madison agreed to have his proposal referred to a select committee that would report within a few weeks to the full House. He doubtless resented having to make that compromise, but he could see that it was the lesser of two evils. It would, however, be only a temporary setback. By the end of the day, the House would agree to debate the amendments in the committee of the whole.[79]

Representative Alexander White, a Virginia colleague, was the first to voice at least partial support for Madison. White thought that the subject of amendments should be postponed "till the more pressing business is dispatched," but he added that "I hope we shall not dismiss it altogether; because I think a majority of the people, who have ratified the constitution, did it under an expectation that congress would, at some convenient time, examine its texture, and point out where it was defective, in order that it might be judiciously amended." White was speaking not for his own constituents, because "I believe a majority of the district which elected me do not require alterations," but he added, "I know there are people in other parts who will not be satisfied unless some amendments are proposed." Even if Congress ended up not proposing amendments, explained White, those who desired amendments would be satisfied because they would know their views were at least discussed.[80]

Madison had to make a quick decision. He could wait to make his presentation to the committee—of which he would be a member—and let the House resume its debate on the revenue bill. But Madison was holding the floor now, and this would be his best opportunity to make his case for amendments to the whole House, without the intermediation of a committee report. For the next several hours, he began the long process of persuading two-thirds of his colleagues that amendments should be approved and forwarded to the Senate.

As a result of the procedural debate that had just taken place, Madison had a better idea of what was ahead. The resistance to amendments— ranging from indifference and inertia to outright antagonism—would be formidable. Furthermore, the popular demand for amendments was not confined to the issue of personal liberty. The ratifying conventions of Virginia, New York, and other states had also demanded that Congress offer amendments to change key provisions of the Constitution to reduce the power of the federal government. If the First Congress added amendments dealing with individual rights but did not make significant alterations in the structure of the new government by returning power to the states, those still suspicious of the new Constitution might move ahead with plans for a second convention.

Supporters of the Constitution, Madison argued, needed to demonstrate that they were "as firm friends to liberty as those who had opposed it." Amendments could be approved without "effecting the essential principles of the Constitution." He recognized that many citizens were concerned about the potentially sweeping powers that Congress would have under the Constitution, and that a bill of rights "to quiet the minds of people . . . may be salutary."[81]

Before outlining the amendments, Madison offered a statement of deference to his colleagues: "I am sorry to be accessory to the loss of a single moment of time by the house." He said that if "congress will devote but one day to this subject, so far as to satisfy the public that we do not disregard their wishes, it will have a salutary influence . . . and prepare the way for a favorable reception of our future measures." Madison promised to confine his list of proposed amendments to those which are "intrinsically proper . . . or proper because [they] are wished for by a respectable number of my fellow citizens."[82]

As he introduced the amendments, Madison explained, as he had during the months leading up to the congressional election, that "I have never considered this provision [a bill of rights] so essential to the federal constitution, as to make it improper to ratify it." But now, he added, "I will candidly acknowledge that . . . the Constitution may be amended; that is to say, if all power is subject to abuse, that then it is possible the abuse of the powers of the general government may be guarded against in a more secure manner than is now done . . . We have in this way something to gain, and, if we proceed with caution, nothing to lose . . . The people of many states, have thought it necessary to raise barriers against power in all forms and departments of government, and I am inclined to believe, if once bills of rights are established in all the states as well as the federal constitution, we shall find that altho' some of them are rather unimportant, yet, upon the whole, they will have a salutary tendency."[83]

Although he recognized the need for amendments, he warned his colleagues about going too far: "It is necessary to proceed with caution; for while we all feel all these inducements to go into a revisal of the constitution, we must feel for the constitution itself, and make that revisal a moderate one."[84]

Madison then proposed a new preamble to the Constitution—one that emphasized natural rights—and nineteen amendments divided into nine articles. The preamble offered by Madison—which the members

of the House were not expecting, and which was adapted from the opening paragraph of the Virginia Declaration of Rights—affirmed the
nation's commitment to the principle that "all power is vested in, and
consequently derived from the people. That government is instituted,
and ought to be exercised for the benefit of the people; which consists in
the enjoyment of life and liberty, with the right of acquiring and using
property, and generally of pursuing and obtaining happiness and safety."[85]
Further, echoing the words of the Declaration of Independence, Madison's
preamble guaranteed that the "people have an indubitable, unalienable,
and indefeasible right to reform or change their government, whenever it
be found adverse or inadequate to the purposes of its institution."[86]

Madison's list of amendments included enlarging the size of the
House; protecting freedom of religion, speech, and the press and the
right to trial by jury in both civil and criminal cases; and prohibiting
arbitrary searches, excessive bail, and double jeopardy. Many of these
were drawn from the two hundred amendments recommended by Massachusetts, South Carolina, New Hampshire, Virginia, and New York,
which, when duplicates were eliminated, offered about seventy-five distinct amendments.[87]

Not surprisingly, Madison drew heavily on the amendments suggested by his state's ratifying convention and those listed in the Virginia
Declaration of Rights. He did not propose amendments that would alter
the structure of the Constitution; he believed that the amendments he
recommended would be the least objectionable and the most likely to be
approved by Congress and the states.

One of the arguments that Federalists had used in making the case
that a bill of rights was unnecessary was that protections for personal
liberty in state constitutions had not been repealed, and thus even after
the Constitution was ratified, citizens would continue to enjoy the rights
they previously had been granted. In referring to the rights granted under state constitutions, Madison noted that "it has been said, that a bill
of rights is not necessary," because the new Constitution has not "repealed those declarations of rights which are added to the several state
constitutions."[88]

What Federalists often failed to discuss was that many state constitutions and declarations of rights omitted protections that others would
consider fundamental. Therefore, when Madison looked for sources for
his list of rights, state constitutions were of limited value. Six states had
no bill of rights, and none had a comprehensive list of guarantees. Although each one secured the right to trial by jury in criminal cases and

protected religious liberty, five either permitted or provided for establishment of religion. Two states had no guarantee of a free press. Four did not
ban excessive fines or bail and did not prohibit self-incrimination or general search warrants. Five states did not include protection for rights of
assembly, petition, counsel, and trial by jury in civil cases. Seven did not
prohibit ex post facto laws, and nine failed to provide for grand jury
proceedings. Ten had no protection for freedom of speech, while eleven
had no prohibition on double jeopardy.[89]

Even the Virginia Declaration of Rights, long touted as a break-
through in the long struggle for human dignity, did not include several
of the rights that became part of the first ten amendments. While the
Declaration recognized the free exercise of religion and freedom of the
press, it did not mention freedom of speech, assembly, and petition; the
right to the writ of habeas corpus (a judicial order requiring authorities to
show that someone is being held for a legitimate reason); grand jury proceedings; the right to counsel; or freedom from double jeopardy. Federalists had argued that because individuals enjoyed natural rights that could
not be abridged by government—rights that were never surrendered—it
was not necessary to include all such protections.[90]

Madison's address demonstrated his knowledge of government, his
sense of what was needed to make the new constitutional system work,
and his commitment to republican principles. But it also showed that he
was not infallible, as he made one of the most serious misjudgments of
his career.

Madison recommended that the list of rights he presented on June 8
be incorporated into the body of the Constitution and not added at the
end. He believed that if amendments were added at the end, it would
not be clear which sections of the Constitution had been modified. In
his view, a supplemental list of amendments would not be treated as a
permanent part of the Constitution but would instead be a potentially
ignored appendix, leading to an endless debate over whether the amendments had actually altered the Constitution. He argued that because each
amendment would modify a specific section of the Constitution, the
new language should be inserted in the relevant section itself.

Today, far from being regarded as a mere footnote or afterthought
to the Constitution, the amendments that make up the Bill of Rights
hold a near sacred status in America—perhaps revered even more than
the original Constitution itself. Yet had Madison's suggestion to insert
amendments into the original text been adopted, the "Bill of Rights" as
we know it would not exist.

The long-term implications of his proposal were troublesome enough. In the short run, Madison's plan of interpolating the amendments would surely have made it more difficult to secure the approval of both houses of Congress. With the two-thirds requirement, there was little room for error. Many of Madison's colleagues in the House were firmly opposed to altering the document by adding amendments at all. They would certainly have found the idea of tampering with its original language even more disturbing. For all of Madison's political instincts, it remains one of the few, but also one of the most conspicuous, examples of how wrong he could be.

Roger Sherman, the congressman from Connecticut, insisted that the amendments not be inserted into the Constitution. Sherman, who had opposed amendments from the beginning, argued that if the original words were changed, the Constitution's legitimacy would be damaged. The document would no longer be the one George Washington and the other delegates signed in Philadelphia or the states had ratified at their conventions.

For much of the summer, as the House discussed the amendments, a majority continued to support Madison's proposal that amendments be inserted into the Constitution. Perhaps they did not realize the implications of such an arrangement, or possibly some of those opposed to Madison's plan believed that inserting the amendments would persuade more members of the House and Senate to oppose them all together.

The awkwardness of inserting the amendments into the text of the Constitution became evident with the very first attempt at drafting them. A passage from the House committee's report at the end of July on what would eventually become the first amendment proposed by Congress—on the size of the House of Representatives—showed how unappealing this method was: "Art. 1, Sec. 2, Par. 3—Strike out all between the words, "direct" and "and until such," and instead thereof insert, "After the first enumeration there shall be one representative . . ."[91] Several other proposed amendments did not simply insert new words into the body of the Constitution, they also deleted words already there. Sherman and several colleagues eventually convinced the House, with Madison's grudging acceptance, to place the amendments at the end of the Constitution.

Madison's failure to choose the best place for amendments notwithstanding, his speech of June 8 was thorough, impressive, and compelling, and it laid the groundwork for the eventual debate on the Bill of Rights. He admitted that "paper barriers" were sometimes too weak to protect individuals against a determined government, but he also believed that the rights included in his list of amendments would have a "tendency to impress some degree of respect for them, to establish the public opinion in their favor, and rouse the attention of the whole community." Madison added that highlighting these rights in the Constitution might serve to "controul the majority from those acts to which they might be otherwise inclined."[92]

Madison outlined the major advantages of enacting a bill of rights. He believed it would persuade Anti-Federalists finally to give up their opposition to the new government: "It will be a desirable thing to extinguish from the bosom of every member of the community any apprehensions, that there are those among his countrymen who wish to deprive them of the liberty for which they valiantly fought and honorably bled."[93] He was careful not to impugn the motives or integrity of those who still opposed the Constitution, but he believed that they would appreciate the "spirit of deference and concession" of those who controlled the government if a bill of rights was offered.

Madison also expected that Rhode Island and North Carolina, which were still holdouts from the union, would quickly agree to join the other states once a bill of rights emerged from Congress.[94] Most people understood that North Carolina in particular was determined to stay out until Congress had recommended a bill of rights.[95]

Madison considered one amendment to be especially important. He knew that state constitutions often failed to provide realistic protection for unpopular speech and religious practice. He had tried at the Philadelphia convention to include in the Constitution authority for the new Congress to "negative" all laws enacted by state legislatures that Congress considered contrary to the federal Constitution.[96] Such a "veto" power, in Madison's view, could be used to prevent states from interfering with the indispensable right of citizens to freely exchange information and criticize government, and to learn through the press what the government was doing, all of which were essential if the people had to replace unresponsive or oppressive public officials. His colleagues at the Philadelphia convention had rejected the proposal, which would have granted the Congress breathtaking powers and was stunningly impractical. The idea that Congress would have the time or ought to have the authority to review the laws enacted by every state legislature—and in the process exercise quasi-judicial authority, thus violating separation of powers—deserved the negative response it received.

Although his proposal was defeated in Philadelphia, Madison saw the chance to resurrect it on a smaller scale in the First Congress. The fifth article in his list of amendments read in part, "No state shall violate the equal rights of conscience, or the freedom of the press, or the trial by jury in criminal cases."[97] In other words, these fundamental rights would be protected not only against abuses by the national government but against abuses by state governments as well. Madison explained that because the Constitution already prohibited states from passing a bill of attainder (a criminal charge brought by a legislative body) or an ex post facto law (punishing an act that was not criminal at the time it was committed), it made sense to further extend the restrictions on states' powers. The states would thus be prohibited from interfering with rights that would eventually become part of the First Amendment and the right to a jury trial in criminal cases. Although his House colleagues eventually gave their support, the amendment was deleted by the Senate.

This had been one of the most important speeches in the nation's history. If Madison had any sense of the eventual importance of the bill of rights, he would have expected at least some approbation from his colleagues. He had put his heart and soul into this address, having worked so hard to get elected to the First Congress and then preparing for months for this moment. How disheartening it must have been for him that, after engaging the attention of his fellow House members for several hours, Madison had barely resumed his seat when one member after another denounced his proposals—primarily arguing that amendments were unnecessary, premature, and certainly less important than other legislative business.

He had heard many of the same comments earlier in the day, before introducing the amendments. Now, as those arguments were repeated, it was as if his colleagues had already decided not to consider the potential value of the amendments themselves. Representative Jackson of Georgia immediately stated that he was "against inserting a declaration of rights in the constitution . . . and if such an addition is not dangerous or improper, it is at least unnecessary." He asked why Madison would seek to protect freedom of the press: "[P]ray, how is this in danger? There is no power given to congress [in the Constitution] to regulate this subject as they can commerce, or peace, or war."[98]

Jackson was especially concerned about the message a prolonged debate about amendments would send to foreign nations, which would view with alarm additional delays in creating a stable government. He noted that such nations will "treat us with the contempt we have hitherto borne by reason of the imbecility of our government. Can we expect to enter into a commercial competition with any of them, while our system is incomplete? and how long it will remain in such a situation, if we enter upon amendments, God only knows. Our instability will make us objects of scorn."[99]

Jackson repeated his earlier point that it was too soon to propose amendments until more experience was gained with the nation's affairs, and because additional amendments would likely be recommended by the states or Congress, the Constitution would be deprived of the stability it needed: "This is not the time for bringing forward amendments; and, notwithstanding the honorable gentleman's ingenious arguments on that point, I am now more strongly persuaded it is wrong . . . The imperfections of the government are now unknown; let it have a fair trial . . . then we can tell where to apply the remedy."[100] He thought it might take a year for the House to deal thoroughly with the subject of amendments.[101]

Representative Samuel Livermore, a Federalist from New Hampshire, said he would consider amendments at a later time. He recommended that the Senate be consulted to see whether it was willing to discuss amendments, because if senators were unenthusiastic about the subject, it made no sense for the House to continue: "If they opposed the measure, all the house did would be a mere waste of time."[102]

The influential Roger Sherman spoke next. He was firmly against considering amendments because he did not see how they could, at this point, improve the Constitution. He argued that since the plan of government had been approved by most ratifying conventions without recommendations for amendments, it was viewed favorably by a majority of citizens. He also doubted whether states that had not offered amendments would vote to ratify them if proposed by Congress: "We shall not be able to propose any alterations that are likely to be adopted by nine states . . . Those states that have not recommended alterations will hardly adopt them, unless it is clear that they tend to make the constitution better."[103] Because the nation had so little experience with the Constitution, no one could know, Sherman argued, how to improve it. He urged his colleagues to find a way to "get rid of the subject," and he recommended against sending it to a special committee, presumably hoping that the committee of the whole would put an end to the discussion.

The previous December, Sherman—writing as a "Citizen of New Haven" in the *Connecticut Courant* in Hartford—argued that the Constitution, without amendments, would protect individual rights because the authority of the states was preserved. He wrote that "the immediate security of the civil and domestic rights of the people will be in the government of the particular states." Sherman added that the "powers vested in the federal government are particularly defined, so that each State still retains its sovereignty in what concerns its own internal government."[104]

Representative William Smith of South Carolina estimated that it would take "three weeks or a month" to resolve the subject of amendments. During that discussion, "every other business must be suspended, because we cannot proceed with accuracy or dispatch when the mind is perpetually shifted from one subject to another." Federalist John Vining of Delaware argued that a bill of rights was "unnecessary in a government deriving its powers from the people," especially in a document that begins "We the people do ordain and establish." If Congress were to take up amendments, Vining believed, it would be the equivalent of "suspending the operations of government, and may be productive of its ruin."[105]

As the afternoon wore on, it must have seemed to Madison that the House might not even take up amendments in its first session, much less approve any of them by a two-thirds vote. Yet if he was dismayed by the resistance of his Federalist colleagues, he might have taken heart that his effort attracted support from some who had earlier opposed the new government. Gerry of Massachusetts had objected so strongly to the proposed Constitution that he refused to sign it at the Philadelphia convention. Now he agreed with those who said it was "improper to take up the business [of amendments] at this time, when our attention is occupied by other important objects." Unlike some of his colleagues, however, he considered the matter to be of great urgency, and he proposed that amendments be the focus of the House's attention on July 1, a few weeks in the future. Gerry agreed with Madison that if the First Congress did not seem serious about considering amendments, more state legislatures would join the call of New York and Virginia for a second constitutional convention. Despite his earlier opposition, Gerry had pragmatically concluded that the current Constitution was as good as the new nation was likely to get: "I am not, sir, one of those blind admirers of this system, who think it all perfection; nor am I so blind as not to see its beauties. The truth is, it partakes of humanity; in it is blended virtue and vice, errors and excellence." If amendments were proposed by a second convention, "we run the risk of losing some of its best properties."[106]

Gerry had a long and distinguished record of public service. He was a member of the Continental Congress—where he signed the Declaration of Independence—and the Confederation Congress. His refusal to sign the Constitution had cost him a seat in the Massachusetts ratifying convention because his hometown of Cambridge solidly supported the plan, but he was invited to attend the convention so he could answer questions about the deliberations at the Philadelphia convention.[107] After his House service ended in 1793 and he served on a diplomatic mission to France for President Adams, Gerry became governor from 1810 to 1812. He and Madison eventually resolved enough of their differences for Gerry to serve as Madison's second vice president in 1813 and 1814, until his death.

Gerry's refusal to sign the Constitution had incurred the wrath of some important people in Massachusetts, including Abigail Adams, whose husband was presiding over the Senate as vice president. She wrote to Cotton Tufts, her uncle, a physician in Weymouth, Massachusetts, about Gerry after the First Congress had met for several months: "[W]hat can I say. you see him always in the minority, you see him very frequently wrong and the poor man looks gastly."[108]

When Gerry sought election to the House, he published a letter in a Boston newspaper. He said that "some have endeavoured to hold me up as an enemy of the Constitution, than which, nothing is more remote from the truth. Since the commencement of the Revolution, I have been ever solicitous for an efficient Federal Government, conceiving that without it, we must be a divided, an unhappy people." He explained that he supported amendments because they "will remove the just apprehensions of the people, and secure their confidence in, and affection for the new Government."[109]

Gerry believed that amendments protecting individual liberty would enhance the stability of the new government because they would remove much of the opposition to it and allay anxiety about its potential for abuse of power. He wanted the House as a whole to debate amendments, and he believed that sending them to a special committee would be an attempt to "amuse [our fellow citizens] with trifles." They would realize that Congress was not truly committed to proposing such amendments, in Gerry's view. He reminded his colleagues that ratification of the Constitution would never have taken place in several states had delegates to those conventions not been assured that Congress would consider amendments with the "candor and attention which their importance requires."[110]

Another Anti-Federalist who rallied to Madison's cause was Thomas Sumter of South Carolina. Sumter, who had opposed the Constitution at his ratifying convention, said, "I consider the subject of amendments of such great importance to the Union, that I should be glad to see it undertaken in any manner." He believed that referring the subject to a select committee would be "treating the applications of the state conventions rather slightly," and he preferred the full House consider the subject. Sumter worried about what would happen if amendments were not proposed: "I think it will give fresh cause for jealousy; it will rouse the alarm which is now suspended, and the people will become clamorous for amendments." At that point, Sumter added, people would no longer apply to Congress for amendments; they would "resort to the other alternative [a convention] pointed out in the constitution."[111]

Madison's colleague from Virginia, John Page, argued strenuously that if Congress did not act, the people and their legislatures would think seriously about petitioning for a second convention. "How dangerous such an expedient would be, I need not mention," he said, "but I venture to affirm, that unless you take early notice of this subject, you will not have the power to deliberate. The people will clamor for a new convention, they will not trust the house any longer."[112]

After the extended discussion on June 8, the House reversed its previous decision to assign the amendments to a select committee and agreed to consider them in a committee of the whole, but they postponed the debate until July 21. During those five weeks and beyond, the lively debate over Madison's proposals continued in letters among his colleagues, their friends, and constituents. If Madison had been shown some of the letters written in reaction to the June 8 address, he would have been even more pessimistic about the chances for amendments to make it through the legislature than he was based only on the debate.

Representative George Clymer of Philadelphia, who had attended the Constitutional Convention of 1787, used a derogatory allusion—one of several times it would be used during the discussion of amendments—when writing to a friend. In a letter he began before Madison's long address, Clymer wondered whether Madison was serious about proposing essential amendments, or if they were "merely a tub to the whale." The expression came from Jonathan Swift's 1704 story, "Tale of a Tub," and it referred to sailors who, when approached by a whale, would sometimes throw an empty tub into the water to distract and amuse the animal in the hope that it would not damage their ship.[113] Clymer wanted the House to be "strong enough to postpone" amendments. After Madison's speech, he finished the letter, clearly disappointed with the proposed amendments: "Madison's has proved a tub or a number of tubs." He dreaded a long discussion of the subject, noting derisively that Elbridge Gerry planned to "treat us with all the amendments of all the anitfederalists in America."[114]

In his correspondence, Representative Fisher Ames, who was a strong supporter of the Constitution, applauded Madison's research in summarizing the amendments proposed by state ratifying conventions, but he saw a selfish motive in his efforts. Ames wrote to a friend that "Upon the whole, it [the bill of rights] may do good towards quieting men who attend to sounds only, and may get the mover [Madison] some popularity—which he wishes." The next day, Ames wrote to another correspondent that Madison's amendments had little substance: "It [the bill of rights] will stimulate the stomach as little as hasty-pudding. It is rather food than physic. An immense mass of sweet and other herbs and roots for a diet drink."[115]

Ames had even more to say about Madison in a letter to a friend in Boston. He recognized Madison as "a man of sense, reading, address, and integrity . . . He speaks low, his person is little and ordinary. He speaks decently, as to manner, and no more. His language is very pure, perspicuous and to the point." But Ames believed that Madison was not well suited to politics: "Pardon me if I add that I think him a little too much of a book politician and too timid in his politics . . . [He] is afraid of their [Virginia's] state politics and of his popularity there more than I think he should be."[116]

Fisher Ames was a representative from Massachusetts in the First Congress. Although critical of the proposed amendments that became the Bill of Rights, he voted in favor of them. *(Library of Congress)*

Perhaps no letter would have been more upsetting to Madison than the one written by Representative Theodore Sedgwick, a Massachusetts Federalist and supporter of the Constitution. Just before the House was scheduled to debate the amendments on July 21, he wrote that Madison lacked the courage to see them through their difficult course: "Mr. Madison's talents, respectable as they are will for some time be lost to the public, from his timidity. His is constantly haunted with the gohst [ghost] of Patrick Henry. No man, in my opinion, in this country has more fair and honorable intentions, or more ardently wishes the prosperity of the public, but unfortunately he has not the strength of nerves which will enable him to set at defiance popular and factious clamors." Sedgwick called the work the House faced on the amendments a "water gruel business" and told his correspondent that "those substantial amendments which would have a tendency to produce a more compleat and natural arrangement of the national union we must despair of attaining at present."[117]

If Madison was not haunted by Henry, he certainly was aware that his adversary in Virginia was corresponding with Virginia's senators and other Anti-Federalists, encouraging them to hold out for substantive amendments that would alter the relationship between the states and the federal government. As early as March 31, a few days before Congress was supposed to convene, Henry told Senator William Grayson that he doubted Congress would consider amendments that would deny the new government the authority to tax citizens directly, or modify the treaty power of the Senate, or make other changes, noting that "whether apprehensions will extort concession to any salutary purpose I . . . cannot guess."[118] He was eager to have Grayson tell him what would likely happen on amendments when Congress met.

A few weeks after Madison announced on May 4 that he would introduce amendments, Senator Richard Henry Lee warned Henry that the debate over proposed changes to the Constitution was likely to be disappointing. He expected that "his [Madison's] ideas, and those of our convention [the Virginia ratifying convention], on this subject, are not similar." He promised Henry that he and Grayson would "carefully attend to this; and when the plan comes to the senate, we shall prepare to abridge, or enlarge, so as to effect, if possible, the wishes of our [Virginia's] legislature." Lee expressed the desire that amendments protecting personal liberty be approved, but "from what I hear and see . . . many of our amendments will not succeed." Lee also told Henry that at this point in their lives, "after all the turbulence we have passed through," making sure amendments securing "civil liberty" were approved by Congress "was, I assure you, the sole reason that could have influenced me to come here."[119]

Richard Henry Lee, an influential Anti-Federalist who strongly opposed the Constitution and became one of Virginia's first U.S. senators. *(National Archives)*

Shortly after Madison introduced the amendments to the House on June 8, Senator Grayson broke the bad news to Henry: "I am exceedingly sorry it is out of my power to hold out to you any flattering expectations on the score of amendments; it appears to me that both houses are almost wholly composed of federalists." Grayson criticized those who were willing to sacrifice the amendments that would reduce the power of the federal judiciary, change the taxation power, and make other needed alterations, in order to gain amendments affecting "personal liberty alone." Grayson told Henry that he had heard from some in the House that Madison was so "embarrassed" by the reaction of his colleagues to the introduction of amendments that he thought of withdrawing his motion, and that the House's willingness to discuss amendments was "owing more to personal respect [for Madison] than a love of the subject introduced."[120]

Grayson reported to Henry that he had wanted to introduce amendments favored by the Virginia General Assembly in the Senate while the House was still considering them, but his colleague, Senator Lee, "thinks it is best to wait till they come up from the representatives."[121] Both Lee and Grayson knew they were badly outnumbered in the Senate and that introducing radical amendments on the Senate floor before the House completed its work would not have helped their cause.

Henry was not impressed with Madison's amendments. He said they were intended only "to lull suspicion" and provide "guileful bait" to North Carolina and Rhode Island. Referring to Congress's decision that the president can remove executive branch officials who had been confirmed by the Senate, Henry noted, "See how rapidly power grows; how slowly the means of curbing it." He told Lee, "While impediments are cast in the way of those who wish to retrench the exorbitancy of power granted away by the constitution from the people, a fresh grant . . . is made in the first moments of opportunity."[122]

Madison would not have been surprised to hear that Henry was continuing to criticize the new government, but he was pleased to learn that his efforts to win amendments had begun to generate some support. As early as May 12, Madison's longtime friend Edward Carrington, writing from Virginia, told him that his announcement eight days earlier that the House would take up amendments had reduced the anxiety of those still opposed to the Constitution: "Our Antifederal districts [in Virginia] have become perfectly calm and generally shew a disposition to acquiesce in whatever fate of the proposed alterations [amendments], relying on their meeting with due consideration."[123]

William R. Davie of North Carolina told Madison that his announcement on May 4 that the House would take up amendments had, in his state, "dispersed almost universal pleasure[;] we hold it up as a refutation of the gloomy profecies of the leaders opposition, and the honest part of our Antifederalists have publickly expressed great satisfaction on this event." Davie noted that North Carolina was holding a ratifying convention in November, so it was "extremely important that the Amendments, if any, should be proposed before that time."[124]

The public was also learning more about Madison's proposals. Soon after his June 8 address, his amendments appeared in newspapers, such as the *New York Daily Advertiser* on June 12 and the *Gazette of the United States* on June 13.[125] That generated even more attention and inspired more of Madison's friends and supporters to contact him about the issue.

Tench Coxe, the influential Federalist from Philadelphia, told Madison he had carefully reviewed the amendments, and he was confident that both supporters and honest opponents would be pleased that they would "meliorate the government . . . by heightening and strengthening the barriers between necessary power and indispensable liberty." He believed that citizens would especially appreciate the amendments protecting freedom of the press and "liberty of conscience." He added that the "proposed amendments will greatly tend to promote harmony among the late contending parties and a general confidence in the patriotism of Congress." Coxe also published an anonymous article in the *Philadelphia Federal Gazette* on June 18 praising Madison's amendments.[126]

Even among Madison's friends, however, there was disagreement about how valuable the amendments would be. George Lee Turberville told Madison he was worried that even though the new government was the "result of the reason and deliberation of The People," if a "Despotic government" became oppressive, the "Constitution with all its amendments will be ineffectual to protect (us or) our posterity from the Evils which will inevitably await them."[127]

Madison must have been especially heartened by the effusive comments of longtime supporter Edward Stevens of Virginia. He told Madison that "It affords me no small pleasure to inform you, that your proposition of amendments to the Constitution, among all my acquaintances that I have had communication with, gives general Satisfaction, and I trust if adopted will shut the mouths of many."[128]

John Dawson, who still considered himself an admirer of Madison—although he had voted against ratification at the Virginia convention—told him that "I rejoice to find that you come forward at an early day with a proposition for amendments, altho I could have wish'd they had been more extensive."[129]

Dawson had hoped that more of the amendments recommended by Virginia dealing with such issues as the securing of the western territories and protecting access to the Mississippi River had been included. But Madison had taken care not to propose amendments that would be seen as catering to his home state or that would not command broad support. He knew that obtaining a supermajority in each house would be difficult, and he told several correspondents that he had recommended only the amendments he thought would generate the least controversy. He told Samuel Johnston that he wanted to remove the "fears of the discontented and . . . [avoid] all such alterations as would either displease the adverse side, or endanger the success of the measure." He made the same argument in a letter at the end of June to Thomas Jefferson, telling him that "every thing . . . that might endanger the concurrence of two-thirds of each House and three-fourths of the States was studiously avoided."[130]

Most of his supporters realized the fine line Madison was attempting to walk. Joseph Jones told him that the amendments were "calculated to secure the personal rights of the people so far as declarations on paper can effect the purpose, leaving unimpaired the great Powers of the government." Jones understood that Congress was more likely to approve such amendments than those that would reduce the power of the new government.[131]

On the last day of June, Madison heard an encouraging report from Virginia. Former governor Edmund Randolph told him that the proposed amendments "are much approved by the strong federalists here [Williamsburg] and at the Metropolis [Richmond]; being considered as an anodyne to the discontented." Randolph admitted, though, that "not even the abolishment of direct taxation would satisfy those, who are most clamorous."[132]

Madison would have about six weeks to prepare for the next round. As he headed back to his boardinghouse, he must have worried that not enough of his colleagues in Congress would agree to propose amendments and keep the promise that had been made to the American people. Madison had confronted unpromising situations before, from the Constitutional Convention to the election in Virginia that brought him to Congress, and his intellect and energy had prevailed. But now he was facing the challenge of securing a two-thirds vote in each House, as required by the Constitution that he helped write two years before. He could hardly have imagined then that he would be in this kind of situation.

~ 9 ~

Congress Proposes the Bill of Rights

THE CONGRESSIONAL SESSION was taking its toll on Madison. The long debates in the House chamber, followed by evenings spent writing letters to friends and political figures throughout the country, were exhausting him. He told his father in the first week of July that "the business goes on still very slowly," and "We are in a wilderness without a single footstep to guide us." Recognizing that so much of what the First Congress was doing would set a precedent, Madison wrote that "it is . . . necessary to explore the way with great labour and caution. Those who may follow will have an easier task."[1]

He asked about his mother's health and said he would like to hear more often from family members. He regretted having little time to write because of the "extensive correspondence" he had to undertake as part of his work. He said that the subject of amendments would be discussed soon, and that he hoped the result would satisfy "moderate opponents." But he said he had no way of predicting what would happen.

On July 21, six weeks after Madison had introduced the amendments, the time for discussing them had arrived. Madison "begged" his colleagues to "indulge him in the further consideration of amendments," and he recommended, as he had before, that the House debate them as a committee of the whole.[2] What followed may have been frustrating for Madison. Instead of focusing on the amendments themselves, House members again argued for hours—just as they had on June 8—over whether his amendments should be considered by the whole House or sent to a select committee.

Madison evidently believed that if he had the chance to explain the amendments to the House himself—and was not limited by a committee report—he could convince two-thirds of his colleagues to support them. A committee, as opposed to the full House, would meet behind closed doors with only a handful of House members, some of whom might be opposed to amendments, and citizens would be unable to witness the discussion as to which amendments to send to the House floor and which to eliminate or combine. Despite the importance of amendments and the limitations of a committee review, several prominent members lined up against Madison, some for practical reasons and others for political ones.

Fisher Ames disagreed with Madison's contention that the amendments should be considered by the whole House. He argued that it had too many other things to do to focus its attention on amendments. Sending the amendments to a committee would "certainly tend to facilitate the business," he said. "If they had the subject [of amendments] at large before a committee of the whole," it would be impossible to see "where the business was likely to end."[3]

Others said that sending them to a committee was not going to save time because any member would be free to introduce amendments on the House floor. Ames himself warned that if the amendments proposed by Massachusetts, his home state, were not thoroughly considered by the committee, he would insist they be discussed by the whole House upon receiving the committee report. Alexander White of Virginia said no time would be saved by appointing a committee because no matter what amendments were offered, "every member would like to be satisfied with the reasons upon which the amendments by the select committee are grounded."[4]

As he had in June when amendments were first discussed, Roger Sherman argued that Article V of the Constitution, which he had a hand in creating as a member of the Constitutional Convention, was "intended to facilitate the adoption of those [amendments] which experience should point out to be necessary." Because the Constitution was ratified by eleven states—and only five had offered amendments—it was unlikely that three-fourths would approve amendments "offered on mere speculative points, when the constitution has had no kind of trial whatever."[5]

Sherman was one of the most highly respected members of the House. He could be temperamental, and he was not considered very

friendly. But like Madison, he had been an energetic member of the Philadelphia convention, and his House colleagues recognized his keen intellect and speaking skills. During the weeks since Madison first proposed
amendments, Sherman had not changed his mind that Congress should
wait until experience with the Constitution had shown its defects. Representative James Jackson of Georgia, as he had in June, said amendments were a "waste of time," but if the House insisted on debating them,
they should be referred to a special committee.[6]

Elbridge Gerry supported Madison's recommendation. He worried that the five states that had submitted amendments for Congress
to consider—Massachusetts, South Carolina, New Hampshire, Virginia,
and New York—would be insulted if their recommendations were referred to and then rejected by a committee, and thus less likely to be
considered on the House floor. He told his colleagues that such a procedure "will give no small occasion for disgust, which is a circumstance
that this government ought carefully to avoid." He noted that the members of the Massachusetts delegation had been instructed to "press the
amendments recommended by the [Massachusetts ratifying] convention . . . at all times, until they had been maturely considered by congress."
Representatives from the other states that had offered amendments, Gerry
observed, had a similar obligation. He urged his colleagues to resist "any
attempt to smother the business, or prevent a full investigation."[7]

South Carolina's Thomas Tudor Tucker seconded the views of those
who had insisted that a matter as important as amendments not be referred to a committee. If the committee report did not include recommendations based on amendments offered by various states, they would
be dissatisfied. States expected, Tucker said, that their amendments "shall
be fully brought before the house . . . [I]f indeed then they are rejected, it
may be some satisfaction to them, to know that their applications have
been treated with respect."[8]

Fisher Ames, Gerry's colleague from Massachusetts, was concerned
about more than how long the amendments would take to consider. He
was among several Federalists who believed it was risky for the House to
discuss amendments in front of galleries packed with citizens who would
witness a painful examination of the Constitution's defects. In colorful
language, Ames warned that a public discussion "would be like a dissec-
tion of the constitution; it would be defacing its symmetry, laying bare
its sinews and tendons, ripping up the whole form and tearing out its
vitals." Continuing with the analogy, Ames said that while the House
debated amendments, the "government [would be] . . . laid prostrate,

and every artery ceased to beat." He speculated that the congressional session would not be long enough to fully debate amendments.[9]

Gerry could see where the discussion was headed, and he rose again to take issue with Ames about debating amendments in front of the public. Gerry warned that if the House appointed a committee and gave it "the whole legislative power" over amendments, citizens would be dissatisfied that so important a subject was discussed behind closed doors. He asked his colleagues, "Are gentlemen afraid to meet the public ear on this topic? Do they wish to shut the gallery doors? Perhaps nothing would be attended with more dangerous consequences—No, sir, let us not be afraid of full and public investigation; let our means, like our conclusions, be justified; let our constituents see, hear, and judge for themselves."[10]

The House moved to a vote and, by a margin of 34 to 15, approved a motion for sending the amendments to a select committee. Although the votes of the individual members were not recorded, it is likely that Madison and Gerry voted with the minority.

Representative Peter Muhlenberg of Pennsylvania said after the vote that he was glad amendments would be considered by a committee because he also worried about a debate in front of the public. He told Benjamin Rush of Philadelphia that the whole day had been "taken up in debating, whether . . . [amendments] should be refer'd to a Committee of The whole House, or a select committee. I was not sorry to find the latter Prevail, as I conceive no one good purpose can be answered by discussing this subject before Crouded Galleries."[11]

The committee would have eleven members, one from each state. It would meet immediately and report to the full House in a week. Madison was to be Virginia's representative, but he would have to contend with a majority that was opposed to amendments. The only other prominent member of the committee was Roger Sherman. Although he had openly opposed amendments, he would play an important role in shaping the committee's report and the ensuing debate on the House floor. His most significant contribution would be in convincing the House—and a reluctant Madison—to accept the placement of amendments at the end of the Constitution. Other committee members included John Vining of Delaware, its chairman; George Clymer of Pennsylvania; Elias Boudinot of New Jersey; and Aedanus Burke of South Carolina.[12]

A week later, the committee report was delivered by Vining. The committee did not keep a record of its work, but Madison, who was sensitive about criticism, must have found the deliberations to be difficult. The committee accepted most of Madison's recommendations—

including his request that amendments be inserted into the body of the Constitution—but it made several significant changes to his proposed amendments. After Vining presented the report, the House voted to let it "lie on the table" until further action.[13]

The committee changed some of Madison's prose, rearranged the order of the amendments, and considerably narrowed the guarantees of religious freedom and equal rights of conscience.[14] The committee also eliminated most of Madison's natural-rights preamble, cutting out the assertion that the people have the right to reform or change their government when it becomes antagonistic of their wishes or inadequate in its ability to represent them, but leaving a statement about "government being intended for the benefit of the people, and the rightful establishment thereof being derived from their authority alone."[15] Sherman had proposed in the committee that freedom of speech and press be confined to words that are decent, but the committee rejected his suggestion.[16]

The committee replaced some of Madison's words with phrases that would eventually be incorporated into the Bill of Rights. It used "freedom of speech, and of the press," language that would become part of the First Amendment; changed the words of the "just compensation" clause of the Fifth Amendment; wrote most of what would become the Ninth Amendment, which stated that the people retain rights not enumerated in the Constitution; and approved the principles that would form the Seventh Amendment, providing for jury trials in civil suits.[17] The committee accepted Madison's recommendation—which he considered the most important amendment—that states and not just the federal government be prohibited from infringing the rights of "conscience," freedom of speech and the press, and trial by jury in criminal cases.[18]

A few days after the committee delivered its report to the full House, Madison told his friend Wilson Cary Nicholas that some of the changes the committee had made "are perhaps for the better, others for the worse." Madison felt somewhat confident that the House would approve the proposed amendments, but he noted that he could not predict their fate in the Senate.[19]

On August 3, Madison asked that the House consider the committee's report nine days later.[20] When August 12 arrived, the House was busy with other issues, and the debate over amendments was postponed until the following day.

Beginning on August 13, and continuing for eleven days, the members of the House, sitting as a committee of the whole, devoted almost all of their attention to the proposed amendments. It was an extraordinary debate in which all of the main arguments for or against a bill of rights were aired. Some members continued to insist that amendments were premature, unnecessary, and potentially dangerous, while others argued about the language of each of the proposed changes. Madison understandably played a leading role in this debate, since he had set the agenda by offering the initial list of amendments. It was all he could do to keep some of the most impatient and hostile members of the House from derailing the entire discussion and postponing all consideration of amendments.

Just as it had earlier in the summer, the House first debated whether to even consider amendments. Some members continued to insist that amendments should not be discussed at that point because the House had more important business. But Madison said that the matter had been "deferred some time," and that it "ought to have been one of the first objects of the legislature." If amendments were not approved, Madison said, the "people would be disappointed and alarmed." John Page, Madison's colleague from Virginia, said the people would not support the government "unless their anxiety was removed." He asked, "Is not the confidence of the people absolutely necessary to support it?"[21]

But others insisted that the business before the House be completed first, including the system for raising money for the federal government. William Loughton Smith of South Carolina worried that the House would take weeks to discuss amendments. Meanwhile, he observed, the "judicial [system] is uncreated[;] . . . not a single part of the revenue system can operate; no breach of your laws can be punished; illicit trade cannot be prevented; greater harm will arise from delaying the . . . judicial system, than can possibly grow from the delay of [amendments]."[22] Despite these arguments, the House agreed to consider Madison's amendments as a committee of the whole.

Sherman, who still opposed adding amendments, again pleaded with the House to move them, if they must be added, to the end of the Constitution. He advised his colleagues that "this house had no right" to alter what had been approved by the people, and that "any alterations of the individual articles of the constitution was a repeal of the constitution." He added that the "original form of the constitution ought to remain inviolate and all amendments which the Congress were authorised to make were only legislative acts which ought to be detached from the constitution and be supplementary to it."[23]

Several members of the House agreed with Sherman, asserting that the original Constitution should not be altered. Representative Jackson worried that as amendments were added, the Constitution would become "complex and obscure" and would "consist of a long train of laws which might fill a volume." "The people," Jackson argued, "would not know where to find it."[24]

Madison energetically disagreed. He believed that by incorporating the amendments into appropriate places in the Constitution, the system would be "uniform and entire—nor is this an uncommon thing to be done." And he argued that if "these amendments are added to the Constitution by way of supplement, it will embarrass the people—It will be difficult for them to determine to what parts of the system they particularly refer—and at any rate will create unfavorable comparisons between the two parts of the instrument."[25]

Ironically, Madison was arguing for the insertion of amendments when his own state's Declaration of Rights was a separate document adopted by the Virginia constitutional convention of 1776. New Jersey's constitution of 1776 did not include a separate bill of rights but instead contained such protections in the body of the constitution. In total, eight of the twelve states that created new constitutions during the founding period adopted separate lists of amendments, while the remaining four incorporated those rights into the body of their constitutions.[26]

By August 24, Madison could see that he was losing the battle over placement of the amendments. He wrote that day to his colleague and fellow Virginian Alexander White that he had no choice but to agree to listing the amendments at the end because of pressure from "a *few* who knew their concurrence to be necessary"—probably a reference to Sherman and others.[27] Madison worried that this would lead to "some ambiguities" because it would be unclear "how far the original text is or is not necessarily superceded, by the supplemental act." He may have complained in private correspondence about being pressured this way, but on the House floor, Madison suggested that he was not fully committed to inserting the amendments: "I am not however very solicitous about the mode, so long as the business is fully attended to."[28]

Madison was not the only one who thought placement of the amendments within the Constitution was better. William Loughton Smith of South Carolina found support for this position in Article V. Quoting from that article, Smith said that amendments would become "part of the Constitution," and therefore, it was the design of the framers that amendments should be incorporated.[29]

Elbridge Gerry grew impatient as the debate continued for hours. He considered the argument over where to place the amendments to be "trifling about matters of little consequence." He said the Constitution did not say its "present form shall be preserved," and thus amendments should be incorporated into the text. Michael Stone of Maryland had an answer to that: "Was [Gerry intending] to have the constitution republished, and the alterations inserted in their proper place?" Egbert Benson of New York did not think that would be difficult, arguing that "congress may order a number of copies to be printed, into which the alterations will be inserted, and the work stand perfect and entire."[30]

Jackson of Georgia echoed the concerns of many when he said that inserting the amendments into the Constitution would be like repealing the present one and "adopting an improved one." If Congress had that power, he said, "we may go on from year to year, making new ones; and in this way we shall render the basis of the superstructure the most fluctuating thing imaginable, and the people will never know what the constitution is." The arguments against inserting the amendments failed to convince enough members, and the Sherman motion was defeated.[31]

Someone also raised the issue of whether the committee of the whole had to recommend amendments to the full House by a two-thirds vote. The chairman, Elias Boudinot of New Jersey, ruled that a simple majority was sufficient, and his decision was upheld by a vote of the members.[32]

Several members wondered whether the debate would be limited to the amendments included in the committee's report. Tucker of South Carolina asked for permission to offer the amendments proposed by his state. He said he was instructed to do so and felt obligated to carry out that instruction.[33] No one objected.

With the issue of where to place the amendments settled for the time being, the House began on August 14 to discuss the amendments themselves. It was a day that Madison had been waiting for with increasing anxiety. He had convinced his colleagues to set aside their resistance to considering amendments at all—which was no small accomplishment—but that did not mean the House would approve Madison's amendments or those offered by the committee.

The House first considered Madison's preamble. The committee recommended that the words "Government being intended for the benefit of the people and the rightful establishment thereof being derived from their authority alone" precede "We the people" in the original Constitution.[34] The ensuing debate revealed an intense disagreement over whether an addition to the preamble was even necessary.

Gerry focused on Madison's initial phrase, "Government being intended," and objected to any "maxim" being included in the Constitution. He noted that in ancient and modern times, governments were not always created based on the authority of the people, and thus Madison's preamble was misleading: "I don't believe that one out of fifty is intended for any such purpose."[35] Gerry offered a motion to insert the words "of right" in the proposed preamble, arguing that the addition of that phrase would show that the new government derived its power from the people. His motion was defeated.[36]

The debate over the preamble then continued. Roger Sherman was unconvinced that it needed to be changed. He said that if the "constitution had been a grant from another power," it would make sense to include in it a reference to the people's authority. But since the constitution emanated from the people's "sovereign will," it was unnecessary to explain its source. Besides, noted Sherman, the proposed alteration "would injure the beauty of the preamble."[37] Madison urged his colleagues to accept the revision recommended by the select committee, which they did by a vote of 27 to 23, though it would not survive the debate in the Senate.[38]

The House then turned to two amendments that would eventually be approved by Congress but would not be ratified by a sufficient number of states. The original first amendment would have increased the size of the U.S. House based on the argument that a larger body would better understand and represent the interests of a diverse population spread over a large geographical area. The debate on that amendment lasted for hours.

In the elections to the First Congress, five states—Pennsylvania, New Hampshire, Connecticut, Delaware, and New Jersey—chose members in statewide elections. Maryland and Georgia adopted a mixed system, in which candidates were nominated by districts but stood for election statewide. Five other states—South Carolina, Massachusetts, North Carolina, Virginia, and New York—elected members by district.[39] Those districts varied in size from James Jackson's in Georgia, with 16,250 residents, to John Baptista Ashe's in North Carolina, with 108,500.[40]

Federalists had generally favored at-large elections, and Anti-Federalists preferred districts, where they believed they would have a better chance of electing those who would work for radical changes to the Constitution. Federalists expected that those who were known widely would have an advantage in a statewide election. If a representative came from a smaller district, he would likely know more about the lives of his constituents. But a member of the House chosen from a large population might be better able to support policies that would benefit the nation as a whole and not just the interests of the local constituents.[41]

Some members, such as Fisher Ames, argued against enlarging the House. He noted that the people had accepted the size of the current

House—fifty-nine members—and "were reconciled to it, and were convinced that a more faithful and more prompt discharge of the business of the Union would take place in so small an assembly." In Ames's view, if each House member represented thirty thousand residents—as proposed by the amendment—the "increase would . . . swell the representation to an enormous mass, whose support [expense] would be insufferable, and whose deliberations would be rendered almost impracticable." Ames also worried that if the size of the House was increased, the government would "depart from that choice of characters who could best represent the wisdom and the interest of the United States . . . and support the importance and dignity of this branch of the legislature— Men would be introduced, more liable to improper influence, and more easy tools for designing leaders."[42] Madison's friend and supporter Edward Carrington, writing from Richmond, also had concerns about the size of the House, telling Madison that "I would prefer a small representation." He said that if the Virginia General Assembly had been smaller, "we should not have been so frequently disgraced by wicked and puerile Acts, nor would our sessions have been so long as we have generally seen them."[43]

Madison said that several states had recommended enlarging the size of the House until it had two hundred members.[44] He recognized that beyond a certain number, the House could not properly function. But such concerns were speculative, Madison argued, and he urged his colleagues to approve the amendment and to do so at the level proposed by the states—one representative for every thirty thousand citizens. Even as Madison endorsed the amendment, he worried that smaller states would oppose it because they would have fewer representatives relative to the entire House. If they thought large states were insensitive to their concerns, they might be suspicious of other amendments, Madison feared.[45] The House approved the committee's recommendation by a margin of 27 to 22.[46]

Today, there are 435 members of the House, a number that has not changed since 1911. Based on the 2000 U.S. Census, the average congressional district has 646,952 residents.

After the debate over the size of the House, its members took up the sensitive subject of compensation. The committee report included Madison's amendment that no pay increase for representatives would go into effect until after a general election, at which time citizens could express their views on the propriety of such a pay increase by voting for or against a House member running for reelection.[47] Members of the House, reflecting the view held by many that government officials should not personally profit from their public service, were worried about how it would look if they set their own salary.

Theodore Sedgwick of Pennsylvania saw the opposite problem. He thought that a future Congress might set its pay so low—in order to "procure popularity at home"—that only those of wealth would be able to serve, and thus "men of shining and disinterested abilities" would not be able to undertake congressional service.[48]

Madison was ambivalent about the amendment. He thought that "representation would be as well secured under this clause as it would be if it was omitted," but because it was "desired by a great number of the people of America," it should be approved, and the House agreed 27 to 20.[49]

The debate continued the next day, Saturday, August 15. What was left of the preamble, and the amendments related to the size of the House and the compensation of its members, had already been approved by the committee of the whole. The House now directed its attention to the amendments on the volatile issues of freedom and establishment of religion, and freedom of speech and press.

It was probably sweltering inside the House chamber. The temperature outside reached eighty-five degrees with no clouds to block the sun.[50] Despite the uncomfortable conditions and the fatigue that would naturally come after six days in a row of intense debate, the House energetically discussed what would become the rights protected by the First Amendment.

The select committee had recommended that the Constitution be amended to include this language: "No religion shall be established by law, nor shall the equal rights of conscience be infringed." The next amendment offered by the committee stated that "freedom of speech, and of the press, and the right of the people peaceably to assemble and consult for their common good, and to apply to the government for redress of grievances, shall not be infringed."[51]

The amendments, which would eventually be combined into one by the Senate, went through various stages as members of the House offered language they believed would best protect such precious rights. Samuel Livermore of New Hampshire immediately offered to make the right of religious freedom more forceful and direct: "The Congress shall make no laws touching religion or the rights of conscience," which the House accepted. Roger Sherman thought the amendment was unnecessary because "Congress has no power to make any religious establishments."[52]

Madison considered the amendment related to religious freedom to be among the most important. He had devoted much of his public life to fighting against religious establishments and for the free exercise of conscience. While accepting Livermore's changes, Madison said the amendment before the House meant that "congress should not establish a religion, and enforce the legal observation of it by law, nor compel men to worship God in any manner contrary to their conscience." He recognized that some delegates at state ratifying conventions thought that the "necessary and proper" clause gave Congress power to legislate in this area, and he maintained that the proposed amendment would dispel that fear.[53] Some members continued to express concern over how the words suggested by Livermore could be interpreted, but the House eventually approved the substituted language 31 to 20.

The debate over freedom of speech had barely started when Thomas Tucker of South Carolina recommended a change that resulted in a lengthy and sometimes heated discussion. He said the amendment should be changed to include the right of citizens to "instruct their representatives." This had been debated for many years.[54] The prevailing view was that representatives should be free to make decisions that were in the long-term interest of the nation, even if those decisions were not immediately popular. Several of Tucker's colleagues noted that there were times when the people did not act reasonably and did not know what was in their best interest. Thomas Hartley of Pennsylvania disagreed with Tucker, arguing that representatives should be able to resist the will of the people when necessary, and that the "power of instructing might be liable to great abuses; it would generally be exercised in times of public disturbance, and would express rather the prejudices of faction, than the voice of policy."[55]

George Clymer, Hartley's Pennsylvania colleague, was more emphatic. He said the Tucker motion "was a dangerous one" and "would take away all the freedom and independence of the representatives, it would destroy the very spirit of representation itself, by rendering Congress a passive machine instead of a deliberative body." Roger Sherman also spoke against the amendment. Smith of South Carolina worried that those states located closer to the nation's capital would have an advantage with access to their public officials that would be unfair to other states "more remote from it."[56]

After Gerry of Massachusetts endorsed the Tucker motion, arguing that "sovereignty resided in the people," Madison rose to warn his colleagues that passing amendments and getting them ratified by the states was going to be difficult enough as it was. If changes "of a doubtful nature," such as the Tucker amendment, were endorsed by the House, it would "have a tendency to prejudice the whole system of amendments, and render their adoption difficult." Madison believed that the people already had the right to express their views to their representatives as guaranteed by the pending amendments on freedom of speech and the press. A formal declaration of that was unnecessary and could create problems. He cited the example of representatives being instructed to take action that was contrary to the Constitution.[57]

Madison also expressed the view that when the people "created" and approved the Constitution, they did so as citizens of the United States and not as residents of a state or district. Therefore, in Madison's view, giving the people the authority to bind their representatives increased the likelihood—as he had warned in *Federalist 10*—that groups would dominate the process because they were organized and committed to a cause. Madison lectured Gerry about this in the middle of the discussion over the Tucker amendment: "My idea of the sovereignty of the people is, that the people can change the constitution if they please, but while the constitution exists, they must conform themselves to its dictates: But I do not believe that the inhabitants of any district can speak the voice of the people, so far from it, their ideas may contradict the sense of the whole people." He added that compelling representatives to vote a certain way is "of a doubtful, if not of a dangerous nature."[58]

The debate on what would become the First Amendment continued. Sedgwick of Massachusetts thought the words "assemble and" in the proposed amendment unnecessary because assembly was "a self-evident unalienable right of the people," and it was "below the dignity of the house, to insert such things into the constitution." He said that if the people have the right to "converse," they must "meet *for* the purpose."[59]

Elbridge Gerry became increasingly irritated as he listened to Madison and the others. He understood how important this debate was, and he resented the suggestion that only those amendments offered by the select committee should be considered by the committee of the whole. During the discussion on instructing representatives, Gerry observed that although his colleagues "seem in a great hurry to get this business through, I think . . . it requires further discussion; for my part I had rather do less business and do it well, than precipitate measures before they are fully understood." He rebuked Madison for suggesting that some amendments should not be debated because they were considered to be of a doubtful nature. "It is natural," Gerry told him, "for us to be fond of our own work. We do not like to see it disfigured by other hands."[60]

Gerry supported the Tucker amendment on instructing representatives and said he wanted all the amendments proposed by the states to be considered. If the people told their legislators to support bills that violate the Constitution, Gerry advised his colleagues, their representatives were free to ignore that directive. But, Gerry insisted, since sovereignty rests with the people—"as the honorable gentleman [Madison] acknowledges"—the people should have a "convenient mode in which they may convey their sense to their agents." If the people, Gerry continued, "have no right to control it [their government], it appears they have divested themselves of the sovereignty over the constitution."[61]

The chairman of the select committee, John Vining of Delaware, defended the committee's decision not to report all the amendments recommended by the states. Some of them, Vining noted, were "superfluous or dangerous," and many were "so contradictory that it was impossible to make any thing of them, and this is a circumstance the gentleman [Gerry] cannot pretend ignorance of."[62]

As the debate over whether the Constitution should provide an explicit statement about instructing representatives continued for several hours—with members who rarely spoke on the House floor weighing in passionately on one side or the other—Madison had finally heard enough. He must have been furious when Thomas Sumter of South Carolina—who had voted against ratification at his state convention—said that because the discussion over amendments was so important and so complicated, it should not be rushed. "It cannot be denied," Sumter argued, that the "present constitution is imperfect[;] we must therefore take time to improve it." He recommended that we "drop the subject of amendments, and leave it until we have more leisure to consider and do the business effectually."[63]

Then Sumter's South Carolina colleague Aedanus Burke—who had also opposed the Constitution at the state convention—insulted Madison's work by characterizing the amendments as "not those solid and substantial amendments which the people expect," and he described them as "little better than whip-syllabub, frothy and full of wind, formed only to please the palate, or they are like a tub thrown out to a whale, to secure the freight of the ship and its peaceable voyage." Burke did not stop with a criticism of the amendments. He said that since several members of the select committee (including Madison) had been delegates to the Constitutional Convention, and "such gentlemen having already given their opinion with respect to the perfection of the work, [they] may be thought improper agents to bring forward amendments."[64] Madison rejected the accusation that he was "not acting with candor," and he appealed to his colleagues to recognize that the people wanted "some security . . . for those great and essential rights which they had been taught to believe were in danger." And, he said, "have not the people been told that the rights of conscience, the freedom of speech, the liberty of the press, and trial by jury, were in jeopardy; that they ought not to adopt the constitution until those important rights were secured to them?" Madison again urged his colleagues not to consider amendments that would change the "principles of government" or that were "of a doubtful nature," because they had little chance of passing.[65]

Madison must have been greatly relieved when the House rejected the Tucker amendment by a vote of 41 to 10, refused to consider Sumter's motion to postpone discussion of amendments, and accepted the amendment prohibiting establishment of religion and protection for religious freedom. Still, several of his colleagues persisted. Fisher Ames moved to set aside discussion of amendments because the committee of the whole did not recommend them by the two-thirds required for eventual passage, and he noted with frustration that a "great deal of time was consumed in unnecessary debate." Sedgwick seconded the motion, saying that "there was little probability of getting through with the business."[66]

But they were too late. Because the House had already spent so much time discussing amendments, the momentum for finishing was clearly established. In the face of objections from several members of the House, Ames withdrew his motion, and the House adjourned after the long day of debate. The first few amendments of what would become the Bill of Rights had survived, despite the efforts of those who demanded more radical amendments and those who believed the Constitution should not be changed until experience had shown its shortcomings.[67]

During the next few days—until August 18—the committee of the whole House debated the remaining amendments. One amendment after another—dealing with the right to bear arms; the quartering of soldiers in any house during a time of peace; the double jeopardy clause; protection against self-incrimination or deprivation of life, liberty, or property without due process of law; the taking of property without just compensation; and the right to trial by jury in civil suits—was discussed at length. The House considered but rejected a motion that those with religious objections not be forced to bear arms. Several members argued that such language would be difficult to administer fairly, and after several attempts to modify the proposed language, the amendment failed 24 to 22.[68]

During the afternoon of August 17, the House took up the fifth proposition recommended by the committee, which Madison considered the "most valuable amendment on the whole list." It said that "no state shall infringe the equal rights of conscience, nor the freedom of speech, or of the press, nor of the right of trial by jury in criminal cases."[69] Madison, who wrote this language, had long believed that because states were not only able but often inclined to interfere with these fundamental rights, which are so essential to the functioning of a republic, they should be explicitly protected in the federal constitution. This was the only one of the proposed amendments that directly limited the authority of the states.

Some members argued that the federal government did not have the right to tell states what protections they must afford their citizens. Such a discussion struck a nerve with those members who believed that the Constitution had greatly diminished the authority of the states, and that the people would oppose any further intrusion into state affairs. Thomas Tucker of South Carolina put it succinctly: "It will be much better . . . to leave the state governments to themselves, and not to interfere with them more than we already do, and that is thought by many to be rather too much." Madison answered that if these essential rights were to be protected from the federal government, "it was equally necessary that they should be secured against the state governments."[70]

Sometime during the debate on August 17, Madison was probably given a copy of the *New York Daily Advertiser.* Noah Webster—the teacher and publisher of grammar textbooks, who had written essays supporting ratification—had published a stinging condemnation of Madison's efforts to push through amendments. The public letter, which was addressed to Madison and referred to him repeatedly, must have alarmed the congressman from Virginia, for if it represented the views of very many people, the prospects for approval of amendments were not good.

Using the pseudonym "Pacificus," Webster, who lived in New York, reminded Madison that when debating the impost bill, Madison had said that legislators should look beyond local interests, and that he,

Noah Webster, the educator and author, opposed the Bill of Rights. While the First Congress was debating the amendments, he published a commentary critical of James Madison in a New York newspaper. (*National Archives*)

according to Webster, "considered yourself not merely the representative of *Virginia,* but of the *United States.*" Now, Webster charged, Madison justified his sponsorship of amendments partly on the basis that he had "pledged yourself in some measure to your *constituents.*" But then, asked Webster, "who are your *constituents?* Are they the electors of a small district in Virginia?" No, answered Webster, because once Madison became a member of the House, his obligation was to the entire nation.[71] He said that Madison "had no right to declare that you would act upon the sentiments and wishes of your immediate constituents, unless . . . the measures you advocate coincide with the wishes and interests of the whole Union." Webster argued forcefully that amendments were not in the interests of the nation at a time when "an excellent government is going into operation." He rejected Madison's argument that they would satisfy the opposition and give stability to the government: "Paper declarations of rights are trifling things and no real security to liberty. In general they are a subject of ridicule." Webster expressed his admiration for Madison but regretted that "his talents should be employed to bring forward amendments, which, at best can have little effect upon the merits of the constitution."[72]

Madison must have been embarrassed by the Pacificus essay. It did not simply criticize the amendments; Webster had also accused Madison of failing to understand the proper role of a representative of the people. To someone who had given so much time and thought to the relationship between citizens and their government, such a public rebuke was surely agonizing.

Madison's spirits were probably not brightened the next day—the last on which the committee of the whole considered amendments—when Elbridge Gerry offered a motion requiring the consideration of all amendments recommended by the states that were not included in the select committee report. The Gerry amendment might well have ended consideration of the bill of rights, because such a discussion had the potential to go on for weeks, if not months, and a majority of members would probably have postponed debate until the next session. The Gerry amendment was rejected 34 to 16.[73]

Finally, the committee of the whole discussed what would become the Ninth and Tenth Amendments, reserving power to the states or the people. Both were potentially explosive because they tried to resolve the question that had lingered since the Constitution was proposed: To what extent could the federal government exercise powers not explicitly granted in the Constitution? Related to that question was a determination of the nature of powers that had been reserved to the states after ratification.

Tucker of South Carolina introduced a motion that showed how a single word inserted into an important section of the Constitution could have changed the nature of the document and the nation's history. Tucker wanted to place the word "expressly" in what would become the Tenth Amendment to confirm that the federal government was one of limited powers. His proposed language would have read "The powers not expressly delegated by this constitution. . . ."[74] The Tucker amendment would have greatly diminished congressional authority under the "necessary and proper" clause, which had granted Congress substantial discretion to carry out the responsibilities assigned by the Constitution. It would become a major issue throughout the nation's history—going to the heart of how a federal system should allocate power between the states and the central government—that has never been settled.[75]

Madison vigorously objected, arguing that "it was impossible to confine a government to the exercise of express powers[;] there must necessarily be admitted powers by implication, unless the constitution descended to recount every minutiae." He told his colleagues that this subject had been raised, discussed, and rejected by the delegates at the Virginia ratifying convention.[76] Tucker's motion was defeated in the committee of the whole, but he would raise it again in the full House, only to see it defeated on a recorded vote by a margin of 32 to 17.[77]

Tucker had other concerns. He criticized his colleagues for not showing sufficient deference to the amendments proposed by state conventions and legislatures and neglected by the select committee. He said the states that offered amendments "would feel some degree of chagrin at having misplaced their confidence in the general government" and would be disappointed that important rights to which their citizens were entitled would be left unprotected. He warned his colleagues that the failure to act could result in a second convention, and that "we may lose many of the valuable principles now established in the present constitution." He predicted that ratification by three-quarters of the states— which would know that their recommended amendments had not been seriously considered by the House—would be unlikely.[78] The House rejected, by a margin of 34 to 16, Tucker's motion to consider the additional amendments.[79]

The committee of the whole had completed its work. It had rewritten the select committee's language related to the free exercise of religion and the banning of establishments of religion; limited to criminal cases the right against self-incrimination; restored protection against unreasonable searches and seizures, which had been dropped by the committee; and added "or to the people" to Madison's recommendation that powers not delegated to the federal government be reserved to the states. Overall, the House largely adopted Madison's amendments with relatively minor changes over the ten days it debated the issues.[80]

The members of the House were tired and becoming increasingly irritable. The importance of the issues and the heat and humidity of a New York summer weighed heavily on them as they concluded the debate on amendments over the next six days. Even before the full House took over for the committee of the whole, William Loughton Smith told Edward Rutledge of South Carolina, a signer of the Declaration of Independence, that "there has been more ill-humour and rudeness displayed today [August 15, 1789] than has existed since the meeting of Congress." He commented to another correspondent that the hot weather and subject of amendments had "Kept the house in bad temper," and a few days later wrote that the "weather was excessive hot, & the blood warm" because of the debate on amendments.[81]

Representative George Leonard of Massachusetts described the tense atmosphere by noting that the "Political Thermometer [is] high Each Day." Representative John Brown of the Kentucky territory of Virginia said he was not surprised that Gerry, Tucker, and others were "determined to obstruct & embarrass the Business as much as possible." The Speaker of the House, Frederick Muhlenberg of Pennsylvania, said he hoped "this disagreeable Business is finished." He noted that Anti-Federalists such as Gerry and Tucker had "thrown every Obstacle they could" by recommending numerous amendments, although they knew there was no chance they would be approved by two-thirds of the members, yet their plan was to "favour their darling Question for calling a [second federal] Convention."[82]

Benjamin Goodhue of Massachusetts also complained about Anti-Federalists who were "perplexing the House and taking up their precious moments" for amendments that have little support, and he thought it possible that the Senate would postpone consideration of the amendments until the next session.[83] The always candid and occasionally caustic Theodore Sedgwick of Massachusetts said that trying to amend the Constitution before the nation had sufficient experience with it "argues a frivolity of character very inconsitant with national dignity."[84] Richard Peters of Pennsylvania, who frequently corresponded with Madison, could not understand why supporters of the Constitution wanted to call attention to its defects by having a debate on amendments instead of waiting for more experience with the new government.[85]

Others were pleased with the House's work, including Rep. Thomas Hartley of Pennsylvania, who said that the amendments would be popular among the new government's supporters, and that the "great Principles of the Constitution are preserved."[86] He wondered why Anti-Federalists, who had supported amendments for so long, were making the adoption of them by Congress so difficult.[87]

Before the full House approved the amendments, Madison had to give up the rest of what remained of his preamble, and he reluctantly agreed to Sherman's demand that the amendments be added to the end of the Constitution.[88] He had to fight off amendments recommended by Tucker and others that would deprive the federal government of the authority to impose direct taxes except when other sources of revenue had proved to be insufficient, and only after states had refused to pay money requisitioned by Congress.[89] Federalists had long maintained that this power was essential if the federal government was to have the resources to carry out its functions and not be subservient to the states. Tucker's motion was defeated 39 to 9.[90]

Madison also had to defeat new efforts by Elbridge Gerry and others to insert "expressly" into what would become the Tenth Amendment. Gerry asked that a recorded vote be taken, and his motion was defeated 32 to 17. Roger Sherman then recommended language that would be submitted to the Senate as the Ninth and Tenth Amendments, and the House approved his motion. Madison had to convince the House to resist the consideration of additional amendments proposed by several members, telling his colleagues that he would not agree to ones that had not been considered by the select committee or the committee of the whole, and that were not likely to be approved by a two-thirds vote in each house.[91]

Earlier in the summer, Madison had written to Richard Peters, the Speaker of Pennsylvania's General Assembly and later a member of the U.S. Senate. Peters, a wealthy lawyer and landowner who lived on a large estate outside Philadelphia, often showed a dry sense of humor in his notes to Madison. He had sent Madison a long poem in which he compared the process of amending the Constitution to having too many cooks in the kitchen, which could spoil the soup because every time one chef would add an ingredient, another would object to it. He said he felt sorry for Madison, who had to "indulge the Anti Soupites in some of their Whims" to gain their support for the proposed amendments.[92]

Madison responded to Peters in kind, enclosing papers that he said would show that the "nauseous project of amendments" had not been completed. His remark was evidently an allusion to Peters's cooking debated, were, upon the question severally put thereupon, agreed to by the House, as follow, (two thirds of the Members present concurring) to wit:

I. After the first enumeration, there shall be one representative for every thirty thousand, until the number shall amount to one hundred, after which, the proportion shall be so regulated by Congress, that there shall be not less than one hundred Representatives, nor less than one Representative for every forty thousand persons, until the number of Representatives shall amount to two hundred; after which the proportion shall be so regulated, that there shall not be less than two hundred Representatives, nor less than one Representative for every fifty thousand persons.

II. No law varying the compensation to the Members of Congress shall take effect until an election of Representatives shall have intervened.

III. Congress shall make no law establishing religion, or prohibiting the free exercise thereof, nor shall the rights of conscience be infringed.

IV. That the freedom of speech, and of the press, and the right of the people peaceably to assemble and consult for their common good, and to apply to the government for redress of grievances, shall not be infringed.

V. A well regulated Militia composed of the body of the people, being the best security of a free State, the right of the people to keep, and bear Arms, shall not be infringed; but no one religiously scrupulous of bearing arms, shall be compelled to render military service in person.

VI. No soldier shall in time of peace be quartered in any house, without the consent of the owner, nor in time of war, but in a manner to be prescribed by law.

VII. No person shall be subject, except in case of impeachment, to more than one trial, or one punishment for the same Offence, nor shall be compelled, in any criminal case, to be a witness against himself; nor be deprived of life, liberty, or property, without due process of law; nor shall private property be taken for public use, without just compensation.

VIII. Excessive bail shall not be required, nor excessive fines imposed, nor cruel and unusual punishments inflicted.

A page from the Journal of the U.S. House on the Bill of Rights, August 1789.
(*National Archives*)

metaphor rather than a complaint about his labors in Congress, for in the same letter he said that the business of amendments must be completed, and that "no apology [was] requisite" for the time spent debating them.[93]

The letter to Peters is one of Madison's most complete statements outside of a legislative forum of his reasons for supporting amendments. He explained why amendments were needed and the positive impact they would have. A bill of rights might be "less necessary in a republic, than a Monarchy," he conceded, but was "in some degree rational in every Govt., since in every Govt. power may oppress." Madison told Peters, as he did his colleagues in the House, that many of the states that ratified the Constitution would not have done so without assurance that amendments would be considered by the First Congress. Commenting on his own election to the House, Madison said that "if the candidates in Virga. [Virginia] for the House of Reps. had not taken this conciliary ground at the election, that State would have been represented almost wholly by disaffected characters, instead of the *federal* reps. now in Congs [Congress]." He also said that if amendments were approved, "it will kill the opposition every where, and . . . [put] an end to the disaffection to the Govt. itself."[94]

Shortly before the House sent the amendments to the Senate, Madison wrote to Edmund Pendleton, the respected Virginia judge who had presided over the ratifying convention, to say that the "work has been extremely difficult and fatiguing" due to the "diversity of opinion and fancies" and the "dilatory artifices" of some of the Anti-Federalists.[95] After the House approved the amendments, Pendleton told Madison how important that action was in "quieting the minds of many well meaning Citizens." Pendleton criticized those who had fought against amendments, observing that some had "covered their Opposition to the Government under the masque of uncommon zeal for amendments" who really wanted a rejection of the amendments or at least a delay. Pendleton took particular pleasure in knowing that those who said they would propose amendments if elected to the First Congress kept that promise.[96]

Madison also told his longtime friend Edmund Randolph that progress on the amendments had been "exceedingly wearisome." He criticized Anti-Federalist House members who opposed amendments that would actually satisfy many around the country who were still worried about the new government. He said that in order to have some chance of passage, it was necessary to exclude any amendments that were "doubtful & unimportant." Even two or three "contentious additions," Madison said, could "frustrate the whole project." He told Randolph that he had no regrets

about not offering all the amendments recommended by the Virginia ratifying convention. Some Virginians who wrote to him, including his distant relative Robert Rutherford of Berkeley County, supported Madison's
efforts. Rutherford said it would be "criminal in [the] extreme to deny
amendments that would firmly secure the rights of the people."[97]

On August 24, after eight days of debate, the House forwarded seventeen amendments to the Senate. Remarkably, the vote on the amendments was not recorded, but at least two-thirds of the members must
have given their approval.[98]

With great effort, Madison had succeeded in persuading his House
colleagues to approve amendments. Considering the resistance of Anti-
Federalists and even some in Madison's own party, it was a remarkable
accomplishment. Now he had to wait as the Senate took over. There was
always the possibility that it would significantly modify his careful work
in the House or, worse, postpone consideration of the bill of rights until
the next session.

The House amendments were formally read in the Senate on August 25. Little is known about the debate because the Senate met behind
closed doors until 1794, and thus the record of their discussion is sparse.[99]
Immediately, Senator Ralph Izard of South Carolina moved that the Senate postpone consideration until the next session, which was rejected.
Senator William Maclay of Pennsylvania noted in his diary that the
amendments were "treated contemptuously" by Izard, John Langdon of
New Hampshire, and Robert Morris of Pennsylvania. He noted that
Morris "spoke angrily but not well" against the amendments.[100] Morris
had previously predicted that the Senate would postpone discussion of
amendments because of other pressing business.[101] He scoffed at their
importance by saying that the House was "playing with Amendments,"
and that Madison supported amendments only because of his close call in
the election to the House: "Poor Madison got so Cursedly frightened in
Virginia, that I believe he has dreamed of amendments ever since."[102] Referring to the "Nonsense they call Amendments," Morris later said, "I never
expect that any part of it will go through the various Trials which it must
pass before it can become a part of the Constitution."[103] Senator Pierce
Butler of South Carolina called them "milk-and-water amendments," and
he even doubted whether Madison was sincere in proposing them.[104]

Senator Lee of Virginia had a more enlightened view of the proposed amendments. He disagreed with some of his colleagues who
wanted to postpone consideration, as "if experience was more necessary
to prove the propriety of those great principles of Civil liberty which the

wisdom of Ages has found to be necessary barriers against the encroach-
ments of power." He was willing to consider amendments, hoping that
"if we cannot gain the whole loaf, we shall at least have some bread."[105]
By doing this, Lee was resisting Patrick Henry, who firmly believed that
approving amendments protecting individual rights would mean that
more radical changes would not be proposed.

Unfortunately, Senator William Maclay of Pennsylvania, whose diary is the only source of information about this debate, was ill when the
Senate discussed the amendments.[106] After what must have been a week
of lively and at times heated debate, the Senate made changes to some
amendments while rejecting new ones proposed by several senators, including Lee and Grayson. The senators from Virginia had urged consideration of amendments approved by the state ratifying convention but
not included in Madison's or the House's proposals.[107] One particularly
troublesome proposal would have revived a plan rejected by the House:
to prohibit the federal government from directly taxing the people unless the states had failed to provide requisitions. It was rejected by an
unknown margin.[108]

Senator Lee knew in advance that he would be disappointed in the
amendments offered by the House, telling the well-known patriot Samuel
Adams that "my wishes are stronger than my expectations."[109] Shortly
after the Constitution was written, Adams had strongly urged that
amendments protecting individual rights and clarifying the powers retained by the states be added. With his concerns about the erosion of
state sovereignty and the lack of a bill of rights, Adams gave every indication that he would oppose the Constitution at the Massachusetts ratifying convention. However, he surprised many Anti-Federalists by voting
in favor of ratification.[110]

Adams replied to Lee that he hoped the amendments would not
significantly alter the powers granted to the branches of government
under the Constitution, and that the "whole people may in every State
contemplate their own safety on solid grounds."[111] After they had passed
the Senate, Lee said that the amendments had been "mutilated and en-
feebled," and that the government under the amended Constitution
would be "very different from a free one."[112]

The scope of the new amendments proposed in the Senate—twenty
in all—was breathtaking. They included declarations that all power is
"naturally vested in . . . the people"; that powers of the three branches of
government be "separate and distinct"; that certain treaties be approved
by a three-fourths vote in each house; that no standing army be raised

during time of peace except by a two-thirds vote in each house; that the president not serve more than "eight years in any term of sixteen years"; and that the jurisdiction of the federal courts be altered. All were rejected.[113]

By the time the Senate completed its work on September 14, it had made twenty-six changes to the House proposals by tightening language and rearranging some amendments and combining others, thus reducing the number from seventeen to twelve. The most significant decision by the Senate—one that would directly shape the nation's history for a century and a half—was the removal of Madison's most favored amendment, the one that prohibited the states from infringing upon freedom of speech, the press, and religion and guaranteed trial by jury. Considering that senators mostly saw themselves as protecting the interests of the states and the legislatures that elected them, it is not surprising that the amendment failed to win the two-thirds required.

Although senators had six-year terms—which would presumably give them some independence to resist the interests of the state legislatures that sent them to Congress—the Constitution did not provide initially a full term to all the senators in the First Congress. Article I, section 3, required that a third of the senators would initially serve only a two-year term; another third would serve four years; while the final third would enjoy a six-year term before having to seek reelection. This was done so not all senators would be up for election at the same time. Thus a third of the senators—enough to defeat any plan that required a supermajority—would face reelection within a short time and would have to explain why they voted for an amendment that would have restricted states from abridging certain rights. The desire to retain political support among state legislatures no doubt affected senators' action on other subjects as well.[114]

Madison was irritated by the Senate's rejection of that amendment, telling Edmund Pendleton that the "difficulty of uniting the minds of men accustomed to think and act differently can only be conceived by those who have witnessed it." A short time later, Madison told Pendleton that it was going to be difficult for the House and Senate to reconcile their differences over several key amendments.[115] The Senate also eliminated the last remnants of Madison's natural rights preamble, weakened the House's ban on establishment of religion, and changed the House's language in what would become the Second Amendment.[116]

Madison may have been disappointed over the changes made by the Senate, but he should have been pleased that it approved most of what the House had proposed and did so by the required two-thirds margin.

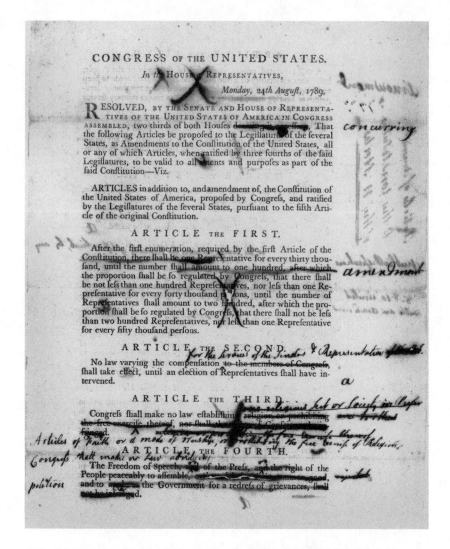

First of three pages of the Senate's working draft of the Bill of Rights, September 2–9, 1789. *(National Archives)*

Still, Madison's frustration was obvious to others. Senator Paine Wingate of New Hampshire said Madison was so dissatisfied with the amendments that "he had rather have none than those agreed to by the Senate." But Roger Sherman thought the Senate had improved the amendments.[117]

The House had previously debated at length, but ultimately rejected, language providing the people with the authority to instruct their representatives. Senators Lee and Grayson tried to insert such language into what would become the First Amendment. They were the only senators to support the motion. Eventually, the Senate combined two House amendments related to freedom of religion and freedom of speech, the press, assembly, and petition into one, which would become the First Amendment.[118]

The House was willing to go along with some of the Senate's changes, but it rejected others. On September 21, the House appointed a conference committee, consisting of Madison, Sherman, and Vining, which met with their Senate counterparts—Oliver Ellsworth of Connecticut, William Paterson of New Jersey, and Charles Carroll of Maryland—to resolve the differences. The conference committee, likely at Madison's insistence, replaced the Senate's version of the religious freedom guarantee with language that would become part of the First Amendment.[119]

Three days later, the House approved the committee's report, 37 to 14. Among those voting against the adoption of the report—and thus against the Bill of Rights—were Theodorick Bland of Virginia, who was closely allied with Patrick Henry, and Elbridge Gerry of Massachusetts, who had long argued that a bill of rights was needed.[120] Gerry's opposition to the amendments drew a rebuke from the chief justice of Rhode Island, William Ellery, who, corresponding from home, said the amendments "will not do any hurt, and they may do some good," and he was glad that Gerry was "disappointed in all his efforts to procure amendments. He is a restless creature, and if he don't take care, he will injure [and] weaken the reputation for honesty to which I used to think he was justly entitled."[121] The governor of Rhode Island thought the amendments had already "afforded some relief and satisfaction to the minds of the People of this State."[122] This show of support for amendments from two of Rhode Island's leading officials was significant because that state, along with North Carolina, had refused to ratify the Constitution until amendments were proposed.[123] For his part, Gerry was content with his opposition to amendments, noting that "I shall . . . console myself with the reflection, that the consequences [of the amendments] be injurious or ruinous, nothing has been wanting [lacking] on my part in Convention or Congress to prevent them."[124]

Burke, Sumter, Livermore, and Tucker also voted against the amendments, with Tucker noting that the amendments were "calculated merely to amuse, or rather to deceive."[125] Surprisingly, Madison's colleague from Virginia, John Page, also voted in the negative. The volatile Fisher Ames voted in favor, having told a correspondent during the debate that he would support amendments, "but they should not be trash, such as would dishonor the Constitution, without pleasing its enemies."[126] Roger

Sherman, who had strongly opposed amendments but played a key role in their passage, also voted in favor. He said they would "probably be harmless & Satisfactory to those who are fond of a Bill of rights."[127] William Loughton Smith of South Carolina, after telling a friend that he would not support the amendments unless the word "expressly" was inserted to limit the powers of the federal government, voted in favor.[128] The following day, September 25, the Senate agreed to the House's version by at least a two-thirds vote, although the exact margin is unknown. The Bill of Rights had been officially proposed by the U.S. Congress.

A week later, George Washington submitted the twelve amendments to the states for ratification. Washington had not been directly involved in the deliberations of the House or Senate. He had allowed Madison to introduce a letter of support—repeating Washington's lukewarm endorsement from the first inaugural address—that Madison shared with his House colleagues toward the end of the debate.[129] But there is no evidence that Washington directly contacted members of Congress to urge passage of the proposed amendments.

The approval of the amendments by Congress was a remarkable victory for Madison. He could look back on the last two years, since the Constitution was signed in Philadelphia, with immense satisfaction. The great document had been written and ratified and had successfully launched a new government. Now twelve amendments that would generate substantial support for the Constitution and end efforts to call a second constitutional convention were before the states.

Madison probably expected fairly quick approval by three-fourths of state legislatures. After all, he had succeeded in keeping Congress from approving those "doubtful" amendments that would create intense opposition. He could not have known at this point that his home state would play a key role in determining whether the Bill of Rights would be ratified.

Facing page: Congressional resolution transmitting the Bill of Rights to the states, September 26, 1789. *(National Archives)*

Congress of the United States,

In the House of Representatives,

Thursday the 24th of September, 1789.

Resolved by the Senate and House of Representatives of the United States of America, in Congress assembled, that the President of the United States be requested to transmit to the Executives of the several States which have ratified the Constitution, Copies of the Amendments proposed by Congress, to be added thereto, and like Copies to the Executives of the States of Rhode Island, and North Carolina.

Attest

John Beckley, Clerk.

United States of America,

In Senate, September the 26th 1789.

Resolved, that the Senate do concur in this Resolution.

Attest,

Sam. A. Otis Secy.

≈ 10 ≈

Ratification of the Bill of Rights

A LESS FORMIDABLE and determined foe than Patrick Henry would have given up by now. Congress had proposed twelve amendments, and indications were that the states would likely ratify them. But Henry was not through. Having failed to obtain the radical amendments he had long demanded, he would do everything he could to prevent Virginia from approving the Bill of Rights. He told Senator Richard Henry Lee that the proposed amendments "will tend to injure rather than serve the Cause of Liberty," and he believed they were intended to "lull Suspicion totally on this Subject," to prevent changing the "exorbitancy of Power granted away by the Constitution from the People."[1]

Earlier, when the House was still debating the amendments, Henry told Leven Powell—who passed the information on to former governor Edmund Randolph—that Henry was, in Randolph's words, "pleased with some of the proposed amendments; but [Henry] still asks for the great desideratum, the destruction of direct taxation." Randolph also said that Henry was "agitated" at learning that Congress had agreed that the president could remove executive branch officials without its approval, even when they had been confirmed by the Senate.[2]

Lee expressed his disappointment as well, telling Henry that the amendments emerging from the House were "very far short of the wishes of our [Virginia's] convention, but as they are returned by the Senate they are certainly much weakened." Lee insisted to Henry that "nothing on my part was left undone to prevent this." The idea of subsequent amendments—agreed to by the Virginia ratifying convention—was, in Lee's view, "delusional," and nothing had been done to reduce the tendency toward a consolidated and powerful federal government, instead of a "Union of Confederated States."[3] Lee criticized supporters of the amendments for searching the English language to "find words feeble in their Nature or doubtful in their meaning!"[4]

Senator William Grayson was even more critical in his assessment of the amendments, telling Henry that "they are so mutilated & gutted that in fact they are good for nothing, & I believe as many others do, that they will do more harm than benefit."[5] When Lee and Grayson wrote a formal note accompanying the proposed amendments to the Speaker of the Virginia House of Delegates, they expressed their disappointment and said that "nothing on our part has been omitted to procure the success of those Radical Amendments proposed by the Convention and approved by the Legislature of our Country [Virginia]."[6]

Although Madison would once again have to do battle with Henry, his amendments won at least some support from George Mason, now living in retirement. While they were being considered by Congress, Mason said he had "received much Satisfaction from the Amendments," and he hoped the Senate would approve them. With two or three additional amendments—dealing with the federal judiciary, with admiralty and maritime jurisdiction and commercial laws, and with limits on congressional control of elections—Mason could "chearfully put my Hand & Heart to the new Government."[7]

The amendments were now before the states, the final step in the long process of changing the Constitution. Perhaps Madison thought occasionally about that day in Philadelphia in September 1787 when Mason said that he needed only a few hours to draw up a list of rights that should be protected in the Constitution before it was submitted to the states and the people for ratification. The delegates told Mason such explicit protections were not needed because the new federal government had no power to abridge individual rights. Only when the people got their first look at the Constitution did the framers realize how badly they had miscalculated. Madison had spent two years making up for that error. If a sufficient number of states did not ratify the proposed amendments, that work would have been in vain, and demand for a second constitutional convention would increase.

Madison must have been worn out by the time the first session of Congress ended on September 29. For almost six months he had worked in committee, on the floor of the House of Representatives, and behind the scenes to sponsor the Bill of Rights. It had been grueling for Madison to convince his House colleagues to support the proposed amendments, while at the same time preventing them from introducing new ones that could have derailed the entire process. Now he looked forward to spending some time at his beloved estate in Orange County before he had to return at the end of the year for the second congressional session.

Even so, instead of leaving New York right away, Madison stayed for another ten days. He wanted to answer the many letters he had received and take care of other business, but he also lingered in the capital because he was hoping that Thomas Jefferson would arrive from Paris. Jefferson had been confirmed as secretary of state by the Senate on September 26 but did not yet know of his appointment. Madison was aware that his longtime friend wanted to return to private life at Monticello, from which he had been absent for so long, and he feared that Jefferson would turn down the appointment before Madison had a chance to persuade him to accept it.

With no sign of Jefferson, Madison left a note just before departing for Virginia by way of Philadelphia, telling his friend it was "of infinite importance that you should not disappoint the public wish on this subject." He pleaded with Jefferson not to "yield hastily to objections" and said that the president "is anxious for your acceptance of the trust." Madison asked him to write "the moment you get on shore."[8]

Madison expected to be in Philadelphia only a few days, but he ended up staying two weeks. The strain of the past months had taken a toll on his health. By the time he arrived at Mary House's hostelry, Madison was so sick he could barely write a letter. He described the ailment as an "indisposition," which probably meant he was suffering from the same stomach disorder that bothered him so much of his life.[9] He was too ill to write to Secretary of the Treasury Alexander Hamilton, who had asked for Madison's thoughts on how to stabilize the nation's revenue system.[10] He would eventually answer Hamilton from home in Orange County weeks later.[11] Despite his ailing condition, Madison managed to have a meeting with Senator Robert Morris of Pennsylvania to discuss the permanent location of the nation's capital and to conduct other business with visitors.[12]

Madison was finally well enough to leave Philadelphia. He arrived at Fredericksburg on November 1 and was home at Montpelier the next day. His delicate system would soon give out again, though, and when Madison journeyed from Virginia back to New York in January, he would be confined for a week in Georgetown with "pretty severe dysentery."[13]

As he tended to business at Montpelier, Madison received reports on how the ratification debate was unfolding. He may have been encouraged when several states quickly endorsed the proposed Bill of Rights. New Jersey was the first to ratify, approving all but the second amendment (on congressional salaries) on November 20. A month later, Maryland assented to all twelve of the amendments. North Carolina finally joined the union and ratified all amendments just before Christmas. By the end of January, three more states—South Carolina (all amendments), New Hampshire (all but the second), and Delaware (all but the first amendment, on the size of the U.S. House) had given their approval.

Despite the promising start, Madison had good reason to be concerned about whether the momentum toward ratification could be sustained. He had been through the ordeal of seeing the Constitution ratified by a number of states in the months right after the Philadelphia convention, only to see Massachusetts, Virginia, and New York come close to rejecting the Constitution or ratifying it with debilitating conditions.

Massachusetts is the first state for which evidence exists of a debate about specific amendments. Governor John Hancock encouraged the Massachusetts legislature to approve the Bill of Rights. In a letter to the members of the House, he said it was the "ardent wish of every patriot, that the plan [the Constitution] may be as compleat as human wisdom can effect it, This resolve [the proposed amendments], I am confident, will demand your serious and careful attention."[14]

Hancock felt so strongly in favor of the amendments that he gave a speech to the legislature a few days later. He told the lawmakers that the citizens of Massachusetts had demanded amendments, and that its ratifying convention had responded by urging Congress to consider them. Now the amendments were before them. He cited several as "of great consequence" and said that "In all free governments, a share

John Hancock, governor of Massachusetts, who urged ratification of the Constitution at the state convention. (*National Archives*)

246 JAMES MADISON AND THE STRUGGLE FOR THE BILL OF RIGHTS

in the administration of the laws ought to be vested in, or reserved to the people; this prevents government from verging towards despotism, secures the freedom of debate, and supports that independence of sentiment which dignifies the citizen, and renders the government permanently respectable." Hancock noted that some of the amendments were "very important to . . . personal security, which is so truly characteristick of a free Government."[15]

By early February, the Massachusetts Senate had approved all but the first and second amendments. The House, however, was troubled by the language of the twelfth amendment, which reserved powers not granted by the Constitution to the people or the states. After an initial discussion, the House postponed consideration for several days. It eventually rejected that amendment, along with the first and second. Thus, by February 2, both houses of the Massachusetts legislature had approved the third through eleventh amendments.[16]

The most contentious debate was to take place, once again, in Virginia. Patrick Henry and other Anti-Federalists wanted the General Assembly to postpone a decision on the amendments. Henry was shrewd enough to realize that Madison's amendments had stalled momentum for a new constitutional convention, but he was not prepared to accept defeat at the hands of Madison. He wanted to attain his goals by having Congress add further amendments, and he believed the best tactic to accomplish that was for Virginia to delay consideration of them for a year.[17] Henry had hoped that North Carolina and Rhode Island would demand new amendments as a condition of ratification, but they joined the union and endorsed the Bill of Rights without such a requirement.[18] Georgia and Connecticut refused to approve the amendments, making Virginia the last of the original states to decide whether they would become part of the Constitution. If Virginia said no, the Bill of Rights would have to wait until additional states were admitted to the union.[19] In such a situation, the amendments might not have been ratified then, or perhaps, ever.

Henry was in his seat in the Virginia House of Delegates on October 19, 1789, as the debate on the amendments began.[20] President Washington had submitted them to Virginia and the other states a few weeks prior.[21] A year earlier, the Henry-controlled legislature had been reliably Anti-Federalist; it had denied Madison a seat in the U.S. Senate and tried to keep him out of the U.S. House. Now, as the debate over the amendments began, the Virginia Senate was solidly in his camp, but Henry found "a much stronger Federal party" in the House.[22] Citizens must have been dismayed by the hostility shown by Henry and his colleagues in the previous legislative session toward the new government—and perhaps Madison in particular—because they voted into office many more Federalists during the spring elections.

As the debate over the amendments began, it was expected that the Senate would reject the proposed amendments until more drastic changes were offered by Congress. Some senators were still determined to seek an amendment to remove the federal government's power of direct taxation.[23] Henry Lee, a supporter of the Constitution and the amendments, wrote to Madison that the "enmity of govt. is I believe as strong as ever in this state."[24] The House, although still dominated by those who had vigorously opposed the Constitution, was more closely divided. Many legislators, in both houses, still wanted to see Congress debate and propose the amendments that had been recommended by the Virginia ratifying convention in June of the previous year but had yet to be discussed in Congress.

Supporters of the Bill of Rights knew from the start that approval would be difficult to obtain, even though it required only a majority vote. At the end of September, Virginia's two U.S. senators—Richard Henry Lee and William Grayson—had forwarded the amendments to the governor of Virginia and the General Assembly with a letter sharply criticizing them. In the note to the governor, the senators complained that the amendments were "far short of the wishes of our Country [Virginia]." They said they had tried "in vain [to] bring to view the Amendments proposed by our [Virginia ratifying] Convention, and approved by the Legislature."[25] To the Speaker of the House, the senators wrote that the amendments would do nothing to stop the "tendency to consolidated empire in the natural operation of the Constitution, if no further amended than as now proposed." They expressed serious concern for "Civil Liberty, when we know of no instance in the records of history, that shew a people ruled in freedom when subject to one undivided Government, and inhabiting a territory so extensive as that of the United States." They wanted the General Assembly to know how hard they had tried to bring about a different result: "Nothing on our part has been omitted, to procure the success of those radical amendments proposed by the Convention . . . and legislature."[26]

The House quickly showed that it viewed the proposed amendments more favorably than fervent Anti-Federalists had hoped. Henry introduced a resolution commending Senators Lee and Grayson for their efforts in trying to secure amendments recommended by Virginia that

Congress had rejected. As Edward Carrington, a member of the House, described the events to Madison, Henry's first effort was to "procure an address of thanks . . . for the great vigilance of our senators . . . in regard to such amendments as will secure our liberties under the Government." But House members voiced strong enough opposition that Henry withdrew the motion. When Henry realized that the motion for commending the senators did not appear to "take well, it was never stirred again." Even some Anti-Federalists were angered by the Lee-Grayson letter, which was, according to Carrington, "considered by some of the most violent of the Anti's as seditious and highly reprehensible."[27]

Henry now realized that the amendments had more support in the House than he had expected, and he would have to change his strategy. Rather than making a frontal assault, he would seek to head off ratification by at least postponing the debate, and he found a creative justification for a delay. Henry argued that because members of the current House and Senate had been elected prior to Congress's approval of the amendments, it was necessary to postpone the debate until the next legislative session, when voters would have the chance to express their view of the proposed changes by choosing legislators who supported or opposed them.[28] As with his motion in praise of the senators, Henry would be disappointed. In Carrington's words, the "disposition of the House [was] otherwise."[29] Former governor Edmund Randolph, now a member of the House, said Henry's motion was "negatived by a great majority."[30] It was not introduced again.

Madison did not accept Henry's argument that the legislature should postpone consideration of the amendments until another election had been held. As he explained to George Washington, "This reason would have more force, if the amendments did not so much correspond as far as they go with the propositions of the State Convention, which were before the public long before the last Election." At least, Madison hoped, if the House put off the amendments until the next session, it "might pass a vote of *approbation* along with the postponement," so the voters would know that the amendments enjoyed strong support and were being postponed only so an ensuing election could be held.[31]

Madison was feeling reasonably confident. He told President Washington that "the great bulk of the late opponents are entirely at rest, and more likely to censure a further opposition to the Govt." He cited the example of a leading Baptist who had sent word that "the amendments had entirely satisfied the disaffected of his Sect."[32]

Henry knew he was in trouble, but he then got help from an unexpected source. Edmund Randolph had been instrumental in persuading the delegates at the ratifying convention to approve the Constitution. But now he objected to the eleventh and twelfth amendments, and he prolonged the debate with a long discussion of his concerns. Despite Randolph's extensive experience in public affairs—as governor, a delegate to the Constitutional Convention, an energetic member of the Virginia ratifying convention, and now a legislator—he did not always know when it was best to remain silent.

This was to be Randolph's last legislative session before he became attorney general of the United States.[33] He had been ill at the beginning of the session, informing Madison that he was "labouring under a violent relapse into the ague and fever."[34] Yet he was well enough to take the floor of the House and lecture his colleagues about the dangers of the last two amendments.

Randolph argued that because the retained rights of the people and the states were not clearly defined in the other amendments, it would be dangerous to add the final two because they could be interpreted to mean that Congress had power to abridge rights not included elsewhere in the proposed amendments.

Randolph apparently believed that amendments should directly limit the power of Congress rather than reserve to citizens and states powers not delegated. Some members of the House, such as Hardin Burnley of Orange County, did not see "the force of the distinction," as he explained to Madison. Burnley worried that if Randolph persuaded very many House members that those amendments posed a threat, it could lead to the rejection of all amendments because "some who have been decided friends to the [first] ten [amendments] think it woud be unwise to adopt them without the 11th. & 12th."[35]

Madison was understandably annoyed by the former governor's actions. He complained to Washington about Randolph's concerns and, using many of Burnley's words, told Washington that Randolph's "principal objection was [to the word] 'retained' in the eleventh proposed amendment, and his argument, if I understood it was . . . that the rights declared in the first ten of the proposed amendments were not all that a free people would require the exercise of, and that as there was no criterion by which it could be determined whether any other particular right was retained or not, it would be more safe and more consistent with the spirit" of the amendments proposed by Virginia if the amendments operated as "a provision agst. extending the powers of Congs . . . than a protection to rights reducible to no definitive certainty."[36]

Madison told Washington that Randolph's attack on the amendments was "really unlucky, and the more to be regretted as it springs from a friend to the Constitution. It is a still greater cause of regret, if the distinction be, as it appears to me, altogether fanciful." To Madison, "if a line can be drawn between the powers granted and the powers retained, it would seem to be the same thing, whether the latter be secured, by declaring that they shall not be abridged, or that the former shall not be extended. If no line can be drawn a declaration in either form would amount to nothing." None of this, in Madison's view, would "justify the risk of losing the amendts" by a contentious debate.[37]

Randolph tried to justify his objections to Washington, saying that in the eleventh amendment Congress had "endeavoured to administer an opiate," and the twelfth amendment "does not appear to me to have any real effect, unless it be to excite a dispute between the United States, and every particular state, as to what is delegated."[38] Washington, who probably received Madison's letter within a day or two of receiving Randolph's, must have wondered why the former governor was jeopardizing ratification of the amendments over this issue.

On November 12, Patrick Henry did something unexpected, considering his long battle to secure radical amendments to the Constitution. He abruptly left Richmond and returned home, with a month to go in the legislative session.[39] There is no obvious explanation for why he would leave then. Randolph told Washington that "Mr. Henry has quitted rather in discontent, that the present Assembly is not so pleasant as the last." Edward Carrington told Madison that Henry was "disposed to do some antifederal business, but having felt the pulse of the House on several points and finding that it did not beat with the certainty in unison with his own, he at length took his departure in the middle of the session without pushing any thing to its issue."[40]

If Henry left because things were not going his way, it seemed uncharacteristic of him, and it put his Anti-Federal colleagues in the House in a difficult position. His absence gave supporters of the amendments a close victory on a matter that could have delayed indefinitely Virginia's consideration of the amendments. On December 5, a motion that had been discussed for several weeks came to a vote. It was a formal request to Congress that it consider all the amendments approved by the Virginia ratifying convention. The vote was 62 to 62, with the Speaker casting the decisive vote against it.[41] Edward Carrington believed that had Henry known how closely divided the House would be on this important issue, "he would not have left us."[42] Both Edmund Randolph and future chief justice John Marshall voted against the motion.

Henry himself did not explain the reasons for his departure, and when he declined to seek reelection in the following spring, his career as a legislator was over.[43] When he returned home in mid-November during the legislative session, Henry is said to have thrown onto a table—with "an expression of much dissatisfaction and distress," in the words of his great-grandson Edward Fontaine—a pamphlet containing the proposed amendments. Henry was then reported to have said to his law clerks in the room that "Virginia has been outwitted, & her reserved rights sacrificed by the ingenious wording of the amendments."[44]

Henry might have left Richmond, but that did not mean the end of his involvement in the debate over amendments. He would continue to work behind the scenes to persuade colleagues—mainly in the Virginia Senate—that they should postpone ratification of the amendments until Congress approved ones that would reduce the power of the new government.

The debate in the General Assembly continued in Henry's absence. The Virginia House initially rejected the eleventh and twelfth amendments in the committee of the whole by a margin of 64 to 58.[45] A few days later, the whole House reversed itself and approved all twelve amendments by a thirteen-vote majority.[46] Randolph had failed to persuade the House to reject the last two amendments.

The Senate, however, postponed approval of the third, eighth, eleventh, and twelfth amendments (which became the First, Sixth, Ninth, and Tenth Amendments), arguing that they did not go as far in protecting individual rights as those proposed by the Virginia ratifying convention and other states.[47] The House declined to go along with the Senate and demanded a conference committee, which was unable to find a compromise. The House, according to Carrington, would not give in to the Senate's "intemperate and unprecedented Conduct" and was left "without a choice of any thing but to adhere also, and thus the whole amendments have fallen." John Dawson, a member of the House of Delegates and longtime correspondent of Madison's, described both houses as "obstinate."[48]

In Carrington's view, the citizens of Virginia "are at ease on the subject of amendments"—which was evident from the fact that the House had approved them—and would have let their senators know more forcefully of their support had those senators "been amongst the people" rather than being cloistered in Richmond. George Lee Turberville asked whether "the senate really are shut up from the world whilst they deliberate as a part of the Legislature."[49]

Carrington predicted that when the next Virginia legislative elections took place in the spring, citizens would replace those senators who opposed the amendments. Madison seemed to share that view. As he calmly explained to President Washington, the failure to ratify the amendments "is no doubt to be regretted. But it will do no injury to the Genl. Government. On the contrary it will have the effect with many of turning their distrust towards their own legislature." Madison thought the public would be especially incensed about the rejection by the State Senate of the third amendment—which would eventually become the First Amendment that protects freedom of religion, speech, and the press, among other rights.[50]

Madison could not foresee that the continued squabbling between the two houses would delay serious consideration of the amendments for two years, and that the contest would drag on until it would fall to Virginia to cast the decisive vote as to whether the Bill of Rights would be ratified.

He might also not have realized that Patrick Henry was working in the background to persuade delegates and senators to postpone debate over the amendments in the hopes that Congress would offer additional ones. John Marshall believed the delay was caused by Anti-Federalists who "contended that they [the proposed amendments] were not sufficient for the security of liberty" and would not "quiet the fears of the people, and check the pursuit of those radical alterations which would afford a safe and adequate protection to their rights."[51] Henry's grandson knew where much of the credit for the delay belonged: "It can hardly be doubted" that by urging the legislature to postpone ratification until more amendments were offered, Henry "caused the delay in the action of that body."[52]

It was two years later, in October 1791, when the Virginia General Assembly again considered ratification of the amendments. As the debate began, Francis Corbin, a member of the House, told Madison that because the Virginia legislature was arranging congressional districts based on the new census, it was timely to propose adoption of the amendment on congressional representation. If that amendment became part of the Constitution, it would enlarge Virginia's delegation to the U.S. House, and the legislature would have to create more districts. Corbin predicted that the amendment would be adopted "without much difficulty," but he wondered how the new districts could be drawn until the legislators heard from Congress.[53]

Corbin was able to report cheerfully to Madison that the House approved the first amendment on October 25 and the rest of the amendments on December 5. Corbin said, "I prevailed upon our lower House to adopt them *all*, without a single Exception, and (Excepting *One Nay*) by an unanimous Vote." But he worried about the Anti-Federalists in the other house, telling Madison: "How they will fare in the Senate—I know not. But I am apprehensive that some impediments will be *there* thrown in the Way of a *Complete* Ratification."[54]

Corbin had a good source for the information he received about the Senate. It was Patrick Henry, with whom he had dined the day before. There was reason to believe that while in Richmond, Henry was lobbying some of the senators who would soon be voting on the amendments. Henry left Richmond the next day, and Corbin told Madison on December 7 that he hoped "that my fears and doubts [about Senate approval] will depart with him."[55]

Finally, on December 15, Corbin was able to give Madison the good news: "I sieze the earliest moment to inform you that *all* the Amendments to the federal Constitution have at length pass'd the Senate."[56] Unfortunately, the Senate debate on the Bill of Rights and the vote were unrecorded.[57] When Madison wrote to Edmund Pendleton three days later to tell him about the debate in the U.S. House over how many members it should have and to ask whether the proposed first amendment had been ratified, he did not know that Virginia had made the Bill of Rights an official part of the Constitution.[58]

Despite the efforts of Patrick Henry and the Anti-Federalists, Madison had succeeded in sponsoring the Bill of Rights and preventing the nation from suffering the consequences of a second constitutional convention. Two days before the Virginia Senate ratified, Madison was feeling generous toward his old adversary. Madison told his brother William that he had "never, in the midst of political contests indulged any personal ill-will to that gentleman [Henry], & at all times admired his eminent talents." William had apparently inquired of his famous brother why he had not responded to one or more of Henry's letters over the years, at which Madison expressed surprise. He told William that Henry and he had not corresponded with each other in years, and that it was "extremely improbable" that Henry had sent Madison a letter that went unanswered. Henry had written Madison a pleasant note in 1784, long before they battled over the Constitution and the Bill of Rights, and Madison referred to this letter in his response to his brother. But Madison added that if he failed to respond to a letter from Henry, the only reason would be that he had not received Henry's note.[59]

This was either gracious of Madison or disingenuous, considering that Henry had worked tirelessly to prevent the ratification of the Constitution at the Virginia convention in 1788, to elect two Anti-Federalists to the U.S. Senate, thus excluding Madison from that body, and to prevent

Virginia's ratification of the Bill of Rights, December 15, 1791. *(National Archives)*

Madison's election to the U.S. House so he would not have the chance to propose the amendments that became the Bill of Rights. Henry had continued his efforts to prevent passage of those amendments indirectly through Senators Lee and Grayson, and more directly as a member of the House of Delegates when the Virginia General Assembly took up the issue of ratification.

On December 30, 1791, President Washington notified Congress that Virginia had ratified all of the amendments, and he submitted the documents written by the General Assembly to confirm each house's approval.[60]

In what has to be the most understated announcement in the nation's history, Secretary of State Thomas Jefferson informed governors of all the states on March 1, 1792, that the amendments had been approved: "I have the honor to send you herein enclosed, two copies duly authenticated, of an Act concerning certain fisheries of the United States, and for the regulation and government of the fishermen employed therein; also of an Act to establish the post office and post roads within the United States; also the ratifications by three fourths of the Legislatures of the Several States, of certain articles in addition and amendment of the Constitution of the United States, proposed by Congress to the said Legislatures."[61]

Jefferson's backhanded announcement—putting the notice about laws on fishing and the post office before the news about the Bill of Rights—may have reflected the ambivalence shared by many over whether amendments should be added to the Constitution so soon after its birth. But if their arrival was inconspicuous, their importance in American history would not be.

~ **11** ~

Epilogue

THROUGH THE EXTRAORDINARY EFFORTS of a small man with a quiet voice, the nation finally had the Bill of Rights. By the time those amendments were added to the Constitution in 1791, the drive to hold a second convention had dissipated, and opponents of the government knew they had no choice but to work within the new system. The Bill of Rights would become of critical importance to the American people, but they would have to wait a long time before those words had much meaning.

The first two amendments proposed by Congress—on the size of the House of Representatives and congressional pay—fell short of ratification in 1789–91. Thus what we know today as the First Amendment moved up to its exalted position not by design but because those original amendments failed to earn sufficient support among state legislatures.[1] Nevertheless, protection for freedom of speech, of the press, and of religion would become the foundation of individual liberty, without which most other rights in the Constitution would be virtually meaningless.

That the Bill of Rights would gradually—but not immediately— become a source of significant protection against government was shown by the passage of the Alien and Sedition Acts of 1798. The Federalist Congress, in response to criticism of President John Adams and fear of war with France, enacted the sedition law to punish "scandalous and malicious" publications, primarily those of Republican newspaper editors.[2] The law allowed partisan judges to impose severe punishment: up to five years in prison and a five-thousand-dollar fine.[3]

Newspaper editors, a member of the U.S. House, and other outspoken critics of the administration—ten in all—were convicted, and they served sentences of at least several months.[4] Many others were afraid to speak out for fear they too would be prosecuted.[5]

James Madison, who had left the U.S. House the year before the Sedition Act was passed, tried to generate public opposition to the law by writing for his home state what became known as the Kentucky-Virginia Resolutions. His friend Thomas Jefferson penned a more radical version for Kentucky. Both men argued that the First Amendment prohibited Congress from enacting a law that punished speech critical of the president and Congress.[6]

Jefferson's resolution, which was adopted by the Kentucky legislature, held that states could nullify unconstitutional federal laws. Madison's resolution, approved by Virginia, took a less contentious approach. It stopped short of nullification and argued that a state could intervene to protect its citizens against an illegitimate exercise of federal power, and it could ask other states to join an effort to convince Congress that it had overstepped its authority. Madison and Jefferson were disappointed when no other states approved the resolutions. Even when Madison drafted a report—endorsed by the Virginia legislature in 1800—restating that the Alien and Seditions Acts violated the First Amendment, no other states followed its lead.[7] Many years later, in the 1830s, Madison, by then very old, was distressed to learn that his resolution and name were being used in the nullification crisis to justify secession from the union.[8]

Citizens were so outraged by the ruthless campaign under the Sedition Act to punish constitutionally protected speech that they threw out the Federalist Congress and elected Jefferson president.[9] The Sedition Act itself expired on the day Adams left office and was never considered by the Supreme Court. If an appeal had been brought, the Federalist judges on the Court, several of whom had already presided at trials under the law, would almost certainly have upheld the convictions. One hundred sixty-three years later, Justice William Brennan spoke for all his colleagues in a 1964 landmark First Amendment case when he wrote that "Although the Sedition Act was never tested in this Court, the attack upon its validity has carried the day in the court of history. Fines levied in its prosecution were repaid by . . . Congress on the ground that it was unconstitutional."[10]

Throughout the nineteenth century, the First Amendment and the other provisions of the Bill of Rights would be confined mostly to symbolic value. They would be of little use in defending the right to speak or write freely in either state or federal court.[11] In fact, Americans would have to wait until 1919—128 years after it became part of the Constitution—before the First Amendment was interpreted by the Supreme Court in a meaningful way. Even when it was then finally applied in a series of cases, the First Amendment was treated with appalling indifference by federal judges who—despite having lifetime tenure and the obligation to protect the constitutional rights of even despised individuals—saw their mission as upholding President Wilson's crusade to punish criticism of U.S. involvement in World War I and the decision to send troops to Russia to prevent the revolution.[12] A concerted effort on the part of the Wilson administration to rid the country—through deportation and draconian prison sentences—of radicals, anarchists, and anyone else who opposed the war was cheerfully upheld by federal judges who had little understanding of the importance of free speech in a democratic society.[13]

It took until 1931 for the Supreme Court finally to hand down a decision that was a clear victory for the First Amendment. In that case, the Court, divided 5 to 4, held that a state could not stop a newspaper from continuing to publish because it had sharply criticized allegedly corrupt city officials.[14]

Several reasons explain why the Bill of Rights lay mostly dormant for so many years of the nation's history. First, as Madison had said, words written on paper cannot always prevent determined government officials or intolerant majorities from abusing the rights of unpopular citizens.[15] A culture of tolerance for even controversial speech has to develop over time. Originally, the First Amendment may have meant little more than protection against prior restraint—when government prevents a newspaper from publishing or an individual from disseminating information—and not protection for harsh criticism of the government or public officials.[16]

Second, during the first half of the nineteenth century, the Supreme Court was preoccupied with determining the relative power of the federal and state governments. Under the leadership of Chief Justice John Marshall, the Court decided many important cases that helped solidify the authority of the national government, nationalize the economy, and settle many issues of federalism that had been left unresolved in the Constitution. During the Civil War, Congress did not enact a sedition law, so the Court had no occasion to consider whether it violated the First Amendment. In the last half of the century, the Court was primarily concerned with the industrial revolution and government efforts to regulate the economy.[17]

Third, from 1791 until well into the twentieth century, the procedural protections in the Bill of Rights applied only to the federal government and not the states. That meant that any state laws punishing
speech or publication, or failing to provide due process rights to criminal defendants, could not be challenged using those amendments. Only
when the federal government passed laws or carried out policies impli-
cating fundamental rights could those amendments be invoked. Few such
laws were enacted during the nation's first century.[18]

Madison understood that when the Bill of Rights was introduced in
the First Congress, it was intended to limit the powers of the new government and not secure the rights of citizens against their states. The
states, it was assumed, already provided sufficient protection for individual liberty in their constitutions, and if citizens' rights were abused,
the public officials at fault would be held accountable and removed from
office at the next election.

But Madison was not satisfied that the states would faithfully guarantee such rights. He had wanted to provide explicit protection for certain essential rights against encroachment by state governments, as well
as the new national government. He introduced this amendment as the
fifth one in his speech of June 8, 1789, to the House: "No State shall
violate the equal rights of conscience, or the freedom of the press, or the
trial by jury in criminal cases." He considered this amendment—the only
one limiting state power—to be among the most important of the ones
he proposed in the First Congress. Although his House colleagues gave
their approval, the Senate—to serve the interests of the state legislatures
that had elected them—refused to go along. Madison lived long enough
to see Chief Justice Marshall and the Supreme Court confirm in 1833
that only the federal government was bound by the Bill of Rights.[19] The
fact that for much of the nation's history the Bill of Rights provided
citizens with no protection against oppressive action by the states had
profound implications.[20]

Eventually, the First Amendment and the procedural rights in the
Fourth through Eighth were applied to the states through the "due process" clause of the Fourteenth Amendment, which was adopted after the
Civil War: freedom of speech (1925); freedom of the press (1931); religion
clauses of the First Amendment (1947); search and seizure protection in
the Fourth Amendment (1961); the "cruel and unusual punishment"
clause of the Eighth Amendment (1962); the Sixth Amendment right to
counsel (1963); the self-incrimination clause of the Fifth Amendment
(1964); right to a jury trial (1968); protection against double jeopardy

(1969); and prohibition against excessive bail (1971).[21] Several rights in the first ten amendments have never been applied to the states.[22]

Madison would have been surprised that it took so long for the Bill of Rights to provide citizens with the protections outlined in those amendments. After eight years in the U.S. House, he left Congress in March 1797, one day before John Adams's inauguration as president. But he was not leaving Philadelphia—the temporary capital—alone. Three years earlier, James had met and fallen in love with Dolley Payne Todd, to whom he would be married for forty-two years. When James completed his congressional service, he and Dolley returned to Montpelier, their estate in central Virginia near the Blue Ridge Mountains.

Dolley Madison, who married James in 1794. She served as unofficial first lady in the Jefferson administration and played an influential role during her husband's two terms as president. *(National Archives)*

Although Madison seemed to be content with a life devoted to helping form the new nation, he became a happier and more fulfilled person after he married Dolley. While his letters from 1787 to 1791 are mostly about politics, the letters James wrote Dolley beginning in 1794 show a thoughtful and affectionate individual who was clearly enamored with his charming and outgoing partner. A few months before they were married, James was vying with other suitors for the attention of the twenty-five-year-old widow, but as might be expected, he was too shy to tell Dolley directly how he felt. He asked Dolley's friend Catharine Coles—who was Elbridge Gerry's sister-in-law—to let Dolley know that he was thinking of her and that he was worried that another man might catch her eye: "[Mr. Madison] told me I might say what I pleas'd to you about him ... [H]e thinks so much of you in the day that he has Lost his Tongue, at Night he Dreames of you ... & he hopes that your Heart will be calous [callous] to every other swain [suitor] but himself he has Consented to every thing that I have wrote about him with Sparkling Eyes."[23]

James and Dolley had not been home at Montpelier for very long when it looked as if he and Patrick Henry would battle once more in the legislative arena. After Henry left the Virginia House of Delegates in 1790, he resumed a successful legal practice and lived comfortably at his 1,700-acre estate at Pleasant Grove in Prince Edward County. But after the Alien and Sedition Acts were passed, Henry, who was then living at Red Hill in Charlotte County, would again be asked to answer the call of public service.

President Washington, now retired, saw the Virginia resolution—which had been written by Madison—as threatening to use the state's authority to prevent enforcement of the Sedition Act, and he became alarmed that the resolution, if pursued, would "dissolve the Union or produce coercion." In early 1799, Washington asked the sixty-two-year-old Henry to stand for election to the General Assembly so he could oppose further efforts in Virginia to interfere with the federal government. Henry, although quite ill, and even though he may not have supported the Sedition Act and the prosecutions under it, reluctantly agreed out of respect for Washington.[24] There was great irony in Henry's willingness to come to the aid of the federal government, which he had so ardently opposed during the ratification period.

Once word spread that Henry would return to the legislature, Madison's friends implored him to run so he would be in Richmond to support the Virginia resolution and denounce the sedition law. Although Henry and Madison were both elected to the House of Delegates, Madison would not have to go up against his venerable adversary again. Henry died in June 1799, before the legislature met.[25]

James and Dolley moved in 1801 to Washington, where he served for eight years as Jefferson's secretary of state, and she was the unofficial first lady, since Jefferson's wife had died years before. This was a difficult time to be secretary of state because the British were creating serious problems for the United States. They frequently raided or destroyed American ships and forced the captured sailors to serve in the British navy. Some of the raids took place in American territorial waters. The United States wanted to stay neutral in the ongoing war between France and Britain, but it became increasingly difficult to do so. Desperate to find a solution, the Jefferson administration convinced Congress to impose an embargo on all American vessels departing for foreign ports so they would not become targets of the British navy. Jefferson hoped the embargo would postpone war with England until the United States could better defend itself. But the embargo seemed to hurt American commerce more than the British government, and it was unpopular at home. The South was cut off from many of its trading partners for its agricultural products, and the embargo greatly curtailed northern shipping. As secretary of state, Madison was involved in all these issues.

Madison was elected to the first of two terms as president in 1808. He had to continue to deal with the hostilities in Europe. When the British attacked the United States in the War of 1812, Madison had to flee the White House. He rode by horseback to nearby Bladensburg, Maryland, where he watched as the militia fought the better-organized British troops.[26] Dolley won the gratitude of the nation by arranging for papers, furnishings, and precious artworks—including Gilbert Stuart's portrait of George Washington—to be removed from the White House before British troops burned it and the capitol building.

Madison was a better legislator than executive, and some historians have argued that he had an ineffective cabinet in his first term, could have avoided war with Britain, and once in the war could have managed it more successfully. But although Madison was probably not among the nation's best presidents, it is hard to imagine that someone else could have done much better in defending the United States, with limited military capabilities, against powerful British forces. The War of 1812 was essentially a draw, and Madison should be commended for protecting the nation from what could have been a more devastating conflict.[27]

Midway through Madison's second term, with the war over, the country entered an "era of good feeling" that lasted through the eight years in office of his successor and friend, James Monroe. Monroe's defeat in the congressional race with Madison in 1789 did not hurt his career. He became a U.S. senator upon the death of William Grayson in 1790. President Washington named him minister to France in 1794, and from 1799 to 1802 he was Virginia's governor. A year later, President Jefferson sent him to France to help secure free navigation of the Mississippi River and the Louisiana Purchase.[28]

Monroe allowed his name to be entered as a candidate for president in 1808, which could have led to another contest against his friend James Madison. But when it became clear that the Republican caucus in Congress preferred Madison, Monroe did not seriously pursue the presidency. Monroe later served in the state legislature, as governor again, and then, from 1811 to the end of Madison's second term, as secretary of state. After serving two terms as president, Monroe briefly interrupted his retirement by agreeing to preside at the Virginia convention of 1829 to revise the state's constitution. Because of financial problems, in 1830

Monroe sold his estate and moved to New York, where his daughter could help take care of him. He died there on July 4, 1831, at age seventy-three.[29]

After Madison's term as president ended, he and Dolley retired to Montpelier in 1817. For the next almost twenty years, he stayed mostly at home. He entertained the many visitors who wanted to talk to the man who had been present at so many of the events that shaped the nation's formative years. He read extensively and became involved in a few public issues by writing letters, giving advice, and making recommendations about some challenges facing the country. But he rarely ventured away from his estate.

He did travel away from home when Orange County citizens elected him as a delegate to the state constitutional convention of 1829. Although the seventy-eight-year-old Madison was treated with great respect in Richmond—he was the sole surviving member of the last Virginia convention in 1776 and the Philadelphia convention of 1787—he worked unsuccessfully behind the scenes for reform, gave only one speech, and was disappointed when the convention failed to adopt his suggestions for improving the state's constitution.[30]

By June 1836, Madison was feeble and tired. He could no longer write; the reliable hand that had penned so many words over the years could not function anymore. During the previous months, it had become increasingly difficult for him to care for himself, and he depended on Dolley and others to help him through each day.[31]

During the last week of June, when it was obvious that he was dying, his doctor offered him medicine that might have prolonged his life until July 4. Thomas Jefferson and John Adams both died on that date in 1826—the fiftieth anniversary of the Declaration of Independence—and James Monroe died on July 4 in 1831. But Madison said no. After having given so much to the nation, he did not want to keep his frail body going just so he could last until that anniversary. Early in the morning of June 28, 1836, Madison was so weak that he could not eat. With family at his side, he quietly passed away at age eighty-five.[32]

It is fair to say that no other person in the nation's history did so much for which he is appreciated so little. James Madison had to overcome one obstacle after another to help give the nation a Constitution and sponsor the amendments that became the Bill of Rights. He had to convince a reluctant George Washington to attend the Constitutional Convention of 1787, then played a central role in writing the new charter of government. He won election to the Virginia ratifying convention and took on Patrick Henry to win approval of the Constitution. He had to seek election to the U.S. House in a district that was designed to make it almost impossible for him to win. In the First Congress, he had to persuade uninterested and often hostile members—two-thirds of them in each house—to propose the amendments that became the Bill of Rights. Finally, he helped to win its ratification in Virginia and other states. If that were not enough to earn the nation's gratitude, he served for eight years as secretary of state and two terms as president, before beginning a twenty-year retirement in which he continued to be involved in public affairs.

It is difficult to understand why Madison is not better known today. Historians have not neglected him. Several excellent biographies have been written about him, his papers have been published in several multivolume series, and he has been the subject of shorter books that illuminated his life and career.[33]

It is impossible to know if we would have a Bill of Rights today had Madison lost the congressional election in February 1789. But there is no doubt that it was a crucial moment in the country's history, and a person of extraordinary ability was there to see that those amendments—on which so much of our freedom depends—became part of the Constitution.

Appendix I

James Madison's Proposed Amendments
(June 8, 1789)

First. That there be prefixed to the Constitution a declaration—That all power is originally vested in, and consequently derived from, the people. That Government is instituted and ought to be exercised for the benefit of the people; which consists in the enjoyment of life and liberty, with the right of acquiring and using property, and generally of pursuing and obtaining happiness and safety. That the people have an indubitable, unalienable, and indefeasible right to reform or change their Government, whenever it be found adverse or inadequate to the purposes of its institution.

Secondly. That in article 1st, section 2, clause 3, these words be struck out, to wit: "The number of Representatives shall not exceed one for every thirty thousand, but each State shall have at least one Representative, and until such enumeration shall be made." And that in place thereof be inserted these words, to wit: "After the first actual enumeration, there shall be one Representative for every thirty thousand, until the number amounts to ——, after which the proportion shall be so regulated by Congress, that the number shall never be less than ——, nor more than ——, but each State shall, after the first enumeration, have at least two Representatives; and prior thereto."

Thirdly. That in article 1st, section 6, clause 1, there be added to the end of the first sentence, these words, to wit: "But no law varying the compensation last ascertained shall operate before the next ensuing election of Representatives."

Fourthly. That in article 1st, section 9, between clauses 3 and 4, be inserted these clauses, to wit: The civil rights of none shall be abridged on account of religious belief or worship, nor shall any national religion be established, nor shall the full and equal rights of conscience be in any manner, or on any pretext, infringed.

The people shall not be deprived or abridged of their right to speak, to write, or to publish their sentiments; and the freedom of the press, as one of the great bulwarks of liberty, shall be inviolable.

The people shall not be restrained from peaceably assembling and consulting for their common good; nor from applying to the Legislature by petitions, or remonstrances, for redress of their grievances.

The right of the people to keep and bear arms shall not be infringed; a well armed and well regulated militia being the best security of a free country: but no person religiously scrupulous of bearing arms shall be compelled to render military service in person.

No soldiers shall in time of peace be quartered in any house without the consent of the owner; nor at any time, but in a manner warranted by law.

No person shall be subject, except in cases of impeachment, to more than one punishment or one trial for the same offence; nor shall be compelled to be a witness against himself; nor be deprived of life, liberty, or property, without due process of law; nor be obliged to relinquish his property, where it may be necessary for public use, without a just compensation.

Excessive bail shall not be required, nor excessive fines imposed, nor cruel and unusual punishments inflicted.

The rights of the people to be secured in their persons, their houses, their papers, and their other property from all unreasonable searches and seizures, shall not be violated by warrants issued without probable cause, supported by oath or affirmation, or not particularly describing the places to be searched, or the persons or things to be seized.

In all criminal prosecutions, the accused shall enjoy the right to a speedy and public trial, to be informed of the cause and nature of the accusation, to be confronted with his accusers, and the witnesses against him; to have a compulsory process for obtaining witnesses in his favor; and to have the assistance of counsel for his defence.

The exceptions here or elsewhere in the Constitution, made in favor of particular rights, shall not be so construed as to diminish the just importance of other rights retained by the people, or as to enlarge the powers delegated by the Constitution; but either as actual limitations of such powers, or as inserted merely for greater caution.

Fifthly. That in article 1st, section 10, between clauses 1 and 2, be inserted this clause, to wit: No State shall violate the equal rights of conscience, or the freedom of the press, or the trial by jury in criminal cases.

Sixthly. That, in article 3d, section 2, be annexed to the end of clause 2d, these words, to wit: But no appeal to such court shall be allowed where the value in controversy shall not amount to —— dollars: nor shall any fact triable by jury, according to the course of common law, be otherwise re-examinable than may consist with the principles of common law.

Seventhly. That in article 3d, section 2, the third clause be struck out, and in its place be inserted the clauses following, to wit: The trial of all crimes (except in cases of impeachments, and cases arising in the land or naval forces, or the militia when on actual service, in time of war or public danger) shall be by an impartial jury of freeholders of the vicinage, with the requisite of unanimity for conviction, of the right of challenge, and other accustomed requisites; and in all crimes punishable with loss of life or member, presentment or indictment by a grand jury shall be an essential preliminary, provided that in cases of crimes committed within any county which may be in possession of an enemy, or in which a general insurrection may prevail, the trial may by law be authorized in some other county of the same State, as near as may be to the seat of the offence.

In cases of crimes committed not within any county, the trial may by law be in such county as the laws shall have prescribed. In suits at common law, between man and man, the trial by jury, as one of the best securities to the rights of the people, ought to remain inviolate.

Eighthly. That immediately after article 6th, be inserted, as article 7th, the clauses following, to wit: The powers delegated by this Constitution are appropriated to the departments to which they are respectively distributed: so that the Legislative Department shall never exercise the powers vested in the Executive or Judicial, nor the Executive exercise the powers vested in the Legislative or Judicial, nor the Judicial exercise the powers vested in the Legislative or Executive Departments.

The powers not delegated by this Constitution, nor prohibited by it to the States, are reserved to the States respectively.

Ninthly. That article 7th be numbered as article 8th.

Appendix II

Amendments Reported by the House Select Committee
(July 28, 1789)

In the introductory paragraph before the words, "We the people" add, "Government being intended for the benefit of the people, and the rightful establishment thereof being derived from their authority alone."

ART. 1, SEC. 2, PAR. 3 — Strike out all between the words, "direct" and "and until such," and instead thereof insert, "After the first enumeration there shall be one representative for every thirty thousand until the number shall amount to one hundred; after which the proportion shall be so regulated by Congress that the number of Representatives shall never be less than one hundred, nor more than one hundred and seventy-five, but each State shall always have at least one Representative."

ART. 1, SEC. 6 — Between the words "United States," and "shall in all cases," strike out "they," and insert, "But no law varying the compensation shall take effect until an election of Representatives shall have intervened. The members."

ART. 1, SEC. 9 — Between PAR. 2 and 3 insert, "No religion shall be established by law, nor shall the equal rights of conscience be infringed."

"The freedom of speech, and of the press, and the right of the people peaceably to assemble and consult for their common good, and to apply to the government for redress of grievances, shall not be infringed."

"A well regulated militia, composed of the body of the people, being the best security of a free State, the right of the people to keep and bear arms shall not be infringed, but no person religiously scrupulous shall be compelled to bear arms."

"No soldier shall in time of peace be quartered in any house without the consent of the owner, nor in time of war but in a manner to be prescribed by law."

"No person shall be subject, except in case of impeachment, to more than one trial or one punishment for the same offence, nor shall be compelled to be a witness against himself, nor be deprived of life, liberty, or property without due process of law; nor shall private property be taken for public use without just compensation."

"Excessive bail shall not be required, nor excessive fines imposed, nor cruel and unusual punishments inflicted."

"The right of the people to be secure in their person, houses, papers and effects, shall not be violated by warrants issuing, without probable cause supported by oath or affirmation, and not particularly describing the places to be searched, and the persons or things to be seized."

"The enumeration in this Constitution of certain rights shall not be construed to deny or disparage others retained by the people."

ART. 1, SEC. 10, between the 1st and 2d PAR. insert, "No State shall infringe the equal rights of conscience, nor the freedom of speech, or of the press, nor of the right of trial by jury in criminal cases."

ART. 3, SEC. 2, add to the 2d PAR. "But no appeal to such court shall be allowed, where the value in controversy shall not amount to one thousand dollars; nor shall any fact, triable by a Jury according to the course of the common law, be otherwise re-examinable than according to the rules of common law."

ART. 3, SEC. 2 — Strike out the whole of the 3rd paragraph, and insert — "In all criminal prosecutions the accused shall enjoy the right to a speedy and public trial, to be informed of the nature and cause of the accusation, to be confronted with the witnesses against him, to have compulsory process for obtaining witnesses in his favor, and to have the assistance of counsel for his defence."

"The trial of all crimes (except in cases of impeachment, and in cases arising in the land or naval forces, or in the militia, when in actual service in time of war or public danger) shall be by an impartial jury of freeholders of the vicinage, with the requisite of unanimity for conviction, the right of challenge and other accustomed requisites; and no person shall be held to answer for a capital, or otherwise infamous crime, unless on a presentment or indictment by a Grand Jury; but if a crime be committed in a place in the possession of an enemy, or in which an insurrection may prevail, the indictment and trial may by law be authorized in some other place within the same State; and if it be committed in a place not within a State, the indictment and trial may be at such place or places as the law may have directed."

"In suits at common law the right of trial by jury shall be preserved."

"Immediately after ART. 6, the following to be inserted as ART. 7."

"The powers delegated by this Constitution to the government of the United States, shall be exercised as therein appropriated, so that the Legislative shall never exercise the powers vested in the Executive or the Judicial; nor the Executive the powers vested in the Legislative or Judicial; nor the Judicial the powers vested in the Legislative or Executive."

"The powers not delegated by this Constitution, nor prohibited by it to the States, are reserved to the States respectively."

ART. 7 to be made ART. 8.

Appendix III

Amendments Passed by the House of Representatives
(August 24, 1789)

ARTICLE THE FIRST.

After the first enumeration, required by the first Article of the Constitution, there shall be one Representative for every thirty thousand, until the number shall amount to one hundred, after which the proportion shall be so regulated by Congress, that there shall be not less than one hundred Representatives, nor less than one Representative for every forty thousand persons, until the number of Representatives shall amount to two hundred, after which the proportion shall be so regulated by Congress, that there shall not be less than two hundred Representatives, nor less than one Representative for every fifty thousand persons.

ARTICLE THE SECOND.

No law varying the compensation to the members of Congress, shall take effect, until an election of Representatives shall have intervened.

ARTICLE THE THIRD.

Congress shall make no law establishing religion or prohibiting the free exercise thereof, nor shall the rights of Conscience be infringed.

ARTICLE THE FOURTH.

The Freedom of Speech, and of the Press, and the right of the People peaceably to assemble, and consult for their common good, and to apply to the Government for a redress of grievances, shall not be infringed.

ARTICLE THE FIFTH.

A well regulated militia, composed of the body of the People, being the best security of a free State, the right of the People to keep and bear arms, shall not be infringed, but no one religiously scrupulous of bearing arms, shall be compelled to render military service in person.

ARTICLE THE SIXTH.

No soldier shall, in time of peace, be quartered in any house without the consent of the owner, nor in time of war, but in a manner to be prescribed by law.

ARTICLE THE SEVENTH.

The right of the People to be secure in their persons, houses, papers and effects, against unreasonable searches and seizures, shall not be violated, and no warrants shall issue, but upon probable cause supported by oath or affirmation, and particularly describing the place to be searched, and the persons or things to be seized.

ARTICLE THE EIGHTH.

No person shall be subject, except in case of impeachment, to more than one trial, or one punishment for the same offence, nor shall be compelled in any criminal case, to be a witness against himself, nor be deprived of life, liberty or property, without due process of law; nor shall private property be taken for public use without just compensation.

ARTICLE THE NINTH.

In all criminal prosecutions, the accused shall enjoy the right to a speedy and public trial, to be informed of the nature and cause of the accusation, to be confronted with the witnesses against him, to have compulsory process for obtaining witnesses in his favor, and to have the assistance of counsel for his defence.

ARTICLE THE TENTH.

The trial of all crimes (except in cases of impeachment, and in cases arising in the land or naval forces, or in the militia when in actual service in time of War or public danger) shall be by an Impartial Jury of the Vicinage, with the requisite of unanimity for conviction, the right of challenge, and other accostomed requisites; and no person shall be held to answer for a capital, or otherways infamous crime, unless on a presentment or indictment by a Grand Jury; but if a crime be committed in a place in the possession of an enemy, or in which an insurrection may prevail, the indictment and trial may by law be authorised in some other place within the same State.

ARTICLE THE ELEVENTH.

No appeal to the Supreme Court of the United States, shall be allowed, where the value in controversy shall not amount to one thousand dollars, nor shall any fact, triable by a Jury according to the course of the common law, be otherwise re-examinable, than according to the rules of common law.

ARTICLE THE TWELFTH.

In suits at common law, the right of trial by Jury shall be preserved.

ARTICLE THE THIRTEENTH.

Excessive bail shall not be required, nor excessive fines imposed, nor cruel and unusual punishments inflicted.

ARTICLE THE FOURTEENTH.

No State shall infringe the right of trial by Jury in criminal cases, nor the rights of conscience, nor the freedom of speech, or of the press.

ARTICLE THE FIFTEENTH.

The enumeration in the Constitution of certain rights, shall not be construed to deny or disparage others retained by the people.

ARTICLE THE SIXTEENTH.

The powers delegated by the Constitution to the government of the United States, shall be exercised as therein appropriated, so that the Legislative shall never exercise the powers vested in the Executive or Judicial; nor the Executive the powers vested in the Legislative or Judicial; nor the Judicial the powers vested in the Legislative or Executive.

ARTICLE THE SEVENTEENTH.

The powers not delegated by the Constitution, nor prohibited by it, to the States, are reserved to the States respectively.

Appendix IV

Amendments Passed by the Senate
(September 9, 1789)

ARTICLE THE FIRST.

After the first enumeration, required by the first article of the Constitution, there shall be one Representative for every thirty thousand, until the number shall amount to one hundred; to which number one Representative shall be added for every subsequent increase of forty thousand, until the Representatives shall amount to two hundred, to which number one Representative shall be added for every subsequent increase of sixty thousand persons.

ARTICLE THE SECOND.

No law, varying the compensation for the services of the Senators and Representatives, shall take effect, until an election of Representatives shall have intervened.

ARTICLE THE THIRD.

Congress shall make no law establishing articles of faith, or a mode of worship, or prohibiting the free exercise of religion, or abridging the freedom of speech, or of the press, or the right of the people peaceably to assemble, and to petition to the government for a redress of grievances.

ARTICLE THE FOURTH.

A well regulated militia, being necessary to the security of a free State, the right of the people to keep and bear arms, shall not be infringed.

ARTICLE THE FIFTH.

No soldier shall, in time of peace, be quartered in any house, without the consent of the owner, nor in time of war, but in a manner to be prescribed by law.

ARTICLE THE SIXTH.

The right of the people to be secure in their persons, houses, papers, and effects, against unreasonable searches and seizures, shall not be violated, and no warrants shall issue, but upon probable cause, supported by oath or affirmation, and particularly describing the place to be searched, and the persons or things to be seized.

ARTICLE THE SEVENTH.

No person shall be held to answer for a capital, or otherwise infamous crime, unless on a presentment or indictment of a Grand Jury, except in cases arising in the land or naval forces, or in the militia, when in actual service in time of war or public danger; nor shall any person be subject for the same offence to be twice put in jeopardy of life or limb; nor shall be compelled in any criminal case, to be a witnesses against himself, nor be deprived of life, liberty or property, without due process of law; nor shall private property be taken for public use without just compensation.

ARTICLE THE EIGHTH.

In all criminal prosecutions, the accused shall enjoy the right to a speedy and public trial, to be informed of the nature and cause of the accusation, to be confronted with the witnesses against him, to have compulsory process for obtaining witnesses in his favour, and to have the assistance of counsel for his defence.

ARTICLE THE NINTH.

In suits at common law, where the value in controversy shall exceed twenty dollars, the right of trial by Jury shall be preserved, and no fact, tried by a Jury, shall be otherwise re-examined in any court of the United States, than according to the rules of the common law.

ARTICLE THE TENTH.

Excessive bail shall not be required, nor excessive fines imposed, nor cruel and unusual punishments inflicted.

ARTICLE THE ELEVENTH.

The enumeration in the Constitution, of certain rights, shall not be construed to deny or disparage others retained by the people.

ARTICLE THE TWELFTH.

The powers not delegated to the United States by the Constitution, nor prohibited by it to the States, are reserved to the States respectively, or to the people.

Appendix V

Amendments Proposed by Congress to the States
(September 25, 1789)

Article the first*. . . . After the first enumeration required by the first Article of the Constitution, there shall be one Representative for every thirty thousand, until the number shall amount to one hundred, after which, the proportion shall be so regulated by Congress, that there shall be not less than one hundred Representatives, nor less than one Representative for every forty thousand persons, until the number of Representatives shall amount to two hundred, after which the proportion shall be so regulated by Congress, that there shall not be less than two hundred Representatives, nor more than one Representative for every fifty thousand persons.

Article the second†. . . . No law, varying the compensation for the services of the Senators and Representatives, shall take effect, until an election of Representatives shall have intervened.

---

* Not ratified by the states

† Ratified in 1992

Article the third ... Congress shall make no law respecting an establishment of religion, or prohibiting the free exercise thereof; or abridging the freedom of speech, or of the press, or the right of the people peaceably to assemble, and to petition the Government for a redress of grievances.

Article the fourth ... A well regulated Militia, being necessary to the security of a free State, the right of the people to keep and bear Arms, shall not be infringed.

Article the fifth ... No Soldier shall, in time of peace be quartered in any house, without the consent of the Owner, nor in time of war, but in a manner to be prescribed by law.

Article the sixth ... The right of the people to be secure in their persons, houses, papers, and effects, against unreasonable searches and seizures, shall not be violated, and no Warrants shall issue, but upon probable cause, supported by Oath or affirmation, and particularly describing the place to be searched, and the persons or things to be seized.

Article the seventh ... No person shall be held to answer for a capital, or otherwise infamous crime, unless on a presentment or indictment of a Grand Jury, except in cases arising in the land or naval forces, or in the Militia, when in actual service in time of War or public danger; nor shall any person be subject for the same offence to be twice put in jeopardy of life or limb, nor shall be compelled in any criminal case to be a witness against himself, nor be deprived of life, liberty, or property, without due process of law; nor shall private property be taken for public use without just compensation.

Article the eighth ... In all criminal prosecutions, the accused shall enjoy the right to a speedy and public trial, by an impartial jury of the State and district wherein the crime shall have been committed, which district shall have been previously ascertained by law, and to be informed of the nature and cause of the accusation; to be confronted with the witnesses against him; to have compulsory process for obtaining witnesses in his favor, and to have the Assistance of Counsel for his defence.

Article the ninth ... In suits at common law, where the value in controversy shall exceed twenty dollars, the right of trial by jury shall be preserved, and no fact tried by a jury shall be otherwise re-examined in any Court of the United States, than according to the rules of the common law.

Article the tenth . . . Excessive bail shall not be required, nor excessive fines imposed, nor cruel and unusual punishments inflicted.

Article the eleventh . . . The enumeration in the Constitution, of certain rights, shall not be construed to deny or disparage others retained by the people.

Article the twelfth. . . The powers not delegated to the United States by the Constitution, nor prohibited by it to the States, are reserved to the States respectively, or to the people.

Abbreviations
and Frequently Cited Sources

AH	Alexander Hamilton
Amar	Akhil Reed Amar, *America's Constitution: A Biography* (New York: Random House, 2005)
AS	Archibald Stuart
Banning	Lance Banning, *The Sacred Fire of Liberty: James Madison and the Founding of the Federal Republic* (Ithaca: Cornell Univ. Press, 1995)
Banning II	Lance Banning, *Jefferson and Madison: Three Conversations from the Founding* (Lanham, Md.: Rowman & Littlefield, 2002)
Brant	Irving Brant, *James Madison: The Nationalist, 1780–1787* (Indianapolis: Bobbs-Merrill, 1948)
Brant II	Irving Brant, *James Madison: Father of the Constitution, 1787–1800* (Indianapolis: Bobbs-Merrill, 1950)
Brown	Robert E. Brown and B. Katherine Brown, *Virginia, 1705–1786: Democracy or Aristocracy* (East Lansing: Michigan State Univ. Press, 1964)
C&K	Patrick T. Conley and John P. Kaminski, eds., *The Bill of Rights and the States* (Madison, Wisc.: Madison House, 1992)
Carey	George W. Carey, *In Defense of the Constitution* (Indianapolis: Liberty Fund, 1995)
Cornell	Saul Cornell, *The Other Founders: Anti-Federalism & the Dissenting Tradition in America, 1788–1828* (Chapel Hill: Univ. of North Carolina Press, 1999)
DGW	Donald Jackson and Dorothy Twohig, eds., *The Diaries of George Washington*, vol. 5, *July 1786–December 1789* (Charlottesville: Univ. Press of Virginia, 1979)

DHF	David Hackett Fischer, *Washington's Crossing* (New York: Oxford Univ. Press, 2004)
DHFFC	Charlene Bangs Bickford et al., eds., *Documentary History of the First Federal Congress* (Baltimore: Johns Hopkins Univ. Press, 1992)
DHFFE	Gordon DenBoer, ed., *The Documentary History of the First Federal Elections, 1788–1790* (Madison: Univ. of Wisconsin Press, 1984)
DHRC	John P. Kaminski and Gaspare J. Saladino, eds., *The Documentary History of the Ratification of the Constitution,* vols. 8–10 (Virginia) (Madison: State Historical Society of Wisconsin, 1988–93)
EC	Edward Carrington
EG	Elbridge Gerry
EIO	Emphasis in original
EP	Edmund Pendleton
ES	Edward Stevens
FA	Fisher Ames
FC	Francis Corbin
Federalist	George W. Carey and James McClellan, eds., *The Federalist* (Indianapolis: Liberty Fund, 2001)
Fontaine	Edward Fontaine, *Patrick Henry: Corrections of biographical mistakes, and popular errors in regard to his character* (transcribed, introduced, and published by Mark Couvillon, 1996)
Freeman	Joanne B. Freeman, *Affairs of Honor: National Politics in the New Republic* (New Haven: Yale Univ. Press, 2001)
G&L	Michael Allen Gillespie and Michael Lienesch, eds., *Ratifying the Constitution* (Lawrence: Univ. Press of Kansas, 1989)
GLT	George Lee Turberville
GM	George Mason
GN	George Nicholas
Goldwin	Robert A. Goldwin, *From Parchment to Power: How James Madison Used the Bill of Rights to Save the Constitution* (Washington: AEI Press, 1997)
Grigsby	Hugh Blair Grigsby, *The History of the Virginia Federal Convention of 1788* (Richmond: Virginia Historical Society, 1890)
GW	George Washington
GWAC	W.B. Allen, ed., *George Washington: A Collection* (Indianapolis: Liberty Fund, 1988)
HB	Hardin Burnley
HK	Henry Knox
HL	Henry Lee
JD	John Dawson
JM	James Madison

Ketcham	Ralph Ketcham, *James Madison: A Biography* (Charlottesville: Univ. Press of Virginia, 1990)
Koch	Adrienne Koch, *Notes of Debates in the Federal Convention of 1787 Reported by James Madison* (New York: Norton, 1987)
Leibiger	Stuart Leibiger, *Founding Friendship: George Washington, James Madison, and the Creation of the American Republic* (Charlottesville: Univ. Press of Virginia, 1999)
Levy	Leonard W. Levy, *Origins of the Bill of Rights* (New Haven: Yale Univ. Press, 1999)
LPEP	David John Mays, ed., *The Letters and Papers of Edmund Pendleton, 1734–1803* (Charlottesville: Univ. Press of Virginia, 1967)
Mattern	David B. Mattern and Holly C. Shulman, eds., *The Selected Letters of Dolley Payne Madison* (Charlottesville: Univ. of Virginia Press, 2003)
Mayer	Henry Mayer, *A Son of Thunder: Patrick Henry and the American Republic* (New York: Grove Press, 1991)
McDonald	Forrest McDonald, *E Pluribus Unum: The Formation of the American Republic 1776–1790* (Indianapolis: Liberty Fund, 1979)
McDonald II	Forrest McDonald, *Novus Ordo Seclorum: The Intellectual Origins of the Constitution* (Lawrence: Univ. Press of Kansas, 1985)
McGaughy	J. Kent McGaughy, *Richard Henry Lee of Virginia: A Portrait of an American Revolutionary* (Lanham, Md.: Rowman & Littlefield, 2004)
Miller	William Lee Miller, *The Business of May Next: James Madison and the Founding* (Charlottesville: Univ. Press of Virginia, 1994)
PGM	Robert A. Rutland, ed., *The Papers of George Mason*, vol. 3, *1787–1792* (Chapel Hill: Univ. of North Carolina Press, 1970)
PGW	Dorothy Twohig, ed., *The Papers of George Washington, Presidential Series*, vol. 1, *Sept. 1788–March 1789* (Charlottesville: Univ. Press of Virginia, 1987)
PH	Patrick Henry
PJM	Robert R. Rutland, ed., *The Papers of James Madison* (Charlottesville: Univ. Press of Virginia, 1962–)
RBL	Richard Bland Lee
RHL	Richard Henry Lee
Risjord	Norman K. Risjord, *Chesapeake Politics, 1781–1800* (New York: Columbia Univ. Press, 1978)
RJM	Reverend James Madison
Rossiter	Clinton Rossiter, *1787: The Grand Convention* (New York: Norton, 1987, orig. pub. 1966)
RP	Richard Peters
Rutland I	Robert Allen Rutland, *The Ordeal of the Constitution: The Antifederalists and the Ratification Struggle of 1787–1788* (Boston: Northeastern Univ. Press, 1983, orig. pub. 1966)
Rutland II	Robert Allen Rutland, *The Birth of the Bill of Rights, 1776–1791* (Chapel Hill: Univ. of North Carolina Press, 1955)

Rutland III — Robert A. Rutland, ed., *James Madison and the American Nation: 1751–1836, an Encyclopedia* (New York: Simon & Schuster, 1994)

Schwartz — Bernard Schwartz, *The Roots of the Bill of Rights,* 5 vols. (New York: Chelsea House, 1980)

Simon — James F. Simon, *What Kind of Nation: Thomas Jefferson, John Marshall, and the Epic Struggle to Create a United States* (New York: Simon & Schuster, 2002)

Sydnor — Charles S. Sydnor, *Gentlemen Freeholders: Political Practices in Washington's Virginia* (Chapel Hill, N.C.: Institute for Early American History and Culture, 1952)

Taylor — *Diary of Col. Francis Taylor, Orange County, Virginia, 1786–1799,* Library of Virginia, Archives and Records Division (typewritten transcription)

TFC — Philip B. Kurland and Ralph Lerner, eds., *The Founders' Constitution,* vols. 1–5 (Indianapolis: Liberty Fund, 2000; orig. pub. 1987 by Univ. of Chicago Press)

TJ — Thomas Jefferson

TS — Theodore Sedgwick

Veit — Helen E. Veit et al., *Creating the Bill of Rights* (Baltimore: Johns Hopkins Univ. Press, 1991)

VHS — Virginia Historical Society, Richmond

VMHB — *Virginia Magazine of History and Biography* (Virginia Historical Society, Richmond)

Wakelyn — Jon L. Wakelyn, *Birth of the Bill of Rights: Encyclopedia of the Antifederalists,* vol. 1, *Biographies* (Westport, Conn.: Greenwood Press, 2004)

WJM — Stanislaus Murray Hamilton, *The Writings of James Monroe,* vol. 1, *1778–1794* (New York: G. P. Putnam's Sons, 1898)

Wood — Gordon S. Wood, *The Creation of the American Republic, 1776–1787* (New York: Norton, 1972)

WWH — William Wirt Henry, *Patrick Henry: Life, Correspondence and Speeches,* 3 vols. (New York: Burt Franklin, 1969, orig. pub. 1891)

Notes

Chapter 1

1. Sept. 17, 1787, Koch, 655.
2. Richard Brookhiser, *Founding Father: Rediscovering George Washington* (New York: Free Press, 1996), 61–62. See also Joseph J. Ellis, *His Excellency: George Washington* (New York: Knopf, 2004), 177–79.
3. For the length of the sessions, see Sept. 17, 1787, *DGW*, 185.
4. For an excellent discussion of Washington's accomplishments in the war, see Ellis, *His Excellency*, 73–146.
5. July 30, 1787, *DGW*, 178–79. For Morris's role at the convention, see Richard Brookhiser, *Gentleman Revolutionary: Gouverneur Morris—The Rake Who Wrote the Constitution* (New York: Free Press, 2003).
6. Noel F. Busch, *Winter Quarters: George Washington and the Continental Army at Valley Forge* (New York: Liveright, 1974), 31–32.
7. July 31, 1787, *DGW*, 179.
8. Leibiger, 58–70.
9. For the Annapolis convention, see *TFC* 1:185–87. For Washington's decision to go to Philadelphia, see Ellis, *His Excellency*, 171–77.
10. Sept. 15, 1787, Koch, 652. John Adams was in England representing the United States when the convention met.
11. Thomas Jefferson was serving as the U.S. envoy in France during the summer of 1787.
12. Sept. 17, 1787, Koch, 659.
13. Ibid., 614–15.
14. Sept. 12, 1787, ibid., 630; Sept. 15, 1787, ibid., 651.

15. *DHRC*, 530–31. See also Brent Tarter, "The Virginia Declaration of Rights," in *To Secure the Blessings of Liberty: Rights in American History,* ed. Josephine F. Pacheco (The George Mason Lectures) (Fairfax, Va.: George Mason Univ. Press, 1993), 37–54.

16. This description of Mason is drawn from Brent Tarter, "George Mason and the Conservation of Liberty," *VMHB* 99 (July 1991): 279–304.

17. Aug. 31, 1787, Koch, 566.

18. Tarter, *VMHB*, 292–97.

19. Sept. 12, 1787, Koch, 630.

20. Ibid.

21. *Federalist 84,* 445.

22. Ibid., 443, 447. See also Banning II, 8–13.

23. Aug. 31, 1787, Koch, 566–67.

24. Sept. 10, 1787, ibid., 612.

25. Ibid., 615.

26. Sept. 15, 1787, ibid., 651–52. See also Randolph, Aug. 31, 1787, ibid., 567; and Sept. 10, 1787, ibid., 612.

27. Ibid. See generally Wood, 306–43.

28. Ibid., 652.

29. Sept. 17, 1787, Koch, 656–58.

30. Ibid., 652–54. See also Walter Isaacson, *Benjamin Franklin: An American Life* (New York: Simon & Schuster, 2003), 457–60.

31. Sept. 17, 1787, Koch, 653.

32. Ibid., 654, 657.

33. Ibid., 659.

34. The incident was recorded by Maryland delegate James McHenry. Earl Warren, *A Republic, if You Can Keep It* (New York: Quadrangle Books, 1972), 1–12.

35. Sept. 17, 1787, *DGW*, 185.

36. The delegates discussed ratification several times during the convention. For the final week's treatment of the subject, see Sept. 10, 1787, Koch, 612–15. See also GM, July 23, 1787, Koch, 348.

37. McDonald, 334.

38. JM discussed this with GW, Sept. 30, 1787, *PJM* 10:179.

39. Article XIII, *TFC* 1:26. For two excellent books on the confederation period, see Merrill Jensen, *The New Nation: A History of the United States During the Confederation 1781–1789* (New York: Knopf, 1950); and Jack N. Rakove, *The Beginnings of National Politics: An Interpretive History of the Continental Congress* (New York: Knopf, 1979).

40. Akhil Reed Amar disputes whether Rhode Island was the only state not to endorse the 1781 impost amendment, 514–15, n. 55.

41. May 29, 1787, Koch, 30–33.

42. Sept. 10, 1787, ibid., 611–15.

43. June 5, 1787, ibid., 70.

44. Sept. 10, 1787, ibid., 613.

45. JM to GW, Sept. 30, 1787, *PJM* 10:180. See generally McDonald II, 279–80.

46. Ibid.

47. Jack N. Rakove, *Original Meanings: Politics and Ideas in the Making of the Constitution* (New York: Knopf, 1996), 108.

48. JM to GW, Sept. 30, 1787, *PJM* 10:179.

49. Ibid., 180.

50. GW to JM, Oct. 10, 1787, ibid., 189.

51. See generally Wakelyn. Sam Adams, the well-known patriot, eventually supported the Constitution at the Massachusetts ratifying convention. Ibid., 4.

52. For a discussion of Madison's role, see Rakove, *Orginal Meanings,* 109–11.

53. Jack Larkin, *The Reshaping of Everyday Life, 1790–1840* (New York: Harper & Row, 1988), 224–31.

54. Sept. 19, 1787, *DGW,* 186.

55. Ibid.

56. See Ellis, *His Excellency,* 147–87.

57. John P. Kaminski and Gaspare J. Saladino, *Commentaries on the Constitution: Public and Private* (Madison: State Historical Society of Wisconsin, 1981) vol. 1, Sept. 28, 1787, Doc. 96-A, 243.

58. Doc. 96-B, ibid.

59. DC to JM, Oct. 28, 1787, *PJM* 10:227.

60. GM to GW, Oct. 7, 1787, *PGM,* 1001.

61. GW to JM, Dec. 7, 1787, *PJM* 10:298.

62. JM to Ambrose Madison, Nov. 8, 1787, ibid., 244.

Chapter 2

1. Grigsby, 314. According to Grigsby, Dawson often wore "fair top" boots. These were tall boots of brown or black leather worn mostly by southern gentlemen in the nineteenth century. When folded over below the knee, they revealed the underside of the leather, usually of a lighter color, thus the phrase "fair top" in the boot's name. Worn more for fashion than to protect against the elements, the boots were rarely seen after 1884. Sir William A. Craigie and James R. Hulbert, *A Dictionary of American English on Historical Principles* (Chicago: Univ. of Chicago Press, 1940), 921.

2. JD to JM, Sept. 25, 1787, *PJM* 10:173–74.

3. JD to JM, Aug. 5, 1787, ibid., 131.

4. Grigsby incorrectly states that Dawson was Monroe's brother-in-law, 314. The accurate information about Dawson's relationship to Monroe was provided by Greg Stoner, library assistant, VHS, March 23, 2004.

5. See, for example, GLT to JM, Dec. 11, 1787, *PJM* 10:315–18.

6. Sept. 28, 1787, *DHRC,* 23.

7. Oct. 2, 1787, ibid., 23–24.

8. GM to GW, Oct. 7, 1787, ibid., 43.

9. LC to GM, Oct. 8, 1787, ibid., 581.

10. JH to Horatio Gates, Nov. 20, 1787, ibid., 582.

11. JD to JM, Oct. 19, 1787, *PJM* 10:198.

12. JM to William Short, Oct. 24,1787, ibid., 221.

13. *DHRC,* 581. The election took place on March 17, 1788. See also EC to HK, Jan. 12, 1789, ibid., 583.

14. ER to JM, Dec. 27, 1787, *PJM* 10:346.

15. JD to JM, Feb. 18, 1788, ibid., 518.

16. James Mercer to John Francis Mercer, Dec. 12, 1787, *DHRC,* 582.

17. EC to HK, Jan. 12, 1788, ibid., 583.

18. *Philadelphia Independent Gazetteer,* April 4, 1788, ibid., 614. EIO.

19. G&L, 14.

20. John Ferling, *A Leap in the Dark: The Struggle to Create the American Republic* (New York: Oxford Univ. Press, 2003), 302.

21. Mayer, 61, 59.

22. Ibid., 61–62.

23. Ibid., 64.

24. Gordon S. Wood, *The American Revolution: A History* (New York: Modern Library, 2003), 16.

25. David J. Vaughn, *Give Me Liberty: The Uncompromising Statesmanship of Patrick Henry* (Nashville: Cumberland House, 1997), 44.

26. Mayer, 65–66.

27. Wood, 28–29.

28. Rutland III, 234.

29. WG to William Short, Nov. 10, 1787, *DHRC,* 150–51.

30. JM to AM, Nov. 8, 1787, *PJM* 10:244.

31. Ibid.

32. See generally Mattern.

33. When Madison was only twenty-one, he wrote to his friend William Bradford that he did not expect to live a long life: "As to myself I am too dull and infirm now to look out for any extraordinary things in this world for I think my sensations for many months past have intimated to me not to expect a long or healthy life." Nov. 9, 1772, *PJM* 1:75.

34. JM to GW, Feb. 20, 1788, *PJM* 10:526–27. See generally Sydnor, 73–74.

35. See especially *Federalist 10,* Nov. 22, 1787, *PJM* 10:263–70. For a speech on citizenship delivered on the floor of the U.S. House on May 22, 1789, see *PJM* 12:178–82. See also Wood, 122, 195–96, 505–6, 510–11.

36. Madison, Aug. 7, 1787, Koch, 403–4. See generally Alexander Keyssar, *The Right to Vote: The Contested History of Democracy in the United States* (New York: Basic Books, 2000), 11–12, 22; and Ketcham, 182–83, 220–21. Madison later modified this view to allow participation by those who paid taxes. Ketcham, 637–38.

37. See generally Gary Rosen, *American Compact: James Madison and the Problem of the Founding* (Lawrence: Univ. Press of Kansas, 1999); and Wood, 344–89.

38. JM to William T. Barry, August 4, 1822, in *James Madison's "Advice to My Country,"* ed. David B. Mattern (Charlottesville: Univ. Press of Virginia, 1997), 41.

39. JM to TJ, Oct. 17, 1788, *PJM* 11:298–99.

40. April 24, 1777, *PJM* 1:192–93. See generally Sydnor, 56; and Brown, 53–154.

41. Sydnor, 73, 51.

42. Ibid., 15.

43. Ibid., 16–17.

44. Ibid., 53–55.

45. Ibid., 21.

46. Ibid., 20.

47. Ibid., 25.

48. Ibid., 32–33.

49. *DHRC,* 17–19.

50. JD to JM, Sept. 25, 1787, *PJM* 10:173; ER to JM, Sept. 30, 1787, ibid., 182.

51. RJM to JM, Oct. 1, 1787, ibid., 184. See also Wood, 150–61; 202–6.

52. RJM to TM, Oct. 1, 1787, *DHRC,* 30.

53. JJ to JM, Oct. 29, 1787, *PJM* 10:228–29.

54. GW to JM, Oct. 10, 1787, ibid., 189–90.

55. JM to WS, Oct. 24, 1787, ibid., 221.

56. JM to GW, Oct. 28, 1787, ibid., 225.

57. ER to JM, Oct. 29, 1787, ibid., 230.

58. Ibid., 231.

59. GW to David Stuart, Nov. 5, 1787, *DHRC,* 147.

60. JD to JM, Nov. 10, 1787, *PJM* 10:248.

61. JM to GW, Nov. 18, 1787, ibid., 254.

62. *DHRC,* 180–83.

63. HK to GW, Oct. 3, 1787, ibid., 33–34.

64. RHL to EG, Sept. 29, 1787, ibid., 25.

65. See generally Oliver Perry Chitwood, *Richard Henry Lee: Statesman of the Revolution* (Morgantown: West Virginia Univ. Foundation, 1967); and McGaughy.

66. *DHRC,* 65–67. Lee's statement was published in newspapers in Virginia and nationally.

67. Ibid., 65.

68. Sydnor, 95–96.

69. Ibid; *DHRC,* 66.

70. Freeman, 114–16.

71. RHL to GM, Oct. 1, 1787, *DHRC,* 29.

72. RHL to WS, Oct. 2, 1787, ibid., 32–33.

73. RHL to ER, Oct. 16, 1787, ibid., 64.

74. RHL to SA, Oct. 5, 1787, ibid., 36–37. EIO.

75. Nov. 16, Dec. 6, 1787, ibid., 59–60.

76. GW to JM, Dec. 7, 1787, *PJM* 10:298.

77. *DHRC,* 60.

78. Ibid., 241–43.

79. Ibid., 40.

80. GM to TJ, May 26, 1788, ibid., 882–83.

81. Ibid., 43–45.

82. John Dawson thought it was Mason. JD to JM, Oct. 19, 1787, *PJM* 10:198.

83. Oct. 17, 1787, *DHRC,* 73.

84. Ibid., 41.

85. JP to HK, Oct. 21, 1787, ibid., 88–89.

86. TL to JL, Dec. 3, 1787, ibid., 196–97.

87. TL to JL, Oct. 19, 1787, ibid., 80–81.

88. Ibid., 41–42.

89. GW to David Stuart, Oct. 17, 1787, ibid., 69.

90. Oct. 31, 1787, ibid., 138.

91. James Monroe to JM, Oct. 13, 1787, *PJM* 10:193.

92. Berkeley, Sept. 28, 1787, *DHRC,* 22; Fairfax, Oct. 2, 1787, ibid., 23–25; Frederick, Oct. 22, 1787, ibid., 91–93; Henrico, Oct. 22, 1787, ibid., 93; Alexandria, Oct. 2, 1787, ibid., 23–25; Williamsburg, Oct. 6, 1787, ibid., 39–40; Fredericksburg, Oct. 20, 1787, ibid., 85–86; Petersburg, Oct. 24, 1787, ibid., 96–97.

93. LT to JM, Dec. 16, 1787, *PJM* 10:329.

94. AS to JM, Nov. 2, 1787, ibid., 234.

95. AS to JM, Dec. 22, 1787, ibid., 344.

96. HL to JM, Dec. 20, 1787, ibid., 340.

97. JG to JM, Feb. 17, 1788, ibid., 516.

98. JM to JM, Jan. 30, 1788, ibid., 446.

99. Freeman, 159–98.

100. ER to JM, Jan. 3, 1788, *PJM* 10:350.

101. WM to JM, Jan. 31, 1788, ibid., 454–55.

102. JD to JM, Feb. 18, 1788, ibid., 518.

103. JM to GW, Feb. 20, 1788, ibid., 526.

104. Ibid., 526–27.

105. JM to EHT, March 25, 1788, *PJM* 11:5.

106. Taylor, March 24, 1788, *DHRC*, 602.

107. Ketcham, 251. There is no evidence that alcohol was provided to voters in this election.

108. JD to James Maury, May 8, 1788, *DHRC*, 604.

109. John Vaughn to John Dickinson, April 19, 1788, ibid., 603.

110. CG to JM, April 7, 1788, *PJM* 11:11.

111. EC to JM, April 8, 1788, ibid., 15.

112. JM to Eliza House Trist, March 25, 1788, ibid., 5–6.

Chapter 3

1. The description of the arrival of delegates and spectators in Richmond is adapted from Grigsby, 25–26.

2. Forest McDonald in G&L, ix. For a discussion of North Carolina's conventions, see Rutland, 279–300.

3. Virginia's bicameral legislature consisted of a popularly elected House of Delegates and a Senate, and it was referred to collectively as the General Assembly. Delegates stood for election every year, while senators served four-year terms. Each county elected two delegates to the House, and the city of Williamsburg and the borough of Norfolk elected one each. Senators were elected from each of twenty-four Senate districts. *DHRC*, xxiv. In reaction to the abuses of power committed by King George III and royal governors in the colonies, the Virginia constitution of 1776 sharply restricted the powers of the executive branch of government. The General Assembly not only had the authority to make laws, it also chose the governor, the eight members of the Council of State to advise the governor, the attorney general, and all judges and other state officials. Emily J. Salmon and Edward D. C. Campbell Jr., *The Hornbook of Virginia History* (Richmond: Library of Virginia, 1994), 30.

4. JM to EP, Oct. 28, 1787, *PJM* 10:224.

5. *Petersburg Virginia Gazette,* Nov. 1, 1787, *DHRC,* 112–14.

6. See also John Pierce to HK, Oct. 26, 1787, ibid., 123–24.

7. *DHRC,* 113.

8. Ibid.

9. Ibid., 114.

10. Ibid., 117.

11. ER to JM, ca. Oct. 29, 1787, *PJM* 10:230.

12. JM to TJ, Dec. 9, 1787, ibid., 311.

13. JM to GN, April 8, 1788, *PJM* 11:12.

14. JM to ER, April 10, 1788, ibid., 11:19.
15. JM to TJ, April 22, 1788, ibid., 28.
16. JM to TJ, Aug. 10, 1788, ibid., 226. EIO.
17. JM to TJ, Aug. 23, 1788, ibid., 238. See also Rutland I, 286.
18. JM to GW, Aug. 11, 1788, ibid., 230.
19. GW to BL, Aug. 28, 1788, *GWAC*, 415–16.
20. GW to TJ, Aug. 31, 1788, ibid., 420.
21. ER to JM, Sept. 3, 1788, *PJM* 11:246–47.
22. Cassius III to RHL, *Virginia Independent Chronicle*, April 23, 1788, *DHRC*, 751–52.
23. Virginia and New York did not list amendments in their petitions to Congress. Veit, 235–38.
24. See GW to David Stuart, Nov. 30, 1787, ibid., 193–94.
25. JM to GLT, Nov. 2, 1788, *PJM* 11:331; JM to HL, Nov. 30, 1788, ibid., 372.
26. JM to TJ, Dec. 8, 1788, ibid., 382–83.
27. John Pierce to HK, Oct. 26, 1787, *DHRC*, 123.
28. JD to JM, Nov. 10, 1787, *PJM* 10:248.
29. GW to JL, Dec. 3, 1787, *DHRC*, 198.
30. Ibid., 116.
31. Ibid., 120, n. 12. White men at least twenty-one years of age who owned twenty-five acres and a house, fifty acres unimproved, or a lot with a house in town, could vote. Special exceptions were made for voters in Norfolk and Williamsburg if there was a "house keeper" who had lived in the town for six months and had an estate of fifty pounds or had served an apprenticeship for five years in the town.
32. Ibid., 185.
33. Ibid., 185–86.
34. JM to AS, Dec. 14, 1787, *PJM* 10:325. See Rufus King to Jeremiah Wadsworth, Dec. 23, 1787, *DHRC*, 258; and GW to JM, Jan. 10, 1788, *PJM* 10:357–58.
35. JM to AS, Dec. 14, 1787, *PJM* 10:325–26.
36. For amendments to the bill, see *DHRC*, 189. For the final bill, see 191. After the words "Federal Constitution," the General Assembly added this language: "in such manner as to keep up that friendly intercourse and preserve that unanimity respecting any great change of government, which it is the duty and wish of the legislature to promote and cherish." Ibid., 191.
37. Ibid., 184–85.
38. AS to JM, Dec. 2, 1787, *PJM* 10:291.
39. *DHRC*, 191. This motion was approved on Dec. 26, 1787.
40. Opponents suspected that mail carriers, sympathetic to the Federalists, sometimes "lost" Anti-Federalist mail. Rutland, 62, 224.
41. See generally Michael Allen Gillespie, "Massachusetts: Creating Consensus," in G&L, 138–67.
42. JM to GW, Feb. 15, 1788, *PJM* 10:510; GW to JM, March 2, 1788, ibid., 553; JM to GW, March 3, 1788, ibid., 555.
43. TJ to Alexander Donald, Feb. 7, 1788, *DHRC*, 1088, n. 7.
44. TJ to EC, May 27, 1788, ibid.
45. TJ to William Carmichael, June 3, 1788, ibid.
46. *Virginia Independent Chronicle*, March 19, 1788, *DHRC*, 504. EIO.
47. Levy, 31–32. For a discussion of the Pennsylvania convention, see George Graham Jr., "Pennsylvania: Representation and the Meaning of Republicanism," in G&L, 52–70.
48. G&L, 6.
49. During a speech at the Virginia ratifying convention, Henry asked the delegates: "When I call this the most mighty State in the Union, do I not speak the truth? Does not Virginia

surpass every State in the Union, in number of inhabitants, extent of territory, felicity of position, and affluence and wealth?" June 7, 1788, *DHRC,* 1040.

50. Henry told the delegates at the ratifying convention that Virginia could join North Carolina as part of a regional confederacy to protect its interests. "They could exist separated from the rest of America," Henry said, although he admitted that this was "not a desirable object." June 9, 1788, *DHRC,* 1059. See also Banning, 67–68, 120–25.

51. GW to David Stuart, Nov. 30, 1787, *DHRC,* 193.

52. Grigsby, 319.

53. June 7, 1788, *DHRC,* 1045; June 9, 1788, ibid., 1055.

54. See generally Carey, 77–121.

55. See Madison's speech at the Virginia convention, June 6, 1788, *DHRC,* 995.

56. June 10, 1788, ibid., 1099.

57. Rutland called the lack of a bill of rights an "Achilles' heel" and said it was of "vital" concern to the public. He argued that the Federalists quickly regretted their decision to reject Mason's offer to prepare a bill of rights before the document was signed. Rutland, 32–33. See also Banning II, 3–4, 9–22.

58. For an excellent discussion of Madison's position on a bill of rights, see Paul Finkelman, "James Madison and the Bill of Rights: A Reluctant Paternity," in *1990 Supreme Court Review* (1991): 301–47.

59. This section on *The Federalist* is based on Finkelman's discussion, 316–19.

60. For a discussion of the Madison-Jefferson correspondence, see Finkelman, 309–22; 328–33; James Morton Smith, ed., *The Republic of Letters: The Correspondence Between Thomas Jefferson and James Madison, 1776–1826,* vol. 1 (New York: Norton, 1995), 518–637; and Ralph Ketcham, *Framed for Posterity: The Enduring Philosophy of the Constitution* (Lawrence: Univ. Press of Kansas, 1993), 93–98.

61. Much of the discussion of the ideology and impact of the Anti-Federalists in this section comes from Cornell.

62. Cornell, 28–29. See also Gerry's support for Randolph's motion at the Constitutional Convention to hold a second convention to propose a bill of rights. Sept. 15, 1787, Koch, 652.

63. Cornell, 25. The dissenting report of the Pennsylvania convention was reprinted thirty times.

64. Ibid., 311. Rutland identifies Lee as the author of the "Letters of a Federal Farmer," which were published beginning in early October. Rutland, 21. Some scholars believe it was Melancton Smith of New York. See McGaughy, 195–201.

65. RHL to SA, Oct. 5, 1787, *DHRC,* 38.

66. RHL to ER, Oct. 16, 1787, ibid., 61, 64.

67. RHL to GM, May 7, 1788, ibid., 785–86. See also RHL to EP, May 26, 1788, ibid., 880. Rutland argues that the improving economy also decreased interest in a second convention. Rutland I, 306–8.

68. EC to TJ, Oct. 23, 1787, *DHRC,* 95.

69. Cornell lists nine issues as having appeared repeatedly in Anti-Federalist writings: consolidation of the federal government; aristocracy (undermining principles of a republic); representation (the people not adequately represented); separation of powers; judicial tyranny; lack of a bill of rights; the taxing power of the federal government; the allowance of a standing army during peacetime and its impact on state militias; and the extent of powers granted to the executive branch. Cornell, 30–31.

70. Rutland, 190.

71. AL to RHL, Feb. 19, 1788, *DHRC,* 620.

72. June 5, 1788, *DHRC*, 955.

73. June 9, 1788, ibid., 1070.

74. Lance Banning, "Virginia: Sectionalism and the General Good," in G&L, 262, 285, 234–64. At its convention in July 1788, North Carolina voted by a two-to-one margin neither to ratify nor reject the Constitution, thus handing Federalists a serious defeat. Willie Jones, who led the North Carolina convention to this "state of suspended indecision"—in the words of Rutland—was influenced by Anti-Federalists in Virginia. Rutland, 275.

Chapter 4

1. John G. Roberts, "The American Career of Quesnay de Beaurepaire," *French Review* 20 (May 1947): 463.

2. W. Asbury Christian, *Richmond: Her Past and Present* (Richmond: L. H. Jenkins, 1912), 29. Quesnay also envisioned the teaching of medicine, astronomy, natural history, and other subjects. Samuel Mordecai, *Richmond in By-Gone Days* (Richmond: Dietz Press, 1860), 202.

3. Martin Staples Shockley, "The Richmond Theatre, 1780–1790," *VMHB* 60 (July 1952): 426–35.

4. *Virginia Gazette and American Advertiser*, June 28, 1786.

5. Mordecai, *Richmond*, 204.

6. Roberts, "American Career," 470. After the fire of 1803, the theater was rebuilt. That structure burned in 1811, with a loss of seventy-two lives. Grigsby, 68, n. 81. See also Grigsby, 67–69.

7. Grigsby called the Virginia convention "the most animated parliamentary tournament of the eighteenth century, at least on this side of the Atlantic." Ibid., 4.

8. Alexander White to Mary Wood, June 10–11, 1788, *DHRC*, 1591.

9. Grigsby, 67; Roberts, 469, 470.

10. WWH 2:341. The author was the grandson of Patrick Henry. On June 8, William Heth said, "The weather [is] extremely warm, as it has been for some days." *DHRC*, 1589, n. 2.

11. AW to Mary Wood, June 10–11, 1788, *DHRC*, 1592.

12. Grigsby, 73.

13. Christian, 33. See also Mary Newton Stanard, *Richmond: Its People and Its History* (Philadelphia: J. B. Lippincott, 1923), 56–62.

14. James Duncanson to James Maury, June 7, 13, 1788, *DHRC*, 1582.

15. The "Socrates" title comes from Miller, 197.

16. Grigsby, 201.

17. Ibid., 326–27.

18. Henry said that Innes was "endowed with great eloquence—eloquence splendid, magnificent, and sufficient to shake the human mind!" But Henry refused to be swayed by Innes's argument that the convention could not ratify the Constitution contingent upon the approval of amendments: "His reasoning has no effect on me. He cannot shake my political faith . . . Subsequent amendments have no higher authority than previous [amendments]. We will be absolutely certain of escaping danger in the one case, but not in the other." June 25, 1788, *DHRC*, 1536. See also Grigsby, 333.

19. GW to JM, Oct. 22, 1787, *PJM* 10:204.

20. EP to William Woodford, May 15, 1777, *LPEP*, 208; EP to RHL, August 30, 1777, ibid., 222.

21. *DHRC*, 912.

22. Grigsby, 65, 77.

23. *DHRC*, 902–3. Mason's comments were in a letter to John Mason, Dec. 18, 1788, *PGM*, 1137, cited in *DHRC*, 903.

24. *Virginia Herald,* June 5, 1788, *DHRC*, 912.

25. GM to John Mason, July 21, 1788, *DHRC*, 1757.

26. *DHRC*, 902–3.

27. WWH 2:345.

28. Ibid., 346.

29. Ibid.

30. Ibid., 347.

31. June 2, 1788, *DHRC*, 911.

32. RHL to GM, May 7, 1788, in *PGM*, 1042, cited in *PJM* 11:77, n. 1. See also June 4, 1788, *DHRC*, 914.

33. GW to John Jay, June 8, 1788, *DHRC*, 1587. See also JM to GW, June 4, 1788, *PJM* 11:77.

34. GW to Henry Knox, June 17, 1788, ibid., 1633.

35. North Carolina's convention adjourned on August 2, 1788, without ratifying the Constitution. Rutland, 254–78.

36. JM to AH, June 22, 1788, *PJM* 11:166. See also JM to Rufus King, June 22, 1788, ibid., 167. For a discussion of how Virginians felt about the Constitution at the time of the convention, see Risjord, 300–317.

37. Miller, 203; WWH 2:350–51.

38. For a discussion of Henry's effect on the delegates, see WWH 2:358–59.

39. Madison wrote to his father toward the end of the convention that he believed he had a majority of three or four votes, but he said to others that the decision could go either way. JM to JM Sr., June 20, 1788, *PJM* 11:157–58. See also JM to Tench Coxe, June 18, 1788, ibid., 151, in which he said that "there will not probably be half a dozen for a majority on either side."

40. June 3, 1788, *DHRC*, 917.

41. Grigsby, 79.

42. June 4, 1788, *DHRC*, 926.

43. See generally Wood, 206–14, 216–18.

44. June 4, 1788, *DHRC*, 929, 931.

45. For an excellent discussion of this, see Akhil Reed Amar, *America's Constitution: A Biography* (New York: Random House, 2005), 5–53.

46. June 4, 1788, *DHRC*, 932.

47. Ibid., 932–33.

48. Ibid., 933.

49. Ibid., 934–35. For Randolph's role at the convention, see John J. Reardon, *Edmund Randolph: A Biography* (New York: Macmillan, 1974), 137–50.

50. *DHRC*, 936.

51. June 9, 1788, ibid., 1081–82. EIO.

52. John Brown Cutting to TJ, July 24, 1788, *DHRC*, 1707.

53. Reardon, *Edmund Randolph,* 143–44.

54. June 5, 1788, *DHRC*, 955–56.

55. June 6, 1788, ibid., 1002.

56. June 7, 1788, ibid., 1015.

57. Grigsby, 4.

58. June 4, 1788, *DHRC*, 936, 938, 940.

59. Ibid., 937.

60. Ibid., 938–39.

61. Pendleton provided a detailed response to Mason's statement the next day, June 5, 1788. Ibid., 948–49.

62. The day before, Madison had briefly spoken when he concurred with Mason's offer to debate the Constitution clause by clause. Ibid., 914.

63. JM to GW, June 4, 1788, *PJM* 11:77.

64. June 4, 1788, *DHRC,* 941.

65. June 5, 1788, ibid., 949.

66. Ibid., 951, 966.

67. Grigsby, 119; WWH 2:359.

68. June 5, 1788, *DHRC,* 968.

69. June 6, 1788, ibid., 971.

70. Ibid., 973.

71. Ibid., 973–74.

72. Grigsby, 165.

73. *DHRC,* 972–73, 985, 977, 981–83.

74. Ibid., 974, 985.

75. Ibid., 987–88.

76. Ibid., 988.

77. *Pennsylvania Packet,* June 13, 1788, *DHRC,* 1004, n. 3. For information about news coverage of the convention, see ibid., 1569–72.

78. BW to GW, June 7, 1788, ibid., 1581. See also James Duncanson to James Maury, June 7, 13, 1788, ibid., 1583; and John Vaughan to John Langdon, June 11, 1788, ibid., 1598.

79. GW to JJ, June 8, 1788, ibid., 1587.

80. Edward Coles to Grigsby, Dec. 23, 1854 (typewritten transcription), VHS, 3. The letter was written in Philadelphia when Coles was sixty-eight.

81. Ibid., 6–7. Coles did not know Madison until well after the ratifying convention, and thus Madison's bald spot may not have been so obvious in 1788.

82. Simon, 23.

83. Coles, 7.

84. June 6, 1788, *DHRC,* 989.

85. Ibid.

86. Ibid., 990.

87. Ibid.

88. Ibid., 990–91. Exclamation point in original.

89. Ibid., 992.

90. Ibid., 992, 995.

91. Ibid., 996–98.

92. BW to GW, June 7, 1788, ibid., 1581.

93. June 6, 1788, ibid., 999–1001.

94. Ibid., 1002.

95. James Breckinridge to John Breckinridge, June 13, 1788, DHRC, 1620–21.

96. *Pennsylvania Gazette,* June 18, 1788, DHRC, 1651. EIO. This letter was reprinted in fourteen newspapers around the nation.

97. *Petersburg Virginia Gazette,* June 19, 1788, DHRC, 1654.

98. Madison told Rufus King that "the vote of Kentucky [delegates] will turn the scale, and there is perhaps more to fear than to hope from that quarter." JM to RK, June 13, 1788, *PJM*

11:133. John Brown, a leading figure promoting Kentucky statehood and later one of its first U.S. senators, wrote Madison to express his disappointment that Madison would not help draw up a constitution for the territory, but also informing Madison that he had written to several Kentucky delegates to the ratifying convention urging them to approve the Constitution. JB to JM, June 7, 1788, *PJM* 11:90.

99. PH to John Lamb, June 9, 1788, WWH 2:342–43.
100. WG to John Lamb, June 9, 1788, ibid., 344.
101. WWH 2:339–40.
102. June 7, 1788, *DHRC*, 1032.

Chapter 5

1. JM to AH, June 9, 1788, *PJM* 11:101.
2. JM to RK, June 9, 1788, ibid., 102; JM to TC, June 11, 1788, ibid.; JM to GW, June 13, 1788, ibid., 134. See also JM to RK, June 13, 1788, ibid., 133.
3. JM to AH, June 16, 1788, ibid., 144; JM to RK, June 18, 1788, ibid., 152; JM to GW, June 18, 1788, ibid., 153.
4. CG to JM, June 18, 1788, ibid.; AH to JM, June 21, 1788, ibid., 165.
5. June 9, 1788, *DHRC*, 1051–52.
6. Ibid., 1052.
7. TJ to AD, Feb. 7, 1788, ibid., 353–54. See also ibid., 1088, n. 7. The description of Donald is at ibid., 155, n. 1.
8. Ibid., 1088. Jefferson wrote to Carmichael on June 3, 1788.
9. June 10, 1788, ibid., 1097.
10. June 12, 1788, ibid., 1202. EIO.
11. Ibid., 1210, 1223. EIO.
12. June 10, 1788, ibid., 1103–4. The length of Monroe's speech is cited by Alexander White in a letter to Mary Wood, June 10–11, 1788, ibid., 1592.
13. June 10, 1788, ibid., 1108–12.
14. Simon, 24–25; Grigsby, 176.
15. June 10, 1788, *DHRC*, 1117, 1121.
16. June 11, 1788, ibid., 1147–50.
17. Grigsby, 195–97.
18. Ibid., 202. In a macabre and detailed description, Grigsby noted that Grayson's coffin was opened after he had been dead forty-six years, and his features were "fresh and full" and had retained the "beloved original." Ibid., 202–3.
19. June 11, 1788, *DHRC*, 1165, 1167.
20. Ibid., 1169. The next day, June 12, Grayson continued with a long speech that focused on taxes and other issues. Ibid., 1184–92.
21. TJ to JM, Dec. 20, 1787, *PJM* 10:336. See generally Banning II, 1–26.
22. Ibid. "Gratis dictum" means a "voluntary assertion; a statement which a party is not legally bound to make, or in which he is not held to precise accuracy." *Black's Law Dictionary* (St. Paul: West, 1983), 358.
23. TJ to JM, Dec. 20, 1787, *PJM* 10:337.
24. June 16, 1788, *DHRC*, 1326.
25. Ibid., 1327–28.

26. Ibid., 1328.
27. Ibid.
28. Ibid., 1328–29.
29. Ibid., 1331.
30. June 17, 1788, ibid., 1354.
31. June 23, 1788, ibid., 1471–72.
32. June 24, 1788, ibid., 1487–88.
33. Ibid., 1489, 1491.
34. Ibid., 1493–94.
35. Ibid., 1500.
36. Ibid., 1500–1501. See also Madison's comments on June 6, ibid., 994–95.
37. Ibid., 1511–12; WWH 2:370–71.
38. *DHRC*, 1512.
39. Ibid., 1512–13.
40. June 25, 1788, ibid., 1518.
41. Ibid., 1519.
42. Ibid., 1520–21.
43. Randolph made a brief comment after Henry spoke in which he again insisted that he had done the right thing by refusing to sign the Constitution. Ibid.,1537.
44. Ibid. Madison commented to Alexander Hamilton that Henry "declared previous to the final question that although he should submit as a quiet citizen, he should wait with impatience for the favorable moment of regaining in a *constitutional way*, the lost liberties of this country." EIO. JM to AH, June 27, 1788, *PJM* 11:182. See also JM to GW, June 27, 1788, ibid., 182–83. The *Philadelphia Independent Gazetteer* observed on July 2, 1788, that Henry "has been powerful, but now appears to be content." *DHRC*, 1698. See also William Nelson Jr. to William Short, July 12, 1788, ibid., 1701–3. Washington wrote to Tobias Lear about Henry's professed support for implementing the Constitution: "Mr. Henry it seems having declared that, though he can not be reconciled to the Government in its present form, and will give it every constitutional opposition in his power; yet, that he will submit to it peaceably; as every good citizen he thinks ought." GW to TL, June 29, 1788, ibid., 1715–16.
45. JM to AH, June 27, 1788, *PJM* 11:182; JM to GW, June 27, 1788, ibid., 183.
46. WG to Nathan Dane, June 18, 1788, *DHRC*, 1636.
47. For example, see GN, June 10, 1788, ibid., 1129–33.
48. John Blair Smith told Madison after the convention had started that Henry "has written letters repeatedly to Kentuckey & as the people there are alarmed with an apprehension of their interests being about to be sacrificed to the Northern States." JBS to JM, June 12, 1788, *PJM* 11:120.
49. For example, see PH, June 7, 1788, *DHRC*, 1039. See also editors' note, ibid., 1179–81.
50. For example, see John Marshall, June 10, 1788, ibid., 1116–17.
51. *DHRC*, 1538.
52. See generally Risjord, 300–306.
53. Ibid.
54. The time of the vote comes from Stephen Austin to Jeremiah Wadsworth, June 25, 1788, *DHRC*, 1676–77.
55. Ibid., 1512–15.
56. Ibid., 1514, 1542.
57. Ibid., 1550–56.

58. Ibid. 1515.

59. Ibid., 1547–58. There was apparently no recorded vote on the motion.

60. Ibid., 1556–57.

61. JM to AH, June 27, 1788, *PJM* 11:181.

62. Ibid., 182, n. 2; *DHRC,* 1560.

63. June 28, 1788, *DHRC,* 1562. EIO.

64. PH to JL, June 9, 1788, WWH 2:343.

65. *Massachusetts Centinel,* July 26, 1788, *DHRC,* 1561. EIO.

66. GW to JM, June 23, 1788, *PJM* 11:170.

67. WWH 2:363–64, 377.

68. Ibid., 357, 376.

69. SR to Philip Aylett, June 26, 1788, *DHRC,* 1713.

70. *Winchester Virginia Gazette,* June 25, 1788; *Virginia Independent Chronicle,* June 25, 1788, ibid., 1680–81.

Chapter 6

1. June 25, 1788, *DHRC,* 1537. See also JM to AH, June 27, 1788, *PJM* 11:182.

2. *DHRC,* 1560.

3. JM to AH, June 27, 1788, *PJM* 11:181–82. See also James Duncanson to James Maury, Feb. 17, 1789: "Henry . . . took every step [he] could think of, that would have a tendency to obstruct, & prevent, as far as was in their power, the new Constitution being put in motion." *DHFFE,* 405.

4. See generally Cornell, 61–74.

5. *DHRC,* 1672–74.

6. AH told Madison that supporters of the Constitution in New York were "eagerly wait[ing] for further intelligence from you [Madison], as our only chance of success depends on you." AH to JM, June 27, 1788, *PJM* 11:183. See also Cecil L. Eubanks, "New York: Federalism and the Political Economy of Union," in G&L, 325–28.

7. *DHRC,* 1709.

8. Ibid., 1683.

9. June 26, 1788 (extract of a letter from Richmond, June 18), ibid., 1688.

10. GW to JM, Nov. 17, 1788, *PJM* 11:351. Randolph described Henry as "all powerful." ER to JM, Nov. 5, 1788, ibid., 336.

11. WWH 2:420–22. See also Mayer, 444–45.

12. Moses Coit Tyler, *Patrick Henry* (New York: Burt Franklin, 1970, orig. pub. 1877, rev. 1898), 400–404; *DHFFE,* 415.

13. Fontaine's material was used by Tyler. Patrick Henry died in June 1799. Fontaine lived from 1814 to 1884. The Fontaine manuscript is at Cornell University Library. Biographical information about Fontaine comes from Couvillon's introduction, i–v.

14. Fontaine, 11–13.

15. Ibid., 8.

16. Ibid., 13.

17. Ibid., 14.

18. Ibid., 12.

19. Ibid., 12, 28.

20. Kevin R. Hardwick, *Patrick Henry: Economic, Political, and Domestic Life in Eighteenth-Century Virginia* (Brookneal, Va.: Patrick Henry Memorial Foundation, 1991), 1–2.

21. Tyler, *Patrick Henry*, 5–7, 189, 241. See generally Jacob Axelrad, *Patrick Henry: The Voice of Freedom* (New York: Random House, 1947).

22. Fontaine, 9. For a discussion of the children, see Edith Poindexter, "Patrick Henry's Children," in *Patrick Henry Essays*, ed. James M. Elson (Brookneal, Va.: Patrick Henry Memorial Foundation, 1994), 39–42.

23. Hardwick, *Patrick Henry*, 7–8.

24. James Gordon Jr. to JM, *PJM* 11:245–46; Joseph Jones to JM, Oct. 20, 1788, ibid., 308; GLT to JM, Oct. 27, 1788, ibid., 319–20.

25. Charles Lee to GW, Oct. 29, 1788, *DHFFE*, 268–69; GW to BL, Oct. 26, 1788, *GWAC*, 424.

26. GLT to JM, Oct. 20, 1788, *PJM* 11:309; GLT to JM, Oct. 24, 1788, ibid., 316.

27. John R. Vile, *The Constitutional Amendment Process in American Political Thought* (New York: Praeger, 1992), 25.

28. See generally Willi Paul Adams, *The First American Constitutions* (Lanham, Md.: Rowman & Littlefield, 2001), 137–42; 298–99.

29. May 29, 1787, Koch, 33.

30. June 5, 1787, ibid., 69.

31. June 11, 1787, ibid., 104–5.

32. Aug. 30,1787, ibid., 560.

33. Sept. 10, 1787, ibid., 609.

34. Rossiter wrote that Hamilton was "far and away the most disappointing" delegate at the convention and that he "had so much to give, and he gave so little." Rossiter, 252–53. See also Charles Cerami, *Young Patriots* (Naperville, IL: Sourcebooks, 2005).

35. Sept. 10, 1787, Koch, 609.

36. James Wilson, Sept. 10, 1787, ibid., 610. Under Article V, Congress chooses whether amendments—proposed by itself or a convention—will be ratified by state legislatures or state conventions.

37. JM, Sept. 10, 1787, ibid., 609.

38. Sept. 15, 1787, ibid., 649–50.

39. Sept. 15, 1787, ibid., 649.

40. JM to GLT, Nov. 2, 1788, *PJM* 11:330.

41. Ibid., 331.

42. Ibid., 331–32.

43. *DHFFE*, 275–76; *DHRC*, 1765–66.

44. *House Journal* (Oct. 20–Dec. 30, 1788) (Richmond, 1789), 12, in *DHFFE*, 274, 276–79; and *DHRC*, 1764–65.

45. Monroe was among those opposing the substitute letter. He thus favored having a second convention propose amendments. *DHFFE*, 278–79.

46. GLT to JM, Oct. 27, 1788, *PJM* 11:319.

47. EC to JM, Nov. 15, 1788, ibid., 345; and *DHFFE*, 276–77. See also FC to JM, Nov. 12, 1788, *PJM* 11:341–43; and GLT to JM, Nov. 16, 1788, ibid., 346–47. Carrington wrote that the "palpable untruths contained in the [Anti-Federalist] drafts ought to fix the condemnation of the people upon them." EC to JM, Nov. 18, 1788, ibid., 352.

48. *DHFFE*, 274–79.

49. The petition was formally presented to the House on May 5, 1789. Both New York's and Virginia's call for a convention were entered in the *House Journal* and ordered to be filed. *DHRC*, 1763.

50. RBL to JM, Oct. 29, 1788, *PJM* 11:323; GLT to JM, Nov. 10, 1788, ibid., 340.

51. *DHRC,* 1556.

52. In General Assembly, Nov. 20, 1788, *DHRC,* 1767.

53. JM to HL, Nov. 30, 1788, *PJM* 11:372.

54. *DHFFE,* 265, n. 3.

55. EC to JM, Nov. 9, 1788, *PJM* 11:337. Henry successfully used a previous version of the Disabling Act to expel Carrington, a member of the Confederation Congress, from the House of Delegates. See EC to JM, Oct. 24, 1788, ibid., 314–15.

56. July 16, 1788, *DHFFE,* 257. The article appeared in newspapers in other states.

57. Madison told Governor Randolph that he preferred the House because, among other reasons, "it will less require a stile of life with which my circumstances do not square, & for which an inadequate provision only will probably be made by the public." JM to ER, Nov. 23, 1788, *PJM* 11:362. See also JM to ER, Nov. 2, 1788, ibid., 328–30.

58. JG to JM, Aug. 31, 1788, ibid., 245–46. See also Joseph Jones to JM, Oct. 20, 1788, ibid., 308.

59. JM to ER, Oct. 17, 1788, ibid., 305.

60. Ibid.

61. EC to JM, Oct. 19, 1788, ibid., 306.

62. Ibid., 311.

63. ER to JM, Oct. 23, 1788, ibid., 314.

64. JM to ER, Nov. 2, 1788, ibid., 329.

65. RBL to JM, Oct. 29, 1788, ibid., 323; JM to ER, Nov. 2, 1788, ibid., 329.

66. ER to JM, Nov. 5, 1788, ibid., 335. There were 170 members of the House and twenty-four senators. *DHFFE,* 273, n. 3.

67. ER to JM, Nov. 5, 1788, *PJM* 11:335–36.

68. The *House Journal* does not mention the nomination. Confirmation comes from Randolph. ER to JM, Nov. 10, 1788, *PJM* 11:338–39.

69. Ibid., 339.

70. This quote is in a letter from Charles Lee to GW, Oct. 29, 1788, *DHFFE,* 269.

71. ER to JM, Nov. 10, 1788, *PJM* 11:339. Henry also argued that Madison was in favor of closing the Mississippi River in return for trading concessions from Spain. Madison held the opposite position, but the charge would have damaged his chances because Virginians supported free navigation of the river. HL to JM, Nov. 19, 1788, ibid., 356.

72. Ibid., 339.

73. GLT believed that if the election had been delayed one day, Madison would have been chosen. GLT to JM, Nov. 10, 1788, ibid., 340.

74. EC to JM, Nov. 9, 1788, ibid., 336.

75. Ibid.; ER to JM, Nov. 10, 1788, ibid., 339; FC to JM, Nov. 12, 1788, ibid., 342.

76. HL to JM, Nov. 19, 1788, ibid., 357.

77. JM to ER, Nov. 23, 1788, ibid., 362.

78. PH to RHL, Nov. 15, 1788, *WWH* 2:429.

79. *DHFFE,* 283–84. The suffrage qualifications required that the voter be a male, twenty-one or older, with either twenty-five acres and a house or fifty acres unimproved. Residents of Williamsburg and Norfolk could vote if they had lived there for six months and either had an estate worth at least fifty pounds or had served an apprenticeship in some trade within the town for five years.

80. Ibid., 289–92. The law provided the same penalty for failure to vote as imposed in elections for the General Assembly. Such laws were rarely enforced.

81. *DHFFE,* 308. Buckingham County was in the presidential election district, but not the congressional district from which Madison would run for election to the House.

82. Ibid., 305–6.

83. U.S. Constitution, Article I, section 2, clause 3. Virginia and other southern states were greatly overrepresented in the House because three-fifths of slaves—there were three hundred thousand slaves in Virginia—were counted for apportionment. For an excellent discussion of the impact of the three-fifths clause on Congress and presidential elections, see Amar, 87–98.

84. Several of these counties would later be divided to create new counties. Thus, the eight counties of the 1789 congressional district would comprise twelve counties on today's map.

85. EC to JM, Nov. 15, 1788, *PJM* 11:346.

86. *DHFFE,* 296.

87. GLT to JM, Nov. 13, 1788, *PJM* 11:343–44; EC to JM, Nov. 15, 1788, ibid., 345.

88. GW to Benjamin Lincoln, Nov. 14, 1788, *DHFFE,* 374; BB to JM, Dec. 8, 1788, *PJM* 11:385.

89. *DHFFE,* 287. Some Federalists supported the measure, "having at an early period committed themselves upon that side." EC to JM, Nov. 15, 1788, *PJM* 11:345–46.

90. *DHFFE,* 294. As it had with the presidential electors, the General Assembly required that anyone who failed to vote be subject to forfeiture of property. Also, no food or drink could be given to a voter as an inducement, with severe penalties potentially imposed on violators. Ibid., 295.

91. Article I, section 2: "No person shall be a Representative who shall not have attained to the age of twenty-five years, and been seven years a citizen of the United States, and who shall not, when elected, be an inhabitant of that State in which he shall be chosen."

92. Robert Luce, *Legislative Assemblies* (Boston: Houghton Mifflin, 1924), 223–24, cited in *PJM* 11:379, n. 2.

93. In *U.S. Term Limits v. Thornton,* 514 U.S. 779 (1995), the Court held that Article I established only three qualifications for service in Congress: age, citizenship, and residence. The Court struck down an Arkansas law that imposed another qualification based on how long someone had already served in Congress.

94. RJM to JM, Nov. 22, 1788, *PJM* 11:360.

95. EC to JM, Dec. 2, 1788, ibid., 378–79.

96. Ibid., 378.

97. EC to JM, Nov. 9, 1788, ibid., 337.

98. Ibid., 363, n. 1. The *Virginia Centinel* (Winchester) reported on November 19, 1788, that thirty-nine legislators voted against Madison's continuing in the Confederation Congress. *DHFFE,* 378. William Wirt Henry said that Madison's reelection to Congress showed Patrick Henry's opposition to him was not personal. WWH 2:432–33.

99. GLT to JM, Nov. 13, 1788, *PJM* 11:344. EIO.

100. JM to ER, Nov. 23, 1788, ibid., 363.

101. GLT to JM, Nov. 16, 1788, ibid., 347. EIO.

102. GLT to JM, Nov. 13, 1788, ibid., 344, EIO; RBL to JM, Nov. 17, 1788, ibid., 348; EC to JM, Nov. 18, 1788, ibid., 352.

103. ER to JM, Nov. 10, 1788, ibid., 338–39; EC to JM, Nov. 15, 1788, ibid., 345–46.

104. EC to JM, Nov. 18, 1788, ibid., 352; Nov. 26, 1788, ibid., 369. EIO.

105. Jan. 1789, *DHFFE,* 329–30.

106. JM to GW, Dec. 2, 1788, *PJM* 11:377–78.

107. Ibid., 377; JM to HL, Nov. 30, 1788, ibid., 372.

108. AW to JM, Dec. 4, 1788, ibid., 380; AS to JM, Dec. 14, 1788, ibid., 396.

109. JM to TJ, Dec. 8, 1788, ibid., 384.
110. GLT to JM, Dec. 14, 1788, ibid., 396. See also GLT to JM, Dec. 12, 1788, ibid., 392–93.
111. HB to JM, Dec. 16, 1788, ibid., 398.
112. JJ to JM, Dec. 14, 1788, ibid., 394.
113. Joseph Jones told Madison on November 21 that Henry had left the legislature and gone home. JJ to JM, Nov. 21, 1788, ibid., 358–59. See also Mayer, 450.

Chapter 7

1. JM to James Madison Sr., Dec. 18, 1788, *PJM* 11:400. Madison was suffering from piles and could not comfortably ride a horse.
2. GW to Henry Lee, Dec. 23, 1788, *PGW*, 202.
3. The Piedmont is one of five major geographic regions of Virginia. Its eastern border is the "fall line," an imaginary line running from north to south between Washington, D.C., and Richmond, while the western edge is the Blue Ridge Mountains. The word "Piedmont" comes from the name of a region of northern Italy and means "foot of the mountains." Emily J. Salmon and Edward D. C. Campbell Jr., eds., *The Hornbook of Virginia History* (Richmond: Library of Virginia, 1994), 3.
4. Michael F. Doran, *Atlas of County Boundary Changes in Virginia, 1634–1895* (Athens, Ga.: Iberian Publishing, 1987).
5. The name of the county seat was changed to Culpeper in 1859. Salmon and Campbell, *Hornbook*, 190.
6. See William C. Rives, *History of the Life and Times of James Madison*, vol. 2 (Boston: Little, Brown, 1870), 655, n. 1.
7. GM to John Mason, Dec. 18, 1788, *PGM*, 1136.
8. *DHRC*, 564.
9. *Virginia Independent Chronicle*, March 12, 1788, ibid., 570.
10. James Duncanson to James Maury, May 8, 1788, ibid., 578.
11. Ibid., 594–95.
12. March 24, 1788, Taylor, 91.
13. "Instructions to the Spotsylvania Delegates to the State Convention," March 4, 1788, *DHRC*, 611.
14. *Virginia Centinel*, April 9, 1788, ibid., 627–28.
15. For the names of the delegates, see ibid., 907.
16. *Winchester Virginia Gazette*, April 2, 1788, ibid., 587.
17. The 1790 Census is printed in *DHRC*, 555–57.
18. The land tax records are on microfilm at the Library of Virginia. Some names could have belonged to either males or females. Property owners with fifty acres or more were counted. Few freeholders owned between twenty-five and fifty acres, thus requiring a house on the property in order to be eligible to vote. These records were kept beginning in 1782, when the General Assembly required counties to keep records of how much land and personal property were owned. Taxes were based on the reported holdings.
19. William A. Degregorio, *The Complete Book of U.S. Presidents* (New York: Barricade Books, 1996), 73.
20. Henry S. Randall, *The Life of Thomas Jefferson*, vol. 3 (New York: Derby & Jackson, 1858), 255. See generally Catherine Allgor, *Parlor Politics: In Which the Ladies of Washington Help Build a City and a Government* (Charlottesville: Univ. Press of Virginia, 2000), 89–90.
21. JJ to JM, April 5, 1789, *PJM* 12:48.

22. Monroe to TJ, Feb. 15, 1789, *WJM*, 199; *DHFFE*, 347. See also W. P. Cresson, *James Monroe* (Chapel Hill: Univ. of North Carolina Press, 1946), 103.

23. Monroe to TJ, July 27, 1787, *WJM*, 174.

24. Harry Ammon, *James Monroe: The Quest for National Identity* (Charlottesville: Univ. Press of Virginia, 1990), 66–67.

25. Monroe to JM, Oct. 13, 1787, *PJM* 10:192–94.

26. *DHRC*, 1111–12. See also ibid., 845. Monroe wrote a twenty-four-page pamphlet outlining his objections to the proposed Constitution that he wanted to distribute shortly before the ratifying convention in Richmond. His intended audience was the voters of Spotsylvania County who elected him and his fellow delegate at the convention. But he was dissatisfied with the job the printer did, and few people saw the pamphlet in its entirety. Stuart Gerry Brown, ed., *The Autobiography of James Monroe* (Syracuse: Syracuse Univ. Press, 1959), 50. Although it is a lucid examination of the Constitution, the pamphlet's length, discussion of the history of nations, and philosophical themes would have made it difficult for most people to read. For the text of *Some Observations on the Constitution,* see *WJM*, 307–43. In the document, he tells his constituents that he was neutral about the Constitution in advance of the ratifying convention and would make a decision in Richmond. Ibid., 307.

27. TJ to JM, May 8, 1784, *PJM* 8:32. See also Cresson, 81.

28. Ketcham, 146, 154–57.

29. Washington thought it was a great investment opportunity. For a detailed discussion of the land purchase, see Brant, 338–42.

30. Ketcham, 147.

31. JM to TJ, March 29, 1789, *PJM* 12:37.

32. Randall, *Life of Thomas Jefferson* 3:255, n. 2. EIO. Brant asks whether Monroe—with his sensitivity to criticism—would have been able, if he had been subject to the same attacks as Madison, to maintain the friendship by separating the political and the personal attacks. Brant indirectly criticizes Monroe for not publicly disavowing the attacks on Madison's character from which Monroe benefited during the campaign. Brant, 241.

33. Dec. 18, 20, 21, 27, 28, 1788, Taylor, 117–18.

34. Taylor's diary from January 1789: Jan. 2, 121; Jan. 13, 122; Jan. 14, 122; Jan 22, 28, 123; Jan. 30, 124; Jan. 31, 124.

35. Burgess Ball to JM, Dec. 8, 1788, *PJM* 11:385–86.

36. RBL to JM, Dec. 12, 1788, ibid., 392.

37. ES to JM, Jan. 31, 1789, ibid., 438. Unfortunately, neither Madison nor his supporters left a record as to his location on Election Day. He most likely would have been in Orange County at the courthouse.

38. DJ to William Madison, Jan. 14, 1789, *DHFFE*, 334; DJ to JM, Jan. 14, 1789, *PJM* 11:419. EIO.

39. ES to JM, Jan. 31, 1789, ibid., 438.

40. DJ to JM, Jan. 14, 1789, ibid., 419.

41. GN to JM, Jan. 2, 1789, ibid., 406.

42. Ibid., 406–7.

43. Ibid., 407.

44. DJ to JM, Jan. 14, 1789, *PJM* 11:419.

45. JM to GW, Jan. 14, 1789, ibid., 418.

46. TJ to JM, Dec. 20, 1787, *PJM* 10:337. Jefferson listed the rights that should be explicitly protected in a letter written to Madison on July 31, 1788. *PJM* 11:210–14.

47. JM to TJ, Oct. 17, 1788, ibid., 297. EIO.

48. Ibid.

49. Ibid., 297–98.

50. The bill for providing religious freedom was first proposed by Jefferson in 1777 but was not approved until January 1786, largely through the efforts of Madison. For the text of the statute, see Banning II, 116–17.

51. JM to TJ, Oct. 17, 1788, *PJM* 11:298–99. For an elaboration of this view, see Madison's *Federalist 10*.

52. TJ to JM, March 15, 1789, *PJM* 12:14. See also TJ to JM, Nov. 18, 1788, *PJM* 11:353–55.

53. TJ to JM, March 15, 1789, *PJM* 12:13. Hamilton had promised in *Federalist 78* that although independent, the new federal judiciary would never be strong enough to interfere with the rights citizens enjoyed under their state governments: "As from the natural feebleness of the judiciary, it is in continual jeopardy of being overpowered, awed, or influenced by its co-ordinate branches." *Federalist,* 403.

54. Sept. 12, 1787, Koch, 630.

55. June 12, 1788, *DHRC,* 1223–24; and June 24, 1788, ibid., 1502.

56. JM to TJ, Dec. 8, 1788, *PJM* 11:382–83.

57. Ketcham, 276.

58. See *PJM* 1:183, n. 7. See also Garrett Ward Sheldon, *The Political Philosophy of James Madison* (Baltimore: Johns Hopkins Univ. Press, 2001), 27–30.

59. Rutland II, 83–87.

60. Ketcham, 57–58.

61. JM to WB, Dec. 1, 1773, *PJM* 1:101.

62. See also JM to WB, Jan. 24, 1774, ibid., 105.

63. Ibid., 106.

64. JM to WB, April 1, 1774, ibid., 112.

65. See editorial note, *PJM* 1:171; and Warren M. Billings, "That All Men Are Born Equally Free and Independent: Virginians and the Origins of the Bill of Rights," in C&K, 340–41.

66. In January 1787, the Virginia General Assembly approved a law to repeal the act incorporating the Protestant Episcopal Church, eliminating the last remnants of the Anglican establishment. Robert S. Alley, "Anglican Church," in *James Madison and the American Nation, 1751–1836, An Encyclopedia,* ed. Robert A. Rutland (New York: Simon & Schuster, 1994), 13.

67. Risjord wrote that Orange County had a "sizable contingent" of Baptists. Risjord, 52.

68. Robert S. Alley, "Baptists," in Rutland, *James Madison and the American Nation,* 30.

69. JM to GE, Jan. 2, 1789, *PJM* 11:404.

70. Ibid., 404–5. One of the nation's leading Madison scholars, Lance Banning, argued that by this time, Madison genuinely believed a bill of rights should be added to the Constitution, and his support was not just political expediency. Banning II, 15–17.

71. "To the Honorable the General Assembly of the Commonwealth of Virginia, A Memorial and Remonstrance," *PJM* 8:298–304.

72. Editorial note, ibid., 297–98. Article XVI states, in part, that "all men are equally entitled to the free exercise of religion, according to the dictates of conscience." "Virginia Declaration of Rights," in Robert S. Alley, ed., *James Madison on Religious Liberty* (Amherst, N.Y.: Prometheus Books, 1985), 52.

73. Editorial note, *PJM* 8:298.

74. EP to RHL, Feb. 28, 1785, in *LPEP,* 474.

75. Editorial note, *PJM* 8:298. See also Rutland II, 87.

76. JM to GE, Jan. 2, 1789, *PJM* 11:405.

77. For reference to Leland's involvement in the election to the ratifying convention, see James Gordon to JM, Feb. 17, 1788, *PJM* 10:515–16; for Leland's note congratulating Madison for winning a seat in Congress, see JL to JM, Feb. 15, 1789, *PJM* 11:442–43.

78. GN to JM, Jan.2, 1789, *PJM* 11:408.

79. BJ to JM, Jan. 12, 1789, ibid., 414–15.

80. Rives, *History of the Life and Times of James Madison* 2:656–57.

81. Ibid. See also Taylor, Jan. 26, 1789, 123.

82. Randall, *Life of Thomas Jefferson* 3:255, n. 2.

83. Ibid. These observations were made by Madison on December 3, 1827.

84. Ibid. See also *PJM* 11:438, n. 1.

85. BJ to JM, Jan. 19, 1789, ibid., 423–24.

86. Ibid., 424.

87. Randolph's oldest son married Thomas Jefferson's daughter Patsy (Martha) in 1790. *PJM* 7:25, n. 1.

88. JM to TMR, Jan. 13, 1789, *PJM* 11:416.

89. *DHFFE*, 338.

90. JM to TMR, Jan. 13, 1789, *PJM* 11:416.

91. Sept. 12, 1787, Koch, 630.

92. HL to JM, Jan. 14, 1789, *PJM* 11:420.

93. JM to GW, Jan. 14, 1789, ibid., 418.

94. JM to John Brown, Jan. 21, 1789, ibid., 425. Brant thought the results of the presidential election should not have added to Madison's optimism because both candidates were pledged to vote for Washington. Brant, 241.

95. *DHFFE*, 336.

96. Ibid., 337. The widespread interest in the race is reflected in an article in the *New York Daily Advertiser* on Jan. 15, 1789. *DHFFE*, 335.

97. Ibid., 338.

98. Ibid., 340; and *PJM* 11:428–29.

99. *DHFFE*, 340–41.

100. Only the close of the letter, the address line to Thompson, and his signature were written by Madison. The rest was written by someone else. *DHFFE*, 344, n. 1.

101. Jan. 1789, ibid., 393.

102. GN to JM, Jan. 24, 1789, *PJM* 11:427.

103. Ibid., 427; ES to JM, Jan. 31, 1789, ibid., 438; GN to JM, Jan. 24, 1789, ibid., 427. Madison did not write about his visit to the county at the time, but recalled years later that he and Monroe addressed a church congregation there. Randall, *Life of Thomas Jefferson* 3:255, n. 2.

104. By 2:00 P.M., the temperature had risen to "33 1/2" degrees, but it had dropped to twenty-eight by 4:00 P.M. "Meteorological Journal of James Madison at his Plantation, 1789–1791," American Philosophical Society, Philadelphia. Madison listed his weather data by year, month, and day. This was broken down into categories of temperature, wind direction, and overall weather conditions. Jefferson and other political leaders kept similar weather information. William B. Miller, "The Weather Log of James Madison," *Journal of Presbyterian History* 40 (Dept. of History of the United Presbyterian Church, 1962), 209. The Presbyterian Historical Society has a weather log covering the period of April 1793 to July 1796 in Madison's handwriting. The journal kept at Montpelier during 1789–91 has entries that were probably written by someone else while he was away.

105. The entry for the next day, February 3, 1786, listed a high temperature of fifty degrees. "Meteorological Journal for Orange County, Virginia, in Madison's Hand," in *PJM* 8:541.

106. *Fredericksburg Virginia Herald,* Feb. 5, 1789, *DHFFE,* 345–46. At Mount Vernon, some seventy-five miles from Montpelier, Washington recorded the temperature in his journal: "Monday 2d. The Mercury was in the Ball of the Thermometer in the Morning—at 26 at Noon and 20 at Night." *DGW,* 444.

107. Jan. 30, 1789, Taylor, 124. Taylor noted on Sunday that it was "very cold last night and to day" and that he could "perceive no thaw." Five days after the election, the snow was only "about half gone." Feb. 7, 1789, ibid., 124–25.

108. Brown, 152.

109. The law approved by the General Assembly on Nov. 19, 1788, said that "persons qualified to vote . . . shall assemble at their respective County Courthouses on the second day in February next." *DHFFE,* 294.

110. Feb. 2, 3, 6, 1789, Taylor, 124. Grigsby wrote in 1850 that the "polls were kept open three days, every voter, sick and well, was brought to the polls." *DHFFE,* 349.

111. *Philadelphia Independent Gazetteer,* Feb. 10, 1789, in *DHFFE,* 305.

112. Information about individual voters was available for one county in the district, Amherst. Risjord found that based on land and slave ownership, poorer citizens were twice as likely to vote for Monroe, while wealthier citizens were twice as likely to vote for Madison. Risjord, 327–28.

113. Sheriffs from the counties met on February 7 to "compare votes for the member of Congress from this district." Taylor, Feb. 6, 1789, 124. Three days later, Taylor recorded that the sheriffs had confirmed Madison's victory by 336 votes. Feb. 9, 1789, 125.

114. Monroe to TJ, Feb. 15, 1789, *WJM,* 199; *DHFFE,* 347.

115. Eleazer Early to James Monroe, Feb. 9, 1824, *DHFFE,* 349.

116. JM to ER, March 1, 1789, *PJM* 11:453.

117. EC to JM, Feb. 16, 1789, ibid., 445; *DHFFE,* 403.

118. EC to HK, Feb. 16, 1789, *DHFFE,* 402–3.

119. James Duncanson to James Maury, Feb. 17, 1789, ibid., 405. Duncanson's support for the Constitution is inferred from his expression of disappointment at the election of James Monroe and John Dawson to represent Spotsylvania County at the Virginia ratifying convention. JD to James Maury, March 11, 1788, *DHRC,* 479.

120. MK to JM, March 3, 1789, *PJM* 12:1–2.

121. GLT to JM, March 30, 1789, ibid., 40.

122. GN to JM, May 8, 1789, ibid., 138.

123. GW to Samuel Powel, Feb. 5, 1789, *DHFFE,* 400; GW to JM, Feb. 16, 1789, *PJM* 11:446.

124. PH to WG, March 31, 1789, *VMHB* 14:203, cited in Mayer, 452.

125. JM to TC, Feb. 16, 1789, *PJM* 11:443.

126. JM to TJ, March 29, 1789, *PJM* 12:37.

Chapter 8

1. For a discussion of British occupation of New York City, see DHF, 81–114. For the financial impact of the presence of the federal government, see Kenneth R. Bowling, "New York City, Capital of the United States, 1785–1790," in *World of the Founders: New York Communities in the Federal Period,* ed. Stephen L. Schechter and Wendell Tripp (Albany: New York State Comm. on the Bicentennial of the United States Constitution, 1990), 1–3.

2. Bowling, "New York City," 3–4.

3. JP to Robert Page, March 16, 1789, *DHFFC* 15:71. BR to JA, March 19, 1789, ibid., 79–82. EIO.

4. TP to Paine Wingate, April 15, 1789, ibid., 269.

5. JA to BR, May 17, 1789, ibid., 573.

6. The travel description comes from *DHFFC* 15:19–22.

7. For an excellent discussion of the decision to locate the capital along the Potomac, see Joseph J. Ellis, *Founding Brothers: The Revolutionary Generation* (New York: Knopf, 2000), 48–80.

8. Ibid., 6. Bowling, "New York City," provides the basis for the description of the renovated city; see 5–6.

9. OE to Abigail Ellsworth, March 8, 1789, *DHFFC* 15:42.

10. Ibid., xxiii.

11. EB to Hannah Boudinot, May 15, 1789, ibid., 557.

12. GC to Samuel Meredith, June 12, 1789, *DHFFC* 16:756.

13. MJS to TC, June 14, 1789, ibid., 779.

14. WM to Benjamin Rush, April 7, 1789, *DHFFC* 15:217. See also WM to Richard Peters, April 16, 1789, ibid., 275.

15. GC to Benjamin Rush, July 3, 1789, *DHFFC* 16:923–24; and [August, 1789], ibid., 1344.

16. Henry Sewall to Benjamin Shaw, Aug. 18, 1789, ibid., 1350.

17. JP to Robert Page, March 16, 1789, *DHFFC* 15:71.

18. WM to Richard Willing, April 2, 1789, ibid., 185.

19. Ibid., xxiv.

20. OE to Abigail Ellsworth, March 29, 1789, ibid., 145.

21. Ibid.; Paine Wingate to Sally Wingate, April 11, 1789, ibid., 252. See also William C. diGiacomantonio, "A Congressional Wife at Home: The Case of Sarah Thatcher, 1787–1792," in *Neither Separate nor Equal: Congress in the 1790s*, ed. Kenneth R. Bowling and Donald R. Kennon (Athens: Ohio Univ. Press, 2000), 155–80.

22. *DHFFC* 15:xviii.

23. EB to HB, April 14, 1789, ibid., 261; and April 21, 1789, ibid., 304.

24. Ibid., 27. For a detailed description of Federal Hall, see ibid., 32–35.

25. WP to Euphemia Paterson, March 24, 1789, ibid., 109; CDM to Comte de Montmorin, June 9, 1789, *DHFFC* 16:730.

26. The description of Federal Hall comes from Kenneth R. Bowling and Helen E. Veit, *The Diary of William Maclay and Other Notes on Senate Debates* (1988), *DHFFC* 9:3–4, n. 1. The description of the marble is from *DHFFC* 15:34.

27. The building was torn down in 1812. The four lots on which it had stood were bought by individuals but later purchased by the federal government. A new building there later served as the New York Custom House and the Federal Reserve Bank of New York. *DHFFC* 9:3, n. 1.

28. R.B. Bernstein, "A New Matrix for National Politics: The First Federal Elections, 1788–90," in *Inventing Congress: Origins and Establishment of the First Federal Congress*, ed. Kenneth R. Bowling and Donald R. Kennon (Athens: Ohio Univ. Press, 1999), 121.

29. Charlene Bangs Bickford, "'Public Attention is Very Much Fixed on the Proceedings of the New Congress': The First Federal Congress Organizes Itself," in ibid., 139.

30. FA to George R. Minot, March 25, 1789, *DHFFC* 15:126.

31. FA to George R. Minot, April 4, 1789, ibid., 196.

32. *DHFFC* 17:1744, 1739; AW to Mary Wood, March 8, 1789, *DHFFC* 15:45.

33. *DHFFC* 10:xi–xxiii. See also Charlene Bangs Bickford, "Throwing Open the Doors: The First Federal Congress and the Eighteenth-Century Media," in Bowling and Kennon, *Inventing Congress*, 166–90.

34. Madison wrote to James Monroe to say that of all the issues debated on the "ratio of particular duties . . . the proper one between rum & Molasses has been the last & the longest question of that sort." May 13, 1789, *PJM* 12:159–60.

35. See generally David P. Currie, *The Constitution in Congress: The Federalist Period, 1789–1801* (Chicago: Univ. of Chicago Press, 1997), 7–115.

36. *PJM* 12:170–74, 232–39.

37. *DHFFC* 15:xxiii–xxiv. On the lack of staff, see Charlene Bangs Bickford, "Public Attention," 158.

38. EB to Hannah Boudinot, April 14, 1789, *DHFFC* 15:260–61.

39. Frank Monaghan and Marvin Lowenthal, *This Was New York: The Nation's Capital in 1789* (Freeport, N.Y.: Books for Libraries Press, 1943), 22–23. For a discussion of President Washington's levees and the social obligations of government officials, see Catherine Allgor, *Parlor Politics: In Which the Ladies of Washington Help Build a City and a Government* (Charlottesville: Univ. Press of Virginia, 2000).

40. The description of the members' routine comes from Bowling, "New York City," 9–10. For a discussion of lobbyists in this era, see Jeffrey L. Pasley, "Private Access and Public Power: Gentility and Lobbying in the Early Congress," in *The House and Senate in the 1790s*, ed. Kenneth R. Bowling and Donald R. Kennon (Athens: Ohio Univ. Press, 2002), 57–99.

41. Bowling, "New York City," 10. Fisher Ames wrote on April 8 that the "Galleries were open for the first time, and crouded." FA to John Lowell, April 8, 1789, *DHFFC* 15:221. For a description of the galleries, see ibid., 34.

42. See generally Leibiger.

43. *PJM* 12:120–21.

44. Leibiger, 97–123.

45. Editor's note, *PJM* 12:120; JM to Jared Sparks, May 30, 1827, cited in *PJM* 11:446–47.

46. *PJM* 12:123.

47. Ibid.

48. GW to JM, May 31, 1789, *PJM* 12:191.

49. Ibid., 133.

50. Reply of the President to the House of Representatives, May 8, 1789, ibid., 141–42; Reply of the President to the Senate, May 18, 1789, ibid., 166–67.

51. The numbers come from Veit, xii.

52. May 5, 1789, *DHFFC* 10:451.

53. *DHFFE*, 359, 364.

54. May 6, 1789, *DHFFC* 10:472.

55. May 5, 1789, ibid., 444.

56. Ibid., 445.

57. Ibid.

58. Ibid., 445–46.

59. May 4, 1789, ibid., 391–92.

60. TL to JI, May 9, 1789, *DHFFC* 15:493–94.

61. JM to ER, June 24, 1789, *PJM* 12:258. See also *DHFFC* 10:xx–xxi.

62. JM to TJ, May 27, 1789, *PJM* 12:186.

63. Address to the House, June 8, 1789, *PJM* 12:196.

64. June 8, 1789, *DHFFC* 11:811.

65. Madison added, "The applications for amendments come from a very respectable number of our constituents, and it is certainly proper for congress to consider the subject, in order to quiet the anxiety which prevails in the public mind." June 8, 1789, *PJM* 12:196.

66. James Madison, Notes for a Speech, *DHFFC* 16:724.

67. Address to the House, June 8, 1789, *PJM* 12:203.

68. Ibid., 207.

69. For a contrary view, see Paul Finkelman, "James Madison and the Bill of Rights: A Reluctant Paternity," in *1990 Supreme Court Review* (1991), 319–47.

70. June 8, 1789, *DHFFC* 11:803. The record does not indicate whether the quote is from Jackson or Burke. Jackson represented the smallest congressional district in population in the nation, with 16,250 residents. *DHFFC* 15:xiii.

71. *DHFFC* 11:804–5, 816.

72. Ibid., 805. See generally Marie Sauer Lambremont, "Rep. James Jackson of Georgia and the Establishment of the Southern States' Rights Tradition in Congress," in Bowling and Kennon, *Inventing Congress,* 191–207.

73. *DHFFC* 11:805.

74. Ibid., 806.

75. Rutland III, 377–78.

76. June 8, 1789, *DHFFC* 11:807, 817, 805.

77. Ibid., 813–14.

78. *PJM* 12:198–200.

79. *DHFFC* 11:804; June 8, 1789, House of Representatives Journal, ed. Linda Grant De Pauw (Baltimore: Johns Hopkins Univ. Press, 1977), 84.

80. June 8, 1789, *DHFFC* 11:815–16.

81. Ibid., 807, 808, 823.

82. Ibid., 818, 819, 820.

83. June 8, 1789, ibid., 820–22.

84. Ibid., 820.

85. For a discussion of the role Virginia played in the creation of the Bill of Rights, see Brent Tarter, "Virginians and The Bill of Rights," *Virginia Cavalcade* (Autumn 1982): 62–75.

86. Address to the House, *PJM* 12:200.

87. Veit, 14–28. See also Levy, 11.

88. *PJM* 12:206.

89. Levy, 21, 23.

90. Ibid., 9, 22–23, 17.

91. House Committee Report, July 28, 1789, Veit, 29.

92. *DHFFC* 11:823.

93. Ibid., 819.

94. Ibid., 820; Gerry made this point at 831.

95. See generally William S. Price Jr., " 'There Ought to Be a Bill of Rights': North Carolina Enters a New Nation," in C&K, 424–42.

96. June 8, 1787, Koch, 88–89, 92; July 18, 1787, ibid., 304–5; Aug. 23, 1787, ibid., 518.

97. *DHFFC* 11:826.

98. Ibid., 827–28.

99. Ibid., 828.

100. Ibid., 830.

101. Ibid., 813.

102. Ibid.

103. Ibid., 834.

104. "A Citizen of New Haven" [Roger Sherman], March 24, 1789, *DHFFC* 15:121. Reprinted in Philadelphia on March 20, 1789, this was an expanded version of an article that was first published in the (Hartford) *Connecticut Courant* on January 7, 1788, with a revised version reprinted in the *New Haven Gazette* and the *Connecticut Magazine* on December 25, 1788.

105. *DHFFC* 11:811, 835.

106. Ibid., 830–31.

107. G&L, 148–49.

108. AA to CT, Sept. 1, 1789, *DHFFC* 17:1443.

109. Elbridge Gerry to the Electors of Middlesex, Jan. 22, 1789, *DHFFC* 15:113.

110. *DHFFC* 11:832–33.

111. Ibid., 834–35.

112. Ibid., 816.

113. Kenneth R. Bowling, "'A Tub to the Whale': The Adoption of the Bill of Rights," in C&K, 46–60.

114. GC to RP, June 8, 1789, *DHFFC* 16:722–23.

115. FA to Thomas Dwight, June 11, 1789, ibid., 748–49; FA to George R. Minot, June 12, 1789, ibid., 755–56.

116. Brant II, 249.

117. TS to Benjamin Lincoln, July 19, 1789, *DHFFC* 16:1075–76.

118. PH to WG, March 31, 1789, *DHFFC* 15:168.

119. RHL to PH, May 28, 1789, ibid., 644.

120. WG to PH, June 12, 1789, *DHFFC* 16:759.

121. Ibid.

122. The Henry quotes come from Mayer, 457, citing the recollections of Edward Fontaine (mss., Cornell Univ.), and PH to RHL, Aug. 28, 1789, WWH 3:398.

123. EC to JM, May 12, 1789, *PJM* 12:156.

124. WRD to JM, June 10, 1789, ibid., 211. After listing the rights he believed North Carolinians preferred, Davie said that "Instead of a Bill of rights attempting to enumerate the rights of the Indivi[du]al or the State Governments, they [those opposed to the Constitution] seem to prefer some general negative as will . . . [confine] Congress to the exercise of the powers particularly granted."

125. Ibid., 219, n. 1.

126. TC to JM, June 18, 1789, ibid., 239, 241, n. 1.

127. GLT to JM, June 16, 1789, ibid., 224–25.

128. ES to JM, June 25, 1789, ibid., 261.

129. JD to JM, June 28, 1789, ibid., 264.

130. JM to SJ, June 21, 1789, ibid., 250; JM to TJ, June 30, 1789, ibid., 272.

131. JJ to JM, June 24, 1789, ibid., 258–59.

132. ER to JM, June 30, 1789, ibid., 273.

Chapter 9

1. JM to JM Sr., July 5, 1789, *PJM* 12:278.

2. *DHFFC* 11:1158.

3. Ibid.

4. Ibid., 1161, 1158–59.

5. Ibid., 1159.

6. Ibid., 1159–60.

7. Ibid., 1160.

8. Ibid., 1162.

9. Ibid., 1161.

10. Ibid., 1163.

11. PM to BR, July 22, 1789, *DHFFC* 16:1105.

12. *DHFFC* 3:117.

13. Ibid., 124.

14. Kenneth R. Bowling, "'A Tub to the Whale': The Adoption of the Bill of Rights," in C&K, 51.

15. House Committee Report, July 28, 1789, in Veit, 29.

16. Bowling, "A Tub," 51.

17. Schwartz, 1050.

18. Veit, 31.

19. JM to WCN, Aug. 2, 1789, *PJM* 12:321.

20. *DHFFC* 3:130.

21. *DHFFC* 11:1208, 1220–21.

22. Ibid., 1218.

23. Ibid., 1209.

24. Ibid., 1209–10.

25. Ibid., 1212.

26. Schwartz, 231–36, 256, 262.

27. JM to AW, Aug. 24, 1789, *PJM* 12:352. EIO.

28. *DHFFC* 11:1212–13.

29. Ibid., 1213.

30. Ibid., 1225–27.

31. Ibid., 1231.

32. Ibid., 1216.

33. Ibid., 1222–23.

34. Ibid., 1232.

35. Ibid., 1232, 1240.

36. Gerry's motion did not indicate where in the clause the words would be inserted. Ibid., 1240–41.

37. Ibid., 1233.

38. Ibid., 1242.

39. R. B. Bernstein, "A New Matrix for National Politics: The First Federal Elections, 1788–90," in *Inventing Congress: Origins and Establishment of the First Federal Congress,* ed. Kenneth R. Bowling and Donald R. Kennon (Athens: Ohio Univ. Press, 1999), 123–24.

40. *DHFFC* 15:xii–xiii.

41. Bernstein, 122–23.

42. Ibid., 1233–34. See also Amar, 76–84.

43. EC to JM, Sept. 9, 1789, *PJM* 12:393.

44. *DHFFC* 11:1238.

45. JM to Edmund Randolph, June 15, 1789, *PJM* 12: 219.

46. *DHFFC* 11:1253.

47. Ibid., 1240. See also Amar, 72–76.

48. *DHFFC* 11:1253.

49. Ibid., 1253–53. Vote: Ibid., 1254. The original second amendment would eventually be ratified and officially become part of the Constitution in May 1992.

50. *DHFFC* 12:1750.

51. Veit, 30.

52. *DHFFC* 11:1254, 1257.

53. Ibid., 1261; Article I, section 8, para. 18.

54. See generally Wood, 189, 191, 252–53, 370.

55. *DHFFC* 11:1255. See generally Alfred De Grazia, *Public and Republic* (New York: Knopf, 1951).

56. *DHFFC* 11:1255, 1259.

57. Ibid., 1255–56.

58. Ibid., 1271.

59. Ibid., 1257. EIO.

60. Ibid., 1272.

61. Ibid., 1273.

62. Ibid., 1274.

63. Ibid., 1277–78.

64. Ibid.

65. Ibid., 1279–80.

66. Ibid., 1280–81.

67. Ibid., 1280.

68. Ibid., 1283–91.

69. Ibid., 1291–92.

70. Ibid., 1292.

71. See generally Wood, 505, 510.

72. "From Pacificus," Aug. 14, 1789, *PJM* 12:334. EIO.

73. Veit, 51.

74. *DHFFC* 11:1300.

75. See generally Amar, 320–22, 327, 333; Amar, *The Bill of Rights: Creation and Reconstruction* (New Haven: Yale Univ. Press, 1998), 123–24; Cary, 99–107; and Levy, 256–59.

76. *DHFFC* 11:1301.

77. Veit, 51.

78. *DHFFC* 11:1297–98.

79. Veit, 51.

80. This section relies on Levy's analysis of the debate, at 38.

81. WS to ER, Aug. 15, 1789, Veit, 278; WS to Otho H. Williams, Aug. 17, 1789, ibid., 280; WS to Otho H. Williams, Aug. 22, 1789, ibid., 285.

82. GL to Sylvanus Bourne, Aug. 16, 1789, ibid., 279; JB to William Irvine, Aug. 17, 1789, ibid.; FM to Benjamin Rush, Aug. 18, 1789, ibid., 280–81.

83. BG to Michael Hodge, Aug. 20, 1789, ibid., 283; BG to the Salem Insurance Offices, Aug. 23, 1789, ibid., 285.

84. TS to Pamela Sedgwick, Aug. 20, 1789, ibid., 283.

85. RP to JM, Aug. 24, 1789, *PJM* 12:353–54.

86. TH to Tench Coxe, Aug. 23, 1789, Veit, 286.

87. TH to Jasper Yeates, Aug. 16, 1789, ibid., 279.

88. JM to Alexander White, Aug. 24, 1789, *PJM* 12:352.

89. *DHFFC* 11:1319.

90. Veit, 52.

91. *DHFFC* 11:1310–11.

92. RP to JM, July 20, 1789, *PJM* 12:301.

93. JM to RP, Aug. 19, 1789, ibid., 346–47.

94. Ibid., 347. EIO.

95. JM to EP, Aug. 21, 1789, ibid., 348.

96. EP to JM, Sept. 2, 1789, ibid., 368–69.

97. JM to ER, Aug. 21, 1789, ibid., 349; RR to JM, Aug. 22, 1789, ibid., 350.

98. *DHFFC* 3:166.

99. Schwartz, 1145.

100. Diary of William Maclay, Aug. 25, 1789, Veit, 289.

101. RM to RP, Aug. 9, 1789, ibid., 272.

102. RM to Francis Hopkinson, Aug. 15, 1789, ibid., 278.

103. RM to RP, Aug. 24, 1789, ibid., 288.

104. PB to James Iredell, Aug. 11, 1789, ibid., 274.

105. RHL to Charles Lee, Aug. 28, 1789, ibid., 290.

106. Schwartz, 1145.

107. RHL to PH, Sept. 14, 1789, Veit, 295–96; RHL to PH, Sept. 27, 1789, ibid., 298–99; RHL and WG to the Speaker of the Virginia House of Delegates, Sept. 28, 1789, ibid., 299–300.

108. Schwartz, 1150.

109. RHL to SA, Aug. 8, 1789, Veit, 272.

110. Wakelyn, 3–4. Adams was defeated by Fisher Ames in the election for a seat in the House in the First Congress.

111. SA to RHL, Aug. 24, 1789, Veit, 286.

112. RHL to Francis Lightfoot Lee, Sept. 13, 1789, ibid., 294.

113. Schwartz, 1151–53.

114. See generally Amar, 35–36.

115. JM to EP, Sept. 14, 1789, *PJM* 12:402; and Sept. 23, 1789, ibid., 418–19.

116. Levy, 40.

117. FA to Caleb Strong, Sept. 15, 1789, Veit, 297; PW to John Langdon, Sept. 17, 1789, ibid.; RS to Samuel Huntington, Sept. 17, 1789, ibid.

118. Schwartz, 1146, 1148, 1149.

119. Ibid., 1159.

120. Veit, 53. EG to John Wendell, July 10, 1789, ibid., 261–62.

121. WE to Benjamin Huntington, Sept. 8, 1789, ibid., 291.

122. John Collins to the President and Congress, Sept. 26, 1789, ibid., 298.

123. See generally G&L, 343–67 (North Carolina) and 368–90 (Rhode Island).

124. EG to John Wendell, Sept. 14, 1789, Veit, 294. See generally Rutland II, 190–218.

125. TT to St. George Tucker, Oct. 2, 1789, Veit, 300.

126. FA to George R. Minot, July 23, 1789, ibid., 269.

127. RS to Henry Gibbs, Aug. 4, 1789, ibid., 271.

128. WLS to Edward Rutledge, Aug. 10, 1789, ibid., 273.

129. GW to JM, May 31, 1789, *PJM* 12:191.

Chapter 10

1. PH to RHL, Aug. 28, 1789, Veit, 289–90.

2. ER to JM, Aug. 18, 1789, *PJM* 12:345.

3. RHL to PH, Sept. 14, 1789, Veit, 295.

4. RHL to PH, Sept. 27, 1789, ibid., 298–99.

5. WG to PH, Sept. 29, 1789, ibid., 300.

6. RHL and WG to the Speaker, Sept. 28, 1789, ibid., 299.

7. GM to Samuel Griffen, Sept. 8, 1789, ibid., 292.

8. JM to TJ, Oct. 8, 1789, *PJM* 12:433.

9. JM to TJ, Nov. 1, 1789, ibid., 439.

10. AH to JM, Oct. 12, 1789, ibid., 435–36.

11. JM to AH, Nov. 19, 1789, ibid., 449–51.

12. JM to GW, Nov. 20, 1789, ibid., 452.

13. JM to GW, Jan. 4, 1790, ibid., 466.

14. JH to Mass. Legislature, Jan. 14, 1790, Schwartz, 1173.

15. Ibid., 1174.

16. There was a problem with the Massachusetts ratification. Apparently, the legislature never enacted a bill formally announcing that it had assented to the amendments and never sent President Washington an official notice of ratification. Although such a declaration is not required by Article V of the Constitution, Secretary of State Jefferson did not count Massachusetts as among the states ratifying the amendments. Almost two years after Congress had proposed the amendments, Jefferson asked Christopher Gore, the U.S. attorney for Massachusetts, why no such notification was given. He replied that the committee appointed to write the bill announcing the approval never completed its work. Christopher Gore to TJ, Aug. 18, 1791, Schwartz, 1175–76.

17. WWH 2:449.

18. Ibid., 449, 451. Rhode Island rejected the second amendment.

19. Vermont joined the union and ratified the Bill of Rights on Nov. 3, 1791, thus requiring the approval of eleven of the fourteen states for ratification of the amendments.

20. WWH 2:448.

21. Washington transmitted the amendments on Oct. 2, 1789. Schwartz, 1172–73.

22. WWH 2:448.

23. HB to JM, Dec. 5, 1789, *PJM* 12:460.

24. HL to JM, Nov. 25, 1789, ibid., 454–55.

25. Virginia Senators to Governor of Virginia, Sept. 28, 1789, Schwartz, 1186.

26. Virginia Senators to Speaker of the House, Sept. 28, 1789, ibid., 1187.

27. EC to JM, Dec. 20, 1789, *PJM* 12:463.

28. WWH 2:449.

29. Ibid.

30. ER to GW, Nov. 26, 1789, Schwartz, 1186.

31. JM to GW, Nov. 20, 1789, *PJM* 12:453. EIO.

32. Ibid.

33. Joseph Jones to JM, Nov. 2, 1789, *PJM* 12:441.

34. ER to JM, Oct. 10, 1789, ibid., 434. Ague is associated with malaria.

35. Hardin Burnley, who represented Orange County in the House, explained to Madison that Randolph objected to the eleventh amendment because the "rights declared in the first ten of the proposed amendments were not all that a free people would require the exercise of; and that . . . there was no criterion by which it could be determined whether any other particular right was retained or not." Therefore, as Burnley interpreted Randolph's objections, it would be safer and more consistent with the wishes of the Virginia ratifying convention that the last two amendments operate "against extending the powers of Congress by their own authority" rather than as a "protection to rights reducable to no definitive certainty." HB to JM, Nov. 28, 1789, ibid., 456.

36. JM to GW, Dec. 5, 1789, ibid., 458–59. EIO.

37. Ibid., 459.

38. ER to GW, Dec. 6, 1789, Schwartz, 1191.

39. WWH 2:458.

40. ER to GW, Nov. 22, 1789, WWH 2:449; EC to JM, Dec. 20, 1789, *PJM* 12:463.

41. Journal of the House, Dec. 5, 1789, 101–2.

42. EC to JM, Dec. 20, 1789, *PJM* 12:464.

43. WWH 2:451–52, 458–59. Henry's biographer, Henry Mayer, offers no explanation for Henry's premature departure. Mayer, 459. When Senator Grayson died in March 1790, Henry declined to be considered for his seat. Ibid., 460–61.

44. Fontaine, 20.

45. ER to GW, Nov. 26, 1789, Schwartz, 1186.

46. Journal of the House of Delegates, Nov. 30, 1789, 90–91. The vote total comes from GLT to JM, Jan. 20, 1790, *PJM* 12:470–71.

47. *Virginia Independent Chronicle,* Jan. 13, 1790, cited in EC to JM, Feb. 5, 1790, *PJM* 13:28, n. 1.

48. EC to JM, Dec. 20, 1789, *PJM* 12:464; JD to JM, Dec. 17, 1789, ibid., 461.

49. EC to JM, Dec. 20, 1789, ibid., 464–65; GLT to JM, Jan. 20, 1790, ibid., 471.

50. JM to GW, Jan. 4, 1790, ibid., 467.

51. WWH 2:457–58, quoting John Marshall's *Life of Washington* 5:209.

52. WWH 2:458.

53. FC to JM, Oct. 25, 1791, *PJM* 14:85; see also FC to JM, Nov. 22, 1791, ibid., 123.

54. FC to JM, Dec. 7, 1791, ibid., 140–41. EIO.

55. Ibid., 141.

56. FC to JM, Dec. 15, 1791, *PJM* 14:151.

57. Levy, 43.

58. JM to EP, Dec. 18, 1791, *PJM* 14:156–57.

59. PH to JM, April 17, 1784, *PJM* 8:18; JM to WM, Dec. 13, 1791, *PJM* 14:149.

60. Schwartz, 1201–2.

61. Ibid., 1203.

Chapter 11

1. Eventually, the original second amendment was ratified in 1992 as the Twenty-seventh Amendment. For a discussion of how this provision became part of the Constitution after 203 years, see David E. Kyvig, *Explicit and Authentic Acts: Amending the U.S. Constitution, 1776–1995* (Lawrence: Univ. Press of Kansas, 1996), 461–70.

2. The term "Federalist" may be confusing here. From 1787, when the Constitution was written, to about 1791, supporters of the Constitution were called "Federalists," while opponents were labeled "Anti-Federalists." As political parties developed early in the decade, Presidents Washington and Adams, and many members of Congress, established the "Federalist" party, while Thomas Jefferson and James Madison formed the Democratic-Republican party, whose members were known as "Republicans" or sometimes as "Jeffersonian-Republicans."

3. The sedition law made it a crime "if any person shall write, print, utter or publish . . . any false, scandalous and malicious writing . . . against the government of the United States, or either house of the Congress . . . or the President . . . with intent to defame . . . or to bring them . . . into contempt or disrepute; or to excite against them . . . the hatred of the good people of the United States." The act allowed the defense of truth, but it would prove to be a hollow

protection. 1 Stat. 596 (1798). The text of the sedition law comes from *New York Times v. Sullivan*, 376 U.S. 254, 274 (1964). The Alien Enemies Act permitted the president, in case of a declared war, to deport citizens or subjects of a foreign nation residing in the United States. The Alien Friends Act authorized the president to detain and deport any noncitizen considered to be dangerous to the nation. Geoffrey R. Stone, *Perilous Times: Free Speech in Wartime, from the Sedition Act of 1798 to the War on Terrorism* (New York: Norton, 2004), 30–31.

4. Jail conditions in the late eighteenth century could only be described as inhumane, and those incarcerated faced serious threats to their health and financial ruin. Some remained in jail after their sentences were over because they could not pay the fine. Twenty-five well-known Republicans were arrested under the act. Fifteen were indicted, and ten cases went to trial, all resulting in conviction. Ibid., 63.

5. Among the best known of those convicted under the Sedition Act was Matthew Lyon, a Republican congressman from Vermont first elected to the House in 1797. In a letter to the editor of a newspaper, Lyon wrote that under President Adams "every consideration of the public welfare" was "swallowed up in a continual grasp for power, in an unbounded thirst for ridiculous pomp, foolish adulation, and selfish avarice." He became the first person indicted under the law and after his conviction, was sentenced to four months in jail and fined a thousand dollars. He was ordered held beyond the four months if he could not pay the fine. Ibid., 20. For a description of Lyon's incarceration, see ibid., 51. Lyon was reelected to Congress while serving his sentence in a federal prison, the only time that would happen in the nation's history. He was released after the four months because his fine was paid by Republicans who raised money on his behalf. Thomas Jefferson, James Monroe, and James Madison were among those who contributed to the fund. Ibid., 53. Among Republican newspaper publishers prosecuted under the law was Thomas Cooper, the publisher of a Pennsylvania paper, who wrote an essay charging that Adams was a "power-mad despot" and an enemy "of the rights of man." Cooper was tried and convicted in Philadelphia in April 1800, with Supreme Court Justice Samuel Chase presiding. Chase, who was as rabid a Federalist as ever served on a federal bench, would come within a few votes in the U.S. Senate of being impeached and removed from office a few years later. Cooper was sentenced to six months in prison and fined four hundred dollars. Ibid., 54–60. In another trial, Justice Chase, after excluding jurors who might have been sympathetic to the defendant, sentenced James Callender, a Republican publisher in Virginia, to nine months in jail and a two-hundred-dollar fine. Ibid., 61–63. This is adapted from Stone's book, which provides an excellent discussion of the First Amendment during times of crisis.

6. Madison, referring to the "Alien bill"—although he could also have meant the Sedition Act—told Jefferson that the law is a "monster that must for ever disgrace its parents." JM to TJ, May 20, 1798, *PJM* 17:133–34.

7. Madison was then a member of the House of Delegates. For a discussion of the resolutions, see R. B. Bernstein, *Thomas Jefferson* (New York: Oxford Univ. Press, 2003), 124–26.

8. For a discussion of Madison and the nullification crisis, see Ketcham, 640–46.

9. See generally John Ferling, *Adams vs. Jefferson: The Tumultuous Election of 1800* (New York: Oxford Univ. Press, 2004).

10. *New York Times v. Sullivan*, at 274.

11. See generally David M. Rabban, *Free Speech in Its Forgotten Years* (New York: Cambridge Univ. Press, 1997).

12. See, for example, *Schenck v. U.S.*, 249 U.S. 47 (1919); *Frohwerk v. U.S.*, 249 U.S. 204 (1919); *Debs v. U.S.*, 249 U.S. 211 (1919); *Abrams v. U.S.*, 250 U.S. 616 (1919); *Schaefer v. U.S.*, 251 U.S. 466 (1920); and *Pierce v. U.S.*, 252 U.S. 239 (1920).

13. For Wilson's efforts to punish dissent and the courts' willingness to go along, see Stone, *Perilous Times*, 136–233.

14. *Near v. Minnesota*, 283 U.S. 697 (1931).

15. See, for example, *Federalist 48*.

16. See generally Leonard W. Levy. *Emergence of a Free Press* (New York: Oxford Univ. Press, 1985).

17. See generally C. Herman Pritchett, *The American Constitution* (New York: McGraw-Hill, 1977).

18. Although Congress did not pass a sedition law during the Civil War, President Lincoln suspended the writ of habeas corpus, and that allowed his administration to punish what it considered to be dangerous speech. Stone, *Perilous Times*, 120–24.

19. *Barron v. Baltimore*, 32 U.S. 243 (1833).

20. For example, in 1937, the Supreme Court had to decide whether a man convicted of first-degree murder could be put to death after he was originally convicted in the second degree and sentenced to life in prison. The state had appealed his conviction because of errors made by the judge, and in a new trial, he was convicted of the more serious charge. This clearly violated the "double jeopardy" clause of the Fifth Amendment that was intended to prevent prosecutors from repeatedly trying defendants until they obtained a conviction or one for which the penalty was more severe. In a decision legendary for its adherence to settled law—but with a depraved callousness to the rights of an individual—the Court ruled that the Fifth Amendment did not apply to the states, and thus he could be executed. *Palko v. Connecticut*, 302 U.S. 319 (1937).

21. Freedom of speech: *Gitlow v. New York*, 268 U.S. 652 (1925). Freedom of the press: *Near v. Minnesota*, 283 U.S. 697 (1931). Religion clauses: *Everson v. Board of Education of Ewing Township*, 330 U.S. 1 (1947). Search and seizure: *Mapp v. Ohio*, 367 U.S. 643 (1961). Cruel and unusual punishment: *Robinson v. California*, 370 U.S. 660 (1962). Right to counsel: *Gideon v. Wainwright*, 372 U.S. 335 (1963). Self-incrimination: *Malloy v. Hogan*, 378 U.S. 1 (1964). Right to a jury trial: *Duncan v. Louisiana*, 391 U.S. 145 (1968). Double jeopardy: *Benton v. Maryland*, 395 U.S. 784 (1969). Excessive bail: *Schilb v. Kuebel*, 404 U.S. 357 (1971).

22. Examples are the Second Amendment's right to bear arms, the Fifth Amendment's grand jury indictment requirement, the Seventh Amendment's guarantee of a jury trial in civil cases, and the Eighth Amendment's prohibition against excessive fines. Kermit Hall, ed., *The Oxford Companion to American Law* (New York: Oxford Univ. Press, 2002), 415–16.

23. Mattern, 27–28. See also Catherine Allgor, *A Perfect Union: Dolley Madison and the Creation of the American Nation* (New York: Henry Holt, 2006).

24. Mayer, 471–72.

25. Ketcham, 397–98.

26. Jack N. Rakove, *James Madison and the Creation of the American Republic* (New York: Longman, 2002), 199.

27. Ibid., 187–203. For a critical account of Madison's failure to prevent the war and to manage it effectively, see Garry Wills, *James Madison* (New York: Times Books, 2002).

28. Wakelyn, 147.

29. Ibid., 147–48. See also Ammon, *James Monroe*, 546–73.

30. Ketcham, 637. For a thorough discussion of the retirement years, see Drew R. McCoy, *The Last of the Fathers: James Madison and the Republican Legacy* (New York: Cambridge Univ. Press, 1989).

31. Mattern, 224.
32. Ketcham, 669–70. See also Virginia Moore, *The Madisons* (New York: McGraw-Hill, 1979), 477–78.
33. Examples of biographies include Irving Brant, *James Madison,* 6 vols. (Indianapolis: Bobbs-Merrill, 1941–61); Ketcham's 1971 biography and Banning's *Sacred Fire of Liberty* (cited in the abbreviations); Robert Allen Rutland, *James Madison: The Founding Father* (New York: Macmillan, 1987); Robert A. Goldwin, *From Parchment to Power: How James Madison Used the Bill of Rights to Save the Constitution* (Washington: AEI Press, 1997); and the works by Drew McCoy, Jack Rakove, and Garry Wills cited above.

Acknowledgments

IT MAY BE ODD TO FIRST THANK people I don't know, but the editors of the collections of the Madison papers, the Documentary History of the Ratification of the Constitution, the Documentary History of the First Federal Elections, and the Documentary History of the First Federal Congress deserve the gratitude of anyone who uses those materials to write about the founding period. Those editors worked for years to acquire letters, newspapers, and other documents. Transcribing the sometimes nearly illegible handwriting from that era is tedious and often difficult. But their efforts made it so much easier for the rest of us to use those resources.

I can't say enough about the people at the Virginia Historical Society in Richmond. Greg Stoner, reference department manager, and Toni Carter, former assistant librarian, deserve thanks for their help in finding materials and suggesting ideas for additional works for the book. I saw them frequently during June 2002, when I spent a week there on a Mellon Research Fellowship. That fellowship, run by Dr. Nelson Lankford of VHS, is an excellent program. VHS is more than a great library and archive; it is also a first-class museum and with its new expansion will be an even better place for people to learn and discuss Virginia history.

I also want to thank the terrific staff at the Library of Virginia. I needed the assistance of people in various departments with research and illustrations, and they could not have been more helpful. The library has one of Virginia's most valuable assets, Brent Tarter. Brent met with me early on to make useful suggestions about the direction of the book. Over the next few years, he always responded quickly to further requests for help. He read the entire manuscript and made useful comments, many of which I included. His knowledge of Virginia history and the founding period is remarkable.

I also gathered materials, including illustrations, at the National Archives and Library of Congress. Even though their staff is very busy, they were always helpful and pleasant.

Closer to home, I very much appreciated the comments that the late Professor Lance Banning of the University of Kentucky's History Department made on the manuscript. Professor Banning, who was one of the nation's foremost Madison scholars, met with me in the earliest stages and made helpful suggestions.

The director of the School of Journalism and Telecommunications at UK, Dr. Beth Barnes, was highly enthusiastic about this project from the time I first mentioned it to her. She read the manuscript and made great comments.

My colleague Dr. Mike Farrell has been of incalculable assistance. He read the book carefully and helped in too many ways to describe. Our friendship did not inhibit him from candidly assessing the strengths and weaknesses of the manuscript, and his many excellent suggestions improved the book.

I received very generous financial support from the University of Kentucky for this research, including from the office of the vice president for research, from the College of Communications and Information Studies, and from my school. All of that support has been immensely helpful.

I also want to thank Professors James McPherson and David Hackett Fischer for allowing me to be a part of the Pivotal Moments in American History series. Both of these distinguished scholars have won the Pulitzer Prize in history, and it is exciting to be associated with this series.

At Oxford, I am immensely grateful to Peter Ginna, editorial director of the trade division, who was enthusiastic about the project from the start. He read the manuscript carefully and made excellent suggestions. He was able to see the book as an editor and a reader at the same time, and his revisions have made it more interesting and compelling. The associate editor, Dr. Furaha Norton, could not have been more responsive and helpful. Joellyn Ausanka did a very good job seeing the book through the production phase.

I also very much appreciate the copyediting work by India Cooper. As I went through her comments and recommendations, I became more and more impressed by her skills. All authors should be fortunate enough to have someone of her ability work on their books.

I also want to thank Steve Wrinn, the director of the University Press of Kentucky. Even though he was not publishing the book, Steve was very helpful and encouraging and provided useful information about the publishing business. Gena Henry of the press gave me helpful advice on gathering illustrations.

My father and stepmother, Stephen and Jeralyn Labunski, have been incredibly enthusiastic and supportive from the beginning of this project.

Now, saving the best for last, I want to thank my wife, Elisa Devera. It is routine for an author to express gratitude to a spouse for helping with the book and making sacrifices that permitted the writer to complete the project. Elisa has been helpful beyond what words can describe. She has read everything and has been involved in every phase, but her most valuable contribution has been in commenting on the multiple drafts of the manuscript. Her suggestions have greatly improved it, and even though her name is not on the book's cover, she deserves a lot of credit for how it turned out. I thank her so much for everything.

Index

Note: Page numbers in *italics* refer to illustrations.

Great Britain. *See* England
Greece, 100
Greene County, 148
Griffin, Cyrus, 47, 97
Grigsby, Hugh Blair, 101, 293n. 7, 296n. 18

habeas corpus, 317n. 18
Hamilton, Alexander
    advice sought from Madison, 244
    on amendment process, 128
    as convention delegate, 299n. 34
    correspondence to, 111
    The Federalist, 22
    Madison correspondence to, 297n. 44
    and the New York convention, 121
    and the Philadelphia convention, 9–10, 16
    and the Virginia ratifying convention, 73,
        96–97, 115
Hancock, John, *245*, 245–46
Hanover County, 29
Hartley, Thomas, 224, 232
health problems of Madison
    and life expectancy, 288n. 33
    and military service, 152
    in old age, 263
    and travel difficulties, 22, 31, 96–97, 144,
        147–48, 244–45
Hebron Lutheran Church, 166
Hell's Gate, 179
Henry, John, 28, 76–77, 82, 95
Henry, Patrick, *74*
    and the Anti-Federalists, 20, 22
    and Bill of Rights introduction, 208–9,
        236, 239
    on centralization of power, 61–62
    on compensation of representatives, 58
    and congressional elections, 148, 151, 158,
        165, 170–71, 176–77
    and Dawson, 24
    death, 261
    on importance of Virginia, 291–92n. 49
    influence of, 27–28, 36–37
    on Innes, 293n. 18
    as Madison's opponent, 263–64
    on navigation issues, 300n. 71
    obstructionism, 298n. 3
    and opposition to the Constitution, 27–
        28, 65–66
    oratorical skills, 73–74
    and ratification of the Bill of Rights, 242,
        245, 247–48, 250–54
    and ratifying conventions, 49–50, 69–74,
        79–81, 83–86, 88–90, 93–95, 97–99, 105–
        6, 108–11, 113, 115–16, 118–19

on regional confederacies, 292n. 50
    and second convention proposals, 52, 58,
        120–25, 132–33, 135, 137–46
Henry, William Wirt, 71–72, 94, 118
Holland, 130
"Hon. Mr. Gerry's Objections" (essay), 63
honor, 153
Hopkins, Samuel, Jr., 57
House Journal, 58
House of Burgesses, 28, 29, 33, 136, 252
House of Commons, 71
House of Delegates
    on amendment process, 57
    and congressional elections, 158
    date for ratifying convention, 55
    and delegate compensation, 56
    and election of senators, 136
    Madison's service in, 164, 261
    and ratification delegate elections, 32, 47
    and ratification of the Bill of Rights, 243,
        245–48, 252
    structure of, 290n. 3
    and support for the Constitution, 25
House of Representatives
    accountability of, 92
    and the amendment process, 131
    and amendments proposals, *233*, 272–74
    and the Bill of Rights, *233*, 240
    conference committees, 239
    congressional districts, 135, 138
    criticisms of, 42
    election of members, 91
    eligibility requirements, 76
    and geographic diversity, 83
    Jefferson on, 103
    Madison's preference for, 300n. 57
    and opposition to the Constitution, 84
    and reserved powers, 114
    size of, 4, 39, 139, 221–23, 252, 256, 265, 269,
        272, 275, 278
    Virginia delegation, 119, 252, 301n. 83
    and Washington's inaugural address, 189
Hughes, James, 26
Humphreys, David, 188

imports, 185
impost laws, 185, 228–29
inaugural addresses, 188–89, 240
Independence Hall, Philadelphia, 3–4, *4*
independence movement, 29–30
Innes, James, 69, 110, 293n. 18
instruction of representatives, 225–26, 238–39
interest groups, 225
Iredell, James, 191
Izard, Ralph, 235

About the Author

RICHARD LABUNSKI is a professor in the School of Journalism and Telecommunications at the University of Kentucky. He previously taught at the University of Washington and Penn State. He has a Ph.D. in political science from the University of California, Santa Barbara, and a J.D. from Seattle University School of Law. Labunski is the author of four previous books and numerous journal articles and newspaper commentaries.

About the Type

MINION is a 1990 Adobe Originals typeface by Robert Slimbach. Minion is inspired by classical, old style typefaces of the late Renaissance, a period of elegant, beautiful, and highly readable type designs. Created primarily for text setting, Minion combines the aesthetic and functional qualities that make text type highly readable with the versatility of digital technology. The Minion family contains black weight, display, and swash fonts, expert sets, and a full range of ornaments, for uses that range from limited-edition books to newsletters to packaging.